CU005311l66

A Way of Life That Does Not Exist

A Way of Life That Does Not Exist

Canada and the Extinguishment of the Innu

COLIN SAMSON

VERSO

London · New York

First published by Verso 2003
© Colin Samson

Published in Canada by ISER Books, Faculty of Arts Publications,
Institute of Social and Economic Research,
Memorial University of Newfoundland

All rights reserved

The moral rights of the author have been asserted

1 3 5 7 9 10 8 6 4 2

Verso
UK: 6 Meard Street, London W1F 0EG
USA: 180 Varick Street, New York, NY 10014-4606
www.versobooks.com

Verso is the imprint of New Left Books

ISBN 1-85984-525-8

British Library Cataloguing in Publication Data
A catalogue record for this book is available from the British Library

Library of Congress Cataloging-in-Publication Data
A catalog record for this book is available from the Library of Congress

Printed and bound in Canada by AGMV Marquis

Contents

Acknowledgements

More than anything else, this book has been made possible by the generosity, kindness, and warmth of the people of Sheshatshiu and Utshimassits.

I have lived with several families in the villages and in the hunting camps of the interior of Labrador. Families that I would like to thank for allowing me to stay with them are those of Marie Angela Pijogge and Sam Pijogge, Christine Rich and Joseph Remi Rich, Lyla Andrew and Ben Andrew, Sheila Blake and Daniel Ashini, Matnen Benuen and Anthony Jenkinson, Janet Jenkinson, Angela Penashue and Basil Penashue. Over the years, I made friends with many residents of the villages, whose observations, insights, and experiences helped deepen my understanding, and in this respect, I would especially like to thank Jean-Pierre Ashini, Daniel Ashini, George Rich, Simeon Tshakapesh, Louis Rich, Ben Michel, Apenam Pone, Etienne Pone, Paul Pone, Sheila Blake, Basil Penashue, and the late Cecilia Rich. While travelling and hunting in the country, I benefited from the expert guidance of Dominic Pokue, Daniel Ashini, Joseph Remi Rich, Sam Pijogge, and Simeon Tshakapesh.

A number of research grants funded my work with the Innu. These started with a grant from the University of Essex Research Promotion Fund. This was followed by grants from the Canadian High Commission in London and the Research Institute for the Study of Man in New York. In 1999, I was hired by the Sheshatshiu Innu Band Council to undertake research on the Innu experience of schooling. Here I must thank Luke Rich and Marcel Ashini and the Sheshatshiu Local Education Committee for their comradeship. The Sociology Department at the University of Essex generously permitted periods of leave, which were necessary to the project as a whole.

Parts of the manuscript were written while a Visiting Scholar at the Institute for the Study of Social Change at the University of California at Berkeley. In Berkeley, my friend David Minkus was a constant source of metaphorical wisdom and humour and Janice Tanigawa made my stay comfortable and pleasant. The trickster hermeneutics and teasing of Gerald Vizenor, also at Berkeley, always inspired. Finally, in 2000, I received a Strategic Research Grant from the Institute for Social and Economic Research (ISER) at Memorial University Newfoundland. This grant enabled me to complete the manuscript in residence in St. John's where I availed myself of the resources at the Centre for Newfoundland Studies. At

ISER I am grateful to Eleanor Fitzpatrick and Rosalind Collins for making me so welcome, as well as the support and conviviality of Adrian Tanner. In St. John's, both Anne St. Croix and Kezban Saki helped me through several months without seeing the sun.

Alternate versions of some portions of the text have been previously published in the following publications: "Sexual Abuse and Assimilation: Oblates, Teachers and the Innu of Labrador," *Sexualities* 6, 1, 2003: 47-54; "Drinking and Healing: Reflections On the Lost Autonomy of the Innu," *Indigenous Nations Studies Journal* 2, 2, Fall 2001: 37-56; "Sameness as a Requirement for the Recognition of the Rights of the Innu of Canada: The Colonial Context," In Jane Cowan, Marie-Benedicte Dembour, and Richard Wilson, eds., *Culture and the Anthropology of Rights*. Cambridge: Cambridge University Press, 2001: 226-48; "Teaching Lies: The Innu Experience of Schooling," *London Journal of Canadian Studies*, Special Issue, *Continuities and Changing Realities: Meanings and Identities Among Canada's Aboriginal Peoples*, 16, 2000/01: 83-102; *Canada's Tibet: The Killing of the Innu*, co-authored with James Wilson and Jonathan Mazower, a Human Rights Report commissioned and published by Survival International, London: 1999; and "The Dispossession of the Innu and the Colonial Magic of Canadian Liberalism," *Citizenship Studies* 3, 1, February 1999: 5-26. Grateful acknowledgement is given to the publishers of these books and journals for permission to reproduce some elements of the text.

Several people have read, advised, and commented on my work. For spending time reading and engaging with me, I am indebted to Michael Asch, Julie Brittain, Andrew Canessa, Rampaul Chamba, Jane Cowan, Heidi Grainger, Lorenza Hall, Jane Hindley, Vivien Hughes, Ernest Landauer, Jony Mazower, Heather Nicholson-Norris, Peter Patrick, Itesh Sachdev, Nancy Scheper-Hughes, Laura Spautz,and Ron Schwarz. I am especially grateful to Anthony Jenkinson for reading every chapter, and for providing valuable historical documents, advice, and suggestions. Hugh Brody helped start me out on the project and his book *Maps and Dreams* was an early inspiration. To James Wilson, I am also greatly thankful. James, not only introduced me to the Innu people, he worked with me during the early stages of the project, and he encouraged me at all times. The anonymous reviewers for the book at ISER Books and Verso Press, as well as the editorial assistance of Richard Tallman, Laurna Tallman, Jeanette Gleeson, and Tim Clark, added polish to the final product.

Nicola Gray always supported me in my many trips to Labrador, made our Innu guests feel welcome when they visited our home, and survived what has been a life-transforming experience for me.

Prologue

"ISN'T IT TIME THEY JOINED THE MODERN WORLD?"

Toronto, *Globe and Mail*, 27 November 2000

"Does it make sense, in the year 2000," asked an editorial in one of Canada's leading national newspapers, "for people to be living a marginal existence in such a remote place? Would it be better for its residents to move to bigger communities where there might be jobs to be had? Isn't it time they joined the modern world?" The "they" of the narrative in the *Globe and Mail* (2000) were the indigenous Innu. The Innu are Algonkian-speaking descendants of peoples who have occupied the Labrador-Quebec peninsula for as much as 8,000 years (Loring and Ashini, 2000: 174). In the midst of a widely reported epidemic of youth gas-sniffing and adult drinking sprees in November 2000, the Innu were being urged finally to cut their ties with the "remote place" that had given them meaning, purpose, and survival for so long. For the editors of the *Globe and Mail*, it was "time to face facts . . . . They must find a way to enter the modern world, even if it means moving somewhere else."

This book is about ideas like this and the policies that have been informed by them. More specifically, it is about the social and political processes involved in the transformation of the unique way of life of the Innu people of *Nitassinan*, the Labrador-Quebec peninsula in what is now Canada. Although these processes are highly complex, by examining the many points of contact between the Innu and Canada, I hope to offer some insights into how these processes have affected a massive transformation of a society and the relationships of the people in that society to their landscape and cosmos.

Social changes of this kind have, of course, occurred to many of the world's tribal peoples. Formerly self-reliant, although by no means isolated, peoples have gradually, or in some cases suddenly, been made subject to the authority of larger social, political, and economic orders. This could be seen, indeed as it often was, as an inevitable consequence of the encounters between Europeans and small peoples such as the Innu or, as is a more fashionable explanation today, as a product of the globalization of Western technology, media, and capitalism. In accounting for social change, some anthropologists even emphasize the "appropriation" of European norms, values, and institutions on the part of indigenous peoples (see Merry, 2001). These kinds of explanations, however persuasive they may be for particular cases, downplay the manipulation and social engineering involved when, having their land claimed by colonists, a people are relocated. And here, the *Globe and Mail* editorial hints at what I am getting at – the conscious destruction of the relationship of a people to the lands that historically gave meaning, purpose, and order to their existence as a society.

If we were creative we might say that what is at issue is not the destruction of such relationships, but the "restructuring" of them. Here, I would agree, but would urge that we not move on so quickly, that we not gloss over how the restructuring is achieved only through destruction of what formerly existed. In my view, this crucial intermediary step as related to the Innu and many other North American Aboriginal peoples can best be summarized in the official term used in Canada (and historically across North America) for the cancellation of the sovereignty over territories or "Aboriginal title" of Native peoples. "Extinguishment" is the end result of political processes used to settle outstanding land conflicts. Formerly, extinguishment was achieved throughout North America through written treaties, but in other cases the same result was achieved through violent displacement, the spread of disease, or by Native peoples fleeing in the wake of advancing Europeans. Today, extinguishment entails the official voiding of what the state recognizes as Aboriginal title to land by agreements between the government and political bodies established (often by Canada) to represent Aboriginal peoples. By extinguishing what are recognized as prior rights, Canada assumes unquestionable legal ownership over Native lands and in exchange confers subsidiary rights and provides cash compensation to Native peoples who have become parties to this process. However, the various social processes that have led up to the extinguishment of Aboriginal land titles also involve the extinguishing of cultural difference. Both types of extinguishment are important topics of this book.

Only relatively recently, in the 1950s and 1960s, were the Innu prompted by Canadian authorities to abandon permanent nomadic hunting, the way of life that had made them such independent and successful occupants of the boreal forests and tundra of the Subarctic. Over these decades a people who had occupied a territory the size of France, and for whom the land, waterways, and animals provided physical, moral, and spiritual sustenance, were settled in government-built villages in northern Quebec and the Labrador portion of the province of Newfoundland.[1] Considering the Innu hunting life incompatible with the "modern world," the government authorities of the day argued that settlement, or sedentarization as it is technically known, would bring "civilization" and "progress." Although it is impossible to say exactly what was meant by these frequently used epithets and whether or not they were simply convenient slogans to use in clearing potentially valuable land of "Indians," with hindsight we now know that settlement coincided with a precipitous decline of the Innu by almost any measure. As the very source of Innu well-being, *Nitassinan*, the land of the interior of the Labrador-Quebec peninsula, has gradually become a separate sphere rather than, as it was, at the centre of their activities; they have suffered from rates of self-destruction – suicide, alcohol-related deaths and abuse, infant mortality, and epidemics of gas-sniffing – that are among the highest in the world. The Innu follow a long line of sedentarized and relocated northern peoples who have been thrown into social turmoil, cultural confusion, and mental and physical breakdown as a consequence of the state-sponsored severing of their links to particular lands (see Shkilnyk, 1985; Tester and Kulchyski, 1994; Bussidor and Bilgen-Reinart, 1997).

Ignorant of the fact that the first removals of the Innu to villages precipitated numerous human tragedies, the exasperated editors of the *Globe and Mail* were advocating the complete separation of the Innu from their lands. To remove them to cities would mean their cultural extinction since the myriad Innu connections with *Nitassinan* provide the basics of life and make them distinctive as a people. The last-gasp final solution called for even more "civilization," with no thought given to the vital relationships the Innu have been struggling to maintain with their land.

Focusing primarily on two Innu villages in Labrador, Sheshatshiu and Davis Inlet or Utshimassits,[2] I attempt to understand this "modern world" that the authorities were so anxious that the Innu enter in the first place. While the Canadian authorities were quick to promote and enforce fundamental changes in the way in which people have lived for hundreds of years, they have been much less eager to consider if there might be connections between these policies and the perilous state of the Innu since they came to the villages. To do so, one needs to examine how the transformation plays itself out in the relationships between government agents, traders, developers, missionaries, and settlers, on the one hand, and Native peoples, on the other. Beyond periodic newspaper headlines of gas-sniffing or suicide epidemics, not much about the condition of such indigenous populations has filtered into the consciousness of non-Aboriginal Canadians.[3] Although the complacency is rocked by tragic revelations of suffering in villages or reserves, as the journalist Geoffrey York (1990: xiii) pointed out, these:

> are treated as an isolated event, a curious aberration, a temporary lapse in the judgement of the administrators and leaders of our civilized society. There is rarely any understanding of the sheer number of similar events taking place in aboriginal communities across the country. And few Canadians realize the connections between all these stories – the recurring pattern of the disintegration of entire communities as a direct consequence of assaults made by the institutions of modern Canadian society.

The point is that, whatever the motive, whether it is planned or unplanned, benevolent or malicious, ignorant or knowing, the sustained efforts to transform and to impose external authority upon Native peoples such as the Innu carry with them consequences that demand to be accounted for.

A WAY OF LIFE THAT DOES NOT EXIST

In the early 1970s, some four years after the village of Davis Inlet was built on Iliukoyak Island just off the northern Labrador coast, the Roman Catholic priest posted in the settlement used a throwaway phrase, "a way of life that does not exist," to depict village life. In the mimeographed text that George Gregoire, an Innu of the community, handed me on one of my first visits, the Flemish Father Frank Peters (1972) observed that the village school was preparing the first generation of sedentary Innu[4] for a life that was neither Innu nor Canadian. Davis Inlet, predicated on sedentary life, was disconnected from the Innu hunting world both literally and figuratively. Hunting trips to the mainland were prohibited during the times of the year when the waters were freezing up and when they were breaking up, leaving the people stranded on the island for several months at a time. The village then became the base from where they would make occasional forays into the interior to hunt and camp. By the same token, even though the Innu were now living in wooden dwellings from inside of which Father Peters often heard the radio crackle of country and western music, everyday life in Davis Inlet did not appear to be Canadian. Few people in Canadian

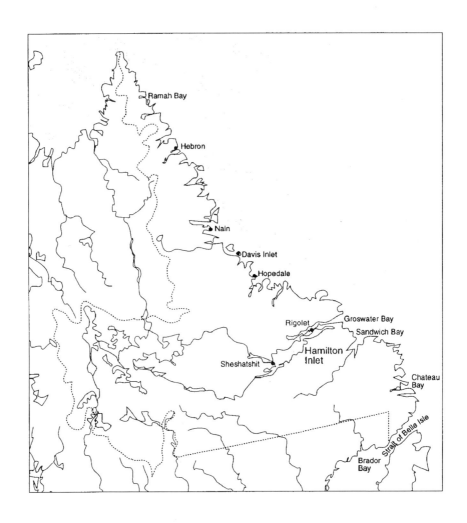

Map of Labrador.

Source: Mailhot, José, 1997. *The People of Sheshatshit: In the Land of the Innu* (St. John's: ISER Books), p. 5.

communities were almost entirely housed in overcrowded shacks lacking basic sanitation and running water. Similarly, even fewer Canadian communities would be populated by relocated people who had been persistently hounded to abandon their most cherished ideas, practices, and beliefs and were now almost entirely "unemployed." Not only did the island instigate a partial isolation of the Innu from the hunting world, but it did little to connect them with the sources of well-being offered by an industrialized society.

Thirty years later after he wrote it, Father Peters's phrase seemed to strike a chord. Yet, I wondered exactly what it meant. Surely village life *exists* and it could be offensive to suggest otherwise. But in what way does it exist? How could a rather crowded village serve as a secure base for the transmission of knowledge important to the Innu people and the succession of the generations? What experience could they bank on to survive in these villages, the social units of agriculturists? Over time, with more visits, more conversations with my Innu friends, and more observations of their contact with the *Akaneshau* (non-Native or, literally, "English speaker" in *Innu-aimun*, the Innu language) authorities, I saw and experienced a certain torpor and lack of purpose in the villages. Settlements, by their mere existence, seemed to be contributing both to the erosion of a meaningful and healthy existence, the vestiges of which I had keenly experienced on my visits, and to the integrity of a particular way of understanding the world. At the same time, I could see few if any meaningful replacements for all that the Innu were losing by abandoning life on the land. A kind of reckless destruction of the nomadic hunting life seemed to be taking shape, but any assimilation, for that was the explicit goal of settlement, was at best superficial.

"A way of life that does not exist," then, is a statement of what the Canadian authorities have, through design as well as ignorant blundering, created in the villages or "communities," as they are often euphemistically called. Many Innu have gradually become neither hunters nor "modern" Canadians. Others, however, have managed to maintain their links with the land and devote several months each year to living in what they would see as an Innu way. Some, a tiny number, have been able to achieve a modicum of success in employment and education, and are gradually entering the Canadian mainstream. A small number of Innu are considered proficient in both Innu and Euro-Canadian terms. That is, while they are skilled at hunting activities, they have also been able to establish themselves by the very different Euro-Canadian standards of employability in the small number of jobs that are available in the villages. But, for the vast bulk of Innu, their connections with the land and, hence, their Innu identity have become compromised, while few meaningful opportunities have arisen to allow them to function, let alone succeed, in the Euro-Canadian society that has gradually encircled them.

As a result, the project of sedentarization has only been a success insofar as the Innu are no longer *permanent nomadic* hunters. They have continued to travel long distances to hunt animals, and many Innu families spend considerable periods of time in hunting camps in the interior of the Labrador-Quebec peninsula. In these areas, which the Innu refer to as "the country" (known as *nutshimit*), they live in small family groupings as confident, skilful, and respected hunters. While they are often pulled back to the villages by the need to obtain money and to send their children to school, *nutshimit* affords the Innu a much greater degree of well-being and autonomy. In contrast, when they return to the village – a transition often fraught with many personal difficulties – they are struck by the ubiquity of Euro-Canadian institutions that regulate almost all aspects of their lives. Imposed authority structures – principally, the state, the law, schools, Christian missions, health and social welfare agencies – by assuming that the villages are *faits accompli*, chip away at the hunting life and provide every possible incentive for the Innu to adopt the ideas, practices, and sensibilities of "modern" Canadians.[5] This process of transformation, however, is still in the balance. While the authorities act to incorporate the Innu within a larger Canadian whole, the people themselves continually resist, insisting on their right to be Innu.

One of the major ironies of the conflicts between the Innu and Canada is that after almost 40 years of directing the Innu to be village dwellers, the authorities have not fashioned a new set of integrated and compliant citizens of the state. Rather, the attempt to change the Innu by creating settlements has generated uncertainty among both the Innu themselves and the white agents in the villages – teachers, social workers, priests, and judges – who are part of the ongoing project of transformation. If we are to take the civilizing project of the Canadian state at face value, the result, partial as it may be, is a seriously bungled operation. The various resistances of the Innu, manifest in the refusal of many to send their children to the schools, resilient attachment to the country, failure to internalize Euro-Canadian values, and their constant opposition to industrial development projects, give the lie to any notion that the Innu are grateful to Canada for altering their way of life. At the same time, village life has been so devastating to many Innu that it has led to astronomic rates of personal and collective self-destruction, making resistance at times impossible, subordination to the imposed order a dull compulsion, and resignation often the norm.

Canada's political control over the Innu is the force that most clearly gives rise to the way of life that does not exist. Past and present government agents and missionaries have exercised authority over the Innu primarily as a necessary accompaniment to the economic development of the Labrador-Quebec peninsula. Industrial development of *Nitassinan* has necessarily involved both transforming and relocating the Innu. If industrialization was to succeed and Labrador was to be an actor on the stage of global capitalism, then nomadic hunters had to be both cleared from the lands and made to see the sense behind resource extraction.

In the process little or no consideration was given to any adverse consequences that might follow from coercing a people to give up a tried, tested, and loved way of life. This blindness is a manifestation of the broader policy of the Canadian state *not* to recognize the Innu as a distinct people. Successive government policies ignored the Innu, treating them as invisible people not worthy of mention or, at best, simply Other Canadians. Aboriginal peoples were never mentioned in the terms of the agreement under which Newfoundland entered the Canadian confederation in 1949. It was simply assumed that they were enfranchised, having the same status as any other Canadian citizen and therefore, not having any specific rights to land or self-determination (Tompkins, 1988: 25). Over the years, they have been "administered by the provincial government under the stated policy of treating them no differently than all other Newfoundlanders" (Tanner, 1983: 18). To date the province has assumed jurisdiction over the Innu in Labrador and the federal government has simply paid the bills.

THE FAILURE OF RECOGNITION

This failure to recognize difference and distinctiveness is one of the more obvious features of Canada's relationships with indigenous peoples. It is mirrored in the attitudes of policy-makers in the distant capitals of St. John's and Ottawa. As I hope to show in this book, a wide spectrum of policies and pronouncements, including "land claims," court cases involving Aboriginal rights, and even official apologies, reflect this failure of recognition. At the other end of this spectrum are acts of simple ignorance that are sometimes wilful and at other times plainly incompetent.

Numerous examples of this failure of recognition could be cited and many of them will be discussed in the chapters that follow, but a couple of events that I closely followed are indicative of this insensitivity. A raft of publicity in the Canadian news media followed the publication of the Survival International human rights report on the Innu that I co-authored (Samson et al., 1999). It provoked a welter of newsprint and TV footage. Just a few months later, in March 2000, the federal Minister of Indian Affairs, Robert Nault, sat through a meeting with the Innu leaders in Ottawa to discuss one of the points in the report, referring to them as "Inuit," and proclaiming that if the Innu received various benefits from the federal government other "Inuit" communities would want the same. Peter Penashue, the President of Innu Nation, politely pointed out to Nault that the Innu were not "Inuit." Canada's highest-ranking official with responsibilities towards Aboriginal peoples had displayed a basic ignorance of the Innu, suggesting that he had no inkling of the very significant differences between the Innu and Inuit. If it did not reflect on the general indifference the Canadian state (and a huge swath of the Canadian population[6]) displays towards Aboriginal peoples, this might seem relatively innocuous. Other meetings between the Innu and the Canadian authorities illuminate more destructive forms of non-recognition.

In November 2000, I attended a meeting between the Mushuau Innu band council from Davis Inlet and provincial health and social services officials at a Best Western motel in St. John's. The meeting was held to discuss the epidemic of gas-sniffing of over 100 children in the village. The Innu had come to the meeting to request assistance for the children. Early on, it became clear that only one of the 15 or so provincial authorities had ever visited Davis Inlet – and that was seven years previously. After some preliminary statements by the Innu leaders of the dangers to the Innu children, a halt was brought to the meeting when the officials refused to accept Innu health co-ordinator Mark Nui's simple statement that the Mushuau Innu band council had "jurisdiction" over Innu children. The provincial authorities assumed that the Innu were to be treated like any other Newfoundlanders and that the children could legally be removed from their homes without parental consent if they were considered to be in "neglect." The remarks of several Innu leaders that the provincial plan of forced removals would backfire because many children were suicidal and because this would be a jarring reminder of the activities of social workers in the past who removed children, never to be seen again, were met only by silence. The Davis Inlet leadership's insistence on the peculiarities of their circumstances, and their collective right as a distinct people to decide the fate of their own children, was simply intolerable to the befuddled provincial bureaucrats. Only several weeks later, after the epidemic continued to grow, was a compromise struck. By agreement, several children were removed to a hospital in St. John's, only later to return to the same conditions in Davis Inlet.

CIVILIZATION IS ON THE NORTHWARD MARCH

Almost any history of Native-white relations in North America will show that onslaughts from the state, the Christian churches, and other imposed agencies produce what settlers long regarded as inevitable – either the physical extinction of Natives or Natives who became compliant or dispirited enough to pose no threat to Euro-American control of the land (see, for example, Dippie, 1982; Wilson, 1998). While the Innu have never ceded their own sovereignty and actively resist the usurpation of their land and autonomy, their "inevitable" transformation has been both recent and startlingly abrupt. In part this is a function of the geographical peculiarities of their territories. In other areas of North America, Natives felt the full effects of European expansion (and for some, this meant physical extinction) much earlier. Stripped of their languages, legends, beliefs, and land, many of the descendants of these groups can only learn of their Native identity from museums or reinvent it with pan-Native iconography. Although the Innu in Labrador, along with the now extinct Beothuks of Newfoundland, were probably among the first Native Americans to experience European contact from the tenth-century Norse voyages onward, the Innu are almost unique at the dawn of the twenty-first century in not having either to display their customs, traditions, and material culture in a museum or to reinvent them.

The Innu predicament would not be remarkable were it not for the fact that these processes are occurring as I write. Until very recently, the Innu were more independent of Europeans and the state than almost any other indigenous people in North America. Consequently, the same forfeiture of land that colonists demanded of other tribal peoples in New England in the seventeenth century, the U.S. South in the 1830s, and the Great Plains in the second half of the nineteenth century have been required of the Innu only over the last half-century. Yet, they are facing the threat of following a long line of Native peoples into the cultural, physical, and psychological decline that has almost always accompanied land demands placed upon them by Europeans. Equally remarkable is that Canadian governments seem to have absorbed so little of these history lessons and appear to be blindly following roughly the same path in their dealings with the Innu and other Aboriginal peoples over which they claim dominion.

Although all peoples change and make adaptations to the ideas and practices of other groups – indeed, human history is littered with disappearing peoples and languages – it is important to understand *why* such changes occur and to distinguish between forced and voluntary changes. While Native Americans did make voluntary changes that benefited them as a result of their contact with Europeans, the most important transformations were prompted by the requirements of dealing with aggressive and domineering intruders. Most changes were fashioned in the crucible of necessity. In many parts of North America, Native participation in education and agriculture and submission to the law, for example, were products of the coercion of either colonizers or, in later times, the state established by settlers.

In the not too distant past, these transformations, as well as the extinction of some Native peoples, were conveniently rationalized by European intellectuals as an inevitable part of the progress of human history, the unfolding of cultural evolution. Although losses of an "old world" would occur and vices such as alcohol might be adopted by Natives who survived the early contact period, such peoples were often said to prosper from improved technologies, education, morality, economies, and other facets of a supposedly more advanced civilization. Although European survival in many of the areas of the world that they colonized, including Labrador, was made possible by adapting local technologies and customs, in almost every case indigenous peoples were thought to make only a negligible contribution to European understandings of the world. The direction of beneficial change brought on by the meetings between peoples was seen to be almost entirely one way.[7] Eight years after Newfoundland and Labrador joined Canada in 1949, Walter Rockwood, the director of the Division of Northern Labrador Affairs and a prime mover in the government-sponsored drive to settle the Innu, provided a stirring rendition of this point of view when he remarked of the Inuit ("Eskimo") and Innu ("Indian") of the territory:

> But one fact seems clear, – Civilization is on the northward march, and for the Eskimo and the Indian there is no escape. The last bridges of isolation were destroyed with the coming of the airplane and the radio. The only course now open, for there can be no turning back, is to fit him as soon as may be to take his full place as a citizen in our society. There is no time to lose. No effort must be spared in the fields of Health, Education, Welfare and Economics. (Rockwood, 1957: 6)

In Rockwood's evolutionary formula, there could be *no turning back* for anyone, least of all the "Eskimos" and "Indians" whom, as is apparent in his correspondence (see Roche, 1992),[8] he regarded as extremely primitive and lazy. Such was Rockwood's sense of destiny that he believed they had only one future, and that would be *in our society.* Anticipating the editors of the *Globe and Mail* by nearly half a century, Rockwood (1957: 4) even considered the prospect of the Labrador Natives so bleak that he, too, contemplated moving them to other areas of Canada.

The Innu, of course, were never static, never enclosed in one timeless culture. "Culture," as a recent wave of anthropologists have been at pains to point out, is hardly a tenable concept since it implies that groups of people are homogeneous, separate, and bounded entities (see Clifford and Marcus, 1986; Clifford, 1988; Marcus and Fischer, 1999). While this reformulation is a necessary corrective to the primitivizing portraits that some anthropologists composed for American Indians and other non-Europeans, one need not assume therefore that Natives and non-Natives are the same or that they stand together in the face of global changes. As the writings of Anishinaabe author Gerald Vizenor (1994, 1998) demonstrate, one can be opposed to "paracolonial" anthropological renderings of "culture" and at the same time maintain a dynamic sense of Native difference in a postmodern world. Native stories, survival, memories, humour, and motion shape difference and autonomy. For Vizenor, a Native absence is connoted by many anthropological studies of Natives, while presence is apparent in Native "sovenance" – a sovereign quality that is never static and includes but also transcends territory. The simulation, the "Indian" or "*indian*," in Vizenor's usage, is created in the compositions of social science and public policy, and signifies the absence of the Native.

Therefore, what I am discussing in this book is not a hermetically sealed Innu "culture," since their dealings with missionaries, traders, government agents, and indeed other Native peoples of the North naturally have influenced them. Although discussed, the subject matter of the book does not primarily consist of detailed ethnographic elaborations of the various Innu ideas and practices, closely bound up with the ancient associations of the Innu with *Nitassinan.* Rather, it is concerned with the processes that attempt to alter the Innu and diminish the many sources of their uniqueness as a people. Among other things, their distinctiveness includes their attachments to the land, respect for animals, communitarian ethos, consensual decision-making, belief in the importance of personal autonomy, as well as their language, religion, medicine, and technologies. As I hope to demonstrate, these broad attributes, in both overt and subtle ways, have become the raw materials for direct transformation in public policy and through the imposition of Euro-Canadian institutions. This does not mean, of course, that they have not made voluntary changes under the influences of the people who colonized them. But changes such as those involved with the adoption of non-Native technologies, for example, do not necessarily diminish their Innu identity, and in some ways these have been able to enhance that identity. By allowing many elderly and infirm people to travel into regions of the country that would normally involve long and arduous portages, the airplane charters organized by the Outpost Program of the band councils have ensured that such individuals have access to *nutshimit*, something that normally would have been denied them as residents of the villages.

ENGAGEMENTS

This study relies on a wide range of theoretical, historical, and practical engagements that are not limited to any single disciplinary or methodological perspective. As Marcus and Fischer (1999: x) have remarked, "the essential characteristic [of intellectual thought] of the moment [is] an exhaustion with a paradigmatic style of discourse altogether." Freed from what would be a wholly unsatisfactory unitary discipline-based approach, I have attempted to understand the Innu predicament by drawing on a wide range of sources inside and outside the social sciences, as well as through my own personal passions, memories, and prejudices. Limiting myself to one approved "method" or one set of privileged sources would have been parochial and resulted, like many academic books on subject populations, in the people themselves being mere "data" to marshal in support of particular intellectual perspectives or theories. Nonetheless, the book is still an outsider's interpretation. I do not pretend to speak for the Innu or to provide any specific prescriptions. Instead, I offer an understanding of how their recent crisis of cultural (and physical) survival came to be in the light of their relations with Europeans and Euro-Canadians. Because the book is primarily about both the Innu and their colonizers, and I am neither Innu nor Canadian, I look at the situation from a distance. While this has certain limitations, it also provides an openness to perceptions and perspectives that the insider might miss or fail to recognize.

Taken as a whole, the time that I have spent in Davis Inlet, Sheshatshiu, and hunting camps of the interior of Labrador amounts to one year between 1994 and 2001. I began my work with the Innu with a visit in 1994 with my friend James Wilson, who had visited the Innu on several previous occasions as a scriptwriter for the BBC documentary film, *The Two Worlds of the Innu* (Wilson, 1994), and as a member of the non-governmental organization Survival International. Our intention in 1994 was to visit Utshimassits and Sheshatshiu to discuss my participation in a research project that would offer help in interpreting and understanding the Innu experience of settlement and would be fashioned towards an international human rights report. With the unanimous agreement of the many Innu we consulted on that trip, my work began in earnest. I returned every year between 1995 and 2001, sometimes for as long as three months, other times for only a weekend. In 1995, during a two-month stay, I spent three weeks with Innu families at Utshisk-nipi, and the following year I spent a week at the Mushuau Innu gathering at Kamesteuishikashish. I have since been to "the country" with the Innu on several other occasions. These were transformative experiences as I lived and travelled with the Innu and came to appreciate the facts of their difference and uniqueness, not simply in the practical ways in which they live but in their special view of the world, which is most apparent in the hunting camps.

In subsequent trips in 1997 and 1998, I visited locations in which I could observe the Innu-*Akaneshau* encounter. Much of my time was spent in school classrooms where I recorded dialogues between the white teachers and the Innu students, and in courtrooms, where I made similar recordings between Innu and non-Innu participants. Over these years, I also attended various meetings between the Innu Nation officials and their advisers as well as meetings between the Innu Nation or band council teams and Canadian officials. However, I did not limit myself to recording dialogue, but also noted the many other activities that surrounded the central focus of the institutional procedures. In 1999, I became a researcher for the Sheshatshiu Innu band council for three months. At this time, I interviewed about 60 people from the community on their experience of schooling. I also interviewed non-Innu and Innu teaching staff. The following year I spent three months in St. John's, Newfoundland, from where I made two additional trips to Sheshatshiu. In connection with the gas-sniffing crisis mentioned earlier, I also accompanied the Mushuau Innu band council of Davis Inlet to Ottawa where I participated in discussions between them and the Canadian federal Departments of Health and Indian Affairs.

As a frequent visitor to Sheshatshiu and Utshimassits, I made friends with many residents of these villages. My days were often spent visiting and socializing, and from these informal occasions much of what I know about how the Innu feel has its origins. I have quoted many Innu in many different contexts, and supplemented my own conversations with them with the spoken records of Innu that have appeared in films, on the Internet, and in the many Innu Nation publications. Some of the material presented was collected for the international human rights report *Canada's Tibet: The Killing of the Innu* (Samson et al., 1999). Other material has been drawn from my periodic work with the Sheshatshiu Innu band council and as a board member of the Tshikapisk Foundation, an Innu organization dedicated to the revitalization of the Innu way of life in the country.

All of this research speaks to the contemporary experience of the Innu, but discussions of what has happened to the Innu since sedentarization can only be understood by an acknowledgement of the experiences of previous generations – the life in the country before the advent of the villages, their contacts with Europeans while they were nomads, and the orientations of Europeans towards them from the seventeenth century on. Particularly pertinent to the understanding of Innu history have been my discussions with a number of *Tshenut* ("elders"). Not surprisingly, their interpretations of the transformations are at complete variance from those of Canadian officials such as Walter Rockwood, whose writings, along with those of other decision-makers, I traced in various archival sources. The memoirs, diaries, and reports of other Europeans, such as missionaries, fur traders, explorers, and anthropologists, also are drawn upon to provide background material and to elucidate the many continuities between past and present perceptions of the Innu. I have consulted a wide range of archival material at the Centre for Newfoundland Studies at Memorial University of Newfoundland, as well as the numerous documents passed to me at the Innu Nation and band council offices, including a number of printed materials and official publications from the Innu Nation Resource Centre in Sheshatshiu. In doing so, I follow the recommendation of Marshall Sahlins (1994: 377) that research should "synthesize the field experience of a community with an investigation of its archival past."

By attempting to maintain a central focus on the edges that surface in encounters between the Innu and Euro-Canadians and their institutions, to a certain extent I have written against the grain of the revisionist anthropology mentioned earlier. While much anthropology of the 1990s – the discipline that would see the Innu as its territory – dismissed as "essentialist" any notion of cultural integrity in peoples, I have attempted to preserve an understanding of the Innu as a people. This is not to fix the Innu as static and bounded, for I recognize that they are not. Such an approach is necessary, in part, because of the peculiarities of Innu history, particularly the very recent abandonment of permanent nomadic hunting, an activity that has a marked effect on the way the contemporary Innu think and operate in the world. Furthermore, the difficult Subarctic terrain of the Labrador-Quebec peninsula lends itself more to the preservation of the integrity of peoples than do temperate landscapes, which are more immediately amenable to the influences of globalization, and this could be why researchers working in the Far North, such as Hugh Brody and Julie Cruikshank, have been at pains to differentiate clearly between white and Native understandings of the world.

My attachment to some concept of the Innu as a distinct people is also driven by the almost unanimous belief in the villages in the value of what is seen as a still palpable and practicable way of life. While I accept that the Innu and Canadians do not and have not spoken with one voice, the scale of the tragedies among the Innu under the impositions of Canadian authority and the magnitude of domination that has led to such a sustained attempt to control a previously autonomous people call for a different approach. The scale of the political, social, and discursive imbalance renders less than helpful any analysis that assumes only collections of individuals with mixed, contingent, fluid, and globalized identities.

While I have employed recognized social science methodological techniques such as interviews, participant observation, and ethnographic fieldwork, for the most part I have been guided by my own experiences and feelings. Preferring to live rather than consciously "study," I have found that the chance encounters and countless conversations with Innu, settlers, and professionals in the course of everyday life furnished much of the material that I fashion. The uncertain conditions of life both in the villages and in the country, along with the proclivities of the Innu always to be flexible, militate against any fixed plans or methodological strategies.[9] Ethically, my first commitment has been to the desires expressed by countless Innu that their integrity as a people be recognized and respected.

Researching the Innu, or any other Native Americans, is an enterprise fraught with difficulties. Their lives can easily become used as mere data. Discovering my own unease at the constant round of asking questions, I tried to keep a balance between my desire to speak to particular individuals in the villages and my reliance on the numerous chance encounters that occur in the course of participating in activities. My drift, however, was to trust my own experiences with people, watching, learning, and, most importantly listening. In the course of my time with the Innu I have heard many stories of life lived in the settlements and the hunting camps of *Nitassinan*. These first-hand stories, along with the excellent narratives of the Innu predicament produced in *Gathering Voices* (Innu Nation, 1995), a sort of autopsy of what had gone wrong in Sheshatshiu and Davis Inlet since settlement, and films such as *The Two Worlds of the Innu* (Wilson, 1994) and *Ntapueu* (Innu Nation, 1998), provide the individual examples needed for an understanding of how larger social and political processes manifest themselves.[10]

Naturally, I have felt the highs and lows that anyone would in a similar project of studying another people's experience. But all has been balanced against the warmth of the Innu, their good humour, and their kindly teasing in which I have always found levity and elevation. The Innu, a generous and sharing people, included me in their lives in the settlements and on their travels on their land. My presence has been made possible by their hospitality, and their continuing endurance as a people deserving of respect and recognition on their own terms is what makes this book possible.

OUTLINE OF THE BOOK

Each chapter in the book is virtually a self-contained essay on the Innu predicament. As a whole, the book examines "the way of life that does not exist" in the context of sustained pressures from a host of non-Innu organizations to assume control over the Innu and exercise powers to assimilate them. The state, developers, the Church, the school, the health authorities, the healing services, and the criminal justice system are the principal institutions that I will look at. Yet, what is important is not simply the legal and other authority of these institutions, but their infusion with European views of the world and of the Aboriginal Other. Both political power and the power of the image have melded in all these attempts to transform the Innu.

Most fundamentally, the imposition of Euro-Canadian institutions takes place under the powers of the state. First Britain and France and then Canada asserted sovereignty over the Innu and their lands. This mere assertion – and this is all it amounts to, since the Innu have never consented to such authority or signed any treaties – is the basis for the exercise of what is in effect colonial domination. Chapter 1 begins with perhaps the central most important facet of the transformation of the Innu, that is, sedentarization itself, with the accompanying imposition of the state and formal authority structures among the Innu. By imposing itself on a formerly autonomous people and acting on prior interventions of missionaries, Canada itself created the conditions for political extinguishment, and it is here that we start. Central to this project was the creation of Innu "chiefs" to give a semblance of legitimacy to it. By the turn of the twenty-first century, chiefs had been accompanied by Innu political organizations. These bodies, the band councils and the Innu Nation, are now integral to the political nexus of the state and find themselves reacting to Canadian policies that assume sovereignty over their lands and dictate the terms upon which they are able to respond.

Chapter 2 looks in more detail at one Canadian policy, the comprehensive land claims procedure, in which the Innu attempt to deal with the political demands of the state. While on the surface this policy is about political extinguishment, it also carries with it elements of cultural extinguishment. To illustrate this, I focus on the role of Euro-Canadian advisers as brokers and narrate how the use of officially sanctioned cartographic techniques influences the particular manner in which Innu identity is presented and compliance to the "claims" procedure is achieved. In Chapter 3 I examine the recent historical circumstances that helps to explain the state's concern with the land of the Innu. Using a number of European representations of the Labrador landscape, I discuss the scramble for the resources that successive waves of explorers, surveyors, and government agents, first hesitantly and then enthusiastically, encouraged. While the earliest of such large developments – significantly the massive Churchill Falls hydroelectric generating project in the late 1960s – simply went ahead with no consultation with the Innu, Canada has more recently put in place consultation exercises, such as environmental impact assessment (EIA), to evaluate potential impacts on affected populations. These processes have thus far dictated only that megaprojects in Labrador get the green light. By drawing on a closely observed meeting on the EIA for a major mining operation on Innu land, I examine the cultural miscommunications and political exigencies that might suggest why resource extraction on Native lands is so often approved. In Chapter 4 I look at the way in which images of Native primitivity have been harnessed to situate the Innu in the nether regions of cultural evolution and to rationalize the attempts made to change them from the nineteenth-century fur trade onward. While numerous Innu starved as a result of their induction into the fur trade and through deliberate policies of the traders, images of backward and improvident Indians became part of the fur traders' stock in trade. Assuming the necessity of toil to civilization, similar representations of the Innu were taken up by policy-makers in the twentieth century to demand that they be transformed into village-dwelling labourers in the market economy.

Chapters 5 and 6 discuss the linked projects of Christianization and education. From the first Jesuits landing on the North Shore of the Gulf of St. Lawrence in the seventeenth century to the current school authorities in Labrador, the educators' calling resided in the Europeanization of the younger generations of Innu who could, it was thought, be relied on to break the cycles of nomadism and the world view associated with it. In Chapter 7 I narrate the interplay of medical images of the Innu, oriented around Native squandering and squalor and the tragic record of sickness and self-destruction in the villages. Chapter 8 deals with the loss of autonomy incurred by the methods of "healing" and treatment for alcohol abuse, sexual abuse, suicide, and gas-sniffing. In this chapter, I also discuss the personal politics of drinking and, while noting the destructive effects of alcohol on individuals and families, attempt to understand it as both expressive of the experience of the Innu and as a means to achieve an autonomy that is largely denied most people in the settlements. Using close observations of circuit court hearings, in Chapter 9 I detail how alien concepts of judgement, guilt, and retribution, incorporated into the criminal justice system, are applied to the Innu, thus undermining their own beliefs that interpersonal conflict is best avoided and that punishment is foolish. In conclusion, I consider the Innu predicament in the light of Canadian self-perceptions and Innu resistance and cultural continuity.

Burdens on the Crown 1

I think that we do have a right to exist as a people. My father or my grandfather have never signed any treaties or any agreements with any governments and yet we are pushed aside . . . to become beggars in our own country.

– Katie Rich, former President of Innu Nation, speaking at New-foundland Supreme Court trial in 1995

POLITICS BEFORE SETTLEMENT

Prior to the 1960s, the Innu now housed in Davis Inlet and Sheshat-shiu were permanent nomadic hunters, constantly moving across the rich and varied terrain of the entire Labrador-Quebec peninsula. They travelled for most of the year, moving camps as the hunting for caribou and other animals in the tundra, lakes, rivers, and forests of the Labrador-Quebec interior demanded. Hunting camps were composed of small and flexible family groups to suit the many environmental and social contingencies. The highly fluid patterns of social organization, communality, and aversion to any type of formal authority may have helped to ensure survival in sometimes unforgiving territories where any type of open conflict could compromise it.

The shift from flexible, constantly changing, and informal leadership on the land to state-imposed and permanent authority structures in the villages has profoundly altered relationships among Innu and between them and others. Before settlement, the

American anthropologist Eleanor Burke Leacock (1994: 165) noted that "there were no permanent chiefs in Montagnais-Naskapi[1] society, and people who could be referred to as 'leaders' were people whose influence rested on their wisdom and ability. They held no formal authority." The only recognized form of leader was the *utshimau* (literally "first man") who took command only temporarily for particular expeditions; thus, different people were *utshimaut* (plural of *utshimau*) on different occasions. Anyone could follow the *utshimau*, but no one was obligated to do so. If they did follow, they were bound only for a particular expedition (see Henriksen, 1973: 42-49). The authority of the *utshimau* was temporary, non-ascriptive, and open to all. Spiritual and moral authority, on the other hand, was often exercised by *kamintushit* or shamans who acted as mediators between the Innu and the Animal Gods, who decided on courses of action, including the *kushapatshikan* or shaking tent, in times of crisis, and generally helped to ensure that respect for the animals was maintained. Researchers observing pre-settlement life have stressed the egalitarian, even "communistic" basis of Innu society as regards both status and the distribution of food and material goods (Tanner, 1944: 602; Leacock, 1994: 157). According to these accounts, personal autonomy among the Innu was highly valued, and it was considered presumptuous for an individual to make decisions on behalf of others. This extended to authority over children who were rarely punished or scolded. In contrast to the subordinate role of women in European society, Innu women played a major role in decision-making, especially on the locations and timings of movements (Leacock, 1980: 29).

In what was the first detailed written description of the Innu by a European, Father Paul Le Jeune wrote of the "Montagnais" of the North Shore of the St. Lawrence in the seventeenth century: "they have reproached me a hundred times because we fear our Captains, while they laugh at and make sport of theirs. All the authority of their chief is in his tongue's end, for he is powerful in so far as he is eloquent; and, even if he kills himself talking and haranguing, he will not be obeyed unless he pleases the Savages" (quoted in Leacock, 1994: 165-66). A missionary in the service of France, Le Jeune was the first to attempt to instill the value of permanent authority relations among the Innu. However, it was not until they were sedentarized by the Canadian, Newfoundland, and Quebec authorities three centuries later that this took any recognized shape. This was because in the intervening period, although many Innu had been "converted" to Roman Catholicism, they were able to maintain their nomadic life and most of the beliefs and practices that went with it, meeting the priests at the coastal posts for only a few days a year.

Settlement, being predicated on the assumption that the Innu would all live together in one location in perpetuity, was seen by Le Jeune's successors, the twentieth-century missionaries, to require some form of permanent authority. This was deemed to be necessary not only for the orderly establishment of relations among the congregated Innu, but between them and the state and Church. It was not until mid-century, however, that the priests met with any success on this score. The turning point came when the Innu, who were becoming increasingly reliant on trade for rifles, canvas, tea, tobacco, and other materials, assembled in larger numbers at Davis Inlet and North West River, the trading post immediately adjacent to present-day Sheshatshiu, as well as similar locations on the North Shore of the St. Lawrence. While the Innu were gathered around these trading posts, the Roman Catholic priests, who began to establish themselves with more frequency at these posts, intervened to create European-style political authority among the assembled Innu.

Among the Mushuau Innu (or "Naskapi"), this process began in the 1920s with Father Edward O'Brien's appointment of Joe Rich as chief. By the 1960s, the resident missionary had "built a house for the chief with his own money while the other Naskapi continued to live in tents" and otherwise lavished favouritism on this "chief" (Henriksen, 1973: 97-98). To a large extent, the chief unwittingly became an instrument of the priest, who even told him what to say to visitors. At Sheshatshiu, according to José Mailhot (1997: 60), the Innu who were placed in the new authority positions were those who were most patronized by the missionaries and, generally, who were most "Europeanized." Even then, however, the new authority was still regarded as transparently imposed and did not translate into anything meaningful within Innu society. For example, Father O'Brien's "chief" in Sheshatshiu, Antuan Ashini, "was a chief in name only, without power," as one Innu informant told Mailhot in the 1960s (Mailhot and Michaud, 1965: 103). During her fieldwork among Innu families summering at Sheshatshiu in 1951, Leacock (1954: 24) pointed out, "as far as the Indians are concerned, there was as yet no band chief, although the man who had served a former missionary as interpreter was so considered by the whites."

By wielding influence as intermediaries with the rapidly encroaching government authorities, the priests, who learned the Innu language, were able to restrict Innu movements and gain control over various aspects of decision-making. At Davis Inlet in the 1960s, the Norwegian anthropologist Georg Henriksen (1981: 671), who was there at the time, describes how the priest operated as money-lender, confessor, mechanic, and doctor. Crucially, the priest "served as the necessary link between the Naskapi and the storekeeper, the storekeeper's superiors, government officials, and other representatives from Euro-Canadian society. Thus he came to control all strategic information flowing between Davis Inlet and the outside world."

Once in the village, the priests went to extremes to ensure that the Innu remained there. Priests worked their persuasion in both direct and indirect ways, and were not above trading upon the spiritual and political powers they encouraged the Innu to attribute to them as "men of God." Elizabeth Penashue, now a *Tshenu* (singular of *Tshenut*) in Sheshatshiu, recalled that shortly after her parents received a house in the settlement at a time when most Innu were only semi-sedentary, the priest would come over to visit, laughing and joking with her parents. Then he would say to them, "Why do you go to the country? Why don't you just stay here in Sheshatshiu?" Although her mother believed that there was not enough wild food in the community to feed her family, the priest reassured her of the benefits of settled life. Her mother took the priest's advice because, "He's like Jesus. When he says something, you got to do it."[2]

Within a short space of time, other authority positions that assumed the primacy of village life were imposed. After the "chiefs" came the establishment of elected "band councils," with limited powers of self-administration in each of the newly created villages. Canada then began funding a number of larger Native political bodies – such as Innu Nation in Labrador and the Conseil Attikamek-Montagnais (CAM) and Mamit Innuat in Quebec – to represent groupings of Innu villages in their dealings with non-Innu political and commercial organizations.

Although the arm-twisting of the priests is still remembered by contemporary Innu, the larger political processes that worked to transform the Innu from egalitarian hunters to loosely hierarchical villagers is still perceived as mysterious by many *Tshenut*. One of the main questions the Innu asked of themselves in the collection of reflections on settlement life, *Gathering Voices*, was "How did we get here?" The question, posed more than 20 years after the establishment of the Innu settlement at Davis Inlet, received no clear answers. There were many stories and these were not tales of smooth transitions from tents to houses, but memories of interpreters' statements, of official visits, of promises. Kaniuekutat (Innu Nation, 1992: 11) remembered a fateful day when:

> A military ship came to old Davis Inlet about thirty years ago. It had many different flags. A priest and other people were all dressed up.

We were told that a government person was on the ship and he wanted to meet with the Innu people. We were told he was a representative of the Queen. I don't know who he was. The priest was the interpreter. After the man finished his speech, we were told what he said, whoever he was. He said that before he came here he was told that the Innu people had everything – good housing, water and sewerage. Now he could see that this was not true. When he went back, he would tell the Queen what he had seen: that the Innu were still living in tents. The former chief told him that the Innu were very poor and that it was cold to live in tents.

The representative of the Queen turned out to be Ross King, director of the Division of Northern Labrador Affairs for the Newfoundland provincial government. King, *whoever he was*, was to go back to tell the Queen about the Innu. It made a nice, if unintended, symmetry. His message was conveyed through the priest as translator and the "chief," Joe Rich (or Shushibish), who had been appointed by the priest. What the Innu understood of what was going to be done can only be surmised. They received and transmitted messages through the priest. The priest's chief represented the rest of the Innu to him, and he then interpreted and represented the chief's statements to King and the authorities. The priest, as a minister and counsel to the Innu, would have had views on what was *good* for the Innu. This, added into the messages, amounts to an almost non-existent level of consent from the Innu as a whole in the decision to build a settlement.[3] As Shimunish and Miste Manian say in *Gathering Voices* (ibid., 17):

> Ross King and Chief Joe Rich were the ones who decided. As far as we know, it just happened. All I know is we were told old Davis Inlet was too small a space for new houses. Most people were working, cutting the trees down for a new lot for each house. We thought the government was doing a good job moving the community here in this island. We were told this island was a good spot. We didn't know there were going to be all kinds of problems. When we knew this it was already too late to do anything. Everyone thought we would get everything, like chairs, furnaces, and water, but it was just empty houses we got.

Those Innu who spoke to interviewers for *Gathering Voices* say that they were not consulted in the move from the old Davis Inlet trading post, where they were camped for summer trading and meetings with the priests. Not only were they not consulted, but they were promised that giving up their lives as nomadic hunters would lead to vast improvements in their fortunes. Davis Inlet was, literally, a "promised land." As a small boy at the time, George Rich (2000: 1) eagerly anticipated the move to Davis Inlet. He recalled the moment of settlement:

The northerly wind calmed as we landed on the beaches of the new Davis Inlet. Waves splashed against our 15-foot punt, in which 10 people were crammed together. We had often traveled to this place before. It was across from the old Davis Inlet. It had been chosen by the missionary and his appointed chief, a respected elder. Now this place had become the promised land. There was talk of a huge store, a church and a big school that would take all children age five and up.

At Sheshatshiu people tell different stories. Shimun Michel told me that Innu were promised houses at Goose Bay airbase, built by the U.S. Air Force during World War II:

When Goose Bay was first established, we were told that it would be a settlement. No matter what they said, we went along. It was the same with Churchill Falls [a hydroelectric development begun in 1967], we didn't speak to them but went along with it. When I first went on the Goose Bay base, the military guys said it would only be temporary, and houses would be left behind for the Innu. As long as we went along, there would be more houses in Goose Bay. When I came back, I realized that there were strange goings on.

Shimun Michel thought that the interpreter tricked him. Yet, perhaps it was this promise, at least for the Michel family, that was used to entice them to settle across from the North West River trading post at Sheshatshiu. They were settled after travelling up from Sept-Îles on the North Shore of the St. Lawrence. For many, then, it "just happened"; they "went along." The lumber and contracts for their housing arrived and they were expected to start building. In a further measure of enticement, their welfare and other benefits, which had only recently been introduced, were made dependent upon their adoption of sedentary life. Once the provincial authorities decided to go ahead with housing, a rental purchase plan was introduced whereby the heads of households were issued with lumber as an "advance" to actually construct the house. All those receiving houses through this Indian Housing Agreement were required to sign a contract stating that they would live in the house for a period of 10 years. At the end of this time, if the house was deemed to have been kept in a good state of repair, the "homeowner" would receive title to it.[4]

However, among the stories of "advances," relocations, promises of a better life, and gifts of welfare money from the white men is bewilderment as to what was actually happening to them as their own ways of making decisions started to become undermined. Pien Penashue, *Tshenu* of Sheshatshiu, was concerned about the role of money in these tricky transactions:

In the early days there was no such thing as government. Joe Smallwood [the former Premier of Newfoundland] said in the 1950s there were no Innu in Labrador. Only in the late 1950s did they realize that Innu existed, living in Labrador. Then we started receiving family allowance and money. We didn't know the purpose of receiving money or what the government was up to. A lot of people don't realize what is behind it today. I still don't know what it is doing to Innu people.

The perception is of mysterious plots. Proposals containing monetary and other inducements were made, and most people went along on the nod of the priest and his appointed chief. While the Provincial Division of Northern Labrador Affairs exerted direct formal control over the Innu communities from 1949, by the 1970s the spread of more liberal attitudes, particular Canadian Supreme Court cases, and a growing international concern for the rights of indigenous peoples began to make state policies of assimilation and incorporation such as these politically untenable. The political exigencies emerging from the 1970s onward demanded more than the nod of the priest. Any such measures, however, would simply be like shutting the barn door after the horse had bolted, for the Innu were already domiciled in shacks in the villages. Whatever reforms would be put forward would at best be a simple amelioration of a *fait accompli* and at worst be subtle methods to bolster the *fait accompli.*

Nonetheless, by the end of the 1970s, any policy directed towards the Innu needed to elicit some level of *Innu* consent. Reliance on priests as go-betweens was unsustainable, although Canadian officials saw nothing remiss about building on the nascent Innu authority structures that the priests had already erected with the appointment of chiefs. In this context, the manufacture of Native political authority has been a key to the legitimacy of the state itself. In funding, and to a large extent establishing, Native political institutions such as village band councils as well as larger associations of Native peoples, Canada has to some degree insulated itself against any criticism that it has not recognized the rights of peoples that it simply absorbed within its borders. In so doing, it has manufactured the negotiating conditions necessary to impose Aboriginal policies and procedures, all governed by one overarching legal system.

CHIEFS

The late nineteenth-century French sociologist, Émile Durkheim, observed that the arrival of the state in previously self-regulating societies was a deeply destructive process. The state, in Durkheim's view, was an accompaniment to the process of modernization, which was characterized by a shift from relatively "simple" societies to more complex ones. People in Durkheim's "simple" societies were bound together by a division of labour based on the replication of tasks and function. In contrast, more modern, "complex" societies were thought to have highly differentiated divisions of labour. As a parallel to the increasingly complex division of labour, the state functioned to create new forms of personal identity and social life. For Durkheim, the state freed individuals from their more immediate ties to community, tradition, and family, and by doing so, encouraged individualistic character formation.

Durkhcim argues that, as a vast and distant institution, the state erodes pre-existing allegiances and forms of solidarity, while it does nothing to replace the sense of communal well-being that individuals had by virtue of their membership in older forms of association. If this is true of the general process of "modernization," it is even more heavily accented in a colonial situation. As modernization takes hold, people orient themselves less to the authority and social order of their immediate group and more towards the state. The disadvantage of this, according to Durkheim, is that the state does little to bind people together, and this is one of the reasons why he believed, for example, that suicide and alienation were virtually unique to allegedly more complex societies.[5] This general destabilization of society can be observed from the first emergence of "chiefs." As Durkheim (1964: 195) puts it in *The Division of Labor in Society*:

> Chiefs are in fact the first personalities who emerge from the social mass. Their exceptional situation, putting them beyond the level of others, gives them a distinct physiognomy and accordingly confers individuality upon them. In dominating society, they are no longer forced to follow all of its movements. Of course, it is from the group that they derive their power, but once power is organized, it becomes autonomous and makes them capable of personal activity. A source of initiative is thus opened which had not existed before then. There is, hereafter, someone who can produce new things and even, in certain measure, deny collective usages. Equilibrium has been broken.

While Durkheim is correct in identifying the general destabilizing effect of the emergence of permanent authority relations, he makes it sound as if the process is inevitable, an accompaniment to the passing of time, the growth of human societies in the grip of "modernization." While the introduction of the state and institutionalized authority has altered Innu society, the colonial origins of these changes – a principle that Durkheim ignored – signify that the policies of an already established state brought them about. Unlike

Durkheim's hypothetical chiefs, Innu "chiefs" do not derive their power from "the group" in the throes of social change, but from the state that has imposed and legitimized such positions.

When he was the "chief" of Sheshatshiu, Greg Andrew told me that "chief" and "band" (as in band council) are the terms of white people. He was uneasy about the title, and didn't want to have authority, particularly over the *Tshenut*. He didn't accept that he was "it." Similarly, Katie Rich, a former President of Innu Nation, remarked that:

> one of the hardest things that I find in being a leader is that I have a lot of responsibilities for the people. As a leader you have to live on both sides, both the Innu and the non-native way. You have to follow the white man's way of living; you have to be able to understand their ways. It is really hard for me as a leader. You have to choose which path you will go for the people. Because people depend on you a lot, you want to take the steps towards what the people want, but the government also pressures me to do things their way. It is dividing the leaders not in the sense that there is division amongst the leaders, but dividing us personally. (Innu Nation, 1993: 35)

Although missionaries attempted to develop the kind of long-term authority presupposed by these imposed political bodies by promoting certain individuals as chiefs, the idea of electing leaders was profoundly alien and still generates intense animosities, especially between the few Innu elected officials and the many others who feel overlooked and spoken for. It also exacerbates the widening rift between old and young. As the 70-year-old Kaniueketat put it in the film, *The Two Worlds of the Innu* (Wilson, 1994):

> I really blame the young leaders, they don't know what to say to the white man and we elders are never invited to meetings . . . . I told my nephew that and he said, "Don't stop us where you were, don't take us back into the past." And I said to him: "You've never seen the past. Take us with you so we can help, you are not as strong as we are, we have seen more . . . . You grew up in the community with the houses." That's what I said to him. But he never said anything back to me.

As well as dividing the generations, the need to participate in these political institutions has made many of the young leaders ambivalent. During a court hearing in 1988, Penote Michel gave vent to these feelings:

> Those of us drawn into positions on the councils find ourselves expected to act in ways which are not only counter to norms of Innu behaviour but which amount to serving as proxies for our colonizers in administering the government villages . . . . Here we are expected to preside over little empires of chronic financial depend-

ency, watching the foreigners' welfare money flow in while our
People and culture disintegrate around us.[6]

While the political institutions impressed upon the Innu are renewed by periodic elections, they have not been the anchors of
political legitimacy that they are supposed to represent in a democracy, but sources of chaos, division, and, occasionally, tragedy. As
George Rich (2000: 35) remarks in his memoir of growing up in
Davis Inlet:

> the election system created division and took away the elders' tradi-
> tional role. It also brought all the kinds of corruption elections can
> have. In our small community, people with large families can con-
> trol band council elections and government. Also, anyone who has
> a lot of alcohol can win a seat on the council. Now every year we
> have elections in Davis Inlet, mainly because people crave influence
> or business contracts or good employment from the council.

Election times are periods of great stress and turmoil as "[p]etty politics grew from a spark into a blazing fire that divides the community
today" (ibid.). Campaigns are commonly accompanied by heavy
drinking sessions as alcohol is often used as a lever to obtain votes
(although certainly not by all candidates in all elections).[7] There
have been instances when outbreaks of election-fever drinking in
Sheshatshiu have caused the schools to close down on account of
children not attending and inebriated adults entering the building.
Due to the serious violence and hostilities between family-based factions, some families deliberately vacate the community by setting up
camp several miles away to avoid the trouble that occurs around
polling day.

Political platforms or ideas are not necessarily what are at stake
in the elections. In many ways, what separates candidates is not ideology, although there may be substantial differences in what
individual candidates say they will do if they are elected. The quest
for a secure income with all the material benefits that may come with
it is a powerful motivating factor in an environment in which hardly
any Innu can obtain employment outside of their communities. Offices are sources of salaries not simply for the candidates, but for
their family and friends who may be able to acquire jobs. Conflicts
over nepotism with accusations of favouritism in job and housing al-
locations, access to the hunting camps through Outpost Program
sponsorship, as well as suspicions and charges of misuse of substantial sums of money have grown with every election and are often
publicized by rival candidates in local newspapers.

The posts of "chief," "president," and the like reinforce distinctions among the Innu that were first cultivated by missionaries by

lavishing favouritism on particularly co-operative people. As Mail-hot (1997: 55) pointed out, "Nowadays the system of distributing favours . . . is the fundamental feature of Innu politics in Sheshat-shit." With increasing amounts of money becoming available in the communities, primarily from the state anticipating a land claims agreement[8] and in response to the numerous press stories of what is portrayed as rampant social pathology, but also from industries en-camped on Innu land, the stakes are escalating. These injections of cash help to create factions, splitting the Innu between those who are able to latch hold of these funds through the political bodies and those who either refuse the funds or are excluded. In addition, the promise and creation of a number of industrial and bureaucratic jobs, including "joint ventures" between would-be Innu entrepre-neurs and corporations, are a convenient tactic of developers to soften resistance to the sequestration of the land.

Nonetheless, the Innu are mostly supportive of the political goals articulated by Innu Nation and band council officials. At times when it has been important to organize people in defence of Innu interests, the leaders have been instrumental in bringing all people together. This was demonstrated in the campaigns against military low-level flying over Innu land in the 1980s and the gas-sniffing crisis in De-cember 2000 when vast numbers of Innu from Davis Inlet converged on Ottawa to publicize their need for assistance and understanding. Innu leaders have been effective and articulate communicators, many tirelessly campaigning for the rights of the Innu to be recog-nized. Whether or not the Innu people in the villages support these various courses of actions, questions of legitimacy of this power still are posed.[9]

LEGITIMACY

A young hunter once told me that he couldn't understand how Innu Nation could tell people to do anything – like protesting, for example. If people wanted to protest, he thought, they would have to come to that themselves. They would have to make up their own minds as to what was right and what was wrong. When I asked about collective Innu interests, he said that you couldn't say that such a thing really existed. Mineral exploration might destroy the Innu, but it is not up to Innu Nation to tell people what to do. "Anyway," he said, turning to the personnel of Innu Nation, "who are they paid by? What hap-pens if they don't get their pay cheque?" The autonomy of the officials to work in the collective interests of the Innu was, in this hunter's view, compromised by their being in the pay of the Cana-dian government. Similarly, Margaret Nuna of Sheshatshiu said that she remembered, "When we came here, we didn't write anything down. When we came here we didn't pay a Chief. Now the Chief is paid by the Canadian government." Thus, although Canada blindly assumes that the articulations of the Innu political bodies are embodiments of representative views, many Innu, including the leaders themselves, recognize the tangled web of inducements that place them in the contradictory position of being paid by their antagonists to "represent" a people who have no tradition of representative authority. Yet, as we shall see, if the Innu do not step forward to fill these almost untenable positions, they risk having their land taken with impunity and their villages mired in endemic poverty.

At the levels both of village politics and of Innu-Canada relations, this frequently leads to a paralysis of decision-making. Innu democracy was always direct rather than representative. Decisions that affected more than one person were generally made through an informal and sometimes lengthy process of deliberation and consultation. Even then, no individual would necessarily be bound, as personal autonomy was deemed a stronger value than the outcome of any collective decision. These conventions were carried over into the settlement so that, although formal institutions have been created to make decisions on behalf of the many, community-wide meetings and consultations are held often to air a wide range of issues. Despite this, members of the community very rarely feel any moral imperative to attend. Meetings can sometimes be full, at other times empty, and more often than not, attended by a few "regulars." Political gatherings are potentially destructive of communal relations because they encourage the kinds of behaviour that many Innu find foolish. In the villages, people still openly avoid conflict and shy away from inviting it by not openly criticizing others, boasting, or placing themselves in positions that could be taken as offensive by others. Political meetings, however, can generate many of the conflicts that Innu normally go to such great lengths to avoid. Even when community meetings are called in response to the increasing demands being placed on the Innu political bodies by the state, many people in both villages either are not included, do not think that they are included, or voluntarily disqualify themselves from participating in any of these deliberations.

Other factors that mitigate against involvement in political decision-making are bound up with the harsh exigencies of settlement living. A life lived in large families, on and off meagre welfare payments, often in the shadow of mass alcohol consumption, abuse, court appearances, suicide attempts, and the ubiquitous gas-sniffing of the children, would hardly put anyone in the mood for lengthy meetings, the agendas of which are almost always dictated from outside the Innu villages. The pain that results from these tragedies, as well as the lack of sanitation and running water (in Davis Inlet) and welfare dependency, is what many Innu spend their days negotiating. Life is suffused by noise. TVs are constantly blaring. Children are running around at all hours of the day and night. There is never enough money to go around. Wood needs to be gathered and chopped for the stoves. Water needs to be found. Snowmobiles need repairing. If money is available, drinking parties may start and continue for several days. Under these conditions, few are able to focus on any of the complicated issues of land claims, environmental assessment, and such questions as the inclusion of the Innu under the terms of the Indian Act, which the political bodies have been dealing with over the decade of the 1990s.

One afternoon, I went to see Nian Rich and his family on the beach road in Utshimassits. The house was sparsely furnished with buckets for chairs, family photos taped up on the walls. Nian proudly showed me a photo of his nephew, Simeon, beaming in his police uniform. On another wall was a photo of Nian's father, Shushebish, the first chief in Davis Inlet. A stench of urine and feces and homebrew permeated the house. A number of family and friends passed around a noggin of homebrew while we talked. The degradation felt by those living in these conditions could not easily be concealed. When I introduced the subject of land rights, all agreed that Canada has acted in a "criminal" way towards the Innu. But it was towards the more immediate indignities that they focused. For Nian and his large family, the lack of sewerage was a big problem. Living in the stench was a more immediate threat to their human dignity than any of the affairs of Innu Nation. For them, the land was "Innu land" and this was transparently obvious to them, as it was to me. However, I knew more of the news of land claims negotiations and of the environmental review of the nearby Voisey's Bay mine than they did, despite having only recently come over from England. Nian's family did not have access to the Internet, as I did, to learn of these things. They were eager to leave the village and get transport out to the hunting camp at Ashuapun where they would join many other families from the village.

SOVEREIGNTY AND CANADIAN INDIAN POLICY

The question of collective rights to the land is perhaps the most pressing issue facing the Innu political leadership as well as the Innu population as a whole. But rights are a foreign concept to most Innu because they necessarily imply the conferring of privileges from a higher *political* power, a power that has not figured in the Innu world until very recently. The Innu have always used their land, *Nitassinan*, and, although they do not claim to "own" it, they are mystified as to how it could possibly "belong" to any other people. One of the oldest people in Davis Inlet, Tshenish Pasteen, recalled that he had been hunting all his life, all over *Nitassinan*. He remembers going to the George River to hunt and fish. His people did not depend on guns. He and his fellow hunters used spears on the caribou fording the river. For many years, he didn't see a white person or an aircraft. The first white person he saw was the American explorer Donald MacMillan.[10] It was news to him that the Canadian government "owned" the land. He wondered how the government could own the land when white people don't hunt and trap on it. "They just stole the land," he sighs. He understands the land "claim" as a kind of white thievery, not in terms of the myriad abstractions that figure into the negotiating processes between the Innu Nation and the various levels of Canadian government.

At this point, it is important to ask how Tshenish's question as to how *Nitassinan* could belong to white people can arise in the first place. How is it that the state can sit in judgement of a land "claim" from them, the people whose ancestors in the area can be traced back to well before European contact? How is it that low-level military flight training can be carried out across the entirety of *Nitassinan*? Or mining at Voisey's Bay, on the migration route of the caribou, the site of births and burials dating back millennia? Or hydroelectric projects on Mista-shipu (the Churchill River) in the heart of the Innu hunting territory? How is it that the provincial and federal governments can sell off rights to land, water, or airspace with no reference to the Native inhabitants? Many Innu besides Tshenish are perplexed. They have never been asked to grant their consent to any sales. They have not ceded land to Canada, Quebec, Newfoundland, or in earlier times to Britain or France by treaty. Even though they are no longer permanent nomadic hunters, Innu have never committed themselves to any course of action that would make any foreign ownership of *Nitassinan* legitimate. Under Canadian constitutional arrangements, their "title" to land has never been "extinguished." In the next few pages, I will trace some of the assumptions of European colonialism and the enactments of Canadian Indian policy that go some way to addressing Tshenish's question. They provide the rationale for the creation of formal Innu political leadership and the largely reactive context within which this leadership is operating.

Questions of ownership never arose until very recently because the British and French states had no pressing need to deal with the Innu in the Labrador-Quebec interior and, aside from some fur trading and meetings with missionaries, the northern Innu in particular had little contact with Europeans and almost no cause to be concerned about the laws of the state. Despite the use of the Labrador coast by numerous fishing fleets, inroads made by fur traders, and both Roman Catholic and Moravian missionaries, European settlement remained sparse and often temporary. However, unbeknownst to the Innu and other Native peoples, these inroads were backed by simple assertions of sovereignty that conferred "rights" to various European interests to trade, possess, and convert. With only the sketchiest of knowledge of the Labrador-Quebec peninsula itself, Europeans gradually started to claim ownership of lands. King Charles granted a charter to the Hudson's Bay Company in 1670 to legally possess whatever land was suitable for trade (Gosling, 1910: 129). None of the Aboriginal peoples of the area draining into Hudson Bay and Hudson Straits ever were consulted on this. It was simply assumed that they had no rights of possession.[11] In 1752 Moravian Brethren from London sailed to the Labrador coast, where, having met Eskimos, they established a settlement and as Gosling (ibid., 252) states, "took possession of the land in the name of King George III, carving his name on a tree." A few years later, sovereignty by tree-carving was replaced by the edict. In the 1760s, the Newfoundland Governor, Sir Hugh Palliser, issued a number of edicts in which it was simply assumed that various "commodities" were there for the taking and that the Indians were under His Majesty's protection (ibid., 173). Palliser made a further allotment of land at Eskimo Bay (Hamilton Inlet) to the Unitas Fratum society of Moravian missionaries in 1765 under the aegis of the Crown. Although there were sporadic episodes of violence on the Labrador coast, mainly between the coastal Inuit and European fishermen, there were no recorded instances of pitched battles or organized warfare to wrench control of the land away from the Natives.

However, indigenous peoples in other parts of North America were not so fortunate and consequently did not view the seizure and settlement of their land in the same light as the Crown, with the result that there was almost continuous friction between Indians and settlers along the ever-expanding western frontier. In 1763, in an attempt to pacify the Indians, the British government issued a Royal Proclamation that fixed a firm frontier between the colonies and "Indian Country" and stipulated that further territory could be acquired only by the Crown and with the full consent of the tribes concerned –

"any Lands whatever, which, not having been ceded to, or purchased by Us, are reserved to them" (cited in Cumming and Mickenberg, 1972: 29).

Although colonists at the time dismissed the Proclamation as no more than – in the words of George Washington, a land speculator himself – "a temporary expedient to quiet the minds of the Indians" (quoted by Williams, 1990: 230), it became the theoretical cornerstone for subsequent "Indian policy" and the treaty was its instrument in both Canada and the United States. The treaty was then extensively employed across North America to further acquire lands "reserved to them." In virtually all cases, Natives would relinquish land, thus extinguishing "title" to it, and in return they would receive various military, economic, and other benefits. However concessionary this may sound, the Proclamation of 1763 was predicated on the notion that the Crown was "sovereign" and held "dominion" over all Native land (Borrows, 1997: 160). Aboriginal rights consisted only of the personal and usufructuary, dependent on the goodwill of the Crown. This was affirmed in the *St. Catharine's Milling* case of 1888 (Miller, 2000: 343), which did, however, recognize that Aboriginal occupation of (later referred to as "Aboriginal title") land pre-existed the imposition of sovereignty and was a "burden" on the Crown. This same basic package of policies and assumptions remains in place in Canada today as a means to extinguish title to "reserved" lands.

As with the Innu "chiefs," an important mechanism for validating extinguishment across Canada has been the imposition of European forms of social organization among Natives that connect them with political institutions of the state. After 1867, the new Dominion of Canada moved quickly to enfranchise individual Indians through a series of Indian Acts that defined Aboriginal peoples as wards of the state, made formal provisions for the creation of reserve land (significantly, under Crown title), and imposed systems of "band" government. Natives brought under the Indian Act were then registered, given "band numbers," designated "status Indians," and defined according to racial criteria of band membership. Status Indians were and still are further bound by a lengthy series of federal restrictions on their activities.

To be relieved of the burden on the Crown of reserved lands (although they are hardly a burden since sovereignty overrides all), a series of numbered treaties were concluded between the Crown and a large number of officially recognized Native peoples during the nineteenth century. Treaties were a means of dealing with the status both of Natives themselves and of various parcels of land that were to be opened for settlement and/or development. In making treaties, the government brought together agents of the Crown and groups of Aboriginal peoples labelled "bands" under "headmen" who were constituted by these agents as legitimate representatives of peoples, who for the most part had no exact counterpart to European-style representative authority. These assemblages were in almost all cases unwittingly made party to treaties that surrendered Indian land to the Crown in perpetuity and in exchange the Crown provided compensation and certain specified rights in particular "reserved" areas.

The treaties went some way to spelling out Native rights, although we now know from Native oral testimony and other sources that they also were spectacularly manipulative arrangements that always ended with a cession of Native land. Some Native peoples did not know what the treaties signified to the whites, especially in view of the fact that so many had no concept of private, let alone state, property, so could only guess at what the agreement meant. "[T]here is a world of difference," as Brody (1981: 68) states in relation to Treaty 8, "between the terms of [the Treaty] and the understanding the Indian signatories had of it . . . Indians did not understand Treaty 8 to be a surrender of rights." Furthermore, the written versions of treaties are widely believed to have been induced by extortion, force, and fraud and have afterwards been characterized by government non-compliance with their terms (among the numerous examples, see Fumoleau, 1974, on Treaties 8 and 11; Treaty 7 Elders and Tribal Council, 1996: 297-303; Bussidor and Bilgen-Reinart, 1997: 25-28, on Treaty 5). Others were negotiated under extreme duress and threats of extinction from the floods of settlers, miners, gold seekers, and land speculators.[12] Fumoleau (1974: 18) presents a succinct description of the function and purpose of the treaty:

> Most treaties and land surrenders were signed after the Indians had lost control of their territory. Their only choice was to lose their land with a treaty, or to lose it without one. Usually they were guaranteed official use of a "reserve," which was held in Trust by the Crown. This was a measure to protect the Indians from further encroachments, and to offer them security against the aggressiveness of their white neighbours. Other treaty gifts: free education, free medical care, cash annuities, groceries etc., also helped to win the Indian people's good will. Protecting the Indian was not the main reason for treaties, however. Overriding all other considerations was the land: the Indians owned it and the white people wanted it. Even when the Indians posed no threat, treaties were still signed, as a moral or ethical gesture: a gentleman's way to take without grabbing.

Treaties were a way to take without grabbing. Gifts were provided as a sign of good faith but land would be ceded in perpetuity in exchange. For a specified quantum of gifts and circumscribed reserves, the "bands" that were signatories to Treaty 8 at Lesser Slave Lake in 1899 had to "CEDE, RELEASE, SURRENDER AND YIELD UP to the Government of the Dominion of Canada, for Her Majesty the Queen and Her successors for ever, all their rights, titles and privileges whatsoever, to the lands included within the following limits . . ." (cited by Fumoleau, 1974: 71). Treaty 3 involving the Saulteaux or Ojibway Indians states, "And with a view to show the satisfaction of Her Majesty with the behaviour and good conduct of Her Indians She hereby, through Her Commissioners, makes them a present of twelve dollars for each man, woman and child belonging to the bands represented, in extinguishment of all claims heretofore preferred" (quoted in Cumming and Mickenberg, 1972: 315). The Dominion of Canada was slightly less generous to the Sayisi Dene of northern Manitoba, who under Treaty 5 in 1910 surrendered their homelands "in return for five dollars per adult per year, and an annual visit by a doctor" (Bussidor and Bilgen-Reinart, 1997: 26).

While modern Canada has cheerfully accepted the treaties' assertion that the Crown extinguished "Aboriginal title," it has not always honoured the range of obligations specified in the treaties, arguing that it was the Crown and not Canada that negotiated the agreements. As Churchill (1999: 55) points out, Canada has it both ways. That is, Canada has established a policy of appealing to the Crown as the ultimate authority, the personification of the state, *and* constituting itself as a sovereign nation. Despite the repatriation of the Canadian Constitution in 1982, however, the Canadian state is not a republic and still refers to the ultimate authority as "the Crown," creating a mercurial situation in which governmental authority emanates from Ottawa, which is under the auspices of the British Crown, although that "Crown" is now mere symbol, "in right of Canada."

In fact, many Innu actually believe that the Queen exercises ultimate authority over them. It is easy to see how this could arise because the symbolism of the British monarchy is pervasive. In court cases involving Innu, the prosecution is referred to as "the Crown," a portrait of the Queen, circa the early 1960s, still hangs in the courtrooms of Goose Bay and North West River. Queen Elizabeth even visited Sheshatshiu in 1997 in connection with the Newfoundland-sponsored celebrations of the voyage of John Cabot from Bristol in 1497. The monarchical symbolism creates the impression of one ultimate "boss" to whom Canadian governmental functionaries are responsible.

The Innu lands, *Nitassinan*, however, have remained unceded by any means. Neither "Her Majesty" nor her royal predecessors has dispensed "compensation" or gifts in exchange for land in perpetuity. To many Innu, the government functionaries' power is mysterious. It is expressed in onerous demands and backed up by an imposed law. The Queen's portrait merely watches, as a supernatural guarantee of the words in the laws. Nevertheless, the authority exercised over the Innu is as close to absolute as possible between two distinct societies. First of all, like the "bands" of earlier treaties in Canada, the Innu have been divided by the colonial border between Quebec and Labrador drawn by the British government in 1927. Each village (or sometimes a small cluster of them) is picked off for separate negotiations. Following this segmentation of one people, Quebec has been quicker to tether the Innu and their lands on its "side" under the Indian Act and has created "reserves,"[13] while Newfoundland has operated for over half a century without any formal agreements. Only preliminary agreements exist between Canada and Newfoundland and the Innu. In the absence of a treaty or other cession, Newfoundland has proceeded as if there were no impediments to its authority over the Innu, not even the flimsy and hollow legal guarantees of "Aboriginal title." It has assumed, and perhaps this is merely a convenient ignorance of an out-of-the-way settler society, that no lands are "reserved for them" and that no formal cession is needed anymore.[14] Thus, Newfoundland's policy on Aboriginal land claims in the 1990s stated that:

> The continued use and occupancy of the land and the harvest of renewable resources are considered fundamental to native lifestyle and economic self-reliance. On the basis of this premise and the requirement of aboriginal use and occupancy of the land, the Province will *contribute* lands and renewable resources to a land claims settlement (Government of Newfoundland and Labrador, n.d.: 8; emphasis added).

Possession has been quietly incorporated into the mythology of Newfoundland. By *contributing* lands and resources, the Newfoundland government represents itself as the sovereign possessor of the land. If it were not for the fact that sovereignty here amounts to no more than words, it would seem as though the provincial authorities are jumping the gun, assuming that they already "own" the land before the juridical conventions for extinguishing Aboriginal title have been completed. Implicit in the manners of the provincial authorities is that the Innu and Inuit of Labrador are merely beneficiaries of a magnanimous state. Sovereignty, a simple assertion of long-dead conquerors in other parts of the continent, no longer even requires enunciation. Burdens are silently lifted. Violation is transformed into benevolence only by the *proclamation* of an agreement to agree to *contribute* something that has never been acquired, even in this vast hall of mirrors created by Canadian Indian policy. The Innu, then, are placed in a most mystifying position. They are led to believe that Canada recognizes their title to lands via Aboriginal title, yet Canada or its governmental subdivision acts as if the state owns the land under the umbrella of sovereignty, making Aboriginal title and the notion of reserved lands from the Royal Proclamation onwards absolutely meaningless.[15]

In the context of the continued commercial usurpation of Native lands across Canada over the last 30 years, several court actions have now been brought by communities outside the treaty areas for the return of seized land – that is, lands to which Natives allegedly possess unextinguished Aboriginal title. Beginning with the 1970 *Calder* decision involving the Nisga'a people of British Columbia, a series of cases affirmed that Natives like the Innu, who had not signed treaties or other cessions, possessed unextinguished Aboriginal title, a burden on the Crown. Nonetheless, according to the rulings, the state was able to violate such titles because Native peoples were considered not to have met the tests needed to establish prior ownership. In the *Calder* case, perhaps the first in this recent sequence of cases to rely on theories of cultural evolutionism, Chief Justice Davey dismissed the claims of the Nisga'a on the grounds that "the Indians on the mainland of British Columbia . . . were undoubtedly at the time of [white] settlement a very primitive people with few of the institutions of civilized society, and none at all of our notions of private property" (quoted by Cumming and Mickenberg, 1972: 48). The ruling established that while Aboriginal title may exist, the Nisga'a were too primitive to qualify for it. Nonetheless, *Calder* was carried only on a split decision, and the minority opinion validating the concept of Aboriginal title provided the opening for a shift in Canadian Indian policy towards the recognition of this underlying title as a burden on the Crown within Canadian law (see Asch, 1984: 47-51; Berger, 1991: 140-53). Although this ruling assisted Aboriginal peoples in establishing the validity of their prior rights to land against developers in particular, the burden on them for the next 20 years became the damning official judgements that their rights were compromised because they were culturally and technologically inferior to Europeans. In addition, this underlying title has never been recognized as a basis for tribal sovereignty vis-à-vis the state in Canadian law as it has been in the U.S. Instead, *Calder* and subsequent cases proceeded from the assumption that

Aboriginal title is no limit on federal or provincial jurisdiction (see Korsmo, 1999: 123).

Two suits, in particular, go right to the heart of the issue. In the 1990 *Delgamuukw* case, the British Columbia Supreme Court considered what rights the Gitskan and Wet'suwet'en peoples had to the land they had occupied prior to European contact. After much deliberation, following Native and expert testimony on both sides, it was decided that they had few rights, not because their title had been extinguished, but because before contact they had merely survived through biological instinct, "eking out an aboriginal way of life" (quoted by Asch, 1992: 227). In the words of Chief Justice MacEachern, "by historical standards, [they were] a primitive people without any form of writing, horses or wheeled wagons" (quoted by Culhane, 1998: 247). That is, the Crown was successful in portraying the Native peoples as so backward that they did not even constitute a society in the European sense of the term. This being the case, they were at first contact – and ever since then – under the sovereignty of the Crown.

This decision built on the earlier *Baker Lake* case, brought by an Inuit community in 1980, which ruled that Native people could only legitimately claim Aboriginal title if they demonstrated that they and their ancestors belonged to an "organized society." The decision in *Baker Lake* to rule against the Inuit injunction to stop mining exploration on their hunting and fishing territory, in turn, relied on a 1919 precedent in British colonial law, *Re: Southern Rhodesia*, which differentiated between various levels of social organization. After prescribing a number of criteria for what constitutes an "organized society," it was ascertained that tribes that were "so low" on the scale of "civilization" were not members of an "organized society" and therefore may not have equal legal rights as either Europeans or those tribes that did meet the various criteria (see Asch, 1992; Cumming and Mickenberg, 1972: 48; Culhane, 1998: 92-97). This same set of cultural evolutionist assumptions was used in *Baker Lake* and *Delgamuukw*.

These court cases demonstrate that Canadian sovereignty, when it does not simply stand alone as a categorical imperative and when it requires amplification in the face of challenges, has fallen back on the related notions of the cultural superiority of Europeans, the right of "civilized" people to seize areas they regard as devoid of meaningful ownership, and the absence of rights for hunting peoples. If the Innu had taken any of their many grievances over the sale and appropriation of their land to the courts in this period they would, like the Nisga'a and Baker Lake Inuit, almost surely have been dismissed on the same grounds. Under the cultural evolutionist presumption, because they were nomadic hunters and hence not an "organized society," they would not be entitled to prevent their land from being seized by self-styled representatives of an "organized society." As the legal anthropologist Michael Asch (1996) has demonstrated, falling back on such concepts merely confirms that Canada has always based its claim to sovereignty on *terra nullius* – the English legal doctrine that prior to colonization the land was empty of people who had any rights worthy of consideration in part because their land was deemed to be "wasted" (see Seed, 2001: 155-56).

An appeal ruling of the *Delgamuukw* case in December 1997 has signalled a modification of Canadian Aboriginal policy. However, how significant it will be in stemming the continual intrusions upon Native land and autonomy remains to be seen. While avoiding the overt racism and images of Native primitivity of its predecessor, the ruling has made the price for land seizure more costly to Canada and its corporate interests. The early news reports in the North American press vacillated between trumpeting the liberal "fairness" of the decision and complaining about the excessive rights accorded to Natives (see DePalma, 1997; Gibson, 1997; St. John's *Evening Telegram*, 1997). Although some extensions of Aboriginal rights are brought about by the decision, these are made alongside statements affirming the perpetual inferiority of such rights within Canada. "Aboriginal title," for example, is continually counterposed to (Canadian) "sovereignty." The former is solidified as both a creature of, and subordinate to, the latter.

The *Delgamuukw* court spelled out what "Aboriginal title" consists of, how it can be ascertained, and what procedures governments must follow in order to extinguish it. Aboriginal peoples can now make land claims through proving ancestry via oral testimony, and significantly, these claims cannot be struck down because justices may deem Natives to be primitive. While "Aboriginal title" was positively defined in terms of exclusive rights to use and occupy the land "claimed," and the land under such title can be used in ways that are not "traditional," these cannot be "irreconcilable" with a group's attachment to the land. Rights to non-traditional uses of the lands are primarily reserved for non-Natives who, under the ruling, must first "consult" with Natives who possess Aboriginal title. While a vast number of Aboriginal peoples prefer to use the land in a non-industrial manner, in effect the ruling requires that this is all they can do under Aboriginal title. This fixes Aboriginal peoples in a rather static "traditional" world in which any movements they make towards activities that have been monopolized by non-Native developers will be countered by removal of their Aboriginal title.

Nevertheless, the trump card held by the state is reserved for a passage near the end of the ruling. In it, both the federal and provincial governments may "infringe" Aboriginal rights to the lands under Aboriginal title. Agriculture, forestry, mining, and general economic development, as well as the building of infrastructure and the settlement of foreign populations, are all listed in paragraph 165 of the ruling as objectives that can be used to "infringe" Aboriginal rights. These limitations and infringements placed upon this title are so severe that they virtually negate the title itself. Although there are obvious concessions to Aboriginal peoples in this ruling, in certain important respects, such as the mandate for traditional uses of the land and the infringements, no advance in Native rights over the treaties of a century ago is signalled by this decision. For example, while creating reserves for the Cree, Beaver, and Chipewyan Indians under Treaty 8 in 1899, the Crown simultaneously demanded that "such portions of the reserves and lands . . . as may at any time be required for public works, buildings, railways, or roads of whatsoever nature may be *appropriated* by Her Majesty's Government of the Dominion of Canada" subject to "due compensation" (cited by Fumoleau, 1974: 72).

COMPREHENSIVE LAND CLAIMS: THE FINAL UNBURDENING OF THE CROWN

Within the Western political tradition, nation-states can operate only in a global order that recognizes the sanctity of the state itself. Their legitimacy rests on mutual recognition of sovereignties that permit absolute power – including, if necessary, police and military force – over defined populations and territories. International trade, diplomacy, and the conduct of all relationships between nations, including border entries, are bound by the conventions, regulations, and laws that these states agree upon. States, of course, require the consent or acquiescence of populations in order to act and to exercise authority. But because it is the state itself that asserts sovereignty, the state is outside the juridical order that sovereignty expresses itself within. There exists what German philosopher Carl Schmitt calls a "state of exception" by which sovereignty defines itself. Sovereignty is "the originary structure in which law refers to itself by suspending it" (Agamben, 1995: 28). In the case of relations with Aboriginal peoples, Canada makes the laws that regulate relations, binds Aboriginal peoples to them, and then positions itself outside the laws so that it is impervious to any violations of them by invoking sovereignty. Aboriginal title, in spite of and because of the *Delgamuukw* decision, is a prime example of this "paradox of sovereignty."

There is no escaping the fact that the nation-state of Canada is superimposed on pre-existing populations that largely had no institutions empowered to exercise authority over vast territories. Although sometimes considered sovereign nations by European powers in the "doctrine of discovery," their autonomy as distinct peoples was dissolved, and in some cases literally terminated, by the colonization of their lands by Britain and France. Britain, having secured victory over the French for North American territories in 1763, simply handed over the land to the settler populations when Canada became a separate confederation in 1867 under the British North America Act (now known as the Constitution Act, 1867). This Act, again without any Native consent, transferred "Indians and lands reserved for the Indians" to the federal government and Parliament of Canada (Miller, 2000: 197). The same process occurred when Newfoundland and Labrador joined Canada in 1949 – the Innu and Inuit simply were handed over to newly created Canadian authorities.

To return to answering Tshenish Pasteen's question of how *Nitassinan* could possibly belong to the government in the absence of any Euro-Canadian history on that land, we end up with the concept of sovereignty. The earnest ponderings of chief justices, lengthy disquisitions on rights, and statements about how land can be "owned" are a function of sovereignty. Sovereignty is a principle of political authority, which, although invented as a means to deal with relations between different European powers in the seventeenth century, makes sweeping assumptions about the character of the relations between European and non-European peoples. The problem in the New World for Europeans was, and to some extent still is, how an alien concept like sovereignty and the assumptions upon which it is based can be made to transcend the cultural, spatial, and temporal specifics of Europe and its diaspora. Prior to the twentieth century, the practicalities of this problem rarely exercised the minds of statesmen. However, after World War II and with the advent of the United Nations, a number of international human rights agreements and non-governmental organizations dedicated to universal principles of human rights and self-determination challenged absolute state sovereignty. Even though these organizations lack any binding power over states and to a certain extent bolster the sovereignty of the nation-state, contemporary conflicts between states and indigenous peoples now take place under international scrutiny.

In order to appear in the light of this scrutiny to be acting fairly as well as to legitimize sovereignty, Canada has imposed various forms of agreement with the Native political bodies (such as the Innu Nation) that have not signed treaties, not come under the Indian Act (in this case because of the late entry of Newfoundland into Canada), and given no written consent to their incorporation under Canadian jurisdiction. Several Aboriginal groups in Canada, principally in the Far North and British Columbia, fall into this category. Although these peoples possess Aboriginal title, this has been scant defence against industrial encroachments and the imposition of Euro-Canadian social institutions, including those of the state, in their affairs. Nonetheless, faced with an original usurpation of their lands under Canadian sovereignty, the only option outside the courts that holds any possibility of decelerating the continued appropriation of their land is the comprehensive land claims (CLC) process.

From the point of view of the state, such negotiations can be viewed as a means of acting fairly and addressing some of these perceived injustices. In doing so, the paramount objective of CLC policy is to bring about "certainty," a "final" settlement of unceded lands so that such lands can be unambiguously Canadian possessions and used or "developed" with clearer rules and, in many cases, fewer hindrances.[16] At the same time, the process can assure Aboriginal peoples that they can legitimately practise self-determination within certain circumscribed territories. However, like the treaty, the central objective of the procedure is to elicit written consent from Natives to Canada's uncontested sovereignty over their lands. In this sense, the specific focus of CLC is the concept of state ownership. Since this is a concept that most Native peoples have never recognized, it easily paves the way for the state to dictate all of the terms under which the concept is to be negotiated. In such negotiations, Native peoples are at a tremendous disadvantage, since to them the idea of ownership of land is an absurdity. Julie Cruikshank gave a vivid example of this conflict in the 1990s in Yukon. "How can you *own* a piece of land? It's like saying you can *own* a cloud," a Native woman involved in land claims negotiations told Cruikshank (1998: 17).

Although the exact conditions agreed vary from case to case, the CLC policy permits only that the Aboriginal group concerned cede its Aboriginal title to its territory. This is the price that Natives have to pay in order to abate the sequestration of their lands. In return for the cession, cash compensation and other benefits, which might include particular proprietorial rights to certain parcels of land, are offered by Canada. This is spelled out in the comprehensive land claims policy document, which states that "the aboriginal rights to be *released* in the claims process are . . . those related to the use of and title to land and resources" (Indian and Northern Affairs Canada, 1987: 11; emphasis added). In other words, from the beginning, Aboriginal negotiators know that Canada will not allow them the option of *retaining* title to their land: the primary issue is the terms on which they *release* it.

The onus for initiating the CLC process rests squarely on the Native group, which has to start by petitioning for the right to make a claim. If the claim is recognized and approved by the federal and provincial governments, the Natives can then apply for federal loans – deductible from any compensation subsequently agreed – to research, develop, and negotiate their claim. Because these negotiations require specialist knowledge of Canadian law, Aboriginal rights, and the manners of official bargaining, the Innu Nation, Mamit Innuat (the body representing several Innu villages in Quebec), and many other Aboriginal organizations are required to spend a considerable proportion of these monies on Canadian professionals to assist them in their negotiations. The negotiations system is not, as is sometimes supposed, a nation-to-nation process, but rather a series of Native-Euro-Canadian encounters in which many if not most of the representations of the Natives are made by Euro-Canadian professionals, who are conversant in legal jargon and the technicalities of establishing a claim. Although the terms used by Canada to describe the process consider Natives as equal partners in a negotiating process, all of the parameters are dictated by Canada itself – which claim is accepted; how much money will be made available to make the claim; when, where, and how negotiations will take place. Although the 1997 *Delgamuukw* ruling may modify this, there has been no impediment to industrial development on Native lands while a claim is being negotiated. Consequently, there is no urgency on the part of the state to conclude CLC agreements, and such cases may take a decade or more (see Miller, 2000: 353).

Two recent land claims agreements, involving the Nisga'a of the Nass Valley, British Columbia, and the Inuit of Nunavut provide slightly contrasting cession arrangements. The Nunavut Inuit signatories clearly agreed to "surrender to Her Majesty The Queen in Right of Canada, all their aboriginal claims, rights, title, and interests, if any, in and to lands and waters anywhere within Canada and adjacent offshore areas within the sovereignty or jurisdiction of Canada." They therefore extinguished all rights "based on their assertion of Aboriginal title."[17] On the other hand, while the Nisga'a escaped a surrender or extinguishment clause, they released all rights not specifically enumerated in the Final Agreement and have agreed not to pursue any claim for past infringements of Aboriginal rights.[18] According to the Chief who was involved in negotiating the treaty, only 8 per cent of traditional Nisga'a territory was retained (Gosnell, 1998). This was a heavy price to pay for "certainty," leading one Nisga'a elder to remark that the treaty "was done by a bunch of young guys on the negotiation committee who don't even know our resources or culture . . . maybe they were just sitting there nodding their heads" (DePalma, 1998: A10).[19]

Let us make no mistake, comprehensive land claims, as a process, already assume that the Innu and other Native peoples are consenting parties to the sovereignty of the state, as if Canada were the "First Nation." They are considered to have already agreed to forfeit their own autonomy to the state, since the procedure itself is a manifestation of the will of Canada. Prior assent to Crown sovereignty is therefore implicit in the process, amounting to the Innu agreeing to give up their lands in advance of any talks across tables in far-flung capitals. Once the Innu participation in the CLC process was set in train in 1991, monies were advanced by the state to the Innu Nation, and it must spend much of these funds documenting Innu existence on the land. This is done through a number of land use, occupancy, and archaeological studies, which become the basis of their claim. If the precedents are anything to go by, this claim will only be accepted by the state if the Innu extinguish their title to the land in exchange for certain specified rights and compensation; or, failing this, as in the Nisga'a case, accept a minute proportion of their territories and subject themselves to a whole host of other restrictions. If, with the help of an army of non-Native professionals, an agreement is reached, they will have to reimburse the government for advancing them the funds that they used to underwrite the documenting of their claim.

The scope of a land claim is further reduced by a number of *a priori* conditions. Non-Natives who have acquired land in a land claim area are considered to have *equal* rights to it, and there is no provision for questioning how they came by it or the legal validity of their title. Furthermore, persons or business entities that have acquired rights of access through a claims area and holders of subsurface mineral rights (for example, Inco, the company that controls the Voisey's Bay mine, 75 kilometres north of Davis Inlet) also are considered to be parties in the comprehensive claims process. Because the process does not allow for any questioning of the legitimacy of the means by which they acquired the land in the first place, it is in the interests of the provincial government (which dispenses mining stakes) to sell off as much of the territory as possible, so that there is increasingly less land left on the table to negotiate over. Signifying that politicians and capitalist ventures work towards the same ends, industrial projects on Native land have been regarded by several government officials as a "spur" to land claims settlements.

Since the Innu Nation entered the comprehensive claims process, first by drafting a claim proposal under the predecessor organization, the Naskapi-Montagnais Innu Association, they have been kept under pressure to "settle" because the continual siting of industrial projects within their claim areas goads them into action. Thus, the longer the Innu Nation land claims team has sat at the negotiating tables, the more their traditional territories have been appropriated without their consent. The provincial government has also attempted to impose further restrictions on any Innu land claim. Through its internal land claims policies, Newfoundland has insisted that the Natives should be denied rights in certain "specified areas," most notably in water and the development and production of hydroelectric energy (Government of Newfoundland and Labrador, n.d.: 8). Furthermore, the Newfoundland Minerals Act under which mining stakes are regulated makes no mention of Native peoples, Aboriginal title, or land claims. While it has encouraged mineral exploration and development, it has effectively conferred ownership of large areas of traditional Innu land to non-Innu interests, at the same time that comprehensive claims negotiations over the *same* areas were under discussion. By authorizing these land sales in the claim area, the provincial authorities are in effect acknowledging that the negotiations are merely symbolic. Psychologically, the Innu leadership is constantly placed in confusing positions whereby land on the table and under negotiation one day can the next day suddenly be appropriated or sold with no reference to the negotiations.

While the Innu are constantly faced with the prospects of land appropriation and extinguishment of their Aboriginal title, provincial authorities have put in place several coercive measures that serve to commit the Innu to these arrangements and head off any acts of resistance. For example, in December 1993 the Mushuau Innu band council under Chief Katie Rich issued an eviction order on Judge Hyslop, who was presiding over the district court in Utshimassits. Hyslop passed judgement on Innu defendants rapidly; he showed disrespect for the ways in which the Innu express themselves; he did not allow defendants to explain fully the circumstances surrounding their alleged crimes. In response to the eviction, the Newfoundland government attempted to reinstate the court by military force, but efforts to achieve this failed as the Innu blocked the

small gravel airstrip. At this point the province withdrew from comprehensive land claims negotiations. This meant that the
community was compelled to accept a justice system that it had no
faith in, and which was presided over by individuals they found in-
tolerant and offensive, in order that even the insubstantial and
subordinated rights to the land presupposed by comprehensive land
claims be recognized by the state.

Ed Roberts was the Newfoundland Justice Minister at the time.
In a CBC interview he said that he "had a choice":

> I could have ordered or directed the police to go into Davis Inlet . . . I
> could have sent them in with all the risks that that was, that some-
> body would be hurt, and it didn't matter whether it was a member of
> the Innu community or a member of the RCMP. . . . Or we could seek
> a political solution which is what we've done . . . So a number of ne-
> gotiations that I believe are very important to the Innu, and have
> importance in their own right are put to one side until the Innu ac-
> knowledge the rule of law.[20]

Roberts actively contemplated a military solution, but neglected to
mention that the political solution was only considered after the
community prevented the RCMP from landing at the airstrip by
blocking it with oil drums. During the conflict, the Innu were threatened with the invasion of 150 RCMP and military personnel. In
response, Newfoundland simply withdrew from land claims negotiations, until the Innu "acknowledge the rule of law." For Roberts, the
eviction of the court was "not an Aboriginal matter," but "a matter
that the Criminal Code won't permit." Katie Rich's gesture towards
Innu autonomy foundered on "the rule of law" which makes *any* exercise of Innu independence superfluous. The Innu, as Roberts
remarked in the CBC interview, *are* Canadian citizens. They therefore have the "right" to the imposition of alien institutions such as a
police force and the court. When the Innu protest about the injustices of these and other institutions they are dealt with in much the
same way that naughty children are – by the removal of privileges (in
this case, though, fundamental rights provided by the Canadian
Constitution) and the promise of the return of those privileges in exchange for desired behaviour.

In the same interview, Roberts commented on an analogous
situation several years earlier when many Innu refused to pay utility
bills:

> So we had a choice. I took what I believe to be the best one and we'll
> see if it works. I can tell you that it did work before when the Innu in
> Sheshatsheits or some of them in Sheshatsheits decided to stop
> paying for electricity by ripping out their meters and actually they

jumped them with a bit of copper. We didn't send the police in. We didn't react by cutting off the electricity. What we did instead was we suspended Provincial negotiations. Well, after a number of months went by, the Innu paid their bills and things went back on stream. Now we'll see.

The ploy again was to suspend negotiations, which were vital to the exercise of Innu rights, in response to their protests over the actions of institutions they believe to be unjust, and which have been forced on them – in this case, the utility company that generates electricity from resources extracted from what was the Innu hunting territory around Lake Meshikimau. The strategy of Newfoundland in dealing with conflict with the Innu was simple: if the Innu were seen to have collectively broken the law that has been imposed on them in one realm, their rights in another, more fundamental to their sense of being a distinct people, were rapidly revoked.

Of course, Roberts's use of intimidation ultimately rests on the assertion of sovereignty. All of the rights that Natives have are only those that the Crown or its representatives, such as the court, invent and then confer. Natives have no recourse to any rights outside of Canadian sovereignty, and Canada has done its utmost to block attempts to have international tribunals hear Aboriginal grievances against the state. Within Canada, the courts have also affirmed the sovereignty of the state, despite the fact that the Innu and other Aboriginal peoples have always proclaimed their independence as an autonomous people. In the contempt of court case brought against three Innu women involved in evicting the judge in 1993, all three women tabled statements affirming Innu sovereignty. Justine Noah's statement included the following claims to sovereignty:

> I honest[ly] and absolutely believe that the Innu Homeland of Ntesinan [variant spelling of *Nitassinan*] incorporates that part of Labrador within which the communities of Davis Inlet and Goose Bay are located. . . . I honestly and absolutely believe by virtue of the Innu people always occupying the Homeland of Ntesinan that the land, its use and occupation is subject to the traditions, values and customs, the will and the law of the Innu people . . . [and] the affairs of those persons who occupy and live upon or within the land of Ntesinan are subject to the traditions, customs, the will and the law of Innu people.[21]

The Map Precedes the Territory   **2**

The tribal people here were all very aware that the whites put great store in names. But once the whites had a name for a thing, they seemed unable ever again to recognize the thing itself.

– Leslie Marmon Silko (1991: 224)

All that was once directly lived has become mere representation.

– Guy Debord (1995: 12)

WORKING WITHIN THE SYSTEM

The complexity of the Innu negotiations with Newfoundland, Canada, and industrial interests now requires expert knowledge in a wide range of technical areas such as environmental science, forestry, water management, engineering, and the law, in which virtually no Innu person in Labrador is professionally qualified. Some leaders have been articulate and effective speakers with a command over the technicalities, but these qualities have not been developed through any formal training. However proficient they may be in negotiating, the leaders remain reliant on *Akaneshau* advisers for the translation of their ideas into the political vocabulary of Canada. To the hunting families, including those of the leaders, the demands of negotiations, state protocol, and scientific research are burdensome and alien.

There are few obvious similarities between the way Innu hunters and Canadian government functionaries think about the world or the land. The protocol of the state lays bare these differing versions of what is known and how what can be known is known. The knowledge of hunters emerges in immediate and direct experience with the land, the animals, and their stories. The knowledge is contingent. It partakes of notions of "absolute truth" only in the real, experiential context, never the abstract. It resists the kind of generalization, classification, and codification of authenticated knowledge presupposed by the procedures of the state for the determination of the rights of the Innu. Thus, "the hunter, alive to constant movements of nature, spirits, and human moods, maintains a way of doing things that repudiates a firm plan and any precise or specified understanding with others of what he is going to do. His course of action is not, must not be, a matter of predetermination" (Brody, 1981: 37). Hunting is motion, movement, contingency, spirituality, and the avoidance of absolutes.

Nonetheless, a rather different kind of knowledge, often both abstract and predictive, is required to be produced in order that the Innu document their land claims case and beat back the continual threats posed by a host of industrial projects on their lands. What is important to their case, especially in the eyes of advisers, is that representations of their knowledge, land, and identity be presented to the state in terms that functionaries can easily grasp and that pose no serious ontological challenges to the scientific materialism upon which much Western knowledge of the world is predicated. This means that credible images must be created that, while they may be far removed from the direct experiential truth of the Innu hunters, can be processed by the state. In order to enter into this dialogue, Innu Nation employs a host of professionally trained advisers. These advisers, whose powers have increased in proportion to the pressure to sign up to a comprehensive land claims deal, are an important source of images of the Innu and *Nitassinan.* They translate what they take to be Innu sentiments and aspirations into terms that will be understood by Euro-Canadian officials, and these must find a place within the political taxonomies and bureaucratic procedures that the state has laid down. To take one example here, an environmental adviser at the Innu Nation office in Sheshatshiu sketches out the "Innu vision" of environmental assessment:

> Traditional Innu values place a great deal of emphasis on the wise stewardship and respectful use of resources. Innu harvesting activities and other uses of the land, plants and animals of Nitassinan are not merely economic or subsistence activities, but are part of the web of ecological and spiritual relationships that exist between human beings and the rest of the natural world. Respect for the land, the animals, and consideration for the needs of the future generations of both human and animal populations are key to the Innu view of the natural world.

This extract was taken from an internal document prepared for the Innu Nation rights negotiations in St. John's in 1998 and was directed to non-Innu, mainly the bureaucratic antagonists in various negotiations. As such, it is not an act of translation, as much as it is a simulation. In Gerald Vizenor's (1998: 15) terms, simulations such as the representations of Natives found in social science and government documents celebrate the invented *indian*, which connotes only a Native absence. The hunting life is rendered into a neat package, scientized by the use of eco-friendly terms like "stewardship," "resources," and "harvesting." Correspondences are created between Innu hunting activities and Euro-Canadian, especially environmentalist, understandings of the natural world. Nature in these "visions" consists of the use of "resources" extracted and "harvested" from some larger whole. In effect, the author creates an absence in order to save the bureaucrats in St. John's from bafflement and to find a fit between what he says the Innu say and the assumptions of the various political processes that can embrace such words as "resources" and "stewardship" with a minimum of adjustment. The environmentalist here is engaging in exactly the opposite of that which Vizenor recommends as promoting Native integrity. Hence, "the point here, in the absence of natives, is to counter the enterprise of reason that sustains the *indian* as a social science simulation of modernity" (Vizenor, 1998: 56). The environmentalist overturns no reason; he merely renders Innu practices into the straitjacket of materialism by representing hunting in the language of environmentalism.

For the Innu to be able to participate in the comprehensive land claims procedures, much of the funds paid to Innu Nation are redistributed to non-Native lawyers, environmental scientists, and anthropologists, who help prepare the land claim. This procedure involves the federal government subsidizing Euro-Canadian professionals to prepare a "case" for the Innu. This "case" has to be intelligible to government bureaucrats and is therefore conveyed, presented, and packaged to conform to the various expectations of state protocol. The advisers are intermediaries, negotiating not so much *for* the Innu, but *between* Canada and the Innu. Their pivotal role as providers of scientific knowledge, technological competence, and images of the Innu serves to shorten the cultural distance between the Innu and Canada. In the long hauls of meetings in conference rooms in St. John's and Ottawa, real difference is affably banished. The interests of the Innu are rendered into the same bland materialist forms – maps, meetings, processes, and procedures – as those employed by their antagonists. The Innu "vision" as simulated by the advisers involves "stewardship," "harvesting," and "resources." The line between their affiliations as Innu Nation officials and as Canadian citizens is fuzzy. Their urgings are for the

Innu to "participate," albeit as hard bargainers, within the terms of the procedures that Canada has established for the definition and circumscription of their rights.

The situation here differs only in minor details from that in other Aboriginal communities involved in rights struggles across Canada. For the Inuit of the Eastern Arctic, as for the Innu, the process began in earnest only in the 1960s. There, the advisers' "generally assimilationist attitudes did much to confuse Inuit cultural practices, family traditions, and cosmologies" (Tester and Kulchyski, 1994: 339). As a consequence, "the presence of these 'experts,' dominated by the idea that integration with the dominant values and practices of Canadian culture was inevitable and essential, placed a colonial (or neo-colonial) non-Inuit decision-making elite on the ground in virtually each Inuit community."[1] Georg Henriksen (1985: 125), an anthropologist with considerable experience in Davis Inlet, relates the somewhat unsettling observation that by reframing Native concerns for the digestion of bureaucratic officials, it is easier for such officials to refute them. This may cause alienation from the political negotiations and, in Henriksen's view, "further the colonial processes." Yet, could it be that the very procedures that official Canada and the Innu advisers (not to mention advocate anthropologists such as Henriksen himself[2]) portray as recognizing the rights of the Innu are actually the final touches of the physical and conceptual appropriation of Innu land?

MAPPING NITASSINAN

The Labrador-Quebec interior is a landscape of which relatively few non-Natives have any first-hand knowledge. While there are settlers in such communities as Goose Bay and North West River, and there are a scattering of industrial encroachments, the vast interior is used, occupied, and known almost exlusively by the Innu. In the absence of any substantial settler population in such a large land mass, its appropriation has involved commandeering how that land is conceptualized. For Canada to grant rights to the Innu, it must take the lead in defining how the space within which these rights exist is known.

In the rights-granting arenas that take shape in the comprehensive land claims negotiations, the knowledge generated by scientific representations of Native land acts as a trump card over all other possible contesting versions. It is this ace in the pack that is played time and again, summoned up by the advisers and government officials as the basis for the common battleground upon which to contest the claim. It is in a world of representation, not experience, that the Innu are urged to dwell for the sake of winning recognition of their land rights. So, the principal skill offered by intermediaries such as anthropologists and environmental advisers is a command of science and technology, which is conceived of as the main source of authority needed to establish the claim.

And here, cartographic representations of *Nitassinan* are crucial. In Labrador, as in many other colonized territories, cartography is the science that has solidified the grip of invaders and pried apart peoples and land. Map-making became the foundation stone of colonial nationhood. The map was never a neutral tool of spatial representation, but as Winichakul (1994: 129-30) has remarked of Siam, "a lethal instrument to concretize the projected desire on the earth's surface." As such, mapping creates new entities, tearing away at pre-existing ways of making sense of the landscape and long established historical connections. "The ultimate loser" in this process, Winichakul (ibid., 129) tells us, "was the indigenous knowledge of political space."

Mapping *Nitassinan* began in earnest relatively recently, taking tentative steps forward as the Hudson's Bay Company (HBC) factors and their clerks ventured inland from the coastal posts at Mingan on the St. Lawrence, Eastmain and Richmond on Hudson Bay, and northerly Fort Chimo on the Koksoak River in the Ungava Peninsula in the early nineteenth century. Although their endeavours to persuade the Innu of the northern areas to abandon caribou hunting in favour of fur-trapping for trade was not highly successful, the Company's explorations into the interior created European geographical knowledge of the region and its peoples. Referring to the efforts of various HBC expeditions at the time, Davies (1963: lxxix) comments:

> A comparison of the 1814 edition of Aaron Arrowsmith's map of North America with John Arrowsmith's map of 1857 reveals the extent to which the explorations of the Company traders had added to the meagre information available about the great peninsula.

But the thirst for knowledge of the land was not quenched by the exertions of Company men. European and American geographers began mapping and describing in more systematic ways at the end of the nineteenth century. Sizing up the task in front of such men, a New England geographer, Alpheus Spring Packard (1891: 20), remarked of the need to traverse the entire peninsula from north to south, because "when this is done we shall be provided with a knowledge of this vast, shadowy, gloomy, forbidding region, of which we now apparently know less than of the interior of Alaska, the tundras of Siberia, or the plateaus of Central Africa." For traders, geographers, and colonists alike, exploration and the map created

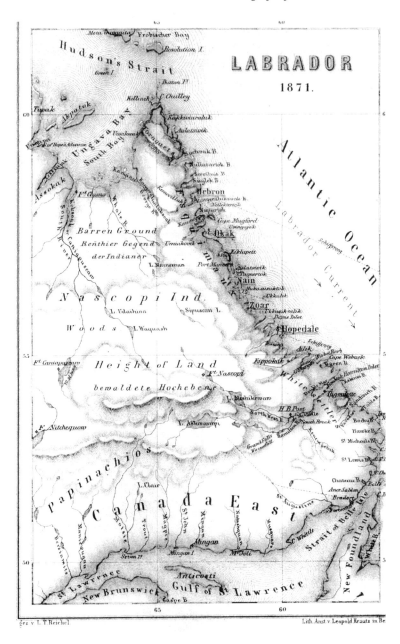

Moravian Missionary map of Labrador 1871 – this and the HBC maps show that although Europeans had extensive knowledge of the coast of Labrador in the
nineteenth century, their knowledge of the vast interior of the peninsula was fragmentary. From Hans Rollman.

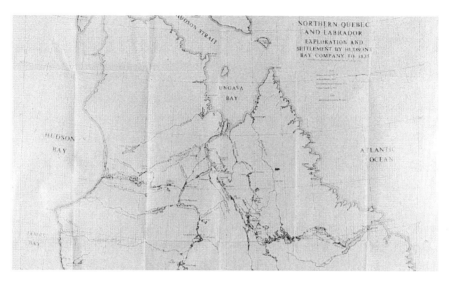

Exploration and settlement by Hudson's Bay Company to 1835. This map shows the routes of various early HBC factors who travelled across the Labrador-Quebec peninsula with the aid of Innu, Cree, and Inuit guides.

Source: K.G. Davies, ed., *Northern Quebec and Labrador Journals and Correspondence 1819-35* (London: The Hudson's Bay Company Record Society, 1963).

structure and order, adding to the "meagre information" of the "vast, shadowy, gloomy, forbidding region." To these pioneers, Labrador represented only a mysterious and probably grim world of uncharted nature, but the excitement of "providing knowledge" spurred them on with a sense of destiny. Eventually, it was hoped, the knowledge of the landscape of trees, animals, lakes, and rivers would become available for commerce and would allow a political delineation of boundaries to guarantee this commerce.

Throughout the nineteenth century, the Labrador-Quebec peninsula was explored, charted, and mapped by HBC employees and then subsequently by geographers, all with the aid of Native guides. Most such explorers bumped up against the value Innu placed on personal autonomy, which was exercised as a reluctance to guide their guests through the land exactly as instructed. Although Native help was essential, as Davies (1963: xlv) comments of the early nineteenth-century HBC treks into the interior, "their reactions had to be anticipated and often firmly combated if successful exploration was to be achieved."[3] Over a century and a half later, the task of comprehensive land claims is not so different. If negotiations are to be successfully concluded, the Innu must be persuaded to accept the reality of the cartographic exercise itself, with its transformation of their living world into gridded and digitized abstractions.

Map of Labrador prepared by A.S. Packard, circa 1890.

Source: Alpheus Spring Packard , *The Labrador Coast: A Journal of Two Summer Cruises to that Region with Notes on Its Early Discovery, on the Eskimo, on its Physical Geography, Geology and Natural History* (New York: N.D.C. Hodges, 1891).

THE MAP PRECEDES THE TERRITORY

The Goose Bay Friendship Centre is a modern multi-purpose building. People from the tiny settlements up the Labrador coast stop over there during the course of hospital and court visits. Some come just to break the monotony of the coast or to escape temporarily from an unpleasant domestic situation. Others use it as a base for shopping in the supermarkets and stores. Many come to Goose Bay to buy booze, and to drink in the bars and nightclubs in town. Inuit come from Nain, Hopedale, and Rigolet and Innu come down from Utshimassits. As well as dormitory rooms that are often crowded with mothers and small children, the Friendship Centre has a cafeteria, and a conference room for meetings.

It was in the conference room that I attended several "land selec-tion" meetings in the spring of 1998. The purpose of these internal meetings was to discuss the strategy that the Innu Nation would adopt at the comprehensive land claims negotiations. The main question to be resolved was how the Innu Nation should present the Innu position on the land. This was from the beginning peremptorily boiled down to a deliberation over how much of it they could "claim" and what kinds of rights they should be accorded on the land. The ultimate goal was to forge out a "proposal" to be presented to Canadian officials. In attendance were representatives of the two Labrador Innu communities, who comprised special teams to carry out community consultations ahead of community-wide meetings. The people in these groups were co-ordinated by a non-Innu woman. The special teams were to explain the proposal to members of the communities and, after receiving comments, redraft it for the high-level talks with the provin-cial and federal governments. Although some of the Innu leaders were present, the meetings were presided over by four non-Native advisers – a lawyer, an environmental scientist, a forestry expert, and an anthro-pologist. I was there to help with the writing of an independent human rights report on the Innu situation (Samson et al., 1999).

Aided by a mass of high-technology computer equipment, which they would individually command while the others addressed the meeting, the advisers began by outlining their conceptual scheme. This consisted of "three landscapes," each of which would be described by one of three experts. After explaining what a "landscape" was ("the whole of the land, culture, and ecology that is claimed"), it was an-nounced that the anthropologist would speak about the "cultural landscape," the environmentalist, the "development landscape," and the forestry expert, the "ecological landscape."

The computer screen pointed out towards us. Microsoft Word for-matting symbols surrounded the Innu Nation logo under which bullet-pointed categories of land were inscribed over an image of a lake surrounded by dark spruce trees. The cultural landscape was described as "travel routes, gathering sites, and hunting and fishing locations." The ecological landscape was "how the land and water work, the whole ball of wax out there." These two landscapes were "tied right together." Another landscape, the "industrial," was also identified. This one was "where non-Innu have taken Innu resources and taken Innu land and water and where they are trying to claim it."

At this early stage, there must have been some concern among the experts that the concept of "landscapes" was not getting through to the Innu, because the environmental scientist repeatedly asked whether "everyone was clear on what we mean by landscape." After a silence, he explained once again. "It is everything you see when you look out at the land. 'Cultural' is putting on your Innu glasses, 'ecological' is when you put on biologist's glasses, 'industrial' is when you put on your glasses and see money." Over the sounds of the hearty chuckles of the advisers, the anthropologist assured us that this was a good analogy.

Although the proceedings were largely controlled by the environmentalist, the forestry expert, and the anthropologist, the lawyer occasionally chimed in with relevant information on how the law governed the three "landscapes." For example, a main focus of the discussions was the existence of three categories of "settlement area" land (Innu core land, co-managed land, and protected land) that could be discussed at the negotiation table. Being well-versed in the legal definitions of these areas and, more importantly, the kinds of rights that could be extended to Aboriginal peoples within them, the lawyer's interventions clarified exactly what kinds of rights the Innu could expect to be recognized for each "landscape." Within the first few minutes, three conceptual "landscapes" were identified and a further three legal categories of land. Not much more time would elapse before three "approaches" would also be unveiled. A certain symmetry prevailed; three landscapes, three approaches, three settlement areas. At this point I glanced up to the screen and noticed that the outline of Labrador formed a triangle.

After sketching out the parameters of the "land selection" procedure, the anthropologist rhetorically asked whether there were any alternatives; that is, could the Innu Nation adopt any strategy other than compliance with land claims negotiations? After a brief pause in which the assembled Innu were silent, he suggested that there were none and, to emphasize the point, ridiculed previous strategies such as protesting and withdrawing from negotiations. The land selection meetings then became exercises in "fine-tuning our proposal," as one expert put it. Forged out of the silence in the room, the foundation stone became the closure of options and the establishing of no alternatives to dealing with the state on its terms.

The advisers then began in earnest by displaying their green credentials, explicating the "approaches" that informed their understandings of the "landscapes." The forestry expert contrasted an "ecosystem approach" to an "industrial approach." The first was diagrammed on an overhead transparency and delivered to the assembled Innu as an "Innu way of thinking." On the screen, phrases such as "Innu wisdom," "traditional ecological knowledge," "healthy Innu communities," "ecologically sustainable Innu economy," and "governance" were printed in boldface type amid a morass of circles, arrows, and bullet points. The expert went on to add that "the Innu economy is part of Innu culture which is part of the land and water." After another pause, he added, "this is another way of saying 'ecosystem,'" thus creating an equivalence between scientific and Innu knowledge.

At this point, the first retort came from the audience, who were in effect being lectured on who they were. Slinking back in his seat, Ben Michel observed that we couldn't really speak of the Innu in isolation, given the rapidly encroaching world. The categories neatly displayed on the computer-generated transparencies had not taken into account all the violations and intrusions into the Innu hunting world by mining companies and other industrial concerns. Whatever "Innu culture" was, it was currently a dynamic engagement with *Akaneshaut* (plural of *Akaneshau*). While the forestry expert looked perplexed, the lawyer, perhaps sensing that the observation might lead to a reassessment of the whole governmental "process" of which this was a part, sidestepped the question, but reassured the Innu that "you have been more successful than a lot of other Native people. The treaty process is the only one that is really out there."

After some questions, some digressions, and a few smoke breaks when we went outside, it became apparent that the centrepiece of the experts' presentations was undoubtedly the maps – colourful, hard-edged, digitized, laminated, overlain with transparencies, cultural as well as physical, metamorphosizing at the tap of a key. According to the anthropologist, the maps were sources of power. Standing beside the overlays, he spoke to a small group of Innu in loud, crisp tones, "When Europeans came here, they asked your people to draw maps so they could find their way around. They then made their own maps, which they used to occupy the land. Now we are making our own maps. That gives us power over them." Like the writing on treaties, a guarantee that Native peoples across the continent were told signified protection for them and future generations, power was now inscription.[4]

To drive home the power inherent in maps, the anthropologist displayed the "available datasets" on the screen. These datasets represented research that had been undertaken on current land use and existing travel routes over the last 20 years by anthropologists. As originary points of the advisers' proposal, these were to be considered the raw data, although they were already severed from the people and the land that were the first sources. The anthropologist's assembled data became further collated on multi-coloured overlay maps of Labrador made with "The Creator," a geographical information system (GIS) computer program specially designed for Innu Nation.[5]

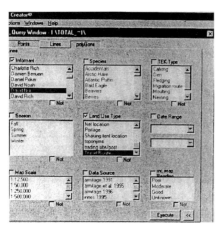

The Creator program used to make Innu land use maps.

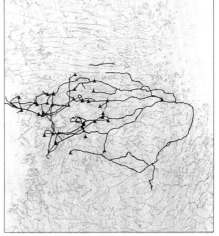

Philip Rich travel routes and camp locations, 1976.

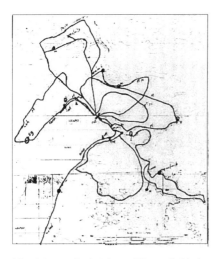

Map biography by Jean-Pierre Ashini, 1991.

Source: Innu Nation, *Money Doesn't Last, The Land is Forever*. (Sheshatshiu: Innu Nation, 1998).

Nevertheless, while power was being invested in these maps, qualifications were continually issued. Political compromises of territory had to be made. So, for example, because land use had "declined" over time, the "land selection" proposal that the advisers were going to advocate necessarily reflected a smaller land base. Despite the apparent thoroughness of the anthropological research, holes in the data started to loom large. Not everyone in the two communities was interviewed because of the time and cost. Only samples were taken. It was also conceded that there were difficulties in translating the maps to the elders as "representations of reality," a frequently used phrase. Some elders had bad eyesight. Others could not read maps, and there were, of course, deceased elders, which made it pressing to obtain information from living elders before they passed on. Thus, the researchers encountered problems of "missing data." There were also elders, and these went unmentioned, who had no faith in maps. "I don't believe in maps," the *Tshenut* Pien Penashue, undoubtedly one of the subjects of the map research, had told me over a year before. "Maps are only pieces of paper. I know ponds and lakes because I was there."

Although the anthropologist argued that the maps gave Innu power, Ben Michel observed that all of the maps contained the sharp lines of demarcation along the 52nd parallel, separating Labrador and Quebec. The map for the Innu land selection stopped at the border, although families use land on both sides. Those in Sheshatshiu and Utshimassits use land in Quebec and those in the Quebec communities use land in Labrador. Indeed, Innu families are and always were tightly connected across the peninsula through kinship ties and frequent travel and communication. For a people who were closely linked through nomadic occupation of a vast territory, straight lines drawn up by a Boundary Commission in London in 1927 have no relevance to their histories or contemporary circumstances.

The process that this meeting was itself a part of, however, demanded not only that the Labrador-Quebec border be recognized as sacrosanct, but that the concept of borders between supposedly discrete communities of Innu be accepted. Thus, separate Utshimassits and Sheshatshiu maps were presented by the experts, demarcating "core Innu land" area boundaries – Utshimassits to the north, Sheshatshiu to the south – between the two communities. The "communities" then became the equivalent of the somewhat mythical "bands" with their attached "hunting territories" proposed by earlier anthropologists (Speck, 1935) and geographers (Tanner, 1944). This move, produced by the advisers as a merely technical aspect of the political process, had the effect of reducing the Innu to a population residing in two discernible communities with bordered "usufructuary" territories attached to each.

The Innu themselves know that both these borders and the notion of discrete communities are fictions. To this day, people who have a house in Sheshatshiu may use areas on the Utshimassits map, while Utshimassits hunters may use more southerly lands. Both may use land in Quebec and those who have residences in villages in Quebec hunt across the invisible frontier. Strong family ties across the entire Labrador-Quebec peninsula, intermarriage, and adoption between people in the two communities also mean that there is a constant flow of people using places that are in both maps or are cordoned off on the Quebec side of the border.[6] As Hammond (1994: 2) has pointed out, the existence of boundaries and the organization of groups of Innu into "bands" with "hunting territories," an assumption of previous anthropologists such as Frank Speck (1935), "deny the mobility that is essential to developing and maintaining the linguistic and cultural unity that Eastern Cree speakers so evidently possess." In 1927, William Duncan Strong (Leacock and Rothschild, 1994: 46) noted that members of the "Davis Inlet band" were drawn from other "bands" between Mingan and Ungava. Just over a decade later, the Finnish geographer Vaino Tanner (1944: 654) observed that the "Davis Inlet band" comprised hunters "from" Seven Islands, Fort Chimo, and North West River. On the basis of extensive genealogical studies, José Mailhot (1997: 31) drives this point home:

> One must realize that the history of a mobile people such as the Innu is completely different from that of village communities, and that the question of whether the people of Sheshatshit are originally from Quebec or Labrador is, consequently, a false issue. When they were nomadic hunters the Innu travelled with ease throughout the whole eastern half of the Quebec-Labrador Peninsula. Each group maintained close relations with its neighbours; there were marriages between members of different groups, and individuals readily changed groups and went to live in new territories. Thus was the groundwork laid for the huge and complex network of kinship that still characterizes the people of Sheshatshit.[7]

If boundaries were important to the Innu, there would be much less cultural similarity between the peoples occupying the entire Labrador-Quebec peninsula, as well as among the Cree inhabiting northern Quebec and the James Bay area. Boundaries would have distanced these peoples from one another and sharpened differences.[8]

Land not believed by the experts to be used by the Innu of the two villages in Labrador was marked on the maps as "Crown land" with no reference to Innu residing in Quebec who have historically used such land. The thousands of Innu not regarded as officially domiciled in Sheshatshiu or Utshimassits were simply ignored and bounded off as outside the "land claim" by the colonial demarcation. When a suggestion from the floor that Innu in the Quebec villages should be involved in the current exercise, the idea was quickly vetoed by the lawyer, citing the complexity of involving another provincial government. This closure was made in spite of all the well-known evidence for long-term use and occupancy of what is now Labrador by Innu now resident in Quebec (see Hammond, 1994). Such a ploy violated the deep-rooted attachment of the Innu people as a whole to *Nitassinan*. All of a territory, even that which is rarely used, is integral to hunting, based as it is on mobility and flexibility. As Brody (1981: 174) states of a similar conflict in northeast British Columbia, "hunters may use parts of this territory infrequently; some locations they may not have seen for twenty years. But no part is therefore dispensable."

As the meeting proceeded, further problems with the cartographic parameters of the land claim were voiced. Etienne Andrew noted that parts of the land where his father had hunted were omitted, and that the areas that had been flooded in the wake of the Churchill Falls hydroelectric project were not included. He also wondered how the advisers could make maps when there were Innu people who could not read maps. Elizabeth Penashue, Etienne noted, was a prominent spokesperson for Innu causes. She had set up camp in areas not marked on the map, but she could not read a map or remember all the details. Daniel Ashini observed that the George River caribou herd migrates over land that is much further south than that indicated on the "ecological landscape" map. Even I was aware from conversations with *Tshenut* that they and their relatives had travelled and hunted on land that the advisers were handing over as "Crown land." Several other Innu believed that the knowledge of the *Tshenut* was not being incorporated completely.

To counter objections, the anthropologist pulled out even more maps, some rolled up in cardboard tubes, others produced by the tapping of the keyboard. One landscape was layered upon another in a quagmire of lines, circles, and shadings over the triangular shape of Labrador. The red beam of his laser pointer zig-zagged across overhead projections. When he ran out of maps, the tack was switched to *realpolitik*, with the anthropologist arguing that the pace of negotiations prohibited more detailed work on where everyone

hunted.[9] The land maps, he conceded, were primarily contemporary. Besides that, and this was the morale booster that was needed,
they could always be changed. "The trick of map-making," the forestry expert reassured us, "is layering." Colours could be changed,
areas could be variously shaded or unshaded, the whole surface
could be reconfigured using "The Creator."

Several of the Innu were clearly uneasy with the maps. Ben Michel noted that "the map is very limited in describing what people
see. There's lots missing from these maps." This was interpreted
with reference to the numerous land-use and occupancy studies by
the anthropologist, who, wielding his laser pointer, countered, "but
your elders identified this area and this area and that area over
there." Teasing empiricism, Ben's riposte was delivered with a grin,
"we should show the maps to the animals, and see what they say."
After a pause, he continued, "I have to scratch my head on that one."
Ben's quick humour indicated a presence that the advisers had no
choice but to ignore since it was an unsettling reminder of lived experience, people in relationships to animals and nature and a far cry
from the protocols of Canada.

His wit echoed that used by other colonized peoples faced with
threats to their connections with land. In Brian Friel's play, *Translations* (1981: 31, 18), the people of Donegal are faced with a mapping
exercise by the British Royal Corps of Engineers. It is to be "the first
ever comprehensive survey of this country." This will entail, Captain
Lancey informs the Gaelic-speaking locals, "a general triangulation
which will embrace detailed hydrographic and topographic information and which will be executed to a scale of six inches to the English
mile." While the English "sappers" were surveying the land, Manus,
a Gael, secretly moved the survey poles, thus confusing the precise
measurements and enjoying the resulting bewilderment of the "sappers." When Manus is challenged by his friends on why he does this
he tells them it was a gesture "to indicate a presence."

Likewise, Ben's humour indicated the presence of the Innu, a
presence that was struggling to breathe in the stuffy room. Ben even
wondered whether the Innu were being locked into one particular
"map." To all the objections, the experts always had a response.
"Mapping costs a lot of money and takes a lot of time. We must train
people for all these projects." The clincher was always a blend of realism that pitted expedience, practicality, and a hard-headed
assessment of the intentions of Canada against the desire to be
truthful to what people see, know, and experience. Each critical observation made by an Innu was met by a defence of both the
mapping concept itself and the colonial procedures within which the

map research is ultimately located. The message to the Innu was always along the lines of "you can take it or leave it, but this is as good
a deal as you are going to get." In other words, they would be foolish
not to treat the fictions that were unveiling themselves in front of
them as true.

In *Maps and Dreams*, Hugh Brody (1981: 175) observes that
hunters were concerned with literal truth. Even slight inaccuracies
in reporting the locations of particular wildlife, and where they are
moving in relation to specific landmarks, can result in starvation or
death. The maps they draw, and are asked to draw by researchers,
he notes, are rarely confabulations. This is perhaps why many of the
Innu who were assembled at the Goose Bay meeting were continually pointing out the shortcomings of the maps. For those Innu who
spoke up, these maps were incomplete. Not all the information from
all the elders was contained on them. Inaccuracies of persons,
places, and animals were frequently noted, as indeed they would be
in the hunting camps of the interior.

I began to wonder about the power that these maps were said to
give the Innu, a power that seemed to slip away in the moments immediately after it was invoked. What power was there in a declining
land base, time and money constraints, numerous factual inaccuracies, and the sharp line along the 52nd parallel? How could
cartography, this science for propagating nation-states, serve those
who were always a people but never a nation except by turning them
into a nation within a nation, a miniature version of their antagonists
at the negotiating table? Just as these two-dimensional projections
miniaturized their land, power became miniaturized also. Were the
maps not about draining rather than gaining power? Were they not
symbols of the belief that power could be acquired only through the
admission, both tacit and explicit, that the stories, the legends, movements, humour, and Innu sensibilities, bound up as they are with the
landscape, are powerless?

Receiving information from *Akaneshau* about their own land
and processing data as they appear on maps are designed within the
structure of the meeting for passive reception. As far as I could tell,
the meeting gave none of the Innu any sense of power. Being on the
land, by stark contrast, is more invigorating and active and this difference is reflected in the disposition of the Innu in these meetings
and on the land. For several days at the Goose Bay Friendship Centre, I watched people who were quietly attentive, yet visibly bored,
slouching back in their seats, walking out for frequent smoke
breaks, patiently listening to the advisers. Simeon Tshakapesh,
then Chief of Utshimassits, was one such participant. Several weeks

after the meetings I went with Simeon and some other hunters on a snowmobile trip to Ashuapun, 135 miles inland from Davis Inlet. We travelled at a brisk pace over bays, brooks, lakes, through forests and the high tundra known as "the barrens." To my eye, the landscape was by turns a featureless and uniform white and an infinitely complex web of ice, snow, trees, and rocks. For hours Simeon controlled the snowmobile over twisted frozen brooks, out in the open of the lakes where the wind whipped up the ice, through the forests, and up on the beautiful, luminescent barrens. His eyes, unshielded by his goggles that he had lent me as I was riding in the komatik, were constantly alert to the terrain and the animals. As we stopped for smokes, he pointed out features of the landscape, places where Innu had camped 20 years ago, the side of a lake where my friend George Rich used to go with his family, signs of animal life: a partridge imprint here, a red fox there, caribou tracks heading for the George River. Six hours in to Border Beacon, where we visited a camp, warmed ourselves by the fires, and accepted a supply of caribou meat. Six hours out, along the same route, stopping for smokes, jokes, and relieving ourselves as darkness gathered. The headlamps on the faint snowmobile tracks and the moonlit outlines of the forests, brooks, lakes, and the hills were his maps. Is this not a form of power? Not over the land, but a power to live with it and to know how to respect it, enjoy it, and derive self-respect from it?

Simeon Tshakapesh at old Innu campsite at *Kashapaushitish* en route to *Ashuapun*. The wooden supports for the stove in the tent can be seen emerging from the snow. Photograph by the author, 1998.

The landscape represented on the maps had little in common with the experience of Innu hunters like Simeon. As Lawrence Buell (1995: 269) notes, "the perfection of orthogonally sectioned mapping . . . opened the way for a 'desubjectified' cartography wildly at variance from the perceived reality." In the inert form of the computer-generated map, a static *Nitassinan* was unveiled. Nothing representational could capture the movements or the visions of the hunters. It is very limited in describing what people see, as Ben Michel observed.

If the hunters do not need maps, to what do the maps refer? They refer principally to themselves and to the protocols of Canadian Indian policy. Jean Baudrillard (1983: 2, 4) describes this general phenomenon:

> Abstraction today is no longer that of the map, the double, the mirror or the concept. Simulation is no longer that of a territory, a referential being or substance. It is the generation by models of a real without origin or reality: a hyperreal. The territory no longer precedes the map, nor survives it. Henceforth it is the map which precedes the territory . . . it is the map that engenders the territory. . . . It is no longer a question of imitation, nor of reduplication, nor even of parody. It is rather a question of substituting signs of the real for the real itself, that is, an operation to deter every real process by its operational double, a metastable, programmatic, perfect description machine which provides all the signs of the real and short circuits all its vicissitudes.

Baudrillard's description applies equally to the conceptual terms used by the advisers – "landscapes" and "approaches" – that were communicated to the Innu as their reality. But the motion of the Innu and that of the animals, the regular changes in the landscape with the icing up of the lakes and rivers in the fall, the spring melts, the rains, snowstorms, and the sudden blizzards that sweep across the land elude the map. This is similar to what Vizenor (1998: 15) calls *transmotion*, a sense of Native motion, an active presence. Its manifestations are in creation stories, totemic visions, and reincarnation.

By contrast, the maps freeze-frame the Innu in a linear history, which recognizes their movements only haphazardly, and then primarily in the past tense. The people's history as rendered in high-technology cartography is one that neutralizes sedentarization, situates the Innu as now permanent village dwellers living in discrete communities. In preparation for the land claim, the maps must still the movements of the Innu, disconnect them from lived experience, and silence their associations with the land. Their nomadic lives are transfigured into symbols. Stories and legends become mere marks, explained by the legend of the map.[10] Even the *kushapatshikan*, the most sacred affirmation of their connections with the Animal Gods, and not just territory, is mocked by wigwam symbols emblazoned on the map of Labrador. The mysterious voices of these Animal Gods, heard only by Innu shamans in the wildly shaking tents within tents, are now re-duplicated ink wigwams, dependent on the service of the toner cartridge.

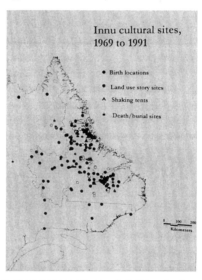

Innu cultural sites map showing locations of shaking tents.

Source: Innu Nation, *Money Doesn't Last, The Land is Forever* (Sheshatshiu: Innu Nation, 1998).

The land used by deceased Innu hunters, the fourth person in some Algonkian languages, does not appear as "Innu core land" on the map. The very living and active presence of the dead becomes annulled by the straight lines, the cardinal points, the shaded layering, the sense of scale, and the border on the 52nd parallel. Some years earlier, the hunter George Gregoire had explained to me, "when a person dies, he is still here with us. You can contact them through dreams and the burned caribou bones. The next day you will see a caribou." Speaking of his dead father and brother, George Rich told me that "they are still with us when we camp there," where they camped many years earlier. The state is never presented with this information, nor is it informed about the dream maps or the maps made on the burned scapula bones (known as "scapulamancy") that Innu have relied on to guide them throughout *Nitassinan*.

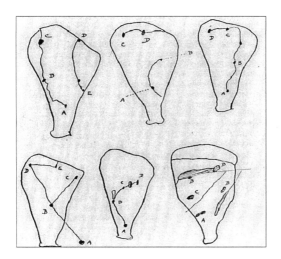

Caribou scapulamancy – examples of various patterns of Innu divination maps assembled by Frank Speck.

Source: Frank Speck, *Naskapi: The Savage Hunters of the Labrador Peninsula* (Norman: University of Oklahoma Press, 1935), 162, Figure 18.

Absent, too, is any land that a hunter might hypothetically use in the future. Because the migration patterns of caribou vary from year to year, it is conceivable that an area not marked on a map by a hunter, and therefore not included in the compilations that create the category, "Innu core land," would be left out of the Innu land claim proposal. This would tie the hunter to the inertia of the map, unable to chase animals who ran off the shaded areas created by "The Creator."

While the map of paper, cloth, or plastic has a certain static quality, its computer origins make it a transformable sign. The experts can move all lines, with the prominent exception of colonial borders, which are, they maintained, fixed. Areas can be redesignated by changing colouring and shading; parcels of space can be re-gridded. What is designated "Innu core land" can be moved this way and that. Its sheer mutability testifies to its ability to create truths, but in contrast to oral and visual experience of the landscape and animals, these are always representational, inert, and, in a certain sense, binary. That is, the map as a document in this context conveys a picture of the world as either one thing or another. It cannot be both. There can be no overlapping, incommensurable, unnameable, unknowable, or intangible entities. All must be transposed as territory and resources, perfectly nameable, claimable, extractable, and controllable. The map is merely the tool for making the real abstract. In doing so, the people who consider themselves part of a living landscape are detached from it. Their lives are now merely symbolized by bold lines, dashes, ink wigwams.

Once such a separation has been achieved, once the real is made abstract, the land can be imbued with the spirit of rationalism, the dull compulsion of official Canada that turns simulations of the Innu into subjects of its own sovereignty. This is achieved almost entirely by representation alone, taking the infinitely flexible sign of the map for the signified people and linking the two by the silent rule of correspondence – representation. Representation needs no justification, because signs constitute a philosophically coherent and logical system taken for granted as not just next best to "reality," but as "reality" itself.[11] To question it would be unthinkable, for the questioner would have to take issue with what are regarded commonly as facts. In this context, the advisers' threat of *realpolitik* became an added insurance against any disturbance to the official procedures. But, as the rebuttals to the comments of Ben Michel and others demonstrated, simply taking issue with the *form* of representation was met by tautological arguments that are, of course, at the heart of *realpolitik*. The retort that Natives cannot challenge the system or the order or the process because "that is the way it is" is the tautology that builds "a dead, a motionless world" (Barthes, 1973: 167). And, we could add, a world stripped of difference.

From a hunting point of view, the maps that the Innu were presented with are not what they are to the comprehensive land claims procedure, a "representation of reality." Although some hunters may use store-bought maps as rough guides, knowledge of the territory always surpasses representation. Native North American map-making is, by contrast, more deeply personal and experiential. Historically, the Innu made maps of travel routes fashioned on birchbark and drawn from personal memory. The more literal maps, however, were primarily made for the purposes of guiding and informing Europeans (Lewis, 1998: 15). Divination maps were made through scapulamancy, a process by which hunters insert the scapula bone of a large animal, usually a caribou, in the fire, and, after withdrawing it, discern certain movements of the animals based on the patterns made by the flames on the bone. In this way, lakes, rivers, forests, hills, as well as animals and people, are identified to correspond with the marks of the fire.[12] As with many other Native North Americans, the Innu used dreams as methods of representing and understanding their lands. Brody (2001: 133) has remarked of the role of dreaming in northern peoples, "dreaming is the mind's way of combining and using more information than the conscious mind can hold. It allows memory and intuition and facts to intermingle."

Vizenor (1998: 170), in discussing Native maps, what he calls virtual cartography, tells us that "Native mappers are storiers and visionaries." The Innu hunters, the *Tshenut* especially, tell stories about what happened at particular places – where a "black fish" was caught; where someone used to set up a summer camp and the stumps of the tents still can be seen above the snow; where a group of hunters were caught in a storm; where a *kushipatshikan* was set up; where babies were born. Innu mapping is these things and more, always surpassing what is represented as territory on the map. Thus, "the memories of the actual territory are not transposed by simulations" (ibid.)

The kinds of maps that the advisers had made are more useful to the paradigms of Western science and the government than to hunters. They file lived experiences into taxonomies. Maps constitute forms of knowledge that are linked to direct personal experience only in a distant sense, perhaps only in a *Tshenu* bending over a table, pointing to a line on a piece of paper, and saying to an interviewer, "I was there." Maps signal the disconnection of people from all but territory, and then only some of the territory. Moreover, they soberly mark the triumph of abstract materialism[13] over visions, dreams, and stories. Cartography, a form of knowledge that lent itself to serving colonial occupation and scientific objectification of lands, has even been thought to mark the progress of civilization. As if technological change signals the passage of time, Norman Thrower (1996: 1) argued, "[v]iewed in its development through time, the map details the changing thought of the human race, and few works seem to be such an excellent indicator of culture and civilization." The map, then, traces the linear march of development and progress. "Indeed," Mónica Amor (1996: 24) writes, "the grid is the quintessential modernist structure, not only in the realm of art but also in that of science and reason."

In the absence of any real, live Innu presence with their sense of motion and experience, it is clear that the maps are both the products and the weapons of the colonial antagonist. The computer-generated GIS map concedes Native sovereignty. It presupposes a giving up, a willingness to simulate as the Same, to be brought into the same materialist universe as those who see the world as gridded, claimable, and ownable. Returning to Vizenor (1998: 174), the map as a document, "is historical, enured by the trustees of dominance, and possessory. Eighty acres and a trustee is never the same as that sense of Native presence in virtual cartography."[14]

The generalized knowledge compiled in the cartographic, environmental, scientific, and much anthropological data constitutes the Innu and their land as entities of a broader Euro-Canadian political taxonomy. Yet, when the people themselves speak, they nearly always reject generalization by prefacing any utterance with "this is only my opinion," as Francesca Snow once started a conversation, or "I speak only for myself," as Pien Penashue began a discussion about the effects of mining at Voisey's Bay. Moreover, the Innu interrelated knowledge of *Nitassinan* and their histories as given expression in their language can only be accommodated within scientific formulas or protocols of the state by layers of reductionism. What the Innu know is never presumed to be definitive, is always personally tied to experiences in time, place, dreams, and visions. Not being limited by privileged methodologies or modes of perception, Innu knowledge, like that of other Native Americans, spills out of the boundaries of Western science.[15] "I find it funny," Paul Pone, a young hunter, said to me on a long walk through Sheshatshiu one day, "that scientists look for life on other planets when there is so much life here like *katshemeitsheshu*, and *Memikueshiu*, the man in the mountain, a spirit my grandfather used to see, and dreams and the *Mistapeo.*"[16] He was bemused that scientists were so worried about "proof," not what people see and feel.

To the advisers, imbued with a hard-headed political realism and a narrowly empirical world view, maps and other documents are the form that Innu engagement with the state *must* assume. The maps were produced to be laid out at future meetings between the Innu Nation and the state, meetings where the representatives of the state would ponder, debate, and negotiate the land claims of the Innu, who with the maps are not only simulated as the same as their antagonists, but must express their aspirations through political and epistemological compromises to Canada. While the state did not dictate that the Innu specifically produce maps, the GIS map has been the usual device used by other Natives to document their claims to the land. Even though the GIS map-making has its origins in the quests of city planners to organize and rationalize urban spaces and peoples, and presupposes contradictory epistemological assumptions about the world, it has become essential to the task of Native peoples to exert their "claims."[17]

The Innu must express themselves through images and protocols that are in many respects at odds with the beliefs and practices that have made them such successful occupants of the Subarctic forests and tundra. They must recognize a science that continually distances itself from its objects until they disappear then reappear as *indians*. The result is a clash in which the modernist visions and political realism of their scientific advisers grind up against their teases and silences. These silences are magnified by the absence of all those hunters, who in several weeks' time would have the maps unfurled to them in the community consultation meetings. This next step along the road to a land claims treaty would be guided by the spirit of *realpolitik*, binary thinking, and the straw man, as the advisers were at pains to contrast Newfoundland's puny offer of a land claim with the advisers' substantially larger chunk of land. The advisers assumed that if the communities did not accept their "proposal" all would be lost, so they presented the Innu with only this limited choice. Options were not provided for them either to choose all of their land or to refuse to participate.

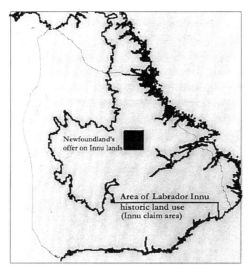

Historic Innu land use compared to Newfoundland's offer on Innu lands.

Source: Innu Nation, *Money Doesn't Last, The Land is Forever* (Sheshatshiu: Innu Nation, 1998).

But all *is* being lost. For the process to operate at all, the Innu way of speaking and thinking about the landscape must be discounted and invalidated. The scientific view of the landscape, with its assumptions about objective, "absolute truth" that can be ascertained by rational methods of investigation and representation, always pushes out alternative means of understanding. As the Arctic scientist and travel writer Barry Lopez (1986: 274) expressed it,

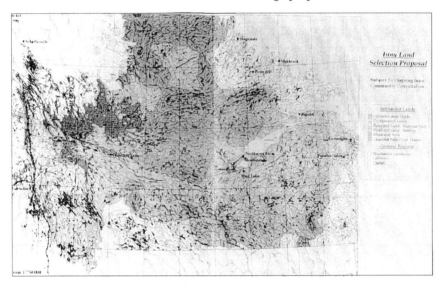

Innu land and resources analysis, Sheshatshiu landscape.

Source: Innu Nation, *Money Doesn't Last, The Land is Forever* (Sheshatshiu: Innu Nation, 1998).

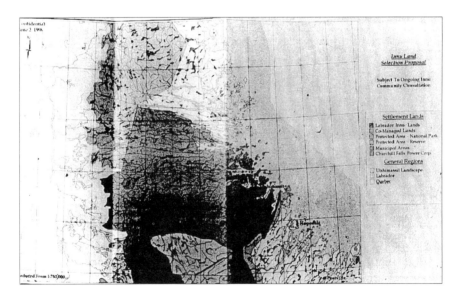

Innu land and resource analysis Utshimassits landscape.

Source: Innu Nation, *Money Doesn't Last, The Land is Forever* (Sheshatshiu: Innu Nation, 1998).

"In the face of a rational, scientific approach to the land, which is more widely sanctioned, esoteric insights and speculations are frequently overshadowed, and *what is lost is profound*" (emphasis added). But what is lost from the point of view of knowledge is a gain for the state, Euro-Canadian developers, and even the advisers whose own scientific world view ultimately triumphs.

A Signature Without A Signified

What maps does the state need to produce? What attachments to the land does it need to document? How many memories does it need to pilfer and sift through? How many scientific interviews must it set up? What archaeological evidence of occupation, travel routes, and campsites does it need to furnish? What folk theories about "landscapes" or "approaches" does it need to concoct? What technologies does it need to appropriate? What computer programs must it devise and purchase? It, of course, needs none of these. If required to prove the existence of European occupation of *Nitassinan* under the same terms as the Innu, it would come up with only a scattering of settlers, missionaries, and traders, who in comparatively recent times, docked on the coast and at North West River and owed their lives to the Innu hunters that they traded with and learned from.[18]

Canadian official history is a history of the extensions of Europe and Europeans. National identity was forged out of an engagement with and, to a certain extent, a disconnection from these origins. Although confederated in 1867, the state and settler population of British claimed regions such as Labrador still draw meaning from the symbolism of the British monarchy. While contemporary Canadians recognize themselves in the symbols of the maple leaf, the Royal Canadian Mounted Police, hockey games, and the notion of the wilderness, they are increasingly oriented to a notion of inclusive (that is, within the nation-state) multiculturalism (see Angus, 1997). When faced with a people whose history is not associated with either European origins or a state established on the territories claimed by emigrants, who have long occupied the land as autonomous peoples, and whose way of life contains deep unfathomable secrets, Canada forces them to document their existence on terms that can only be inclusive of itself. Again, Baudrillard (1990: 16) helps us reflect upon this when he writes that history "exists only if you can prove that there was in fact history before it – which becomes impossible once you have passed the point [when history ceases to be real] . . . history itself can no longer reflect or prove itself. This is why we call on every previous epoch, every way of life, every mentality to historicize itself, to recount itself with proof and documents in hand."

In contrast to the painstaking, burdensome, and laborious efforts that the Innu Nation undertakes to prove that Innu exist as a distinct people *within* the state, the state need only rest on the assertion of sovereignty. Sovereignty, that magical instrument of the state, guarantees that Canada merely judges the validity of these claims, and in doing so dictates the pose *its* subjects should strike up in order to be judged. It forces *its* Native populations to press their claims to lands that have never been ceded. It becomes the arbiter of claims made against it and that can only be resolved within it. No source of authority outside the state can be invoked by the Innu. Their claims against the state must be recognized, considered, and given verdict by the state itself.[19]

And here, the state wants Natives who are versatile enough to appear in a pose that celebrates incorporation and appropriation. This is in effect what the attorney hired by Innu Nation was getting at when he suggested a "ceremony" for the future meeting at which the land selection proposal would be tabled. He envisioned elders talking about what the land means to them, as well as women's groups and young people, perhaps all "in costume." After this, an Innu Nation official would unveil the map. As he did so, television cameras would zoom in to record the event and beam it across Canada. Although objections to this imagery at the Goose Bay meetings came thick and fast – Daniel Ashini said that the Innu were not a ceremonial people and the elders would be in the country at the time – they did not tarnish the desire for ceremonial enactment. The anthropologist followed through by stressing the need to further stage-manage the presentations. "We don't want any loose cannons," he asserted. "Can that be handled by creative translations?" Daniel Ashini then stressed the importance of allowing people, even those who might contradict the proposal, to express their opinions freely. Nonetheless, a week later in Utshimassits when I was in the Innu Nation office the anthropologist phoned the Chief to urge the community to prepare for a "ceremony." Under these promptings, Innu were to dress up in white canvas jackets with bead and hide trimmings, and someone should be asked to perform a drum dance.

In effect, the land claims agreement is not an agreement at all. It is a signature without a signified. Contrary to the assumptions of the advisers and Canada, the signature can never stand in for *people*, especially people who have always valued personal autonomy and practised direct democracy and who are only configured into quasi-political bureaucracies such as the Innu Nation, in order to meet the demands of the state and to decelerate the sequestration of their land. How can a signature to a document drawn up by the protocols of the state and steered by *Akaneshau* advisers, ever be legitimate? Save for the "compensation" that will flow into the communities, how can the *Tshenut* ever feel vindicated by such a signature? When the advisers drive off for the last time in the rental cars paid for by the money fronted to the Innu Nation by the Canadian government, will they be thanked for their tenacity or their magnanimity?

Shortly after the performances at the Goose Bay Friendship Centre, one further act to elicit complicity was required. "Consultations" took place with *Tshenut* in the upstairs conference room of the Innu Nation with its three sides of windows overlooking Lake Melville. Cookies, fruit, and coffee were laid out for the *Tshenut*. Only nine turned up. Others did not want to come, some had clinic appointments, and another group were in the country. Each *Tshenu* was allowed to speak his or her piece. Several, though not all, spoke. When the translations came through, it was clear that they had had great conceptual and political difficulties with the proceedings. Shimun Michel wondered how it was possible for the Innu to "select" land that was used by so many people. "We cannot select our own lands. Why is it up to the Government to tell us which lands are ours?" As the meeting proceeded notes were taken on what was said. The advisers in attendance, ignoring the clear message that the whole process was illegitimate to the *Tshenut*, showed the *Tshenut* the scope of other land claims agreements in Canada. These were presented as the parameters set for the Innu. They stressed that their "proposal" was to match that for the largest agreement settled by Canada. This translated into 14 square miles per person (or the equivalent of a square area of 159 miles), meaningless statistics to hunters. Other *Tshenut* pointed out that the Innu had always shared *all* of the land on each side – did they ever invoke ownership to settlers? They shared *Nitassinan* with the people now at James Bay and the people at Sept-Îles, as well as the settlers. Land should not be set aside for particular groups or families. The implication was that if it was recognized that the Innu were the original people and all parties stuck to a respectful sharing of the land, no formal boundaries need be drawn and certainly no land cession needed to be signed for.

Over time it became abundantly clear that the advisers already had a plan worked out independently of any consultation. The meeting functioned more to sell the "proposal" than to think through a conflict with momentous implications for the Innu. Perhaps sensing this, the *Tshenut* insisted on playing for time. First of all, they were not all there. Many were still in "the bush," not here on this sunny morning enjoying the high-technology presentations and refreshments. Others started to angrily denounce the plans and proposals, stating, as one man put it with a sweep of the arm, that "there is no doubt that this is *Nitassinan*." With these worrying signs of dissent, along with the tendency of the *Tshenut* to speak for long periods of time uninterrupted, the advisers started to steer the proceedings. This was done by urging an orderly turn-taking of discussions that specifically focused on the issues that they themselves had sketched out as relevant beforehand – that is, those issues that fit with the demands of the CLC process itself. No conclusion was reached, but afterwards the advisers persisted with selling the proposal at other community meetings. It was no surprise, then, that almost a year later the Innu Nation Land Selection Proposal tabled an area of Innu land described as of exactly the same proportions as the advisers were advocating *before* the community consultations (Innu Nation, 1999a).

When the high-level land claims negotiations take place between the Innu Nation and Canada, the Innu Nation will wield its maps, injected with scientific power, in battle with Canadian sovereignty. Yet, the battle that actually ensues will have already made an important concession of Innu sovereignty, the sovereignty of their sensibility, their outlook on the world, their stories, and the history, never literal or two dimensional, of their lives with the land. Maps, Louis Owens (1998: 211) tells us, silence a people's stories. They "write the conquerors' stories over those of the conquered." Or, as the geographer Robert Rundstrom (1995: 45) put it, "GIS technology, when applied cross-culturally, is essentially a tool of epistemological assimilation, and as such, is the newest link in a long chain of attempts by Western societies to subsume or destroy indigenous cultures." Maps, in other words will be the instruments of the dispossession of so much more than land. Cartography represents the colonization of Innu views of the world, the supplanting of secrets, visions, experience, stories, and memories by two-dimensional abstractions.[20]

With this hanging over them, perhaps it was fortunate that one night in Utshimassits, almost on the hour of a community consultation meeting to look at the maps, I saw a steady stream of hunters setting off across the bay in search of the spring geese. Hoods up over their parkas, rifles tied across their shoulders, their gazes were fixed on the trails around the newly thickening ice.

Odes to Labrador 3

Ode to Labrador

Dear land of mountains, woods and snow,
Labrador, our Labrador.
God's noble gift to us below,
Labrador, our Labrador.
Thy proud resources waiting still,
Their splendid task will soon fulfil,
Obedient to thy maker's will,
Labrador, our Labrador.

The stately forests soon shall ring,
Labrador, our Labrador.
Responsive to the woodsman's swing,
Labrador, our Labrador.
And mighty floods that long remained,
Their raging fury unrestrained,
Shall serve the purpose God ordained,
Labrador, our Labrador.

– First and second verses. The lyrics were written by Harry Paddon
of the International Grenfell Association, circa 1927. The tune is
traditionally that of "O Tannebaum."

A YOUNG GIANT

Almost unanimously, the earliest Europeans arriving on the
Labrador-Quebec coast declared it a bleak, desolate, and inhospita-
ble region. While the unpredictable climate with its long winters and
fly-infested summers had something to do with this, at the centre of
many depictions were the slim chances of agriculture, and hence the
European settlement dependent upon it could make few inroads
here. In 1534 the French explorer Jacques Cartier sailed from St.

Malo across the Atlantic and up the Gulf of St. Lawrence, probably as far as the present-day Innu community of Ekuantshit, across from Anticosti Island. Cartier was in awe of the harbours and islands and the immense volume of fish. He was less impressed by the land itself. In perhaps the most quoted phrase to describe what became "Labrador," Cartier called the interior, "the land that God gave to Cain." And here, as the text of his remarks makes clear (Cartier, 1906: 9-10), his pessimism embraced both land and peoples:

> If the soile were as good as the harboroughes are, it were a great commoditie: but it is not to be called The new Land, but rather stones and wilde cragges, and a place fit for wilde beastes, for in all the North Iland I did not see a cart-load of good earth: yet went I on shoare in many places, and in the Iland of White Sand, there is nothing else but mosse and small thornes scattered here and there, withered and dry. To be short, I beleeve that this was the land that God alloted to Caine. There are men of indifferent good stature and bignesse, but wilde and unruly; they weare their haire tied on the top like a wreath of hay, and put a wooden pinne within it, or any other such thing instead of naile, and with them they binde certaine birdes feathers. They are clothed with beastes skinnes as well the men as women . . . they paint themselves with certaine Roan colours.

Despite this early pessimism, neither the stones and stunted wood nor the "wilde and unruly" folks would turn out to be insurmountable obstacles to settlement or the extraction of fish, pelts, wood, and other raw materials. The first attempt at permanent European settlement in the Innu territories, principally along the North Shore of the St. Lawrence where Cartier had traversed, has been credited to Augustin Legardeur, Seigneur de Courtemanche, in 1702 (Gosling, 1910: 131). Courtemanche, having secured a "concession" from the King of France, established a fort on the southern Labrador coast, employing "thirty or forty families of the Montagnais to come and settle on his seignory" (ibid., 132). French occupation of the fort lasted most of the eighteenth century. After Courtemanche's death, his son-in-law, de Brouague, became the commander of the fort until at least 1760 when it was abandoned. Courtemanche had great plans for the settlement of Labrador, believing it to be a land of abundance capable of sustaining colonists and natives. A memoir penned by an anonymous writer at the garrison of Courtemanche in 1715-16 mentions:

> [t]he abundant fishery of salmon, codfish, porpoises, seals, walrus and whales: the walrus teeth which are finer than ivory and are used in fine arts: the skins of seals, seal oil, walrus oil and whale oil; an infinity of caribous and other animals are in the vast country of

Labrador, and will furnish an infinite number of skins and furs, the handsomest, the finest, and most precious in the world. . . . All this with mines of copper and iron, that can certainly be found in Labrador, is capable of making the proposed establishments both rich and flourishing, and of such great advantage to the State of Labrador should be regarded as its Peru.

In effect, it will furnish France with fish and oils, whalebone, skins of seals and caribous, furs, ivory, and eider-down, and all in such abundance that a large trade can be established with foreign countries . . . .

The abundance of all these things will be increased in proportion as the country becomes peopled and establishments become numerous. (Quoted by Gosling, 1910: 136-37)

While the English soon appropriated most of the good Newfoundland fishing grounds, the French virtually monopolized the fishing on the Labrador coast for most of the eighteenth century. However, from the instant of British victory in the Seven Years War in 1763, the British Governor of Newfoundland, Sir Hugh Palliser, encouraged British vessels to fish extensively along the Labrador coast. This was extended to salmon fisheries on the rivers that flowed into the Atlantic and St. Lawrence and sealing posts that took many thousands of seals every year, principally for their oil (Gosling, 1910: 379-85). These vessels obtained large catches of cod, and by the nineteenth century, British dominance gradually gave way to the ships of Newfoundland and New England. By the end of the nineteenth century, a residual population of salmon fishermen and furriers, called "liveyeres," occupied the various hamlets along the coast.[1]

By the 1830s the Hudson's Bay Company established trading posts throughout the region, stationing factors at the posts for long periods, and unlike Courtemanche or the fishermen, these men gradually began venturing into the depths of "the interior" from their bases on the coasts. HBC men were principally concerned with prizing commercially viable resources from the land. This involved making solicitations to the Natives, who had unique knowledge of the complex geography. The traders principally conceived of the Innu and Inuit as toilers who would retrieve furs and skins, as well as guides to their own independent appraisal of the land. This necessitated arduous exploration of the coastal and interior areas and the continual refinement of maps. Although the efforts of the HBC and other traders to open up the interior of the peninsula failed in the eighteenth century on account of the inclement weather, labyrinthine waters and forests, and the lack of Native enthusiasm for trade, more extensive incursions were made by a succession of traders in the nineteenth century.

As they gradually extended their forays into the interior, the fur traders, like Cartier and others before them, recorded considerable ambivalence about Labrador in their diaries, journals, and notebooks. Having to establish trading posts in cold and barren locations and blaze trails with the assistance of Native guides in search of inland routes, they were rarely effusive about their commissions, constantly complaining about the hardships of the place. The widely travelled trader and explorer from the Isle of Mull, John M'Lean, was particularly pessimistic about Labrador. After four years at the post at Fort Chimo on Ungava Bay from 1837 to 1841, M'Lean recommended to the Governor and Committee of the Hudson's Bay Company that the post be abandoned altogether on account of the enormous costs of supplying it by sea (M'Lean had concluded by then that there were no easy overland routes), which "precluded the idea of any profit being ever realised" (M'Lean, 1849, vol. 2: 90). The picture presented by M'Lean is altogether discouraging. Standing somewhere north of Meshikimau, possibly in the "barrens" area of the northerly Mushuau Innu ("Naskapi"), he remarked: "The face of the country being level, the least elevation commands a most extensive view; but the eye turns away in disgust from the cheerless prospect which the desolate flats present!" (McLean, 1968: 211).[2] And, after exploring the coast west of Fort Chimo, M'Lean observed:

> While the coast proved inaccessible [because of dangerous currents and ice floes in Ungava Bay], the interior of the country wears a still more dreary and sterile aspect, not a tree, nor shrub nor plant of any kind, is to be seen, save the lichens that cover the rocks, and a few willows. (M'Lean, 1849, vol. 2: 62)

While they were reluctant to ascribe Labrador much importance as a settling place for Europeans, some did rate its potential, risky as it was, as a resource colony. Although the amount of fur traded was never prodigious in Labrador, other commodities soon attracted the attention of those who were willing to overlook its "cheerless" – to use M'Lean's favourite adjective for the landscape – appearance. Another Scot, Donald Smith at the North West River trading post, predicted "that there are minerals here which will one day astonish the world" (quoted in Newman, 1991: 31). In addition to the fur trade and mineral prospecting, Smith advocated the commercial exploitation of salmon fisheries and the promotion of a seal oil industry.

Nonetheless, the development of efficient and economical agriculture always remained elusive. Despite some tortured successes with a few plants and vegetables,[3] most explorers regarded the prospects of agriculture as dismal. Looking over the country "far and near," the nineteenth-century ornithologist, John Audubon, could not see "a square foot of earth." On his voyage to capture, name, categorize, and draw the birds of the south coast, Audubon declared Labrador "a poor, rugged, miserable country" (quoted in Townsend, 1918: 8). Other explorers, such as Alpheus Spring Packard (1891: 3), regarded it as primarily of academic interest, noting that although "less is known of this vast region . . . than of perhaps any region of similar extent in North America . . . the results of exploration, might be of more value to geographical and geological science than to trade and commerce." The only exception Packard (1891: 240-44) made was fisheries and he went to some lengths to provide a detailed statistical summary of the catches in the waters off the Labrador coast and in the Gulf of St. Lawrence. By the 1880s an estimated 30,000 Newfoundland fishermen on 1,000 to 1,200 vessels were spending the summer up and down the Atlantic coast and along the Gulf of St. Lawrence. Even here, though, Packard (1891: 243) noted a decline in the stocks by 1887, which was perhaps not surprising given the extent of the summer fishing, arguing that the Labrador fisheries were "precarious and uncertain," and noting that vessels had already shifted to the outer banks.

In the face of the hard and often fruitless struggles of the fishing merchants and fur traders, commentators on Labrador began to overlook both the gradual depletion of the fish, furs, and seals and the absence of agricultural potential. By the latter half of the nineteenth century, the image of Labrador as a resource colony able to support a small settler population grew in acceptance. Writing in his *Explorations in the Interior of Northern Labrador* of 1863, the explorer Henry Youle Hind foretold: "the Labrador Peninsula, with the coast and islands of the Gulf of St. Lawrence, possesses a colonial and imperial interest which can scarcely be over-estimated in contemplating the possible future of British North America" (1863: v). Fisheries, timber, fuel, salt, and curing, as well as some soil for growing vegetables, were possible pretexts for a small British trading settlement on the Labrador-Quebec peninsula. Citing the bountiful supply of fish off the coast and in the inland lakes, Hind (1863: vi) envisioned "the day . . . when the hitherto desolate shores of Labrador, north, east and west, will possess a resident population capable of contributing largely to the comfort and prosperity of more favoured countries." This "resident population," however, would necessarily be small because it was "unfit for the permanent abode of civilised man." By the turn of the century, in the first comprehensive history of Labrador, W.G. Gosling (1910: 427) concurred in Hind's estimations, noting "[e]normous areas of wood for paper pulp," and "unlimited water-power," but holding out "little promise for the white settler."

Nonetheless, the "liveyeres" in Labrador did establish a rugged and independent presence. These settlers gradually increased in number and, exploiting fish and furs, expanded their territories into the interior from the coast and inland from Hamilton Inlet and Lake Melville. Their subsistence was almost entirely dependent on a small-scale barter economy, trading furs and fish for manufactured goods with fur traders and fishing merchants. By the early twentieth century, settlers had begun to extend their trapping paths up the river valleys further and further into the interior. At this time the number of traps on the Naskapi and Hamilton (now Churchill) rivers was estimated at 15,000 and one settler alone had 500 traps on a 60-mile trap path (Tanner, 1947: 704). Gradually, the trappers, who trapped one area continuously, came into conflict with the Innu, who varied their trapping from one territory to another as a result of their constant movement. By changing the locations of their trapping activities, Innu practices helped to ensure that the number of animals did not become depleted, while the settlers' continuous attachment to more limited areas had the opposite effect. Raoul Thevenet, the manager of the Revillon Frères, a French rival to the HBC, reported that the Indians were "continually complaining to me about the matter, as hunting is their only means of living, they are getting poorer every year" (quoted by Zimmerly, 1975: 152). Unsurprisingly, because the "liveyere" trappers were basically sedentary dwellers of the Lake Melville area,[4] they eventually asserted trapping rights over all of the major river valleys of the region. As Zimmerly (1975: 177) puts it, "the ecological niche occupied by the settlers was being filled by them at the expense of the Indians." Likewise, Tanner (1947: 608) confirmed that the Innu had deserted the adjacent coastal area between Double Mer and Makkovik "because white trappers and the Eskimos have begun to take possession of it for their fur paths."

In his *Labrador Doctor* (1920: 83-84) memoir, Sir Wilfred Grenfell, travelling physician to the "liveyeres" and intrepid adventurer,[5] records the thrill of first sighting of the Labrador coast, where "practically *no man* had ever lived . . . and few had seen it" (emphasis added). Dr. Grenfell watched with excitement as "the shoals of fish everywhere breaching the water, and the silver streaks which flashed beneath our bows as we lazed along, suggested that the whole vast ocean was too small to hold its riches." Comparing his odyssey to the first British voyage to North America, that of John Cabot on the *Matthew* in 1497, Grenfell shared with the Venetian sailor "the exhilaration which only such experiences can afford the human soul, and the vast potential resources for the blessing of humanity of this great land still practically untouched." The wealth of Labrador, especially the fish procured by "the hardy fishermen of these northern waters," was vital, "not merely to the British Empire, but to the entire world" (Grenfell, 1920: 99). However, once out of the waters and into the "hinterland," Grenfell described Labrador as a "wilderness," "a kind of mental and moral sanatorium." But for Grenfell (ibid., 288) this peace would only be temporary, given the necessity of European settlement:

> Some believe that the future of this population depends solely on the attention paid to the development of the resources of the coast. Not only are its raw products more needed than ever . . . still there is ample to maintain a larger population than at present. This can only be when science and capital are introduced here, combined with an educated manhood, fired by the spirit of co-operation.

By the time Sir Wilfred rewrote his memoir as *Forty Years For Labrador* (1933: 100-01), the more immediate temptations of untold riches were enough to transform the sanatorium into a vast outdoor factory:

> It has long been known that Labrador possesses mineral deposits, which in the future may prove of great value, but difficulties of communication, transportation, and mining operations have left these sources of wealth practically untouched, even until today. It is the production of paper from wood pulp, the development of hydroelectric power, wireless, aeroplane communication, electrical prospecting which is bringing to the front this land, so rich in forests and water power. We now know, both from the reports of exploring parties and from aerial surveys, that the hinterland of Labrador possesses huge preserves of timber, unlimited water-power from her tremendous falls, and, in addition, the potentiality of minerals indicated by the nature of her rock formation, it being the same as the Canadian Shield which only a little farther west has yielded the largest gold and silver, nickel and copper deposits in the world.

Around the same time, the Methodist missionary Arminius Young (1931: 97) was recommending "extensive farming" and a railway terminus at Hamilton Inlet because "Labrador is near the markets of the world."

After an exhaustive geographic survey of Labrador in the 1930s, the Finnish geographer Vaino Tanner (1947: 826) confirmed Grenfell's glowing report, concluding that, "it is potentially relatively rich in natural resources: soil, timber, iron ore and hydraulic energy, and these will enable the introduction of modern civilization even into the darkest wilderness." Although sporadic waves of European explorers had made maps of the coast since the sixteenth century, the interior country itself remained not only "unexplored," but unbounded. As the accounts of resources within it started to accumulate, a pressing need arose to demarcate territory. However, until the Labrador Boundary Decision was elaborated by the Judicial Committee of the Privy Council in London in 1927, "more than 100,000 square miles of territory . . . remained so long undecided" (McLean, 1998).

The use of the Labrador coast by English fishing fleets had established an English interest in the area. King Charles had issued charters to the Hudson's Bay Company in 1670 for posts to facilitate the fur trade with the Indians. This charter issued to the Company an award of lands draining into Hudson Bay and Hudson Straits at Ungava, and according to Gosling (1910: 129) made it "the first legal possessor of any part of Labrador." However, it was never clear as to where this area, known as Rupert's Land, gave way to New France (or Canada) in the south, along the St. Lawrence, and the east, along the Labrador coast. The peninsula in many parts was, again in Gosling's (ibid., 130) words, "a no-man's land, free to be adopted by any claimant." Undisputed British sovereignty over the "no-man's land" was simply asserted with the final defeat of the French in the colonial wars for North America and written into the Treaty of Paris in 1763. The eastern coast was strongly linked to the island of Newfoundland, the "great ship provisioned and fitted out by the Mother country" (McLean, 1998: 5), and back to Britain through trade. On the other hand, the southern coast, what is the North Shore of the Gulf of St. Lawrence, was populated primarily by French-Canadian settlements, although there were numerous hamlets containing British "liveyeres."

After Canadian confederation in 1867, there was still ambiguity as to where Canada, specifically the province of Quebec that was partly fashioned out of Rupert's Land, ended and the British colony of Newfoundland began. At this time, the sale of the several parcels of land granted by charter to the Hudson's Bay Company was made. In the absence of clear demarcations, a scramble for resources arose between French-Canadian and British interests. This "gargantuan real-estate transaction" (Miller, 2000: 199) took place with no consultation with the Native peoples of Rupert's Land, which would have included the Innu who travelled as far north as Fort Chimo on Ungava Bay and west to the posts on Hudson Bay. However, into the twentieth century, no clear boundary separated this land which was "bought" from the HBC by Canada and the British colony of Newfoundland. It was in the context of the need to decide how the riches of these lands were to be divided that the Boundary Commission set about its tasks. The 1927 commissioners' report (McLean, 1998: 1) began by explaining why so vast a territory had remained "undecided":

> the region in dispute consists mainly of dense forests and bleak and inhospitable table-lands, of which the greater part is *uninhabited* (except by a few Indian families) and was until recently *unexplored*, being visited only by a few trappers in search of furs. The country has accordingly been regarded as having little or no value, and it is only in recent years, when the growing demand for paper has attracted attention to the vast quantity of timber suitable for pulping, that a serious controversy as to its ownership has arisen. (Emphasis added)

Conflict between Newfoundland and Quebec settlers over the forests of this largely *uninhabited* and *unexplored* terrain had required the Privy Council to draw the line. After much bluster over the various sectional European claims to the two coasts (the Atlantic and the Gulf of St. Lawrence), the unfolding of many maps, and questions about the "hunting grounds" of the "Red Indians," the commissioners sitting across the Atlantic Ocean drew the demarcation to the maximum advantage of the Newfoundlanders. They decided that a "coast" included all of the territory that encompassed rivers that drain into the sea from the "height of land." This meant that, although the settlers were primarily only using the coasts, the land allocated to the island of Newfoundland, a British colony, stretched well over 400 miles inland. The boundary was so self-evident to Vaino Tanner (1947: 41) that he remarked, "it seems scarcely necessary to argue that Newfoundland is the proper country to have jurisdiction over Labrador." Citing W.G. Gosling, Tanner states that this is on account of "law, custom and logic."

A few decades later, after Newfoundland had entered the Canadian federation, the new authorities in Newfoundland keenly encouraged the industrial development that previous explorers, geographers, and adventurers had been urging for so long. Initially, this meant mining camps, sawmills for logging, and fishing, but later larger-scale activities were included. Premier Joey Smallwood entered into negotiations with British financiers only three years after confederation to "combine timber, mineral and water resources for industrial development in Labrador" (Froschauer, 1999: 109). For Smallwood, Labrador was "the one lucky break that nature gave to Newfoundlanders, a compensation for their climate, isolation and sparse natural resources" (Gwyn, 1972: 240). In 1955, Walter Rockwood, who from 1952 to 1964 was Director of the Division of

Northern Labrador Affairs for the provincial government of Newfoundland, was confidently predicting that a new "economic base"
would be found in Labrador. This would involve "mining developments" and "timber resources." With Rockwood, we find the first
attempt to actually include the Innu in these grand plans, albeit primarily as a "backward" population that would be taken along for the
ride. Where the Innu were concerned such a shift in the "economic
base" represented "the transition from a primitive hunting economy
to an industrial one." Two years later Rockwood predicted that
"[t]owns will spring up and ultimately the entire population of
Coastal Labrador will flow into a growing industrial area." In 1959,
with the passing of two more years, Rockwood described Labrador
as "a young giant . . . fast approaching maturity" (Roche, 1992).

     In the grand scheme of development, the Labrador-Quebec pen-
insula was a late bloomer. Even by the mid-1960s, Premier
Smallwood was becoming apprehensive that the hour was late and
that Newfoundland's suit was growing cold. "If we are not big
enough, if we are not daring enough, if we are not imaginative
enough to colonize Labrador," he warned the provincial legislature
in St. John's in 1966, "someone else will do it" (quoted by Gwyn,
1972: 276). As a "young giant" in the mid-twentieth century, Labrador was ready to burst on the global economic scene. If it could not
jostle up against the metropolitan hubs, it could feed their needs for
continuous supplies of raw materials, enriching distant capitalists,
local entrepreneurs, and settlers seeking a stable wage, while at the
same time elevating and advancing the Aboriginal population.

LABRADOR: **THE** PLACE TO EXPLORE

The same sense of wonder, articulated by Hind, Grenfell, Gosling,
and Tanner, and the eager anticipation expressed by the early Newfoundland government, ring through in a Newfoundland government
flyer issued by the Economic Development Department for Happy
Valley-Goose Bay. In the wake of the 1994 mineral discoveries at
Voisey's Bay, about 75 kilometres north of Utshimassits, it describes:

> Labrador . . . a land of immense proportions . . . a frontier of great
> potential: mineral exploration; energy development; scientific re-
> search; hunting and fishing; world class military flight training – a
> land of rich and diverse opportunity.

It is as if, after the wait, wealth is finally realizable. Prosperity is im-
pending. Exploration, adventure, and riches are there for the taking.
The excitement brought on by the prospect of mineral extraction
was infectious. Ever since deposits of nickel, cobalt, and copper

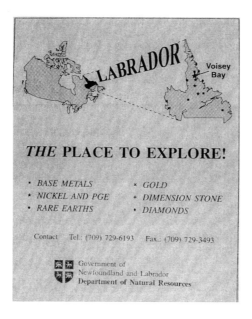

THE PLACE TO EXPLORE!

- BASE METALS   × GOLD
- NICKEL AND PGE   + DIMENSION STONE
- RARE EARTHS   • DIAMONDS

Contact   Tel.: (709) 729-6193   Fax.: (709) 729-3493

Government of
Newfoundland and Labrador
Department of Natural Resources

Advertisement in *The Labradorian*, Special Report Voisey Bay, 19 June 1995, 12.

were discovered at Voisey's Bay, the area has become the object of a $3-billion megaproject. The Canadian mining company, Inco, the world's largest nickel producer, which bought the land in the area, estimated that the rich ovoid deposits would produce 270 million pounds of nickel during the first seven years. The company's publicity stated that the "discovery" was the largest in Canada for 30 years, that it may become the lowest-cost source of nickel in the world, and that the aggressive exploration program will help assure Inco's prosperity for many years to come.[6] According to one trade journal editorial, "Voisey's Bay is the best thing to happen to Newfoundland and Labrador for decades" (*The Northern Miner*, 1998: 4).

The mineral deposits were understood as vast underground reservoirs of future prosperity for enterprising individuals and companies with vision enough to accept the challenge of removing them. In an *Atlantic Canada* magazine article applauding the mineral discoveries, Victor French, president of Newfoundland Goldbar Resources, underlined the sense of uncharted wonder:

> The mineral exploration activity in this Province, as we understand it today, and the ability to go out and stake large tracts of land such as what recently happened in Labrador with the discovery of Voisey's Bay, is a fairly new situation in this Province. This is still

basically *virgin territory* to a large extent. Granted it had been explored and looked at by the companies which held those land
concessions, but it is still largely *virgin territory* for the everyday
prospector, and geologist. (Quoted by Rumbolt, 1996: 17; emphases added)

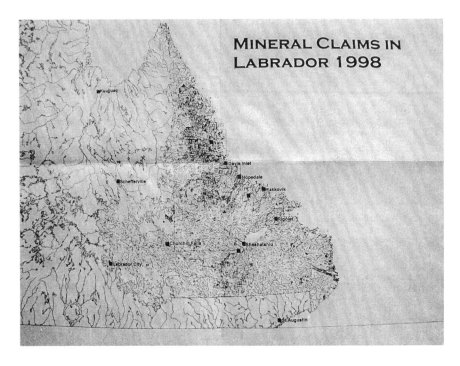

Labrador Mineral Claims Map 1998.

Source: Innu Nation.

By 1996, a total of 280,000 claims had been staked on large tracts of
what the Innu regard as their homeland (Innu Nation, 1996b), but
which the mining industry treats as "virgin territory." It is highly
likely that Voisey's Bay (known to the Innu as Kaupiskatish-shipis
or Emish) is only one among many other locations where minerals
might be found. Since the Voisey's Bay find, another company has
started exploration at Pants Lake, southwest of Utshimassits. A further set of mining claims is located north of Sept-Îles, close to the
Nipissis River, a tributary of the Moisie River, one of the most prolific
salmon spawning rivers in North America.

A process known as "map-staking" permits the claiming of minerals on lands used by the Innu for perhaps thousands of years. For

a refundable fee of $240 individuals and companies can claim 500-square-foot plots of land for the purposes of mineral exploration. They may do this without physically going to their claim site. All they need do is place a pin on a map. If they end up working the claim, all but $5 of their payment is returned to them. One consequence of this procedure is that virtually all of the land around Utshimassits and Natuashish, where construction for a voluntary relocation of the Davis Inlet people to a mainland village began in the late 1990s, has at some time been "claimed."

Amid the Labrador boosters' gleeful anticipation of transforming "virgin territory" to riches, the Native peoples are not even deemed worthy of prior consultation. In this regard, there is little to differentiate the early accounts of exploration that emphasized the *uninhabited* and *unexplored* nature of the interior, and the more recent statements, which simply omit any mention of the prior occupation of the Innu. In the histories of colonists, settlers, explorers, and scientists they are principally invisible, but occasionally emerge as nebulous figures in the forests and at the posts, illuminated only by the light of exploration or commercial activities. For the most part, however, in the more recent surge of industrial development, the Innu have disappeared completely. When a light is shone on them, it is quickly ascertained that they are no hindrance. The main significance of the land to Euro-Canadian developers, to borrow Victor French's imagery, is that some of it has been "explored and looked at by companies." The landscape is a hollowed out space, a void to be filled with exploration and productive activity, creating wealth and prosperity. Only later, as we shall see, when the Innu have protested have they been enjoined, after the fact, to be "partners" in these industrial ventures. Yet, for the Innu, Kaupiskatish-shipis is prime hunting and fishing territory and rich in cultural and personal associations. Many Innu were born in the area and relatives and ancestors are buried there. The Inuit also have had long associations with the area.

Acting spontaneously and through all of the Innu political bodies, the Innu Nation as well as Mamit Innut and Innu Takueikan Uashat mak Maniutenam in Quebec, Innu people have acted to make themselves visible. In February 1995, Innu Nation served an eviction notice on Archean Resources and Diamond Fields Resources, two of the companies involved in establishing the mine, and Innu from Utshimassits and Sheshatshiu set up a protest camp at the site. When the mining companies began building a dock and airstrip before any environmental approval had been granted for the mine, a joint Innu-Inuit protest in September 1997 took place against Inco, which by then was the "owner" of the site. Heavily armed police eventually squashed these protest actions and the eviction notice was ignored. Innu Nation has since contested the legality of the mining operation through the official governmental channels. They have registered their deep sense of violation, but preparations for mining, including new drilling sites, have continued, checked only by the financial difficulties of the mining company and fluctuations in market prices for nickel, which plummeted in 1998.

The Innu Nation Task Force on Mining Activities (Innu Nation, 1996a: 49) summarized the feelings of people surveyed in the two communities as follows:

> Some people talked about it [mining at Kaupiskatish-shipis] as Innu culture being destroyed. Others said it would be lost and still others described it as the culture eventually disappearing. Some thought the consequences of this could be fatal. A number worried about the future of the Innu. They said the future of their children and generations to come was very uncertain. Some thought their grandchildren would be lost like other Native children across Canada who have lost their language and their culture, and who don't know their ancestry. They were worried that their children would no longer think of themselves as Innu and think like whitemen.

The concern was not simply over mining per se. They were worried that they, as a distinct people, as Innu, would remain invisible to the company and "the consequences of this could be fatal," that is, ethnocidal. According to the Task Force survey, mining was viewed by many Innu as a means by which Innu youth would lose their identity. It would encourage Innu to adopt the manners of the whites – greed for material wealth – as well as orienting them to the scientific cosmologies that view nature as under the dominion of humans. Speaking to me around the same time, Prote Poker, a former chief, said that simply taking ancient Innu land for mining was experienced by many in Davis Inlet as a humiliation. "We lose all self-confidence when these developments take place and feel that we can't do anything." He continued, "There is a lot of anger created by Voisey's Bay. People feel powerless. Their anger is not directed at the government, but to each other and towards ourselves."

While they were concerned about the fatal strategies of being transformed into whites and being consumed with inwardly directed anger, the Innu, of Utshimassits particularly, were almost unanimous in sensing environmental catastrophe, pointing out that mining would wreak immense ecological damage, polluting air, land, and water and destroying much of the habitat of the animals on which they still depend. In the presence of open cast mining, the smaller animals and fish would simply become extinct in the area. Larger animals, like the caribou, would change their migration route to avoid the mining. Bears would be attracted to the site when they should be hibernating. Eighty-year-old Tshenish Pasteen, like many older people in Utshimassits, was worried about the destruction of animal habitats. One day when I spoke with him, his son-in-law George Gregoire translating, he said that the tailing ponds would drain out and kill the animals and fish in the salt and fresh water. If acids leeched out into the marshes, the feeding grounds of water-fowl, ducks, and geese, some of them endangered species, would be killed too. Tshenish is old enough to remember what happened when the area called Knob Lake, near Schefferville, was mined in the early 1960s: "There are big holes full of dirty water," and at Knob Lake there was only one site instead of the multi-site complex pro-posed for Kaupiskatish-shipis, so, "it will be a lot worse."

The physical damage to the animals and the landscape is always closely linked not just to the physical survival of the Innu, but to the continued vitality of their distinct identity and world view. Violations of the animals and their habitats are seen as strikes against both the self and the people as a whole. Just before the death of *Tshenu* Pinip Rich, in 1997, Mark Nui told me that he had prophesied, "Today we call ourselves Innu. If we don't have the land, we are not Innu. Then we are nothing." The taking of lands such as that at Voisey's Bay, close to the heart of hunters such as Pinip Rich, precipitated the sense of emptiness, and here he meant personal as much as cultural loss. In his own personal descent, Pinip choked to death on his own vomit while drinking.

Many Innu see the taking of land – and what could be more bla-tant than mining an area that is still used by hunters and is rich in the collective memory – as a kind of personal disgrace. According to many in Utshimassits, people have begun to lose self-confidence as a result of such developments. They feel as if they cannot do any-thing to prevent these violations and out of their powerlessness, a destructive and bitter anger is forged. Having little or no opportuni-ties to externalize the anger towards the state and the developers, it is focused inwardly on self and significant others. In the period just after the "discovery," there was much anxious speculation in the two communities as to what might happen at Voisey's Bay. Some people thought a town would be built there, and that this would lead to an influx of miners, who would further corrupt the Innu. Others thought that it would become a magnet for young Innu workers, who would spend their paycheques on booze and neglect their families.

Most people, however, knew very little that was certain. The mine existed in a cloud of ambiguity and their information about it was nearly always vague, fuelling their worst fears of dispossession, a fear well-grounded in the experiences of other northern peoples faced with the rapid intrusion of "development."[7]

"STEAM RISING"

One of the most significant landmarks for hunters was *Patshetshu-nau* ("Steam rising"), an enormous waterfall, taller than Horseshoe Falls at Niagara, which could be seen and heard from more than 10 miles away. It was located near Lake Meshikimau, an important base for Innu hunting activities and a meeting place for Innu from different parts of *Nitassinan*. The construction of a hydroelectric plant, completed in 1972, turned the waterfall into a trickle, flooded thousands of square miles with an ensuing loss of Innu equipment, hunting camps, graveyards, and burial sites (Ryan, 1988b: 17). It altered the water levels in the rivers, lakes, and brooks, and thereby drastically changed the habitat for the waterfowl, fish, and fur-bearing mammals of the area. Sir Winston Churchill, who was involved in establishing Brinco, the consortium that financed the dam, referred to the damming as "putting a bridle" on the waterfall. For him, Brinco was "a great imperial concept" (Rowe, 1985: 30, 39) and for the first Newfoundland Premier, Joey Smallwood, it was "the biggest real estate deal on the continent in this century" (Gwyn, 1972: 157). In the process, Smallwood memorialized Churchill by the naming of the waterfall itself, the hydroelectric complex, and the nearby settlement as "Churchill Falls." The massive body of water created by the flooding became the third largest artificial lake in the world. It was named "Smallwood Reservoir," in honour of the Newfoundland Premier who went to London in the 1950s to negotiate with Churchill and the British financiers.

John M'Lean, allegedly the first European to set eyes on the waterfall in 1838, described it with his characteristic mixture of awe and pessimism. After hearing "the roar of a mighty cataract," M'Lean's party "soon reached the spot, which presented to us one of the grandest spectacles in the world, but put an end to all hopes of success in our enterprise" (M'Lean, 1849: II, 75). Yet the majesty of the place could not help but touch the usually prosaic diarist who here describes it (ibid., 76) as it might be imagined before the "bridle":

> About six miles above the fall the river suddenly contracts, from a width of from four hundred to six hundred yards, to about one hundred yards; then rushing along in a continuous foaming rapid,

finally contracts to a breadth of about fifty yards, ere it precipitates itself over the rock which forms the fall; when, still roaring and foaming, it continues its maddened course for about a distance of thirty miles, pent up between walls of rock that rise sometimes to the height of three hundred feet on either side. The stupendous fall exceeds in height the Falls of Niagara, but bears no comparison to that sublime object in any other respect, being nearly hidden from view by the abrupt angle which the rocks form immediately beneath it. If not seen, however, it is felt; such is the extraordinary force with which it tumbles into the abyss underneath, that we felt the solid rock shake under our feet as we stood two hundred feet above the gulf. A dense cloud of vapour which can be seen at a great distance in clear weather, hangs over the spot.

About half a century later, the explorer and cartographer Randle Holmes had declared *Patshetshunau* "the most stupendous falls in the world." Citing this, Alpheus Spring Packard (1891: 231-32) had recommended exploration to "any one who is sufficiently enterprising and has sufficient knowledge of geology and natural history to make the journey profitable." His recommendation would appeal to young academics and moneyed New England adventurers, but not industrialists.

However, the potential of this waterfall had gradually "stirred the imagination of many industrial minds" (Tanner, 1947: 804-5), including other nineteenth-century fur traders who referred to it as Grand Falls.[8] Noting the "enormous amount of energy going to waste here," Vaino Tanner recommended the industrial use of the waterfall in his treatise on the land and people of Labrador. Eventually, it was Hydro-Québec, the Quebec utility company that obtained from the Newfoundland government the rights by contract to the power generated at Churchill Falls. It now sells the electricity in Quebec and the United States. The complex is the single largest hydroelectric generating station in North America.

The people whose ancestors used the area for thousands of years were never referred to in the contracts between Newfoundland and Hydro-Québec. Nor did Sir Winston Churchill, Joey Smallwood, or even the Scandinavian academician, Vaino Tanner, ever mention them in the same breath as "hydroelectric power." In the midst of wrangles with Quebec and the British capitalists over the development of the project, Smallwood bellowed into a bank of micro-phones, "this is *our* river, this is *our* waterfall, this is *our* land. We are developing it mainly, chiefly, principally for the benefit of Newfoundland" (quoted by Gwyn, 1972: 274). Shimun Michel, a *tshenu* of Sheshatshiu who travelled and lived much of his life in the Meshikimau area near the development, told me that none of the hunters were contacted or asked about what was going to happen to the land. In fact, hunters were specifically prohibited from observing the construction of the dam. They had no idea that the river, waterfall and land of the territory belonged to Newfoundland.

In a book celebrating the project, Philip Smith (1975: vi) evoked a combination of vast natural richness and astonishing Native primitivity – 10,000 years behind Europeans – as the backdrop to the "largest construction job ever tackled by a private company anywhere":

> Summer comes late to Labrador, and the first snows of winter follow swiftly on its fleeting heels. Gaunt and empty, a place of ancient rock and rivers, of lakes and swamps and stunted, tattered trees, it has never been an easy land to live in. Few men have even tried the experiment: the earliest traces of human habitation found on the Labrador plateau go back only a thousand years. And in those comparatively recent times, the men who roamed that wilderness had no tools more advanced than the chipped flints wielded by the cave-dwellers of Europe ten thousand years before.

The only Native trace here, and elsewhere in the book, is of wandering savages wielding chipped flints. Even this faint and risible presence dissolved altogether in the deal that was cut first in 1952 between Newfoundland and Brinco, privatizing all hydroelectric and hydraulic rights in the province, and then between Brinco and the Hydro-Québec utility company. Brokered in 1969, the second deal allowed for Hydro-Québec to buy power from the dam at a fixed rate until the year 2041. Brinco operated in a nakedly commercial way, operating out of offices in Montreal, contracting to foreign companies for the infrastructure, and freezing Newfoundland out of the vast bulk of financial benefits of the project until 1974, when the provincial government bought back Brinco's remaining water rights in Labrador. The contract with Hydro-Québec, however, still holds. Market rates, since 1969, have, of course, increased, causing the Newfoundland authorities to regard themselves, and not the Innu, as the real victims in the transaction. Eyeing the annual $750 million profits made by Hydro-Québec from Churchill Falls in 1996, the Premier of Newfoundland, Brian Tobin, sought to renegotiate the contract so that power and profits could flow into Newfoundland. While earlier attempts to cut a "fairer" deal with the Premier of Quebec failed (Yakabuski, 1996), a new agreement signed in 1998 between Premier Tobin and Premier Lucien Bouchard of Quebec addressed the Newfoundlanders' sense of inequity and victimhood.

The new accord established the basis for a co-operative venture between Newfoundland and Quebec utility companies to create another hydroelectric project, this time on the Lower Churchill River. This is in the heart of Innu hunting territory, used by people in Sheshatshiu as well as those in the North Shore villages, and like Voisey's Bay is included in the Innu Nation land claim. If built, it will be the second-largest hydroelectric generating station in the world, behind the Three Gorges dam in China. The early newspaper accounts reported that the complex would cost $12 billion and would generate up to 3,500 megawatts of electricity, about triple the requirement for the entire island of Newfoundland. The surplus power generated would be sold to power companies across North America. By diverting two rivers (the Romaine and the St. Jean) that have traditionally and are currently used by the Innu, especially those living in Ekuantshit and Natashkuan in Quebec, two dams would be built on the Churchill River, and an underwater cable would stretch 1,100 kilometres, bringing 800 megawatts of power to St. John's.[9] An additional power line would link northern and southern Quebec. Added to all this, the existing Churchill Falls complex would be boosted by two new 500-megawatt underground turbines. By 2001, again with no reference to the Innu, Newfoundland had reached a preliminary deal with the multinational corporation, Alcoa, the world's largest producer of aluminum, to form an associated development. This proposal, if put into operation, will see an aluminum smelter in Labrador as well as significant investment in the hydro-electric project from Alcoa (Barron, 2001).

For the Newfoundland authorities, Lower Churchill turns the effrontery of having Quebec profit from resources it considers its possessions into an economic revitalization, which is made all the more pleasing because it is, according to Brian Tobin, a "green energy supply." It will help Canada meet its commitments under the global warming treaty signed in Kyoto in 1997. Rounding off what the Newfoundland authorities publicized as a great triumph, the long-standing embarrassment over being outwitted by Quebec in the 1960s was alleviated by Tobin's re-negotiation of the original deal with Hydro-Québec, by which the company will "buy back" a certain proportion of the power at "market rates."

While the perceived inequity of the first Churchill Falls agreement to Newfoundland was a major preoccupation of the Newfoundland government, no parallel consideration was granted to the Native hunters using the area that came to be flooded. The same silence was conspicuous in the period leading up to the second Churchill Falls deal. In fact, the authorities in Quebec and Newfoundland steadfastly refused to consult the Innu before the signing of the pact by the two premiers on 10 March 1998. In the newspaper reports of the deal, the Innu first appear as protesters, wielding placards and surrounding the van escorting Premiers Tobin and Bouchard to the press conference. Only then, as they are about to announce a *fait accompli*, are the Innu remembered, and only then because angry people demanding explanations surrounded the officials and their entourage. But the Innu protesters received no explanations. It was just as well, since the premiers would have been hard-pressed to explain how Aboriginal title land, that is, land not ceded by any treaty, could be appropriated for the sake of selling "power" to people in Newfoundland and elsewhere.[10]

ROADS

There are few paved roads in Labrador. But tarmac is slowly covering the lands, creeping northward from the Quebec North Shore at Baie Comeau and eastward along the same shore towards the Innu villages of Natashquan, Unamen-Shipit, and Pukua-Shipit. Another paved road is expanding eastward and westward from the existing Red Bay to Old Fort Road in the Labrador Straits and the Quebec Lower North Shore area. To provide access to yet another Hydro-Québec impoundment on Innu lands a new 150-kilometre paved road has recently been completed from the Quebec North Shore near Sept-Îles to the Lower Churchill dam site. From Red Bay a rough gravel road has recently been punched through to Mary's Harbour. These roads will remove one of the major impediments to an industrial takeoff in Labrador, which has hitherto required expensive air and sea transportation of supplies to its scattered settlements. At present the only land communication link between the hinterland hub of Goose Bay and the rest of North America is a long gravel road that is impassable for parts of the year, especially during the spring thaw when the road becomes flooded at numerous stream crossings. It is along this road that the supplies needed to support the townspeople and military personnel are ferried up to Goose Bay. The length of time needed by truckers to reach their destination under perilous conditions ensures that Goose Bay shoppers pay high prices for consumer items.

In April 1997, it was suddenly proclaimed that, as a result of intense secret lobbying, $340 million of federal funds would be made available for upgrading the current track running between Churchill Falls and Goose Bay, and then continuing the road from Goose Bay to Cartwright and eventually to Mary's Harbour on the southern Labrador coast. I remember listening to the CBC Goose Bay radio news broadcast the day after the news when, shortly after the playing of the *Ode to Labrador*, a spokesman from the Combined

Labrador Councils hailed the highway as the harbinger of development, transportation, and communication to ease isolation, stating that "Labradorians would be pleased with the announcement." On the same CBC station several days later, local politicians from settler communities from Goose Bay to Forteau were interviewed. Citing forestry, the sale of under-utilized species and resources, and the creation of restaurants, convenience stores, and gas stations in what had hitherto been regarded as a wilderness, the politicians enthused about an economic growth spurt that would accompany the road. "People have to get ready to take advantage of it," one spokesman remarked. His news could have only been met with welcome glee by settlers in depressed communities along the southern Labrador coast and in Goose Bay, perilously over-reliant on NATO and the military air base. When Premier Tobin was asked on the program about the possible interests of native groups, he mentioned only the Labrador Métis,[11] stating that their objections on account of a possible land claim did not really measure up to the concerns of south coast communities fighting for thcir vcry survival on the edge of the continent. He was confident that the road would fully meet the test of environmental impact assessment. Tobin's words, "We will grow and prosper," ended the broadcast.

Already by 2000 the Trans Labrador Highway had been significantly altered by resurfacing, rerouting, and the building of bridges over some of the most frequently flooded streams. Beside the new bridges are highly visible new road signs emblazoned with new settler names – "Ozzie's Brook," "Bob's Brook," and "Divers Brook" – which are clear symbols of the obliteration of the existing Innu names for these locations. As it is "improved," the highway provides far greater settler and industrial access to Innu territory. Many families from Sheshatshiu set up spring and autumn camps along the road, which is already sprouting weekend cabins for the settler population. The final phase of the scheme would cut through *Akamiuapishk*, home of the Mealy Mountain caribou herd and a vital hunting and camping area to the Innu of both Sheshatshiu and the North Shore community of Pukuat-shipu. Numerous graves are located in the mountains of *Akamiuapishk* and extensive Innu associations are held in these mountains. The aim of the project, literally, is to pave the way for more rapid and intensive industrialization, especially logging of the abundant spruce forests along the proposed route.

MILITARY FLIGHT TRAINING

During the spring and summer flying seasons, young, clean-cut Europeans train to be low-level fighter pilots, evading hypothetical

enemy radar over the spruce forests and lakes of the Labrador-
Quebec peninsula. The simulated anxiety of war radiates across *nutshimit*. Since 1979, Canada has leased the air base at Goose Bay,
originally built by the U.S. Air Force during World War II, for low-level
flight training, air-defence exercises, and bombing practice by NATO
air forces. Low-level flight training takes place through a Multinational Memorandum of Understanding between various NATO
partners that permits the British Royal Air Force, the German Air
Force, the Royal Netherlands Air Force, and the Italian Air Force to fly
training flights from Goose Bay airbase. In addition to low-level flight
training, Goose Bay also hosts air-defence exercises and NORAD exercises involving the U.S. Air Force. Bombing ranges at Minai-nipi and
targets at Seal Lake, areas favoured by Innu for spring hunting, are
also used as part of the exercises, and in 2002 the Canadian Defence
Department approved an extension of these ranges to include laser-
guided bombs. Since low-level flight training was initiated in 1979 the
annual number of sorties has increased 2,000 per cent, from 274 in
1979 to 6,558 in 1996 with a peak of 7,355 in 1992. These flights often skim the ground as low as 100 feet at very high speeds. For the
first time, supersonic testing was undertaken in 2001.

By 2000, the French had also entered negotiations to start sub-
sonic low-level flights, particularly a "fast-jet training program." The
following year, pilots from the Norwegian and Belgian military joined
the growing ranks of European low-level flying trainees. The Goose
Bay program is vigorously promoted by the Canadian Department of
National Defence, indicating that far from being chastened or even
mindful of the well-publicized Innu objections (see Wadden, 1991) to
low-level flying, Canada is enthusiastically acting to expand it. The
Reuters news report announcing the French participation referred
to the land only as a "resource rich area" (White, 2000). Innu objections to low-level flying have continually been overruled, and in
1996 the Canadian government renewed memoranda of agreement
permitting enlargements of the number of sorties – to 18,000 per
year – and an expansion of the area covered. In 1997, the British RAF
announced an increase in the use of the training facilities at Goose
Bay. Shortly after, in a deal worth $120 million, the Italian Air Force
announced that it would be joining the other allied countries in participating in low-level flight training. While Innu opposition is
always noted, and indeed the French military authorities were
alerted to it, this has never been considered worthy enough to halt
low-level flying. Once again, as with mining and hydroelectric projects, it is the transformation of the land into mere territory and of
Native people into absences that makes the intrusion possible.

In 1995, Daniel Ashini, Innu Nation Director of Innu Rights and the Environment, wrote to participating NATO defence ministries asking whether European air forces would not conduct low-level flying over their own territories. To this question, A.J. Bluck, a lower-ranking member of the British Ministry of Defence, replied:

> I would just like to pick you up on a point you make regarding low level flying in the U.K. In fact the whole of the U.K. is in principle open to military low flying; and while major conurbations and built up areas are avoided, many comparatively less populated areas will see some military low flying activity. We do not undertake any type of low flying activity in Labrador that we do not undertake in this country. [12]

Hence, it was only "conurbations and built up areas" that were exempt from low-level flight paths. The ministry clearly did not consider the Labrador-Quebec peninsula to be "populated" enough to warrant avoidance. "Labrador" was equated with "this country." Any distinctiveness the nomadic life of the Innu had – their necessary attachment to the land, the open spaces, and the animals – was simply ignored. Besides that, as Bluck pointed out in the same letter, the contract was with Canada. The British government, he stated, was happy to continue low-level flying in line with its agreement with Canada.

While the Innu hunting families that are under the flight paths of the jets are largely invisible to military leaders and pilots, hunters say that they are regularly subjected to deafening screeching noises and sonic booms. They are frequently startled by the sudden noises, causing them to duck down and wince. Their hearts pound. They breathe hard. Some people fall to the ground, immediately fleeing and dropping their rifles, logs, and chainsaws to the ground. Older people and children often become frightened and anxious in anticipation of the jets. As a result, some people avoid altogether areas that are thought to be overflown. The Innu hunting families believe that low-level flying has affected many animals by reducing their numbers and altering their behaviour. Jean-Pierre Ashini , an avid hunter, told me that animals have definitely been hurt by the jets. In the areas that have been overflown he has found dead fish floating on the surface of lakes, baby ducklings on marshes in November, well after they should have flown south, and caribou dead with no wounds. For the hunters, there is little doubt that low-level flying is antithetical to the vitality of the animals they depend on.

The low-level flight training is sensed as a violation of the people, animals, and land that comprise the *nutshimit* life. The overflying tears away at the relationships – between people, between people and animals, between animals and people and their surroundings – that are essential to country life. This sense of defilement was communicated ad infinitum by Innu people throughout the period of sustained protest against low-level flying in the 1980s. In 1994, Elizabeth Penashue gave expression to such feelings in a CBC interview in her sister's house in Sheshatshiu. I was sitting on the floor while reporter Austin Green and his camera crew staged the event. Rose Gregoire, Elizabeth's sister, translated:

> Austin Green (AG): Do the Innu have a special relationship with the land?
>
> Elizabeth Penashue (EP): Yes, because we were born here. Our parents were born here and survived on the land. My father delivered [my mother of] me in the country. I was out in the country since I was a child.
>
> AG: Are the flights a violation of the land?
>
> EP: Yes, because they are not only destroying the people, but the culture and the land. White people have different respects. We respect the land and do not want it to be destroyed.
>
> AG: How have the flights changed the life of the people?
>
> EP: When I was a little girl in the country, we could play outdoors and not be scared of anything and my parents were not scared. Today, I'm not saying it's because of low-level flying, but because the land has been destroyed, the animals are fewer. The fumes go out of the planes and onto the land. The animals don't talk. We do. If they could talk it would be different. I know what a caribou tastes like and you wouldn't know. I remember when I was younger, everything – all kinds of animals – tasted good. This summer five families killed a caribou and the caribou wasn't fit to eat. It seemed as if there wasn't enough blood in the caribou. It was really pale.

Elizabeth then outlined a long list of physical effects of low-level flying on people in the hunting camps until Austin Green moved to bring the interview to a natural closure:

> AG: What would you like to see happen?
>
> EP: People have lived here for thousands of years. I would like to see the Canadian government listen to people. In your culture you have things that are important to you and we have things that are important to us. The government is trying to please these people. If this was white territory, it wouldn't be happening here. People in Germany don't want flights.
>
> AG: Do you feel powerless that people are making decisions on your land?
>
> EP: The government is like a child having a tantrum, tipping over a toy with impunity. I know because I have nine children and twenty-one grandchildren.

After some polite but disingenuous chat, including an inquiry as to whether the Innu spoke the Inuit language, the reporter and his crew soon vanished to Goose Bay in their rental van. The media presence in the community, like so many others that I have witnessed, was brief. Other than through sound bites, there were no attempts to come to grips with how the Innu experience low-level flying or anything else. The crew were on a tight time schedule and appeared edgy to vacate the village. Once they had left, Elizabeth said that she couldn't understand why they didn't ask her more questions. If they really wanted to know about how the Innu felt about low-level flying, they would have stayed longer. Perhaps they were from the government, she joked. But the joke was bittersweet. She was not cheered by the thought. Her sense of the interview was that of having been duped, of being brought close, only to be distanced. She felt the journalist had interviewed her only to appear "fair" and to be seen to be taking account of how Innu looked at low-level flying. Her visibility was momentary and transitory, but she rejected the role of victim. When the journalist set the lure for her to express her powerlessness, she turned the tables, likening the government to a child having a tantrum.

ACTS OF RESISTANCE TO DEVELOPMENT

The Innu presence is always momentary when it is forced into the neat, but pre-emptive, institutional spaces of Euro-Canadian development strategies. These arenas expect, even demand, Innu acquiescence to pre-established formats and the materialist sensibilities of their antagonists. The resistance of the Innu is most potent when it is not constrained by Euro-Canadian conventions. When the Innu Nation asked people in Utshimassits and Sheshatshiu about mining at Voisey's Bay, Edward Piwas articulated his worries in terms of the complex interrelationships between animals, land, water, *Akaneshau*, the mining company, and the Innu:

> There will be no fish, caribou, ducks, geese at Emish after the mining starts. The bear is different. The bear is like the whiteman, but he can't live with them in the winter. He will walk around in the Emish camp. He will eat at the whiteman's table because the *Akaneshau* has killed the fish in the river. The white people will keep the baby animals for pets and these animals will starve – they will not know how to hunt for themselves. Take for example the goose that was seen at Black Ash. It was lost and didn't know its migration route. Even the moose – he is the brother of the *Akaneshau*. He will walk on the streets of Emish with a tie. The *Akaneshau* has three friends – bear, moose and raven, but he can't be friends with

the squirrel because it steals from them. The smog from the milling plant will kill the plants and animals. And it will float into our community. We will not see the smog – it will slowly kill the animals and us. They will probably not just drill in one place – they will drill all around us. The wildlife officer will know when he can't find any animals. He will blame us for the lack of them but he will not think about the drilling. (Innu Nation, 1996a: 38)

The mining is at once destructive of the very living and natural relationships that hunters like Edward Piwas see all around them. Bizarre changes will take place in the animals. They will be disoriented and lose their wildness around the mine. Yet, the *Akaneshau*, oblivious to the living world and its complex interrelationships, will blame the Innu hunters for any adverse changes that are detected. Put another way, *Akaneshau* science, obsessed as it is with empirical cause-and-effect relationships between phenomena that are objectified as things, will not be able to account for the complex changes in the animals and their relationships to the living world.[13]

Edward Piwas had every reason to be skeptical of *Akaneshau* approaches to nature. Generations of fur-trappers, fishermen, and sealers within his and his parents memory had severely depleted animals, fish, and marine mammals, causing the Innu hardships, including starvation.[14] Although there have been some recent attempts at re-thinking human relationships to the environment through the ecology movement, nature, in the more modern scientific and industrial world views, is analogous to a machine, a transformable entity of interconnected components (see Oelschlaeger, 1991: 129). Many of the activities of contemporary big business are oriented towards technological advances, whether these be in medicine, resource extraction, or the business of business itself. Loosely regulated capitalist enterprises constantly are improving their techniques for expanding consumption by transforming nature, whether this be through the Human Genome Project or mining. But in order to do this they must take nature to be a thing, abstract the elements from one another, treating it either as dead or as a controllable life force. As Edward Piwas's statement suggests, this is at great variance from the way in which Innu hunters see nature.

The mining company will not see the moose wearing the tie,[15] the lost geese, and the starving bears until it is too late, and even then, their own acts of destruction will largely escape the noose of reason that they apply to all else. Edward Piwas gestures towards what Gerald Vizenor (1998: 15) calls "native *sovenance*," a real Native presence brought forth by articulations of creation and natural reason, a recognition of the wildness, not the predictability of the world. Yet the natural reason that Edward Piwas lucidly expresses is banished from the arenas within which the Innu are required to speak to Canada. Most expressions of *sovenance* remain subtle. When *sovenance* dissipates, what is left over are acts of resistance, brief moments when Euro-Canadians are jolted into a realization that the Innu exist. Unlike Edward Piwas's statement, these acts are engaged with the representatives of social institutions that presuppose Canadian, not Native, sovereignty. They occasion brief catharsis, followed by a callous denial of their existence.

In October 1994, I accompanied a large group of people from Sheshatshiu to a meeting at the Lions Club in North West River. The meeting, to discuss the environmental impact of low-level flying, was part of a "consultation" exercise being carried out in all of the various communities within a short radius of Goose Bay. Of all the communities where such consultations were taking place at the time, only the Innu villages on the Quebec North Shore, in Labrador, and at Schefferville and Kauauatshikamatsh contained substantial numbers of people (up to more than half of the population) who spent stretches of time (up to half of the year) in the country, hunting under the roar of low-level flying. Because the Innu Nation had no confidence in the fairness of the proceedings, they refused to take part in the consultations. They did not host a meeting with a panel of scientific experts in their villages. These consultations, however, like similar exercises for other industrial projects, were entirely *ex post facto.*

The Innu contingent, about 100 people including numerous children, arrived about one hour before the start of the meeting. They quickly availed themselves of the coffee and cookies that were neatly set out for the North West River residents. The kids, fueled by several styrofoam cups of coffee, were in exuberant mood, chasing each other around the room, flicking coffee at one another with plastic spoon catapults, and creating a party atmosphere. By the time the residents of North West River arrived there were few chairs left and few refreshments. The carnival feeling gave way to tense anticipation as the all-white panel of environmental assessors, and CBC and RCMP camera crews filed into the hall.

The first speaker was a representative from the Canadian Department of Defence, but he was interrupted by Peter Penashue, President of Innu Nation, who took the floor. The stoney-faced panel wearily listened to young Penashue denounce the meeting procedures as flawed because "the land is still claimed by our people; the land was used by our forefathers. We will make sure this process

fails because it affects our civil and human rights." Penashue maintained, "We are the main people affected by it." Within a short time,
the settlers had had enough. Tempers frayed as shouts of "this is a
North West River meeting" shifted attention back to what was supposed to be the non-Native business at hand. But this was
short-lived as women and children with placards pronouncing "Un-
lawful Occupation of Homeland by an Alien Nation" sang and
chanted in front of the rather bored panelists, conspicuous by their
mute reactions to the emotions being expressed right in front of
them. This 20- minute disruption was eventually followed by statements from irate residents of North West River.

Mrs. McLean, the mayor of North West River, began by affirming
support for the "Innu cause," commenting on the generally amicable
relationship between people on each side of the river. "But now
things have changed because of their complaints. It is time to let the
Innu know that they shouldn't have any say over what happens in
North West River. The Innu have turned the tables. They are in
charge here. We shouldn't let Mr. Peter Penashue and his friends tell
us what to do here. This land is part of our heritage, too. The low-
level training is vital in the case of an outbreak of war." With a pause
in the mayor's oration, another Innu leader, Ben Michel, took control of the microphone. A panelist quickly informed him that he was
"not from the community" and therefore not allowed to speak. North
West River residents were then called upon to take the microphone,
as the Innu kids resumed their playful crawling around the floor, tag
games, and catapulting the now-cold coffee. Before they spoke, Mrs.
McLean declaimed her disgust at the Innu leadership for allowing
children "who don't know anything about the issue" to disrupt the
meeting.

Eventually, a coherent settler line emerged. Proprietorship over
"here" and the "community," all-important for wresting control over
the meeting, soon extended to the territory overflown by the jets. The
land was equally part of the settlers' "heritage." "Roots," extending
back to a time when people lived off the land, became all-important
to the residents. These claims established the residents' legitimacy
in the face of the more obvious and threatening Innu appeal to indigeneity.[16] "My ancestors arrived here in this area in the late 1700s,
and for the last 200 years we have observed the traditional lifestyle
that has become synonymous with the Labrador way of life," Lean-
der Baikie's statement began. Others, such as Maharla White,
invoked indigeneity themselves: "I am of Aboriginal descent. My
family originates from Inuit, Innu, and settlers from Europe and I
have lived in North West River since birth. My ancestors hunted for

meat as food, and used the fur for clothing or trading, they harvested wild berries, hunted waterfowl and other birds such as partridge, gathered eggs, grew vegetables, caught and sometimes preserved with smoke and salt whatever sea life was in season, be it trout, salmon, smelts, cod, seal." Attachments to the land, including those of the Innu, were situated in the past and spoken of in the past tense. The vast differences between settler and Innu associations with the land were never mentioned.[17]

The settlers' line was straight and unambiguous. It began to sketch out a moral tale that rested on evolutionary tropes. Life moved from being sustained by hunting, fishing, and trapping to being supported by low-level flying and the cash economy. "We use land now as a convenience, not as a necessity," Mr. Williams pointed out. Another man told the panel, "Everyone cannot live off the land like they did before. This is 1994, not 1904." North West River, as the self-designated "oldest *community* in Labrador," built over Innu graveyards and archaeological sites, symbolized this movement from nomadic pursuits to settled life. Resident after resident testified to the "necessity" of the air base as a place of employment that sustains life. In effect, the land was emptied of content, meaning, and life. It was finished. Land was no longer needed because the change from hunting as subsistence to the air base as sustenance was a "natural" increment, an accompaniment to the evolutionary unfolding of time.

By expending so much energy on planting aboriginal roots and fending off the Innu ambush of "their" meeting, the residents devoted relatively little attention to the "environmental" question of whether low-level flying posed a hazard to animals, water, land, and hunters. While all deferred to scientific knowledge and admitted their own technical ignorance, the environmental damage of low-flying jets was repeatedly represented as minimal, especially in contrast to the disruption caused by locals who used the lands. And here, the residents' wrath turned against what they perceived to be sham Innu environmentalism as they lambasted the use of snow-mobiles, rifles, and outboard motors in hunting. The Innu, their vital presence looming large, became the trespassers, intruders, and violators.

For the residents, the trick was to make the visible invisible; to make these people, full of life, fertility, and humour, disappear. Part of it was to make the Native become an all-embracing category. All had "roots," but these were situated in the past, relevant only to a way of life that no longer existed. Even where these ways of life were practised, such as in the Innu hunting camps, for example, this was deemed to have established no special Innu privilege; it was said to damage the environment even more than low-level flying. The general image drawn was that all people in Labrador were part of one vast democratic order. Each had their own "community" with equal legitimacy. Each had to play by the same rules, which the "consultation" would guarantee, but which the Innu had rejected. The Innu, after their moments of cathartic disruption, were to blend into the whole, to cease to exist as a separate people. Their only distinction became their obstreperousness. The settlers had claimed a parallel indigeneity, giving the Innu no distinctiveness on questions pertaining to the use of the land and skies. The circle was tightening and was completed in May 1995; the panel for the environmental impact study of low-level flying eventually passed judgement that the impacts of the flights ranged primarily from "negligible" to "minor."

TRADITIONAL ECOLOGICAL KNOWLEDGE AND ENVIRONMENTAL
IMPACT ASSESSMENT

Whereas projects such as Churchill Falls went ahead without even a pretense of consultation or environmental review – the land simply was appropriated – the government has since established an environmental impact assessment (EIA) process to consider the likely social and ecological consequences of more recent projects such as low-level flying and mining. Even this, however, is merely administrative – as opposed to legislative, as in the United States – and operates at the discretion of federal ministers (Notzke, 1994: 264-65). If ministers agree to it, final permission for the proposed development is given only if, and when, the required scientific and sociological studies have shown that the effects will be acceptable.

The dominance of the state is reinforced by the mandatory adoption of Western scientific methodology, governed by certain rationalist assumptions: that land, animals, and people can be abstracted and commodified; that accumulated measurements can produce relevant predictions; and that "risk" can be assessed and managed. As Shapcott (quoted in Notzke, 1995: 263) argues, "the values of the dominant culture are so embedded in the process of EIA . . . that alternative values cannot even be considered." Even the seemingly magnanimous inclusion of "traditional ecological knowledge" as relevant data merely reinforces epistemological imperialism. In the Innu communities, "traditional ecological knowledge" (TEK) has been gathered and its collation supervised primarily by non-Innu researchers who employ social science methods comprised of various kinds of paid interviews with the *Tshenut,* as well as film documentation and map-drawing. The interview responses of those surveyed are then collated into a format that can be "fed into" the EIA panel as it was for the comprehensive land claims procedure discussed in the previous chapter.

Perhaps to stem any objections to the state-controlled process itself and to ward off accusations of insensitivity to Natives, the methods of EIA almost always incorporate TEK in some fashion. In much of the literature on the subject, it is frequently stressed that "traditional ecological knowledge" is "a way of life" (see Inuit Circumpolar Conference, 1996), although this knowledge is extricated from the "way of life" so that it can be incorporated as TEK. Thus, Berkes (1993: 3) defines TEK as:

> a cumulative body of knowledge and beliefs, handed down through generations by cultural transmission, about the relationship of living beings (including humans) with one another and with their environment. Further, TEK is an attribute of societies with historical continuity in resource use practices; by and large, these are non-industrial or less technologically advanced societies, many of them indigenous or tribal.

While it is supposed to convey the impression that difference is being respected, TEK is of course, a Western rather than a Native creation. A simulation of hunters and hunting, TEK is a referent to the codifications of "less technologically advanced" societies, an absence rather than a presence.[18] Its main aim is to assist with contemporary land management and industrialization strategies of the state. As a result, TEK becomes Native knowledge that is rendered consistent with "sustainable development" ideologies that attempt to manufacture an affinity between the continued use of natural products as fuel for economic growth and ecological principles as defined by Western science. With its claim to represent the knowledge of Native peoples with associations with the land in northern Canada, TEK is a perfect bridge. "Thus reformulated," Julie Cruikshank (1998: 59) observes, "Native Americans held long term perspectives and engaged in highly rational behavior that sounds suspiciously like intuitive foresight of modern management strategies."

By contrast, hunting wisdom emerges in immediate and direct experience with the land, the animals, and the stories. All that is known is contingent. Knowing is an active process; it is always dynamic. Truth is found in real experience, including dreams, stories, and visions, not in the abstractions or representations of social science. Knowing in hunting actively resists the kind of generalization and codification presupposed by "traditional ecological knowledge." To the state bureaucracies that facilitate these exercises, hunting has no ontological or practical status unique to Native peoples. It is a practice that can be reified as separate from the experience and connections of hunters and granted a badge of legitimacy through state-sponsored science.[19] What was fluid, changeable, non-material, and rooted in a people's experiences with the land and the animals that inhabit it becomes forced into contributing to a predictive objective of a state regulatory process.

In her absorbing study of the stories of Yukon Aboriginal peoples, Cruikshank (ibid., 52) paused to consider how these stories were becoming enmeshed in the political and environmental policies that had begun to affect the peoples that she worked with. As she points out, Native "knowledge is encoded both in distinctive paradigms and in seminal institutional arrangements for converting those observations into everyday practice, and these may get stripped away in translation because they do not travel easily across cultural boundaries." In my observations, not only does hunting knowledge get "stripped away," but it is ignored if it could be perceived to deliver messages that would divert from fundamental Euro-Canadian ontological or political principles. Animal-human relationships that presuppose animal powers over human beings, such as those attributed to the Caribou God in the Caribou House in the Torngat Mountains, are either quietly marginalized or rejected as inconsistent with evidence-based research.

Part of the reason why this type of knowledge is not seriously considered is political. The link between spirituality, hunting, and the land could be taken as an important indication of the deeply rooted relations between the Innu and the areas being prepared for resource extraction. Evidence that particular areas of land (or even the whole of the land) is "sacred" or "holy" would surely raise ethical and moral questions about the contemporary ascendancy of megaprojects on the Labrador-Quebec peninsula. By rejecting spiritual, or even personal, conceptualizations of the land on the basis that there are no means to verify, measure, or empirically observe them, the interests of science and the state coincide. Using an example of her work with one Aboriginal woman, Cruikshank (ibid., 70) explains the conflict between Native knowledge and the epistemological assumptions of science:

> One of the many things I learned from working with Mrs. Ned and her contemporaries is that their extensive knowledge is not amenable to direct questions, nor can it be easily formulated as a set of rules. It must be demonstrated so that others can see how it is used in practice. Such knowledge is a relational concept, more like a verb than a noun, more process than product, and it cannot easily be construed as a written, formally encoded, reified product.

At this level, "traditional ecological knowledge" is blind to the frequent personal disclaimers of the Innu and to the avoidance of
generalized knowledge that was discussed in relation to cartography
in the previous chapter. Innu knowledge largely defies categorical
statements and only with great caution do most *Tshenut* make general pronouncements. Hunters' vast store of knowledge is nearly
always tentative, personal, and attached to particular experiences
and places. To turn this, via social science methods, into TEK is to ignore its complexity and fluidity. Western science, of course, is also
fluid, as even the most hardened positivists admit, but its goal is always to stem the fluidity, to transform hypotheses into theorems
and laws, to discover the Holy Grail of ultimate irreducibility.

ENVIRONMENTAL FABLES DU RICOCHET

Although the Innu communities were encouraged to participate in
the various EIA studies, they have had no authority to determine
what values were accorded importance or even how their views and
"knowledge" would be considered. That authority is vested in the
state and an appointed panel of consultants. As it happened, the research into the probable impact of the Voisey's Bay mine largely
ratified a preordained plan of action to industrialize the land. By assuming that Canada already had the right to adjudicate over
unceded Innu land by implementing the EIA process itself, it effectively reduced the Innu to participants who, even in the face of their
opposition, could be included as parties to the decisions that would
radically alter the land. The final guidelines for the Voisey's Bay EIA –
reached, again, through a seemingly "fair" process of "consultation,"
but drawn up by the panel – specifically and categorically excluded
any consideration of the land claims of the Innu and the Aboriginal
title to the Voisey's Bay land. Although the EIA could have considered these factors, and indeed several submissions, including those
of Innu Nation and third parties including myself, urged the panel to
attend to land claims *before* considering the approval of the mine,
such pleas were ignored.

Like most other EIAs, the Voisey's Bay impact assessment was
entirely *ex post facto*. At the time of the EIA implementation, the mining site had been identified, drilling had begun, workers and
managers had been employed, the provincial and federal governments had promoted the enterprise, millions of dollars had been
invested, and indeed the company openly referred to the area as its
"property." Moreover, the "proponent" of the project is the principal
funding agent of the EIA studies, in this case the Voisey's Bay Nickel
Company, a subsidiary of Inco. According to the company's own rec-

ords, some $14 million was devoted to conducting the EIA. By comparison, Innu Nation was allocated $136,000 to organize its case for the EIA. Newfoundland Premier Tobin tirelessly lobbied for the project, inferring in numerous television and newspaper interviews that environmental approval was merely a formality.

In 1996 I was invited by the Innu leadership to participate in a two-day meeting in Sheshatshiu to discuss the strategy towards a series of environmental and social impact studies. After making a separate $500,000 one-time payment to the Innu Nation, the Voisey's Bay Nickel Company, as the "proponents" of the mine, financed both the meeting and the studies. The agenda was drawn up by a Mennonite volunteer from New Zealand who had been resident in Sheshatshiu for two years. Discussions of particular subjects were strictly limited by time parameters set out in the agenda. In attendance over the two days were several white "experts" – predominantly environmental scientists and anthropologists – a small section of the Innu Nation leadership, and a few *Tshenut* from Sheshatshiu and Utshimassits. The vast majority of the Innu in the two villages were unaware that the meetings were taking place.

The first morning's events opened with the Mennonite telling the delegates that the Voisey's Bay Nickel Company had decided to fund the meeting in order for some clear "outputs" to be achieved. From the start, it was apparent that fundamental questions of land use and rights to land were outside the scope of the meeting. After the representatives of the mining company had provided a thumbnail sketch of the history of the mining activities and, peripherally asserted the need for significant "progress" on land rights, an anthropologist laid down a shared assumption: that it was impossible for the Innu to stop the mine. Although there was some debate of that position, including my own remark that simply assuming inevitability helped create a self-fulfilling prophecy, the meeting proceeded, at least for the bulk of the experts, as if this were literally true.

As the meeting continued each set of contributions was translated to the *Tshenut* into *Innu-aimun*. This proved difficult for the translator because of the incommensurability of words and concepts – the jargon of "process," "deliverables," and "work-scoping," for example, have no equivalent in *Innu-aimun*. Increasingly, the voices that were heard were those of the white experts. The language used became more abstract and scientific. At one point an expert called for the need to "functionally de-link the deliverables." The silences of the Innu, particularly the *Tshenut*, stood in stark contrast to the vocal animation of the experts. After sitting patiently for two whole days the *Tshenut* were finally asked their views. Akat Piwas

was the first to speak:

> What the Innu say should not be translated into Western science. It should be taken in the context of what is being said. We have no real information on Voisey's Bay. There are stories told by Innu of water that is polluted flowing into Voisey's Bay as well as other negative impacts. This needs to get out and be shared. The impacts on the land as expressed by Innu people have to be brought out.

Dominic Pokue, also silent and patient for two days, offered his perspective:

> *Tshenut* care that their children and grandchildren will have land to sustain them. The area is close to the hearts of the Utshimassits people, but this will be no factor in the decision-making arena of the government. It's crazy for us to pretend otherwise. The project has already started. The project is here and that's a fact. It is important to collect information and have on record the opinions of *Tshenut* and put this on paper. But let's not pretend that there is no mine. Already wildlife is being affected, but white people don't see it and this is going to be rammed down our throats no matter what we say.

Akat Piwas then continued:

> Dominic is right. There is a place where Innu people used to get Arctic char when they were hungry. Now they don't go there anymore. This may be because they think that oil and lubricants have contaminated the water. In spring people went to an area near Voisey's Bay and found a decline in the wildlife. There were no black bear, porcupine, or other animals. Before, there was a lot to be hunted. This will not happen when the mine is in place. I can predict myself what will happen to the Innu without going through all of these studies that we are talking about today. There will be a loss of culture. Young people will not know their way of life. Our children will be walking on the pavement, not the barren ground.

For the *Tshenut* the signs were ominous. Mining would lead to a decline in wildlife, contamination of the environment, and the loss of ways of being and thinking. This is what needed to be said and "put down on paper," as Dominic Pokue put it. Yet, it was not put down on paper or, at least, it was not put down on any paper that would mean anything to the authorities. Like so many of the opinions, observations, and stories of the *Tshenut*, they were sidelined almost as soon as they were uttered. These were not the words that could be counted on as TEK, and hence they were of little value to the EIA. Not only were they not elicited by any approved social scientific interview, but they stepped outside of the boundaries of the "traditional" by critically commenting on industrialism, science, and the proclivities of the *Akaneshau*. While much of what the *Tshenut* now present to interviewers naturally ventures into speculations about the relationship between the Innu and non-Innu, such statements are routinely ignored as they were at this meeting.

After the *Tshenut* had said their piece, a few people from both communities expressed their concerns about dealing with these important issues when so many people were suffering from the trauma of alcohol, gas-sniffing, suicide, and abuse. According to David Nui, a man from Utshimassits, the healing process was failing badly. It was, he asserted, necessary for people to heal before they could do anything else. He didn't know how people would cope if mining started. While he spoke Mary May Osmond whispered to a small group of us that the whole affair was like handing a dying man a dinner menu.

These unsettling observations were quickly brushed over, as the meeting resumed its scientific and technical tone. The movement away from heartfelt and ruminating Innu reflections was swift. Any time to dwell on what the *Tshenut* and others had said was killed by the urgings of an anthropologist to identify people with the relevant "skill sets" necessary for particular aspects of the EIA studies. What was needed, he asserted, was someone with particular "skill sets" that included administrative skills. He or she would have to be a bossy person who could keep researchers in line, be able to work well with an Aboriginal person, and have a knowledge of both "good" Western social science and TEK. The Mennonite facilitator signalled that this line of discussion was going in the right direction. The process had been long and unwieldy. There was a need, now at nearly five o'clock on the final day, to move ahead smoothly by identifying a process to "operationalize a proposal." Helpfully, another white expert volunteered to access the community and come up with a "boiler plate."

Over the course of the two days, these discussions became something like the *fables du ricochet*, stories where the narrator constantly evades the hearer's questions. In this case, the expert narrators' story was conveyed without ever taking account of the hearers' melancholy responses. The inelegant and abstract terminology of social and environmental science ricocheted back on itself, turning the people and land in question into objects. As humans, they were barely visible beneath the smoke of reason. The identification of "key elements," "key objectives," "assessing costs of purchasing data," and "arriving at a community participation profile" became the ultimate concerns. According to one expert, the Innu Nation should push for a big enough budget from the mining company and then "integrity will flow." As the huddled and now silent people from Utshimassits became backdrops, the untranslatable verbosity gestured towards particular "outputs." These were framed in terms of the need for more time to do the studies in question and an increased budget to pay the environmental consultants, many of whom were in the room, who would carry it out. Nothing from what any of the *Tshenut* had said was factored into the "outputs." They had been made invisible, only pretexts for the meeting.[20]

Several months later a job advertisement came over the Internet: "Wanted. Coordinator for a Participatory Research project with Communities of Utshimassits and Sheshatshiu, Labrador." The job required the holder to be conversant with "community development and facilitation," "training skills," "video documentation," and "computer bases." Interested persons should apply to an office in Saskatoon, thousands of miles away from *Nitassinan*.

After all of these ethnocentric, laborious, and crushingly dull procedures, it was little surprise that the final government decision in August 1999 gave the mining company the green light, subject to "appropriate safeguards," and ignored key recommendations of the panel. An underground exploration shaft was scheduled for development the following summer. At the time of the announcement of the approval Inco estimated that 137,000 tonnes of nickel ore lie underground (Sullivan, 1999). The Innu communities had participated in the procedures diligently by complying with demands for various reports on how the mine would affect their way of life, completing video projects, repeatedly bringing out often frail elderly people to speak to the issue, and inviting panel members to visit. The green light for the mine indicated to them that once more they had been duped. Among all the solemn promises, earnest pleas of honesty, and dollars thrown to them, they had yet again been ignored. Control of their land and their future had been spirited away from them by a deadly combination of liberal poses and tedious bureaucracy. The sense of being deceived again brought unsettling reflections from members of the Innu communities.

"I am angry with the government now," stated Utshimassits Chief Mark Nui.

> When the panel came to Davis Inlet, we told them about our life at Voisey's Bay, and how the mine would affect our culture. The elders told the panel about how mining at Emish could damage the land and the animals there, and about how they are already seeing the effects of exploration activities. We told the panel that our land had to be protected. The panel listened to us, and recommended that a land rights agreement had to be settled before the mining could begin. Now the government has refused. Why does the government pretend to listen to us and then do what they want anyway? The government makes a lot of promises, but they don't live up to them. (Quoted in Innu Nation, 1999b)

The Evolution of Civilization and Toil   **4**

. . . whatever the derivation may be, the name [Labrador] *fits. Cabot, Corte Real, Davis, Hudson and a long line of adventurous spirits, have toiled along its rugged coasts.*

– W.G. Gosling (1910: 55)

. . . the Northland promises all the physical and material satisfaction which the labour of man's hands and the sweat of man's brow can afford.

– Sir Wilfred Grenfell (1933: 101)

Several years ago when Innu men went to Social Services or the hospital and were asked their occupation, they said, "hunter." Now they say "unemployed."

– Jean-Pierre Ashini, Sheshatshiu, 1997

THE NORTHERN RANGER

A great many people were gathered on the tiny quay. It seemed as though the whole Davis Inlet community was out on this sunny summer evening. I had never seen so many Innu all in one place. As the *Northern Ranger* tour ship docked, kids scurried up the gangplank and tried to get on board while stewards, only loosely prepared for the onslaught, shoved them back. The kids all resisted, but were eventually turned around.

A handful of bewildered passengers ventured ashore, bemused and stunned, stepping around the children and making beelines for Joyce Marshall, a volunteer worker for an Ontario-based charity organization, and myself, the only two white people in the crowd. With wan smiles, a few made-up suburban women with big, fluffy sprayed hairstyles and men clad in clean, pressed slacks and shirts walked timidly through the crowd. Here, on this night of blackfly infestation and teeming humanity, the tourists kept a fearful distance. There was nothing to buy, not even handicrafts. There was just excited activity, a lot of children running around, adults sitting on ATVs, smoking and joking. A few Innu men helped while a crane off-loaded supplies for their grocery stores: case after case of Pepsi Cola. As the ship hoisted up anchor and pulled away into the bay with the tourists safely back on deck, they smiled and waved to the raucous crowd. As if sensing hypocrisy, some Innu kids picked up stones and debris and launched them at the waving passengers, the staccato metallic pings echoing into the night air.

Having docked at Nain overnight and been treated to a cultural tour of the Inuit community, the *Northern Ranger* passengers returned, almost 24 hours later, to the again tumultuous Davis Inlet dock. The second visit was different. This time, the passengers were more cautious. No one disembarked. They kept a safe distance high up on the decks of the ship, gawking and taking photographs of the multitudes of Innu below them. This time they were not smiling. The presumed innocence of the encounter had worn off.

The stewards were more prepared to prevent the kids running up the gangplanks and onto the ship. But they could succeed only by rough handling them and when this didn't work, taunting them by removing their baseball caps and gesturing to toss them into the water. Despite the more organized strategy of passengers and crew, the Innu children managed to climb acrobatically up every possible rope tethering the ship to the dock and its anchor. By hauling themselves about 20 feet up the ropes and facing deadly drops if they slipped, even the very smallest children evaded the stewards and heroically got on board. Eventually all were rounded up, ejected from the ship, and with some relief the horn sounded to signal the departure of the *Northern Ranger*. This time, the kids pelted it with renewed vigour. With each stone launched into the air, they yelled variously, "Fuck you" and "Fuckin' Eskimo," the latter epithet directed towards a group of Inuit children who boarded at Nain.

Judging by the remarks of some of them, the tourists had been surprised that so few concessions to material and cultural consumption would be made at their first encounter with the Innu. The perceived indifference of the Innu towards these vacationers – there were no greeting parties, organized tours, or signs of anything consumable – made it difficult for them to play the role of tourists. The massed ranks of the village were displaying no badges of Native authenticity, but neither were there any indications that they were assimilating by rising to the opportunities of the money economy.

They were selling nothing and soliciting nothing, and they asked nothing of the tourists. Innu parents simply watched as their children gleefully scaled the ropes, uttering only jests such as *tshiskueu autuminish*, crazy monkey. Instead of the tourists being allowed to consume or be treated to any staged entertainment, the *Northern Ranger* and its cargo became the Innu kids' amusement. The tourists' flickering recognition of this turning of the tables, evident by their fearful and distancing observations on the second visit, was obvious to all.

Child climbing rope to board *Northern Ranger*. Photograph by author.

Innu children boarding *Northern Ranger*. Photograph by author.

DEPENDENCE AND STARVATION

This arrival scene recalls earlier Anglo-Saxon impressions of the Innu in which observations of Native indolence and disorder were fashioned into critical judgements. Later these observations would form the basis for attempts to transform the Innu. The stern Presbyterian Donald Smith was the Hudson's Bay Company factor stationed at Tadoussac in Quebec and later at Rigolet and North West River in the 1850s and 1860s. Smith, who in later life became Lord Strathcona the financier, philanthropist, and politician, crisscrossed the entire peninsula with either Innu or Inuit guides. A champion of prudence, Smith was appalled by the very Natives he depended on. "[Y]ou would have to travel the whole world over," he wrote, "to find a greater contrast to the Scotch than to these same Indians." In a letter home Smith wrote, "if civilization consists in frugality and foresight, then the Montagnais are far worse than dogs, who at least have sense enough to bury a bone against an evil day" (quoted by Newman, 1991: 21). The Protestant ethics of thrift, postponed gratification, and possessiveness were absent among these Natives, who, at least in respect to Smith's view of the fundamentals of civilization, were "far worse than dogs."

Smith was so determined to uphold these yardsticks of civilization that he allowed his trading partners to die of starvation. According to documents presented at British Parliamentary Select Committee deliberations in 1857, Smith's refusal to provide the hunters with sufficient ammunition was directly responsible for the deaths of "a great number" of Innu in the mid-1850s. Henriksen (1993b: 4) estimated the "great number" to be 200. Similarly, HBC factor Donald Henderson at Fort Nascopie in the interior of the Labrador-Quebec peninsula also refused ammunition to Mushuau Innu, who subsequently starved to death (see Newman, 1991: 29-30).[1] Newman (ibid., 30) notes that individual Innu were rarely mentioned in Smith's reports or diaries, "the natives were simply there, like trees or the wind." The trader, as other white pioneers in Labrador at the time, saw Natives principally as uncivilized peoples, meriting consideration chiefly as fur harvesters. Adding to his own prestige and advancement, Donald Smith "always showed a balance on the right side of the ledger" in the elaborate bookkeeping of the HBC (Wilson, 1902: 36). In order to achieve this, Smith had to ensure that the Innu become reliable trappers.

Just over a decade earlier, the HBC trader John M'Lean had acted similarly, also in pursuit of a lucrative fur trade in the interior. Writing some fairly detailed accounts of his explorations, in his

Notes of a Twenty-five Years' Service in the Hudson's Bay Territory, M'Lean mentions several instances of near starvation and perilous survival. In one description of a journey in which a party including himself was forced to split up, M'Lean notes without elaboration that an Eskimo servant of the Fort Chimo post had "abandon[ed] himself to despair" some 60 miles from the post (McLean, 1968: 219). In another risky venture, this time involving an attempt to establish a trading post in the interior, an "Indian lad" had to be recruited from Fort Chimo to bring the traders and guides back. Their long return journey home was made possible only by eating their dogs and then going without food for the final three days of the journey. They returned "in so deplorable a state of emaciation that we could scarcely recognize them" (M'Lean, 1849: II, 86).

In order to keep the Hudson's Bay Company stockholders in London happy and to guarantee his own advancement, Lord Strathcona and other traders like M'Lean were prepared to act ruthlessly to ensure that the Indians played the game according to HBC rules. This process involved making Natives dependent on trade goods for both basic subsistence and for the work the Company wished them to carry out, then denying these very goods to them if their work was deemed unsatisfactory. Unlike Strathcona, M'Lean, being much less successful in the Company, could be more candid as to the effects on the Natives. While M'Lean (ibid., 119-20) had observed that the Nascopie (earlier spelling of "Naskapi") were "most averse to locomotion; many of them grow up to man's estate without once visiting a trading post," he clearly perceived how conscious manipulation brought about changes to them. As trading posts and missionary stations were springing up all around them – Ungava Bay, James Bay, the North Shore of the Gulf of St. Lawrence and the North Labrador coast – M'Lean (ibid., 125) predicted:

> I doubt not but artificial wants will, in time, be created, that may become as indispensable to their comfort as their present real wants. All the arts of the trader are exercised to produce such a result, and those arts never fail of ultimate success. Even during the last two years of my management, the demand for certain articles of European manufacture has greatly increased.

Despite their desires for the goods of the traders, causing starvation to the Innu on account of their impeding "the right side of the ledger" by not bringing in sufficient furs was a fairly regular occurrence in the nineteenth century. In a letter to William G. Smith in London in 1858, Donald Smith remarked that, "being far away from their hunting grounds and failing in procuring from Messrs Hunt's people [traders at Nain] a supply of provisions as they had no furs to give in return, . . . it is said upwards of 50, including women and children, died of a state of destitution" (cited by Hammond, 1994: 71). In 1905, on her expedition from North West River to Ungava, Mina Hubbard (1981: 173) came across an encampment of Innu on the George River who spoke of similar meanness on the part of the traders. As one elderly man told Mrs. Hubbard, "We can get nothing from the Englishman, not even ammunition. It is hard for us to live." The anthropologist William Duncan Strong (Leacock and Rothschild, 1994: 133-34) also recorded several accounts of starvation occurring subsequent to refusals of traders to render assistance in the form of food and ammunition.

> Some forty years ago, (?) [this would have been in the late 1880s] a Naskapi band came out of the country near Upatik Bay and went to Davis Inlet. The storekeeper there (a new man) would give them no food and all nineteen in the band starved to death except two women and one small boy – who went to Upatik River on the ice, found a deer killed by wolves, made a trout net from the skin, and managed to live until they met another Naskapi on George River.
>
> About twelve years ago [circa 1915-16] Edward, Joe and Mishin . . . and their families – went from George River to White Whale River. There were no deer and while there were plenty of partridges they were very wild and the group had no cartridges. They went to the store [on White Whale River, Strong thought], but could get nothing as they had no fur. (Job Edmonds, the trader at White Whale River, was very hard on Indians, charging high prices for food and paying low prices for fur). Finally they were forced to eat berries – Mishin went out hunting but did not come back at night. They followed his trail and found his body; he had starved to death. His widow wanted to drown herself but they prevented her.

Similar consequences have been faced by other Natives of the Far North brought into the fur trade. Brody (1975: 166) cites an Inuit man, probably in northern Quebec, who claimed that many Cree starved to death in the early twentieth century on account of the policies of one particular trader.[2] It was not simply that Natives starved because of the meanness of the traders, the trade itself could lure them into starvation as hunting slowly transformed from a way of life to a means to procure European trade items, including the guns and other supplies needed to bring in furs. Henry Youle Hind (1863: II, 104) was forthright on this linkage, observing that starvation occurred "chiefly . . . on account of their [the Innu] leaving their proper hunting grounds to seek the *robes noires* [Catholic priests] or follow the fur traders who, from diminishing returns are compelled to abandon outposts and concentrate their strengths." Although new European trade items, such as firearms, in and of themselves did not diminish the numbers of animals, the use of guns in connection with trade did.[3] Anthropologist Julius Lips (1947: 394), observing that "reports about Indians dying of hunger run through the annual reports of the Hudson's Bay Company managers like a red thread," remarked on how the fur trade had not improved the "economic security" of the Innu. The technological gains to the Innu from trapping were a dubious advantage since European traps and guns hastened the depletion of animals and the food the Innu received from the traders was mere "seasonings and supplements to the principal meat diet."

Independent of the activities of the traders, starvation sometimes occurred on account of other factors. Caribou populations, for example, fluctuate and migration patterns may alter from one year to the next. This means that the principal source of food was never a certainty, and as a result Innu were known to go hungry and occasionally starve. Although hunters had developed means to cope with such fluctuations by drying, storing, and curing meat, the gradual erosion of wildlife by first the fur trade and eventually settlers caused additional sources of uncertainty in procuring food.[4] In some cases, European observers noted that this led the Innu to plunder fragile stocks in ways that would have been alien to them before the fur trade, which had altered their hunting activities and increased competition for animals with European trappers and settlers.[5]

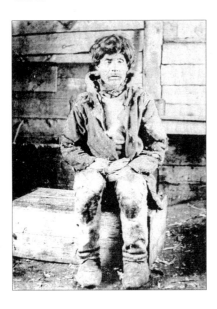

"Starving Indian. G.W.R. [Great Whale River] 1904" by A.A. Chesterfield.

Source: William C. James, *A Fur Trader's Photographs: A.A. Chesterfield in the District of Ungava 1901-4* (Montreal and Kingston: McGill- Queen's University Press, 1985), 61. Of this photo, Chesterfield wrote, "This Indian from the interior of Labrador staggered to a trading post on the coast just in time to be saved from starvation."

If ultimately unsuccessful in commercial terms, the fur trade in Labrador was an audacious and sometimes deadly attempt to manufacture dependence among Native peoples who had up to that point been extremely self-reliant. The Innu had developed a wide range of techniques and technologies to thrive in the rigorous Sub-arctic environment. Innu resourcefulness, especially with the caribou, an animal used to supply food, shelter, and clothing, meant that they had little incentive to engage in a trade that required long hours trapping fur-bearing mammals and animals for little gain. Time spent trapping was time not hunting caribou and not maintaining camps and enjoying leisure time and family life.

The goal of the fur traders, however, was always to combat this independence. This meant turning self-sufficiency into dependence on the traders, and transforming what was seen as laziness on the part of the Innu into "work" involving regular paid employment. Providing "grog" was one mechanism used to induce this dependence, particularly in the southerly areas of the Innu territory. Speaking of the fur trade in the 1927 Privy Council Boundary Dispute debate, Mr. Macmillan was "sorry to see the temptation of fire water used in many instances to attract the Indians. They were most liable to go to the posts where they got most drink" (Great Britain, Privy Council, 1927: 436).[6] Nonetheless, the slow pace of change among the Innu was always a source of irritation and, although not for want of trying on the part of these traders, the northern groups of Innu were always marginal to the fur trade (see Henriksen, 1993b: 1-2).

The attempts to effect such a transformation for the sake of commerce can be traced to the eighteenth century with the final French capitulation to the British in 1763. Although the French retained some fishing rights on the Newfoundland coast and Gulf of the St. Lawrence, in 1765 the British Governor of Newfoundland, Sir Hugh Palliser, issued an Order for Establishing Communications and Trade with the Esquimaux Savages on the Coast of Labrador. In his order, Sir Hugh remarked on the great advantages that "would arise to His Majesty by establishing friendly intercourse with the Indians on the Coast of Labrador" (quoted by Gosling, 1910: 172). The British were to act kindly and generously to the Natives, abandoning the wanton murders that had occurred on the coast, initiated by both fishermen and Inuit. Thus, "by all fair and gentle means," His Majesty's subjects were to "encourage them to come with their commodities to trade," now that "His Majesty [had] taken them under his protection" (quoted by Gosling, 1910: 173).

Despite every encouragement, these entreaties to take part in trade were met with a sluggish uptake as a result of the less than enthusiastic Native participation. In his *Geography of Hudson's Bay*, Captain William Coats (Barrow, 1852: 89) described the Labrador Natives as so independent "that hardly one in twenty have taken the trouble to go to ours or any of the French settlements." Coats interpreted this as both a result of "indolence and idleness" and "a mark of great wisdom in them." He went on to describe the snare that the fur trade was designed to effect, clutching dependence with the bait of trade goods:

> However, those few that has frequented the setlements, begin to like our commodities better; their women like our nicknacks and guegaws, and the men begin to love brandy, bread and tobacco, so that a litle address and management will bring these happy drones out of this profound lethargy.

In 1814, during the earliest days of the trade extending into the Labrador-Quebec peninsula from Hudson Bay, Thomas Alder, the clerk at the Eastmain post, had observed:

> nothing but necessity or extreme want, will ever produce a spirit of exertion, in such Indians as these; their dependence on us is very trifling, the Deer furnishes them with both food and raiment, and so long as they can procure a supply of Powder, Shot, Tobacco, and a hearty swill of grog at times, their wants are wholly supplied. (Quoted by Davies, 1963: xxxvii)

Several years later, James Clouston, an HBC factor also based at Eastmain, lamented the independence of the Indians he encountered as he pushed into the interior, largely with their assistance. For Clouston, "[k]ettle, hatchet, knife, gun, powder and shot and sometimes a net is all they consider necessary, so that they are much more independent of European goods than any other Indians whom I have seen" (ibid., 40). The traders commonly reported that the "Nascopie" preferred to trade minimally, confining themselves to bringing meat and caribou hides to the Fort Chimo post. When the Mushuau Innu did bring pelts and other trade items to the posts, their offerings of fur in particular frequently offended the traders. In 1833, Nicol Finlayson, the trader at Fort Chimo, observed that "the two Indians I engaged are always coming in with nothing, begging their little wants" (ibid., 173-74).

John M'Lean, a blunt diarist, devoted an entire chapter of his *Notes* to the Nascopie. With some irony, he records the persistence of their autonomy. "Fortunately for themselves," M'Lean (1849: II, 124) notes, "they are at present the most independent of the whites of any other Indians on this continent, the Esquimaux excepted." M'Lean noted that this relative independence had kept the Innu "an unsophisticated race of aborigines" (McLean, 1968: 219), insulated from various European corruptions, but nonetheless barely human. Wishing not to "disgust the reader," M'Lean held back on the "grosser passions" that the Nascopie were alleged to indulge in. However, he did observe that they had "no sense of shame" and not one "article of domestic utility." He observed them lapping up food "like dogs" and devouring meat "like the gorged beast of prey" (M'Lean, 1849: II, 120-21).

While a treasury of proto-anthropology, the nineteenth-century fur trade with the northern groups of Innu largely failed to enrich the HBC stockholders. Nevertheless, what the traders missed extracting in furs they gained in assistance with exploration of the interior of the peninsula, as Indians zig-zagged the region, guiding traders on journeys of hundreds of miles. Despite their reliance on Native knowledge of the land, traders frequently quarrelled with Indians and badgered them into taking unwise routes at a pace dictated by commercial and other external pressures. Even so, the traders often could not persuade their guides to take them exactly where they wanted and at the desired speed. Thus, in the midst of his uncompleted Fort Chimo-to-Mingan journey, a trip in which the Innu guides were often stricken with snowblindness, Erland Erlandson, a Danish HBC employee, complained that "these are the most indolent, spiritless Indians I ever saw, they are equally insensible to persuasion or threats" (Davies, 1963: 248). Yet, here it was the "indolent and spiritless" Indians charitably delivering up knowledge of their lands and saving traders such as Erlandson from starvation.[7] M'Lean, with Indian guides and Eskimo helpers from Ungava ventured into "the interior," a sort of El Dorado of fur, but this trip occasioned both ill-tempered impatience on the part of the trader and starvation. In his *Notes*, M'Lean frequently registered annoyance at either the refusals of Natives to guide him into the interior or to do exactly as he wished once they were on the route. In one instance, after failing to persuade an Innu guide of the necessity of expediting a journey, he angrily exclaimed, "I addressed a thing without reason and without understanding." But because he was dependent for his life on his guides, M'Lean was "accordingly obliged once more, to yield" (McLean, 1968: 218). Following M'Lean, Henry Youle Hind (1863:4), a seasoned explorer and scientist, found similar problems in simply recruiting Innu guides to take him inland from Sept-Îles in the early 1860s. He put their reluctance down to "sickness and habitual indolence."

THE FORECOURTS OF CIVILIZATION

By the late nineteenth century, explorers of the Labrador-Quebec peninsula became engaged in more directly scientific missions designed to refine the basic knowledge of the Natives and their terrain that had already been acquired by the fur traders. This involved the compilation of information about the flora, fauna, geology, and geography of a relatively unknown part of the North American continent. In these adventurous scientific quests, the Natives were scarcely considered distinct from the general natural history. Although the images of the Innu produced by explorers and scientists were more nuanced than those of the fur traders, both shared a crude comparative analysis in which Natives and Europeans were lined up against presumed measurements of cultural advancement. Explorers, geographers, and anthropologists of the period from about 1860 to 1935 groped to place the Innu within the taxonomies of cultural evolution that became fashionable as Europeans encountered ever more Natives in their colonial exploits.

Imbued with the idea of history as linear chronology and incremental improvement, nineteenth-century European social thought tended to position non-Europeans as either inert or temporally prior to Europeans.[8] This was fundamental to cultural evolutionism and easily fed into the pervasive scientific, literary, and popular depictions of the "vanishing Indian." The generally accepted theories of cultural evolutionism, which flourished in the social sciences until relatively recently, became a prism through which scientists, explorers, and travellers viewed the Innu and other indigenous peoples. Early anthropology embraced the idea that humans had made progressive transitions between different modes of subsistence and that these leaps had occurred unevenly around the globe. By referring to biological metaphors of growth, it was thought that all life, including human cultural life, moved towards improvement, which was indicated by the "complexity" of social and cultural forms. By analyzing the contemporary non-European cultures, it was possible for scientists to conceive of the span of human development and the origin of certain cultural forms.[9] Those social groups living by what were seen as "simple" modes of subsistence, with similarly uncomplicated social structures, filled in gaps of knowledge as to how human societies developed. By looking at them, Europeans could glimpse their own past and mark out the extent to which they had progressed.[10]

Witnessing the continual defeats of Natives in wars and the effects of European diseases, scientists, politicians, and settlers alike believed that assimilation, population decline, and perhaps the eventual extinction of Indians were inevitable accompaniments to cultural progress (see Dippie, 1982). While the Innu were sheltered from the slaughters, warfare, and, to a lesser extent, the epidemics that ravished more southern and western parts of the continent, different encroachments and natural calamities, such as shortages of caribou and brush-fires, had reportedly thinned their numbers by the time a series of European and American explorers, scientists, and naturalists made contact with them and began to leave more detailed records of encounters.

Despite the paucity of contact with the Innu, these visitors were quick to measure and judge by reference to evolutionary metaphors. Alpheus Spring Packard (1891: 239), who cruised the coast twice in the 1860s as a student of the geography of Labrador, thought the Innu might be "the only truly wild, untamed red-men of North America." Most, especially those explorers appealing to science for the legitimation of their travels, could not resist comparisons against various yardsticks of civilization. One such commentator was Lucien Turner, whose *Ethnology of the Ungava District and Hudson Bay Territory*, written in the 1880s, presents a rich ethnographic account of the material culture of the Innu and Inuit of the Fort Chimo region. While Turner (1979: 105), like many other nineteenth-century observers, had great respect for the physical endurance, hunting acumen, and egalitarian qualities of the "Nenenot," as he called them, he was in no doubt as to their basic inferiority:

> In comparison with a white man under the same conditions the natives of either class [Indian and Eskimo] would soon show signs of inferiority, and under prolonged exertion but few, even the Eskimo, would endure the strain. The principal strength of these people is shown in their success in the chase.

Observers of the last two centuries singled out hunting skill, "success in the chase" as Lucien Turner put it, as the chief accomplishment of the Innu. Successive visitors to the Labrador-Quebec peninsula also praised the sheer physical dexterity, endurance, and practical resourcefulness of the Innu in what they acknowledged was a highly taxing environment. The Innu also came in for compliments for their ingenuity in making tools and weapons and keeping themselves warm in a frigid climate.

However, Innu achievements in the hunting economy were nearly always seen as impediments to their adaptation to more "advanced" ways of earning sustenance. After an exquisitely detailed description of the complexities of salmon spearing, for example, Henry Youle Hind (1863: I, 101) rhetorically asked, "is this the languid drowsy savage which you have often seen slouching through the day, indolent and listless, a sluggard and a drone." For Hind and numerous others, the highly developed hunting and fishing abilities of the Innu afforded them leisure time, and, by implication, retarded their capability of participating in an economy that required more disciplined orientations toward toil and time-keeping.

Being rooted in "subsistence," hunting tethered the Innu to a kind of static existence in the eyes of these visitors. Cultural evolutionism provided the unstated assumptions behind off-the-cuff judgements such as that of Hind, who remarked of the Montagnais that they had "never succeeded in rising above the level of first-rate hunters in the woods" (ibid., 19). This quality, he thought, made them "wholly unfitted for a settled mode of life." In Hind's view, the very instability of the hunting way of life with its dependence on often scarce wild animals would "weaken the intellect" and cause "habitual improvidence" that would eventually "destroy that self-reliance which might be sustained under a more regular and secure mode of life" (ibid., 104).

Hunting was also regarded as a mode of production that called for a "simple" division of labour that mired hunters in a state of underdevelopment if not stagnation. As Julius Lips (1947: 389) remarked:

> In contrast to higher forms of cultural development or to our own civilization with its manifold differentiations and divisions of labor, the Naskapi culture knows division of labor almost exclusively as between the sexes. Generally speaking, every Indian family has the same economic abilities and performs the same type of work.

Thus, while "manifold differentiations" propelled European history forward, hunters seemed locked into a homogeneous and unvarying existence. Speaking of "the nearest part of our Empire across the Atlantic," Sir Wilfred Grenfell told his BBC audience in 1929 that he was not going to deal with its history because, "[a]s a matter of fact, it scarcely has any history, except for an occasional visit from explorers from John Cabot onwards." The Native population, whom Grenfell referred to as "remnants," had no history apart from that which was thrown into relief by European expeditions. It is as if they had been waiting for millennia for explorers, anthropologists, and tourists to cast their eyes down towards them. Although he had little contact with Natives, in his numerous memoirs Grenfell reports the occasional encounter with Eskimos or Indians. But, on the whole, they feature only as backdrops to his heroic tales of civilization and Empire in a harsh climate.[11]

At about the same time, the turn of the twentieth century, the Bostonian William Cabot made several summer expeditions to Labrador, which are recorded in his travel book, *In Northern Labrador*. His accounts of meetings with Innu are frequently tinged with respect for their speed, agility, and skills in the country. Less preoccupied with Empire than British explorers, Cabot's Labrador adventure writing represents an ethnological turn showing him a keen observer of Innu manners. This was extended to photography as Cabot took pictures of the Innu that he encountered in various poses and actions. Although he clearly had great respect for many aspects of their sensibility and way of life, Cabot judged the Mushuau Innu to be in the "primitive hunter stage," "living substantially in the pre-Columbian age of the continent" (Cabot, 1912: 189). Cabot's first impression of the Mushuau Innu was "vivid and a little mixed":

> Their irresponsible thin legs and bare thighs, and their horsetail hair, are decidedly not of our world, though the latter is usually docked at the shoulders. They have a nasal twang, which in the excitement of arrival . . . becomes almost a whine. Their travel clothing is nondescript and dingy; though as to this, again, they know how to do better, and in new white skin clothing are wholly picturesque. But as untamed aborigines, Stone Age people, they lay hold of one. The look in their eyes is the look of the primitive man of the open. (Ibid., 86).

Innu woman making moccasins with a young girl behind her at the Tshinutivish camp on Indian House Lake, George River, Quebec, 8-9

Innu mother and child at camp on Mistinibi Lake, Quebec, on the tundra east of the George River.

Source: William Brooks Cabot collection, 1906: 90, 110, National Anthropological Archives, Smithsonian Institution.

Their bodies and gaze gave away what many Europeans had always suspected – the material impoverishment and the primal wildness of a timeless people. "All in all, the life of these people remains singularly unchanged," Cabot reported in Wilfred Grenfell's edited travelogue of Labrador. These "primitive hunters" were an anachronism, often compared unfavourably to the "savages of temperate America," as Cabot (ibid., 210) put it.[12]

The explorer Dillon Wallace (1977: 25), a survivor of the ill-fated Leonidas Hubbard expedition[13] to Lake Meshikimau, also at the turn of the century, states that one of the intentions of Hubbard was to study "the habits of the Indians who are the most primitive on the North American continent." So bleak were the prospects for these primitives that it hardly needed saying that they, like their cousins in the United States in the nineteenth century, were a vanishing race. As resources began to dwindle, they would go the way of the animals. As W.G. Gosling (1910: 427) predicted early in the twentieth century, "the fur bearing animals and the caribou . . . will disappear with the forests, and with them the Indians and the trappers."

Some years later, in 1935, the anthropologist Frank Speck published *Naskapi: The Savage Hunters of the Labrador Peninsula*. Speck was particularly concerned with "Naskapi" religious life and the intimate interrelationships between the people and the natural world. At the time, Speck provided important insights into a people who had largely been bypassed by European settlement and about whom little was published in the academic records. Filling a gap in anthropological knowledge, Speck felt obliged to consider the Innu within the context of cultural evolutionism. Like so many others, he depicted them as the most primitive people on the North American continent, bar only the Eskimo "whose contemporary existence represents in act and thought the behavior of man of an early stone age." As for the Innu, Speck (1977: 5-6) emphasized their cultural immobility:

> A glance at the culture history of these seminomadic bands shows strikingly their lack of material progress since some period of culture history coincident with the Mesolithic age. Sheltered only in draughty caribou-skin or bark tents, clad in caribou-skin raiment, using mostly bone and wooden implements, and professing neither political institutions nor government, they follow no occupation or industry other than hunting wild animals and fishing amid the most physically exacting and rigorous climatic environments of the continent.

He then continued, "In general, we may imagine . . . that progress has stopped because their civilization was completed ages ago."

Vaino Tanner (1947: 658), whose massive geographical survey of Labrador included several hundred pages on the Innu, was similarly stunned at first contact in 1939. "Already their outward appearance indicates poverty and primitiveness," Tanner declared. "Never before have I had so overpowering an impression that I stood face to face with people of the stone age, or perhaps even cave people." Although the geographer observed their healthy bodily condition, he could not help but note that "all appeared in their savage primitive dirtiness." Their friendliness was an expression of "the natural joyfulness of primitive people." The Nascaupee, however, were more agreeable than the "repulsive Montagnais" he had encountered earlier on the North Shore of the Gulf of St. Lawrence (ibid., 658, 659).

Even though Europeans commonly referred to Native people in relation to what they imagined to be universal laws of cultural and material development, in comparison to others, the Innu appeared to them as especially primitive. Speck compares the Naskapi to other "backward" tribes of North America. Even the word "Naskapi," which originated from an Innu word indicating people hunting "beyond the horizon" further north, became adapted in the English idiom as a synonym for primitivity and applied to disparate groups of Innu (Mailhot, 1986). Building on the idea, championed by anthropologists such as Speck, that the Natives of the Labrador-Quebec peninsula were migrants from more southerly Algonkian-speaking areas, Tanner (ibid., 697) categorized the Innu as being in a "deculturized stage of Algonkian culture." The harsh landscape, inclement weather, and low population density were all signs of "the stage of cultural development." Tanner even noted a certain cultural and psychological degeneration, believing that the more elaborate artistic and institutional forms of the southern Algonkians were absent among the Innu. Thus, Tanner (ibid., 699) concludes, "[p]ushed into the barren region where they now live, they abandoned their earlier higher customs and adhered to the old primitive cultural survivals; only slightly have they been influenced by the coastal Eskimo and the whites in recent times." As a result, the Innu presented Tanner (ibid., 605) with "something of a psychological paradox . . . in mentality he seems to have stopped in the forecourts of civilization at the stage reached by a Northern boy of at most 14."

Until the research of Georg Henriksen in the 1960s, ethnographic accounts were agreed that the Naskapi were not simply living embodiments of a stage of social development that was prior to the contemporary European, but they represented some form of humanity that was peculiarly inert. Their example showed explorers and anthropologists more clearly the roots of cultural development. Encounters with the Innu helped to bring into sharp focus what were to be considered the characteristics of civilization and the progress and development that it was said to embody. When Julius Lips (1947: 379) set about his search for the origin and development of law and legal institutions in North America, he began with the Naskapi on account of "their relatively homogeneous and primitive form of economy." By selecting them for his first study, he could "clarify the problems of the development of primitive law and of the growth of legal institutions of early American primitive law." The contemporary Innu therefore afforded a glimpse at the very origins of fundamental aspects of human culture.

In the cause of evolutionism, the ethnological, ethnographic, geographic, and philosophical studies were supplemented by biological investigations in the continuing quest of academicians to map out the cultural trajectories of humankind. Anthropometric measurements of brain size, weight, and capacity were enthusiastically applied to Indians and freed slaves throughout North America in the nineteenth century. The advent of intelligence tests in the early twentieth century fuelled the drive to compare non-European and European capacities. The Innu did not escape these scientific experiments. Their heads were measured and compared with the statistics for the neighbouring Inuit by the anthropologist William Duncan Strong in the 1920s under the direction of A. Irving Hallowell (1929), an anthropologist with considerable interest in the intelligence and "emotional structure" of Indians of the Eastern Woodlands (see Hallowell, 1955: 125-50). Even without the benefit of measurements or intelligence tests, other researchers would speculate on the "stage of development" of the Innu. Vaino Tanner (1947: 447), attentive as previous commentators such as Lucien Turner had been to Eskimo-Indian differences, noted that, "the Indian on average is at the stage of a north European youth at fourteen, the Eskimo at eighteen in the best instances."

Labrador provided a useful laboratory for more minutely refined measurements of civilization because of the presence of another native group, "the Eskimo," and within the Innu, the construction of a division between the southerly "Montagnais" and the northerly "Naskapi," besides a number of "bands" inhabiting different territories. Many of the written accounts of the Labrador-Quebec peninsula already mentioned were quick to size up the Innu and Inuit in relation to each other. Except in some rare cases, including Speck – the Montagnais or especially the Naskapi – came out less favourably.

Although Speck, Strong, Lips, and Tanner expressed views that were steeped in academic discourses, cultural evolutionism itself became a fairly pervasive means of understanding ethnic differences within the broader lay population. Walter Rockwood, director of the Division of Northern Labrador Affairs for the provincial government of Newfoundland in the period leading up to and including sedentarization, provided a more refined three-way comparison when in an official memorandum of 1956, he wrote, "the North West River Indians are almost if not quite as primitive as the Davis Inlet band, and more primitive than the majority of Eskimos of Northern Labrador" (Roche, 1992). The following year, Rockwood (1957: 9) was prepared to contemplate that the primitivity of the Innu was not an inherent quality but followed from "less intimate contact with our civilization." Even in more recent times, the belief that the Innu were primitive hunters who merely "survived" has been found to be common among Euro-Canadian settlers in North West River (see Plaice, 1990: 107). As recently as 1992, a Canadian Broadcasting Company (CBC) news broadcast on the tragedies in Davis Inlet referred to the Innu as "Stone Age Arctic nomads" (Wilson, 1994).[14]

Primitivity, however it was conceived, may have been of academic interest, but to the colonizing authorities in British North America and, later, Canada, it was a cause for concern, a clarion call for action to transform the Innu. The method for determining this need for change was always comparative and the universe on which its beam shone was one of high and low values, gradations of sophistication, developed, and undeveloped ways of life. The Aboriginal peoples that the twentieth century Europeans encountered jolted them to reflect on how coexistence with what they knew to be civilization could ever be achieved. It was at these moments that they moved out of the shadows of cultural evolutionism (and social Darwinism, from which it was scarcely distinguishable) to reveal what they conceived to be universal truths. For the explorers and later the Newfoundland policy-makers, the Natives' isolation had sheltered them from the realities of a bleak, competitive, and disenchanted world where races would meet, where struggles over territories and resources would take place, and where the superior European would always prevail. Hence, by the mid-twentieth century, the Newfoundland authorities assumed that certain primordial weaknesses would be exposed by the intensified contact between Natives and settlers. The incremental and, importantly, competitive ground of human progress would be laid bare by the closer contact between the Innu and Euro-Canadians. Echoing U.S. Indian policy a century earlier, the stark choice for Natives such as the Innu would be between assimilation and extinction.

These social representations all implied the need for transformation. In particular, there was an urgency in the calls for the Innu to be productive, to adopt European rhythms of time, and to forge out a role in the money economy. In many ways "work" was the backbone of these urgings. After all, work was always the irreducible factor – bridging Scottish Presbyterianism, the teachings of classical economics, anthropological representations, and the narratives of European settlement – that drove notions of human progress in this colonial outpost. Earnest application, dedication, surpluses, trade, and productivity propelled Europeans from the Stone Age to their present industrial ascendancy over the entire globe. In a world of such certainties, work was the baseline from which the Innu could progress. If they did not apply themselves to work in a cash economy, as several twentieth-century commentators had remarked, they would go the way of the extinct Beothuks of Newfoundland, or at best remain marginal to the social and economic takeoff that almost all commentators on Labrador in the twentieth century were confidently predicting.

FROM A PRIMITIVE HUNTING ECONOMY TO AN INDUSTRIAL ONE

By the mid-twentieth century, a strong current of opinion had built up to suggest that Innu nomadic hunting could not be sustained. At the same time, there were obvious difficulties in conceiving of an alternative economy in the Subarctic. While the pattern of colonization in other areas of North America had been to transform hunters and mobile agriculturists to sedentary agriculturists, important practical obstacles to the development of farming loomed large in Labrador. With hard rocky soil, long winters, the necessity of clearing the forests, and the problem of constructing buildings for the storage of crops, the region, even the southerly areas, hardly commended itself to farmers. Only through truly Herculean efforts, involving heated greenhouses, the removal of vast quantities of soil, and measures to prevent crops and animals from freezing, could agriculture be made feasible. While attempts to enforce an agricultural way of life were common in more temperate zones of North America,[15] such schemes would be problematic, to say the least, in the Subarctic.

Some early efforts were nonetheless exerted in this direction. Although the Labrador-Quebec peninsula is icebound and covered in snow for over half the year, as early as 1933 the International Grenfell Association was urging that the Indians be "centralized" and introduced to farming (Roche, 1992). Vaino Tanner (1947: 816-25) had also recommended agriculture for the region. Despite the fact that "there is no land asking for crops in Labrador," he maintained that "it seems perfectly possible to keep cattle, goats, sheep and poultry in the inner districts of Labrador south of 55° lat. It is also possible to be self-sufficient as regards all common vegetables . . . every year, and as regards potatoes eight years out of ten." On the whole, however, the agricultural "stage of development" was skipped over, as the Newfoundland authorities advocated an industrial mode of production for Labrador.[16] In 1955, Walter Rockwood saw the southward migration of the Inuit and the sedentarization of the Innu as "a phase in the movement from a primitive hunting economy to an industrial one" (Roche, 1992).

Starting with the fur trade, this mingling of images of primitivity with the insistence on assimilation took on even greater urgency in the context of the need Europeans generated for the industrial use of the lands of the Innu. The tomes on Innu manners and deficiencies provided a convenient lever of expropriation. The projected Innu deficits made them rather "poor relations" to the Europeans, claimants and dependants that the colonizing authorities believed they must support. The strength, agility, resilience, and wisdom required of hunters, and frequently mentioned by these observers, were increasingly overshadowed by images of the Innu as work-shy, lazy, and improvident. By the mid-twentieth century these images started to take real force as the imminence of a cash economy in Labrador began to be forecast. Hence, Vaino Tanner (1947: 601-02) articulated what many thought when he observed, "[t]he Labrador Indians impresses [*sic*] the 'pale face' in that he is so carefree with regard to the morrow. People say he is like the wild animals of the woods; he is in good condition in the autumn but thins off towards the spring, and the reason is his improvidence in the matter of food . . . the Indian persists in the same care-free attitude from custom it may be said, for if there is a main thread running through the life of the savage it is the power of custom." Tanner went on to note the lack of any "ambition" beyond caribou hunting. Adaptation to European ideas of work and trade would obviously lessen the burden that whites perceived the Innu to be. If Natives adopted the work ethic, they could be made party to the development of the land while also uplifting themselves. Decision-makers such as Walter Rockwood (1957: 9) advocated the same course, urging that the Eskimo and Indian "minorities" in Labrador "must be prepared to pass over into the industrial society now ready to burst upon them."

SPENDING POWER

This reluctance to adopt European rhythms of work and enterprise would have been galling, but perhaps not unexpected, to those who would execute the initial settlement of the Innu in the 1950s and 1960s. Walter Rockwood forcefully articulated the need for "economic rehabilitation" of the Innu on many occasions. His correspondence reveals that he exerted much energy in devising and advocating schemes to channel them into "productive" activity. This always involved some type of wage labour scheme – a sawmill, fur trapping, cod fisheries, trout pickling, work at the Goose Bay airport and at the Grenfell hospital in North West River founded by Dr. Paddon, and relocation to areas of labour demand, such as Schefferville and Wabush where mines had been established. The hunting activities of the Innu, although alluded to, were not considered productive "economic" activities. Rather, the Innu were thought to have only one salvation to save them from "loafing" around the posts and depots at North West River and Davis Inlet and collecting welfare relief. As Rockwood wrote with great urgency in 1956, "Unless a strong positive approach is adopted NOW there is a danger that the Indians will become loafers whose only aim is to extract more and more handouts from the government; indeed there is grave danger that this stage has already been reached" (Roche, 1992).

Fur trapping was one answer to loafing. Trapping and other work schemes such as a cod fishery were encouraged by Rockwood and others in the 1950s and 1960s, in part to enable Innu to qualify for unemployment insurance rather than the more stigmatizing welfare relief. These new schemes differed from the earlier trapping activities of the Innu in that they not only engaged them in the trapping of animals, but tied the trapping to the receipt of unemployment benefits out of season. In the process hunting transformed into "work," an economic activity, useful as the means to procure unemployment relief. Unemployment relief became preferable not only because it paid marginally more, but because it signified that the recipient "worked" rather than "loafed." For the provincial government, such schemes were a means of assimilation – they discouraged loafing and promoted behaviour thought to be rewarding and rational. The barter system, which had operated until well into the twentieth century, was replaced by the use of money to pay for incoming furs and to use in the purchase of supplies and other goods at the company store. Money was a means of achieving assimilation as Wilfred Grenfell (1933: 81) had predicted some 20 years earlier when he complained of trappers who "lived and died in debt to the merchant." With the advent of a "standard medium of exchange," Grenfell believed the Native and settler trappers would come to know "the independence of a dollar in their pockets and the consequent incentive to and value of thrift."

Yet, this "standard medium of exchange" in a colonial context is hardly "standard" since the monetary units themselves, the terms of trade, and the necessity of a material profit, are largely dictated by established European conceptions of worth and value. All traders were in business to secure surpluses and would not be able to continue operating unless they exchanged items of less value for those of more value in terms of the "standard medium of exchange." While Natives may have made some gains from the fur trade and other transactions with Europeans, as they were dragged into the cash economy, they clearly started to be at more of a disadvantage than they would have been had they not entered into the exchange in the first place.[17]

The system itself, at least as it operated at North West River by the 1950s, involved a financial advance being given for the supplies needed for trapping (referred to as "outfits"). The Indians were then liable to repay 50 per cent of their earnings up to the full value of their outfit to the government depot. Between 1958 and 1962, however, Rockwood notes a steady decline in repayments. This was because the Hudson's Bay Company was operating a parallel scheme, but its advance to the Innu was made against social assistance or "relief" benefits. When the furs were brought in, the HBC made payments against the relief and then scooped in further money by selling trade goods. After their purchases, the remainder – an increasingly slender amount – was left over for the Innu trappers to repay the depot for their advances. Since it was the depot, owned and operated by joint agreement between the federal and provincial governments, that seemed to be losing in this three-handed game, Rockwood was led to recommend decreasing welfare payments. Although these work schemes operated only sporadically, they created a kind of welfare peonage where the line between concepts that are thought to be distinct – "work," "welfare," "trade," "productivity" – became increasingly blurred. Innu were "working" in this system in order to collect welfare from the provincial government, and this welfare was then siphoned into the HBC coffers. In effect, in these pre-settlement years the government was generating profits for the HBC by luring the Innu to work for welfare.

The welfare peonage that the Innu became subject to was similar to projects used in other areas of the world to bind colonized people to the will of their colonizers. Michael Taussig (1987: 66-73) has demonstrated how the nineteenth-century Indians of the Putumayo region of the Upper Amazon were primarily producing "debt" by their work on the rubber plantations. They were paid an advance for their bare subsistence, which they could pay off only by working on the plantation. This was enforced by terror exercised by hired thugs of the rubber company, and differs from the starvation inflicted by traders on the Innu in the mid-nineteenth century only insofar as it is a more violent form of killing. While violence was not employed in Labrador in the twentieth century, money in the form of welfare was substituted as an enforcement of the peonage. Like guns and ammunition in the fur trade 100 years previously, this snared the Innu in the colonial trade relationship. In relation to another similar situation in nineteenth-century Tierra del Fuego, Taussig (1993: 94) confesses to "a deepening confusion . . . as to where gifts stop and trade begins, it being obvious that objects here take on the burden of negotiating between might and right." If we substitute "welfare" for "gifts" and "money" for "objects," we have a hint of the colonial peonage of the Innu. Welfare payments took on the burden of negotiating between might and right.

However, an extraordinary state of affairs in the early 1960s demonstrated the unreliability of welfare for the purposes of binding the Innu into Canadian society. Dr. Paddon of the International Grenfell Association complained that the Innu were "misusing money they need for living expenses" and were "simply too well off as far as cash goes" (in Roche, 1992). In a relatively short period of time, Rockwood's consummate loafers had catapulted into monetary surplus. In a somewhat irritable letter to Max Lane (quoted ibid.), Newfoundland Minister of Welfare, Paddon describes two cases in point:

> Three times in the last three days I have wanted an airplane for some purpose related to patient movement and each time none was available because the Indians were using the plane. Last week an Indian named Peter Jack came in from Grand Lake in our ambulance aircraft which he had chartered on his own with his winter catch so far of mink and other fur, paid the pilot $103 in cash, went to the store and sold his fur and then went to the Indian Agent for his relief. A month ago I was on my way to Happy Valley in our ambulance and met three taxis, at $30 charter each, bringing three families of Indians from Mud Lake over here to draw their relief. I suspect, but do not know for sure, that they had in addition chartered a snowmobile from Mud Lake to Happy Valley to get to the taxi station.

What was objectionable to Paddon was not the fact that Innu had cash, but rather that these funds were often welfare handouts, and such proceeds appeared to be used in the wrong ways. That is, the money was going on travelling rather than what he termed "living expenses." It was being used innovatively by the Innu to maintain their nomadic ways, rather than to purchase the consumer goods incumbent upon sedentary life. If this continued, Paddon claimed without irony, "they will never be anything but paupers" (ibid.). For the Grenfell Association, with its philanthropic public health mission, Native assimilation through work and settlement was crucial to the good mental and physical hygiene that they were attempting to promote for the entire Labrador population. Episodes like these prompted many of the white intermediaries, such as the Belgian Oblate priest in Sheshatshiu, Father Joseph Pirson, Rockwood, and Paddon himself, to advocate less "coddling" and generosity from welfare relief. These figures, along with other missionaries, vital links in the chain of events that led to settlement, were able to suggest that welfare be curtailed at various times in accordance with the satisfactory conduct of the Innu. Thus, when the missionary at Davis Inlet in the 1960s contrived a cod-fishing work scheme, he requested that the government suspend welfare relief during the short cod season (Henriksen, 1973: 94).

In 1962, the depot manager at Sheshatshiu, Roy Hammond, spelled out the nature of the solution. Although Hammond noted that the repayments to the Division on outfits were declining, "the Indians" had done well with fur and were obviously working assiduously as trappers. Thus the question Hammond asked was, "how far should this diminution in reimbursement occasion gloom?" He seemed to answer "not very" when he contended that "our object in all that is done in relation to the Indian is his integration into an admittedly economics-dominated world of which he is so far, abysmally ignorant, and [with] which he would seem to prefer to be contemptuously uncooperative." The key to Innu integration was the inculcation of a motivation for rewards to be gained from fur trading through monetary surpluses following the repayment of debts from outfits. Once debts were repaid – and Hammond kept a publicly displayed list of payers and debtors at the post – monies would be available to purchase goods. "The more the Indian is able to get spending power the more he will learn of economics. He will learn nothing of them without it; that he meets his financial obligations more readily when he cannot evade them is but a sure sign that there has already been some progress toward the white way" (Roche, 1992).

The authorities over time hoped that the Innu would gradually transform from hunters to trappers. As hunters they had been an almost totally independent people. The fur trade would catch them up in a cycle of work, debt, and ideally, surplus. The aim of this surplus was to motivate them to buy things that would bind them into the "economics-dominated" world that was to signal progress towards "the white way." If this strategy worked, they would then never be free again to practise a way of life separate from capitalist economics. Life would entail a round of debt (for outfits), work (trapping), debt repayments to the depot, surpluses for material goods that would create a desire for more and hence necessitate another trip through the cycle. The authorities dream was that "work" would become a lifelong necessity and a life of consumption would be the Indian's desire. Work was equated with social evolutionary advancement, and with it would eventually come a conforming to European and Christian norms.[18]

The fur trade enabled a more frequent Innu presence at the coastal posts and this led to a partial sedentarization by the 1950s. It reoriented Innu life towards the trading posts where they handed in their furs and collected their debts, leading commentators in the pre-settlement era such as Tanner (1947: 648) to say that the "Indian hunter is becoming only a kind of intelligent hunting-dog for the trader, kept alive by him to bring him skins." However, as furs became less profitable and scarcer, the insistence of the priests on permanent sedentary life instead of semi-sedentarization was met with less opposition.

While the Newfoundland authorities flailed around unsuccessfully searching for a role for Innu labour in the cash economy, the Innu themselves never completely abandoned hunting after the advent of the settlements. Henriksen portrayed Innu life at Davis Inlet in this period as rife with conflict and bouts of drunkenness amid the often heavy-handed intrusion of the white intermediaries. While the hunting camps provided communal meaning and purpose, at the coast the Innu lived out a pointless existence characterized by boredom and fractious inebriation. When stuck at Davis Inlet, they longed for the day when they would return to the interior.[19] "While the hunting camps were marked by great congeniality, the common purpose of obtaining caribou meat, and the universal participation in communal meals," Henriksen (1973: 74) observed that:

> the social life in Davis Inlet is characterized by heavy drinking and many conflicts . . . through a diversification rather than a unification of activities. . . . The most salient features of community life in Davis Inlet are the many quarrels and the incessant drinking of spruce beer in which more than half the adult male population, and some of the wives, indulge.

Active non-commercial hunting, however, was never abandoned and was a more pleasant alternative to the drinking and quarrelling in the village. But in the 1970s and 1980s Innu hunters were often on the wrong side of the rigid enforcement of game laws by Newfoundland game wardens who patrolled Innu hunting territories in planes and helicopters, seizing animals and on occasion physically removing hunters, trying them, and even sentencing them to prison terms. In the early 1980s, a series of interviews were conducted to document the impact of the enforcement of the game laws on the Innu residing in Quebec and Labrador villages. It is clear from these testimonies that the Innu felt as if the Newfoundland authorities were deliberately trying to cut off their connections to *nutshimit*. This would mean not only quarantining them in the villages, but preventing them from doing what they think is the right thing to do – to live from the land – as these extracts (Innu Nation, 1983) illustrate:

> This incident took place in the year of 1974 or 1975 in *nutshimit* at a river called Uapush-Shekas. There were five of us there . . . . Two *Akaneshaut* Wildlife Officers and one *Akaneshaut* RCMP approached us by helicopter . . . . They told us that we were in the Labrador Border province of Newfoundland and that we would be charged for it. They confiscated our moose and lynx that we killed . . . . They also confiscated our three rifles. They tried to do the same thing to our skidoos but we told them we were so many miles from our community that if they took our skidoos we would have to walk home . . . . We never did get our rifles back . . . . During this incident we had to sign some papers given to us by the RCMP and the Wildlife Officers. We signed them but we didn't understand what the papers said.
>
> – Jerome Mistanapeu
>
> I was at Nekapashakamau when this incident took place. There were a lot of Innu people there at the time . . . . Two Wildlife Officers and one RCMP Officer came to our campsite. The Wildlife Officer tried to take our caribou meat. They wanted to take our caribou meat so they could take us to court . . . . I don't know why we went to court. We were fined five hundred dollars each. The Innu people were only trying to make a living in *nutshimit*.
>
> – Sebastian Rich
>
> Once I went across the bay to the marshes near Kanemich. The Wildlife Officers approached us by helicopter. There was also *Akaneshau* RCMP. I had my 30-30 rifle with me, but hadn't killed anything at the time. They took my rifle. That rifle had cost me $200 at the Hudson's Bay store . . . I went to court. The magistrate . . . . asked me why I kill caribou. I simply said that I want to eat caribou meat and that my family also wants to eat caribou meat. I feel I did the right thing. I don't see any wrong in killing caribou because this is how the Innu people survive in *nutshimit* . . . . But *Akaneshau* thinks that's wrong.
>
> – Pien Penashue

WORK AND THE END OF EVOLUTION

Enforcement of the Newfoundland game laws did not end Innu hunting. Continued hunting has made it possible for them to subsist
without resort to full participation in the market economy. Now, several decades after these attempts to prevent the Innu from hunting,
the Innu still hunt for food and resist the assimilation that is signalled
by the "cash economy." But this is an ambivalent resistance and is increasingly only signified by default. Their displacement from
permanent nomadic hunting in the 1950s and 1960s, the replace-
ment of wild animal meat with the dubious hauls in the community
and Goose Bay stores, and the necessity of money in the community
mean that many people actually want jobs, but few are available. By
2001, unemployment rates in Utshimassits and Sheshatshiu were
widely reported to hover around 80 per cent. Survival in the community depends on both jobs and government transfer payments. In
the country, the Innu can live perfectly well from the wild animals
and fish they kill, but money is necessary to procure supplies,
equipment, and the aircraft charters to transport large families into
the interior. Some of this can be obtained from the band councils,
but additional income is almost becoming a requirement of participation in country life. Since welfare payments in the province of
Newfoundland are the lowest in Canada, virtually every adult Innu
is on the lookout for a job.

However, virtually all the wage labour that is available occurs either in the service of an assimilationist mandate or in dealing with the
consequences of its failure (in Sheshatshiu employment at the group
home, the school, the youth treatment centre, the woman's shelter,
the clinic, the addiction services agency *Innu Uauitshitun*, the Department of Social Services and Child Welfare all fall into this category).
Most employment is operated through the Innu political bodies or
other imposed institutions such as the school and the clinic. There
being almost no jobs in the "cash economy," family and other connections to these political bodies are often the best guarantee of work. In
the community, although co-operation and sharing occur, they are
not necessary, and even counter-productive, for those who wish to
succeed, not simply within the Canadian economy, but within the
small world of Innu politics. Predictably, rivalries and jealousies develop because particular individuals or families obtain certain "plum"
jobs or other benefits, especially from the band councils, who also
control and allocate village housing. Accusations of corruption and
nepotism are a constant feature of the relationship between the band
councils and many members of the communities.[20]

For many Innu, especially those who are not the prime beneficiaries of the band councils, pressures threatening dignity converge
on all sides. At the end of the 1990s, many large Innu families made
do on $500 to $600 per month. While there are some outdoor jobs,
much of the work is in the form of deskbound office chores – filing,
manipulating the computer, answering the phone. Many Innu experience such work as dull and onerous. The "offices" in Sheshatshiu
and Utshimassits project purposelessness. Lobbies, corridors, public areas, and individual offices are generally spartan. When I visited
the Alcohol Program office in Davis Inlet in 1995, for example, I
could not help but notice the reek of gasoline from under the floor-
boards where the basement was used as a holding room for children
high from sniffing. There were usually many people sitting idly,
passing the time and chatting with no visible "work" being carried
out. Sometimes one person would be on a computer playing a card
game. The Innu Nation and band council offices also exude torpor.
Although they were created to be bureaucratic organizations, very
little bureaucratic work actually gets done. Paperwork is largely, although not entirely, produced by white advisers. Energy levels for
this kind of work appear low. As if recognizing the domestication
that the office represents, people lounge around, bide their time,
and often use it to take care of their personal business.

Very little employment is available to the Innu outside their own
communities. When these kinds of job opportunities do arise, they
are mostly in industries involved in exploiting Innu land against the
wishes of most of the people in the communities, presenting the pro-
spective Innu worker with a dilemma. If they want to work, and a
great many do because welfare provides such a bare minimum for
survival, quick cash can be obtained by working at the Voisey's Bay
mine. While the few Innu workers who have been employed at
Voisey's Bay are never stigmatized by others in the communities,
and most people do in fact sympathize because of the need to have a
job to support a family, mining work effectively makes them participants in the desecration and theft of Innu land. As in the case of
Schefferville in the 1960s, where Mushuau Innu from the Fort
Chimo area were relocated by the government as part of a plan to
transform them into labourers at the iron ore mines, it is well known
that almost all Innu who have worked at the Voisey's Bay mining
camp were given the most junior and exacting physical jobs. It is
also suspected, like Schefferville, that when the ore has been extracted, the mining company will simply leave with the tailings piled
up high on the land, leaving the Innu jobless in an adulterated landscape.

Kanikuen Nuna worked at the Voisey's Bay mine in 1995. His experience there was difficult and troubling, leading him to quit after just two months. These are his reflections on working as a miner:

I arrived with another fellow at the Voisey's Bay camp early spring 1995. We were the first few people hired from our community of Sheshatshiu. There were also a few more from Davis Inlet. We started our morning at 6:30 a.m. with a wake-up call. Seven to nine choppers would be going up each morning to the drill sites for the drillers' shift change. They worked around the clock on 8- to 12-hour shifts. The camp personnel, including me, worked 8-hour shifts, 7 days a week for three weeks straight and then we got 10 days off to go home . . . . It was quite difficult for married men to live like this day to day. We constantly thought about our children. There were times when we were only allowed to phone home once a week for five minutes. This was not enough time to talk to the family, the wife and kids . . . .

The Innu and Inuit workers held a few meetings among ourselves to see how we felt about what was happening and who should be doing what about it. We felt we were being hired for many jobs – for example, core shack technicians, prospectors, line cutters and drillers, but none of us was getting promoted. In the meantime people from outside were working only 2 or 3 weeks and getting the promotions. We felt this was discrimination, but it seemed like nobody wanted to speak up, fearing they would lose their jobs. I, for one, really felt that people from the outside were taking our jobs away . . . . Another Innu talked about a problem he was having at camp. He was being called "Chief" by a few of his co-workers and he was offended by this. We talked about this at our meetings. There were other comments being made to us that we found offensive. We took it up with the foreman. But these were his friends and relatives who were saying these things to us, so he really couldn't do anything. He wasn't going to fire his relatives.

There were a lot of problems with the environment – pollution, oil spills, cut trees and garbage all over the place around the camp. They were burning garbage, but sometimes they would leave it for a week. Bears and small animals would take it out into the woods and make a mess. Also the workers would feed the bears, so they would come back to the camp or drill sites for food. Sometimes the workers would taunt the bears and throw sticks at them. The bear would start approaching them and then turn back into the woods. It would eventually end up getting shot. There was a no-feeding policy for bears, but everybody seemed to ignore that. I was upset when they shot the animals. There was no need. They weren't doing anything they naturally didn't do like feeding on berries and small plants. Sometimes the choppers would come in and try to scare the bears away. They would hover over treetops to scare animals. The poor animals must have been having heart attacks running for miles and miles to get away. Bears are not meant to run like this. One time we saw a bear on the hill about a half-mile away. It was huge; it must have been about 8 feet tall and weighed 500 pounds. About 10 workers headed for the hill with knives and sticks to have a look at it and scare it.[21]

Etienne Pone, another Innu employee, working for the Innu Nation Fisheries Department, had to check the nets of Innu fishermen, ask them how many fish they had caught, and if necessary take action against those violating the regulations on catches. The uniform that he was told to wear, he likened to a mask. He felt like the scout in the cowboys-and-Indian films. The message he got from the government was that he was getting paid for working *for* Innu people, but what he was being told to do could not be reconciled with the Innu use of fish as a summertime staple. In his perception, processes like this place so many Innu under severe personal stress. Innu adults are simultaneously confronted with strong reasons both to work and to avoid it. According to Etienne, it is in the context of this double bind that they often regard themselves as failing, turning to alcohol and other expressions of desperation.

In the process of transforming hunters into village dwellers, Euro-Canadian authorities created only the most tenuous of relations to the "market." There has been only a chaotic and partial transition to nuclear families, breadwinners, and consumption. While part of the reason for the failure of assimilation is obviously the relatively depressed economy of Newfoundland and Labrador, the mandate to work in the cash economy contradicts some of the most important values held by contemporary Innu people. For example, the capitalist employment relationship encourages workers to put their own narrow goals and aspirations first, a negation of the attributes of sharing and collectivism that made the Innu so effective as nomadic hunters, and that carry over into their outlook on the world. There are some Innu who short-circuit the individualism of employment by deliberately holding jobs temporarily, giving way after an allotted period of time to a friend or family member so that others can benefit from the wages. The period of time they work often coincides with that required to obtain the more generous unemployment benefits. However, sharing jobs in this manner has become less frequent, as the pressure to obtain money becomes more acute.

With time, village life has become increasingly monetarized. As Innu have realized that *Akaneshaut* charge for everything,[22] they have begun to require fees for interviews, tours, and cultural knowledge sought by outsiders, including those who work with the Native institutions such as Innu Nation. Recently, one *Tshenu* charged a $5

fee for every person who entered her tent, which was strategically located on the shore near where a cruise ship full of foreign tourists
was docked. Another *Tshenu*, camped on the Churchill road, requested $250 from an Innu Nation researcher simply to enter his
tent and exchange greetings. If not initiated by it, this tendency has
certainly been encouraged by the various social science studies that
have been required of the Innu as part of the comprehensive land
claims and environmental impact assessment procedures. The
Voisey's Bay EIA paid *Tshenut* $200 per day for their memories.
"Consultation exercises" for the CLC similarly rewarded them for
simply expressing their views (which were almost entirely ignored)
or for their assistance with making Innu "land use" maps.

The conviction that the Innu would undergo a cultural "ad-
Despite the monetarization of Innu life, when Innu do acquire
cash through formal employment, government payments, or other
means, they rarely use it as would a "rational consumer" within a
capitalist economy. Lying in the sun at our camp at *Utshisk-nipi*, Dominic Pokue told me that when he got his money from his beaver
pelts, he would spend it all at once. When he received his old age social security, it would not last long, because he and his family would
spend it all. This is hardly the behaviour of a prudent retiree. Money,
for Dominic, and I believe many other Innu, is not a universal medium of exchange, investable capital, or a badge of status. Rather, it
is something to be used and consumed, not hoarded or invested. In
the country and to a lesser extent in the community, stinginess is
seen as an absurdity. Objects that have value are to be used for their
function. One cannot ever rely on hoarding for the future because
the future is unpredictable. Plans are temporary, changeable, or
avoided altogether. You cannot predict anything in life so why try to
predict what money you *will* have in the future and what that money
will buy?

The conviction that the Innu would undergo a cultural "advancement" through becoming absorbed in paid employment and
capitalist market relationships has obviously been found wanting as
a result of the structure of opportunities presented to them and by
their own reactions to those attempts to transform them. The justifi-
cations for these policies – cultural evolution and the idea of
progress – have also reached their limits conceptually. That is, the
story of universalistic development predicated on the conceptual,
economic, and political models of the European Enlightenment has
been exposed as a convenient rationale for cultural imperialism and
territorial expansionism.

As Baudrillard and his colleagues noted some time ago (Kamper
and Wulf, 1989), the notion of one united "world" is crumbling be-

cause of obvious difficulties inherent in its relations to the institutions of political power; and here we could cite those of colonial rule. The more such a vision of the world was invoked, with evolution as a unifying theme, the more the chaos of that which could not be predicted needed to be steered; hence were the workings of political power exposed. In our case, the more the *Akaneshau* have sought to control the direction of Innu society, the more has chaos emerged. Although paid work and money have become more available, Innu rarely work in the deliberate and dedicated way that would be demanded by a private company, and often do not use the proceeds in a manner consistent with *Homo economicus*. What has happened can be seen in Baudrillard's (1989: 29) vision of late twentieth-century society:

> This process can be compared best to cancerous metastases – conditions in which the body's organic rules of the game are lost, enabling such a formation of cells to manifest its invincible and fatal vitality, partially leading it to stop obeying its own genetic commands, and finally to grow rampantly instead of following an organized pattern of development.

To the tourists gingerly treading down the gangplanks of the *Northern Ranger* at the Davis Inlet wharf at the end of the twentieth century, notions of organized development of "the world" are quickly banished. There is little or nothing to soften the blow of what must seem to them a remote society that shows signs of material "progress" – why else would snowmobiles and crates of Pepsi Cola be hoisted down onto the dock? – yet looks like a slum, populated with a people who neither buy nor sell. If the visitors were to have explored further, which they could not since the ship docked only briefly, they would have seen what the local Mennonite described as a "war zone." "Any piece of glass is a target," he told me a few nights before the *Northern Ranger* arrived. Even the trucks brought there to construct new houses, whose very presence was for "their" employment and improvement, sat idly with smashed windshields.

Ashamed and Confused 5

. . . anyone who knew their language perfectly, would soon make them laugh at their own stupidity; for sometimes I have made them ashamed and confused, although I speak almost entirely by my hands.

– Father Paul Le Jeune, 1634 (Thwaites, 1897, VI: 225)

Perhaps that's how the Normans will destroy us. Not in war, but by a spell that makes us like them.

– Brian Moore, *Black Robe* (1985: 134)

To the Innu, dreams are visions. To the white man, visions are hallucinations.

– Jimmy Nui, Utshimassits, 1997

HOW MUCH DUST THERE IS IN THEIR EYES

The political and largely secular attempts to radically transform the hearts, minds, and movements of the Innu through their induction into the processes of the state, the sequestration of their lands for development, and the demand that they labour in the cash economy are paralleled by the more long-standing efforts of Christian missionaries. While the state is clearly fundamental to the social transformation, longer-term psychological and cultural change involving the way in which Innu think about the world has involved persistent and systematic pressure from missionaries and educators over several centuries.

Missionaries on the Labrador-Quebec peninsula saw the Native world as a chaotic amalgam of backwardness, superstition, and libertinism. Nomadism was believed to be one of the single most important barriers to conversion. Frustration at the seeming anomaly of what many Catholic fathers saw as a naturally intelligent people attached to "wandering" is a theme that runs equally through the accounts of the missionaries of seventeenth-century New France and the Oblate priests visiting the Innu at the coastal posts in the mid-twentieth century.

Perhaps the earliest attempts to end the nomadism of the Innu (and other Algonquin groups of the lands bounding the St. Lawrence) were those of the French Roman Catholic orders of Recollets, Franciscans, Capuchins, and Jesuits who travelled to the colony of New France beginning in 1611 with the landing of priests at Port Royal in Acadia, the settlement of Sieur de Poutrincourt.[1] Once Samuel de Champlain established a fort at "Kebec" (Quebec) in 1608, the Jesuits became the pre-eminent missionaries along the St. Lawrence. Quebec became the principal settlement, military base, and mission in New France. From there, other forts were established at Trois-Rivières and Tadoussac. Records show that the "Montagnais" frequented the Tadoussac post on the Saguenay River north of Quebec and there the priests met them, occasionally accompanying them inland for winter hunting.[2]

The first attempts at education were indistinguishable from conversion. They were explicitly premised on the notion that Natives required social and mental transformation so that they could be saved from what the *robes noires* (or "Black Robes") saw as certain damnation. This would require toil and dedication by both parties over a long period of time, perhaps even generations. Christianization was always a long-term strategy. While the missionaries were persistent, they did not always push conversion as strenuously as their counterparts elsewhere in North America,[3] lest they provoke too strong a negative reaction. The priests were well aware of their dependence on the Innu and other Algonkian for help in the interior, and against "hostile tribes," particularly the well-organized Five Nations or League of the Iroquois. Champlain himself established a policy of extending French goodwill and military aid to the Natives. According to Kennedy (1950: 21), Champlain's experiences with Natives of the areas along the St. Lawrence led him to "consider the Indians as much more than purveyors of pelts. Chiefly as a result of his astuteness and humanity, the French developed a policy towards the Indians that always remained far wiser and kinder than that of their European rivals." In contrast to the English, the French placed less emphasis on property, permanent colonial settlement, and outright dispossession, operating more subtly to transform Natives through closer association, thus making them more amenable to a variety of colonial designs.[4]

Nonetheless, in the eyes of the early Fathers as recorded in *The Jesuit Relations* (Thwaites, 1896-1901), the Jesuits own detailed recollections, the Natives of New France were "Sauvages," untamed people of the forests, rivers, and wilderness, living a way of life that was severely deficient of all the institutions that the priests believed made society both possible and meaningful. As such, the *sauvage* was the opposite of the civilized person, and the collectivity of *sauvages* was anarchic and inchoate in contrast to French society with all of its rules, laws, strictures, and institutional structures. The more graphic contrasts between the two emerge as the Fathers described in gory detail how they had to witness the cannibalistic torture inflicted on enemies of the Algonquins, Hurons, and Southern Innu, who were eaten only after limbs had been removed, flesh had been torn away, and bodies had been roasted. The same treatment, they record, was meted out to these groups by the Iroquois, infuriated at Champlain's arming of them with arquebuses. Native life, according to the Jesuits, was barbarous, knowing no manners and obeying no God; it was guided by "superstitious" beliefs in the power of dreams and animal spirits. Most Jesuits were appalled by what they perceived as a lack of authority structures, political institutions, or formal religious organizations. In the Black Robes' more reflective moments, Natives were to be pitied for their ignorance of God, which led them to lead such a life. They were surely ripe for transformation, and in the narratives of the missionaries, they play a central role in building up a picture of saintliness or even martyrdom in the lives of the Fathers (see Greer, 2000).

Having little permanent material wealth, Native life was seen as poverty-stricken and destitute of amenities and comforts. In *The Jesuit Relations*, the Fathers shuddered at the Native society, which was described as possessing sexual mores and open sexuality wholly unbearable in the light of their own celibacy. As one missionary described, "one thing seems to me more than intolerable. It is their living together promiscuously, girls, women, men, and boys in a smoky hole" (Thwaites, 1897, V, 169). The strong emphasis of the Innu on personal autonomy gave women far greater freedom than their European counterparts: not only could they make significant decisions, but they were free to court the men they liked, to take on other sexual partners while married, and to divorce easily. This independence scandalized the Jesuit missionaries, who tried repeatedly to impose European standards by making Innu women subservient to their husbands.[5]

Jesuit methods of instruction involved converting *sauvages* to Christianity through a careful pedagogy known as the *Ratio Studio-*

rum. This was a rigorous program of religious and practical instruction developed by the order during the sixteenth century. The missionaries sent to New France to implement it were hand-picked by Provincials and later by Cardinal Richelieu for their scholastic and practical abilities. This required the Fathers to undertake the difficult task of learning the Indian languages, and to do so they had to travel with them and to suffer the depredations for which they were scarcely prepared. As one missionary put it:

> To sleep on the earth, covered with a few branches of pine, nothing but the bark between the snow and your head; to drag your baggage over mountains, to let yourself roll down into frightful valleys; to eat only once in two or three days, when there is no hunting, – and that is the life you must lead in following the Savages. (Ibid., 169-71)

According to *The Jesuit Relations*, the Fathers baptized a large number of Innu, although they never achieved complete devotion to the faith, monogamy, or sedentary life. The many obstacles to conversion included nomadism itself, polygamy, the perceived lack of self-discipline among the Natives, the power of shamans, the lack of vocabulary in the indigenous languages for abstract concepts, little curiosity about Christianity, and most critically what was regarded as the excessive personal autonomy characteristic of Innu society. The missionaries made vigorous attempts to deal with this difficulty by trying to impose chiefly authority, but this was never really successful even in the twentieth century, among a people who evidenced a strong aversion to such notions. It was thought that once converted to Christianity the Natives would be more readily accepting of "reason" and the civilized society which, they held, it made possible. From the point of view of the French state, conversion would make Natives less attached to living on the land and this then could be made more open to commercial exploitation and military control against rival powers. In order to accomplish this, France saw the Jesuits as indispensable.

Under Father Paul Le Jeune, who became the Superior of the Jesuit Mission in Canada from 1632 to 1649, the Jesuits encouraged the sedentarization of the "Montagnais" of the northern shores of the St. Lawrence River. A few settlements for Indians were established on the North Shore at this time and agricultural production was initiated. Although neither villages nor farming were stable, they were seen to provide the socio-political structure that opened the way to schooling, and hence conversion. In the early settlements, the Black Robes taught religion, the French language, singing, agricultural techniques, and vocational subjects such as carpentry. In addition, under Le Jeune, seminaries for Native girls and boys were set up in Quebec, and some Native children were eventually sent to colleges in France for instruction.

However, contradictions soon arose within the French campaign of colonization. While the merchants in the Quebec colony were keen to preserve the nomadic way of life of the "Montagnais," since the fur trade depended on it, control over them as political allies and Christians required a sedentary, preferably a farming, life. Agriculture, thought by the Jesuits to have a biblical mandate, was attempted several times in the first half of the seventeenth century, culminating in the advent of the Sillery reserve in 1641 for Indian would-be farmers. Although "nomads had been led to settle down and even to clear land for farming" (Trudel, 1973: 233), this experiment was short-lived and the Innu "took to roaming the woods again." Father Paul Le Jeune argued to his Provincial in France that conversion of *sauvages* was dependent on settling them in one location and then quickly introducing agriculture. They would, in his view, be so impressed by the superiority of this way of life that they would not want to return to hunting. In 1634, he wrote:

> The . . . means of commending ourselves to the savages, to induce them to receive our holy faith, would be to send a number of capable men to clear and cultivate the land, who, joining themselves with others who know the language, would work for the savages, on condition that they would settle down, and themselves put their hands to work, living in houses that would be built for their use; by this means becoming located, and seeing this miracle of charity in their behalf, they would be more easily instructed and won . . . it seems to me that not much ought to be hoped for the Savages as long as they are wanderers . . . we shall work a great deal and advance very little, if we do not make these Barbarians stationary. (Thwaites, 1897, VI, 147-49)

However, as Le Jeune points out, this was an uphill battle on account of the preferences of many hunters themselves, and the opposition of "the Sorcerers," who were threatened by the growing demands of the priests for change. As perceived by Le Jeune, many of these shamans developed a personal rivalry with priests, and one Mestigoit is mentioned on several occasions by Le Jeune as a particular source of hostility. Nevertheless, if change were to come to the Innu it would, in Le Jeune's view, entail "the difficulty that men accustomed to a life of idleness have in embracing one of hard work, such as cultivating the soil" (ibid., 151).

Le Jeune, however, constantly stumbled against practical impediments to his mission. He often doubted his own capacities to carry out Service to God. One of the difficulties in settling the Innu was, of course, the necessity of travelling with them and undergoing the associated hardships. Again in 1634, Le Jeune reports:

I do not believe that, out of a hundred Religious, there would be ten who could endure the hardships to be encountered in following them. I tried to live among them ["Montagnais"] last Autumn; I was not there a week before I was attacked by a violent fever, which caused me to return to our little house to recover my health. Being cured, I tried to follow them during the Winter, and I was very ill the greater part of the time. (Ibid., 149)

Portrait of Father Paul Le Jeune.

Source: Reuben Gold Thwaites, *The Jesuit Relations and Allied Documents*, Vol. V (Cleveland: Burrows Brother, 1897).

Le Jeune's writings display a constant attention to the need for the suppression of nomadism as a precondition to education. Hunting itself was not only practically incompatible with education and conversion, it signalled spiritual poverty. The Innu, according to Le Jeune, were "descended from Cain, or from some other wanderer like him" (quoted in Blackburn, 2000: 53). He was far more optimistic about the prospects for the semi-sedentary Hurons who lived "in towns, not wandering about after the manner of wild animals, or even like other savages" (ibid., 52). In 1633, he alluded to the necessity of educating both sexes because if only the boys were educated "in the knowledge of God, when they marry savage girls or women accustomed to wandering in the woods, [they] will, as husbands, be compelled to follow them and thus fall back into barbarism"

(Thwaites, 1897, V: 145). The belief systems developed from the nomadic way of life were also a constant hindrance to Le Jeune's aims.
In 1634, he devoted a lengthy chapter of his relation to "superstition," ending with the remarks, "how much dust there is in their
eyes, and how much trouble there will be to remove it that they may
see the beautiful light of truth." Le Jeune then goes on to describe
his own efforts at correction, "anyone who knew their language perfectly, would soon make them laugh at their own stupidity; for
sometimes I have made them *ashamed and confused*, although I
speak almost entirely by my hands" (ibid., VI, 225; emphasis added).

One of the most problematic impediments to the Europeanization of the Innu was their different approach and attitude to
child-rearing. While the French demanded discipline and obedi-
ence, the Innu like other Algonquins favoured tolerance,
indulgence, and freedom for children. Hence, in 1633, after observing the protests when a French boy was about to be physically
punished by adults for wounding a Native man with a drumstick, Le
Jeune wrote, "all of the Savage tribes of these quarters . . . cannot
chastise a child, nor see one chastised. How much trouble this will
give us in carrying out our plans of teaching the young!" (ibid., V,
221). In other places, he echoed the same theme:

> How necessary it is to educate the children of the Savages. We shall
> have them at last if they see that we do not send them to France. The
> savages prevent their instruction; they will not tolerate the chas-
> tisement of their children, whatever they may do, they permit only a
> simple reprimand. Moreover, they think they are doing you some
> great favor if they give you their children to instruct, feed and dress.
> (Quoted by Leacock and Goodman, 1976: 88)

One of Le Jeune's most prized projects was the building of a seminary. He planned this early in his tenure in New France, suggesting
it as "a means of making ourselves welcome to these people." The
seminary was to be for girls and boys, "under the direction of some
brave mistress, whom zeal for glory of God, and a desire for the salvation of these people, will bring over here, with a few Companions,
animated by the same courage." Le Jeune continued hopefully,
"may it please his divine Majesty to inspire some to so noble an enterprise, and to divest them of any fear that the weakness of their sex
might induce in them at the thought of crossing so many seas and of
living among Barbarians" (Thwaites, 1897: VI, 151-53).

To accomplish their goals, the Jesuits closely associated themselves with the Natives. They became keen observers of the details of
Native social and mental life. Le Jeune spent considerable time
praising "savages" for a variety of mental and physical qualities.

Among other things, Le Jeune noted their physical superiority over Europeans, lack of avarice and of ambition, their tolerance, humour, and patience. Just as the priests lived in close proximity to the Natives, French settlers, under the encouragement of the *robes noires*, often married with the more southerly Innu. Intermarriage was a means to achieve Christianization and it assisted French control over Native territories.

This, however, proved to be short-lived. With the final British defeat of the French in North America, the Jesuit influence diminished. The last French Jesuit in the territories passed away in 1800, "and with him Canada lost the living reminder of that teeming Jesuit band who for almost two centuries had fought infidelity and barbarism on *her soil*" (Kennedy, 1950: 54; emphasis added). Despite the hardships they endured, their friendships with the Innu, and their powers of reasoning, the Jesuits' ambitions to sedentarize and Christianize the Innu were only partially and temporarily attained.

The Innu further north, however, were only marginally influenced by the struggles between the rival colonial powers, and European treaties that divided up Native land and remade it, in the revealing phrase above, "her soil." As a result, they had contact with missionaries only sporadically with the growth of trading posts on the coasts, although priests did become a fairly regular feature of the lives of those Innu who ventured south to the posts on the North Shore of the St. Lawrence. Arriving in Canada in 1844, the Oblates of Mary Immaculate mounted concerted efforts to Christianize the Innu both on the North Shore and in the interior. From 1867 to 1896 the Oblates held missions at Sheshatshiu, Fort Nascopie, and Fort Chimo. Some of these Fathers also pushed inland and were proselytizing at Sheshatshiu throughout the nineteenth century. They performed marriage ceremonies, baptized babies, held funeral rites, and instructed the Innu on Catholicism at Mass (Mailhot, 1997: 14-23).

Even by the latter half of the nineteenth century, however, it appeared that the missionaries had made little progress. Meeting the Innu on the North Shore only sporadically, and sometimes fleetingly, the priests still had to contend with the lure of nomadism, which maintained the distinct religion and way of life in the interior. Commenting on this situation at mid-century, Henry Youle Hind (1863, I: 190) thought he had witnessed a minor breakthrough: "Happily the labours of the missionaries are fast dispelling these superstitions from the minds of those who frequent the coast, but it is still to be feared that the medicine men still exercise a powerful influence among the different bands who spend the greater part of their time in the interior." Hind, like other commentators of his generation, was certain that whatever headway the French Roman Catholic priests could make on the North Shore would signal a major moral advance for the Innu. Attending a mass with the Natives at Sept-Îles provoked a melancholy and stirring reflection on the souls of all those Innu missing out on the occasion:

> I thought of the condition of their wild brethren wandering through the dreary forests or over the moss-covered rocks of the Labrador peninsula, who had never heard the name of Christ, who had no real knowledge of sin, none of redemption, and none of the life to come – who were steeped to the lips in superstition, holding imaginary communion with evil spirits, and endeavouring to appease their malice with miserable offerings of food, blood and sometimes human life. (Ibid., 338)

Hind (ibid., 339-41) proceeds to contrast the virtues of the Christian religion with "their own foolish and vain imaginings, full of corruption and sensuality." The Innu, he claimed, were mired in "impure thoughts and words." The *robes noires* were "instilling into their minds the germs of better hope."

Roman Catholic Procession of Montagnais and Nasquapees at the Mission of Seven Islands, drawing by William George Richardson Hind.

Source: Henry Youle Hind, *Explorations in the Interior of the Labrador Peninsula, the Country of the Montagnais and Nasquapee Indians* (London: Longman, Green, Longman, Roberts & Green, 1863).

These germs, however, were not planted in the minds of the Innu living and travelling further north. It was some time into the twentieth century that they were attended by Father Edward O'Brien, who extended his mission to Davis Inlet in 1927 (Mailhot, 1997: 22-23). Father O'Brien, from the diocese of Harbour Grace in Newfoundland, ended his ministry among the Innu in 1946 when the missions were again entrusted to the Oblates. However, perhaps the most persistent of the attempts to "educate" the Innu who are now living in Sheshatshiu and Utshimassits had to await the entry of Newfoundland and Labrador into the Canadian confederation. Only after 1949 was religion truly fused with education in a more directed fashion, consonant with the aims of Canada to become recognized as a state and spread its dominion over "her soil" in the wilderness of the Labrador-Quebec peninsula.

INTEGRATION

At the middle of the twentieth century, the binary division of savagery and civilization was still an antagonism to be overcome. The calls for transformation by the administrators and their agents – missionaries and traders – were made just as urgently as those of the Jesuits. Conversion was still what was required, but this referred not simply to inculcation of Christian religious dogma, but also to Innu acceptance of the principles of "reason" that created and sustained industrialism, capitalism, settled life, political authority, and the state. Yet unlike Le Jeune, the demands of the newly arrived Euro-Canadian authorities and those of the latter-day missionaries were not informed by close association with the Innu. These men were driven by fewer insecurities concerning their own presence and they possessed a much greater sense of certainty and inevitability. In comparison to the *robes noires* who saw time as revealed by events in the Bible and encompassing all peoples, the secular emissaries of science and industry made distinctions between peoples on the scale of evolutionary time (Blackburn, 2000: 48-49). With the benefit of hindsight into successive waves of occupation of the continent and the force of evolutionary theories of social development, the settler authorities in Newfoundland could hardly harbour the kinds of nagging doubts that often plagued the Black Robes.

Being so far north, the Innu travelling in what is now Labrador and northern Quebec were denied the benefit of *Ratio Studiorum* and seminaries. They became heirs to a more rational, bureaucratic civilizing mission, beginning, like their ancestors on the Saguenay several centuries earlier, with calls for an end to their "wandering" but ending with their more systematic induction into schools. While the British authorities up to 1949 had been fairly indifferent to the Innu, the newly confederated Newfoundland authorities pushed through a vigorous sedentarization policy in the 1950s. As we have seen, this was driven foremost by a desire to develop Labrador industrially as speedily as possible. The existence of nomads occupying a sizeable proportion of the peninsula did not resonate well with rapid industrialization. Hence, even before schooling was a real possibility, the authorities in 1955 considered how "these people" fit the plan. On April 16 of that year in a letter to his counterpart, R.L. Andrews of the Department of Public Welfare, P.J. Murray, Deputy Minister of Natural Resources for Newfoundland, addressed the problem of the seemingly destitute Indians at the Davis Inlet post. "It is difficult to envisage any form of economic production in which these people could presently engage in order to look after their needs," Murray pessimistically wrote. "I suggest," he continued, "that the Indians be organized along military lines into Conservation Development Corps . . . . Under this arrangement the able-bodied men of the tribe would be put under the direction of a competent officer who could be assisted by the Chief and other important men of the tribe, aiding in the capacity of non-commissioned officers . . ." (Roche, 1992).

Although this military model of a more secular conversion was not optioned, it assisted the thinking as to how to effect an orderly disposal of these nomadic Natives. From the mid-1950s onwards the authorities argued that settlement in villages should come first, closely followed by what they referred to as "integration," meaning education and employment. Measures to bring about these outcomes were usually presented as compassionate and as indispensable to the survival of "the Indians." Earlier in the same letter quoted above, Murray had even mused that "it would be far more merciful to let them die off quickly than to merely prolong the process with inadequate help." Coming upon these Indians, apparently backward escapees from the westward march of progress, the eager Newfoundland authorities offered a benevolent paternalism. to abate the natural propensity of the Indians to "die off" in the aftermath of contact.[6]

For officials such as Walter Rockwood, education was absolutely vital to the "economic rehabilitation" of the Innu. Their ignorance of the English language had, he maintained, prevented them from obtaining jobs at the air base built at Goose Bay during World War II. Because any work with the Innu would be labour-intensive – at this time, they were dividing their time between the interior and the Hudson's Bay Company posts at North West River, Davis Inlet, Fort

Chimo, and others on the Labrador coast and the North Shore of the Gulf of St. Lawrence – the government was happy to make agents of the Oblate missionaries who visited them. At the posts, the Oblates became preachers, teachers, doctors, and intermediaries between the Innu and the new state. Joining church and state, the priests doubled as evangelists and assimilators. Schooling became the key to the changes in the Innu the missionaries were attempting to effect.

Not only was schooling an excellent means of compelling village life, but the Oblates believed that without education the Christian message could be dangerously and syncretically alloyed with other beliefs, thought to be superstitious at best and satanic at worst. Such beliefs, associated with shamanism, the Animal Gods, and the shaking tent or *kushapatshikan,* were nurtured, of course, by nomadic hunting life – a life that had not been stamped out despite the best efforts of Jesuit, Oblate, and Eudist missionaries since the seventeenth century. Not needing Indians as military allies in a nuclear age, the Oblates of the 1950s were less circumspect, often suppressing Innu religion with a directness that would have made Le Jeune blush.

The priests chipped away at Innu independence by continually portraying nomadic life and the beliefs associated with it as the work of the devil. Those who participated in Innu religious activities were verbally and sometimes physically scolded and many priests did their utmost to foment ostracism of the *kamintushit.* Others were beaten simply for spending time in hunting camps in the country. In *Gathering Voices,* the first publication produced by the Innu in an attempt to take stock of what had happened to them since they were settled in the villages, Iskuess Pasteen, a Sheshatshiu woman, described her experience of the priests during the intensive sedentarization drive:

> The priest would come to visit us where we were camped. He would ask the families to come and reside in the community. The priest would do this with other people living in the community. My mother says that the priest got really angry because there was no one living in the community. The Innu people were afraid of the priest. He controlled them and told them what to do. He christianized them. The Innu would still be living in the country if it wasn't for the priest, and people would still be living their spiritual beliefs if there weren't white people around. The church was always filled up because the priest controlled the people. I never liked the priest telling us what to do and other people as well. (Innu Nation, 1993: 27)

The effects of these attacks on Innu philosophical and religious structure went beyond aggression against "pagan religion" in the Judeo-Christian sense. With hindsight, it is now evident that these assaults profoundly affected the self-confidence of many Innu and assailed the underpinnings of Innu society itself. The activities of the clergy at this time were important factors precipitating the cultural vacuum that began to become apparent in the 1970s. The Innu religion was integral to everyday life – their church was the world in which they moved; everything, including the spring ice, the different winds, the rising and falling of the water levels in lakes, was believed to be possessed of animate character or controlled by forces that were considered animate. The notion of "god in a building" was not only bizarre, but inimical to the notions that ordered Innu life and invested it with meaning. The Innu *Mantushiun* is a religion of hunters and requires nomadism and intimate daily interaction with non-human life to nourish it.

Looking back on the first days of settlement, the stories Innu tell of priests' hostile attitudes towards their religion in the 1960s are similar to those of other Aboriginal groups who were Christianized by the Oblates. The Oblates were notorious for their harsh discipline and authoritarian orientations towards work and time.[7] Driving along the Churchill road in his truck, eyes peeled for animal life, Greg Penashue told me about his school years under the Oblates in the 1960s. "The priests, who were our teachers, used to say that our beliefs were devil worship. There would be drums, bones, and other things hanging in the tents, and when the priest came in he would tell our parents that these objects were bad, sick, and should be thrown away." Many Innu parents were verbally scolded and sometimes physically beaten for taking their children into the country when, as the priests maintained, they should have been in school. A woman in Davis Inlet told me that some people, who were still in their tents at the allotted time for Mass, were dragged by their hair to the church. The priest also removed any drums he heard in the village, and scolded Innu for dancing to the drum. Drum dancing often occurred both in the settlement and in the interior as an essential accompaniment to the *mukushan* feast, a meal of the marrow of the bones of caribou eaten to celebrate and reaffirm the connections between the Innu and the most important of their deities, the caribou god or *Kanipanikasikueu*. While the priests discouraged the older generation from such spiritual practices as playing the drum and respecting the bones, they also concentrated on indoctrinating young Innu into the Christian world view. In the 1960s, Henriksen (1973: 79-80) observed that Innu "religious beliefs have been forced 'underground' by the Church. They no longer play drums, sing or dance, and are extremely reluctant to talk about their religious traditions." Paul Le Jeune in his account of 1634, "On the Belief, Supersti- tions, and Errors of the Montagnais Savages" (Thwaites, 1897: VI, 157-227), reveals similar sentiments, although his views were min- gled with a greater appreciation of the Innu cosmology than was the case for the Oblate priests. While the Oblates are reported to have used physical force in their attempts to eradicate Innu spiritual practices – hitting people with sticks, and smashing drums and bones – Le Jeune narrates stories of singing, praying, drumming, feasting, and sweating. The *Relations* are tinged with his own com- mentaries on the error, falsehood, and superstition of such practices, but never does he record any acts, other than verbal ex- change, designed to end Innu spirituality. Even here, Le Jeune often concedes that his Native interlocutors came out on top.

The correspondence at mid-twentieth century between Rock- wood and other central figures in the sedentarization drive (Father Pirson, the Belgian Oblate at North West River, Dr. Tony Paddon of the International Grenfell Association, and other government repre- sentatives in Labrador) rings with cries for "integration" of "the Indian" as the only, and perhaps, inevitable, course of action. Left to their own devices, the Innu would ultimately become extinct or live a miserable life on the edges of white society. Rockwood provided an evocative rendition of this scenario in a June 1959 memorandum in which he compared the Innu to the Beothuks of Newfoundland, killed off completely by European disease and violence:

> For the Indians and many of the Eskimos, there is no easy, short
> term solution, unless it be the solution found for the aborigines of
> Newfoundland more than a century ago. They, the Beothucks, have
> been no bother since June 6 1829. The writer does not advocate
> this solution for the Labrador Indians, but it would be almost
> kinder than to allow them to live off the garbage dumps, and be-
> come prey to unscrupulous persons. (Roche, 1992)

Diverting the Innu from another Final Solution required education. Rockwood, assumed that the inevitable transformation of the Innu would be through a kind of cultural evolution. He continues with a stirring rendition of the "vanishing Indian" rationalization[8] common in the United States a century earlier:

> The Montagnais and Nascaupi Indians, very largely because of the
> efforts of the Oblates and the Grenfell Mission, have even given up
> their propensity to die out. The correct solution, and it is a long
> term one, is to prepare them for the kind of world they must live in,
> and this must begin with children. Or, to quote from a report on the

Greenland administration, published by the Royal Danish Ministry for Foreign Affairs in 1952: "The foundation of any social evolution truly democratic in character, in Greenland or anywhere else, is public education." (Ibid.)

Following the dire sentiments expressed by Rockwood and others, the priests established schools as the very cornerstone of settlement life at Davis Inlet and Sheshatshiu. Like the missions to the sister Innu villages on the Quebec North Shore these came under the Diocese of Labrador, Schefferville. Similar institutions were established in the 1950s and 1960s in the new settlements for the Innu in Quebec. While the Innu were still living in tents, a school was set up by the Oblates in Sheshatshiu in 1954, but it was not until 1956 that government funds were made available for the construction of a building. In 1959 the first professional teachers arrived, and in 1960 the school came under the authority of the Labrador Catholic School Board. At this time, the professional teachers required "total immersion" of the Innu students, mandating a standard calendar year in which students were expected to attend continuously from September to June. Another school was set up by the Oblates in old Davis Inlet in 1953. This was some 15 years before the "permanent" move to the settlement on Illiukoyak Island. Even though they were living in mobile shelters, the school was intended to give the Innu at the North West River and Davis Inlet posts a sense of order, limitation, and attachment. At the same time, the Grenfell Association in North West River set up a boarding school for the Inuit and settlers of the coast. The motivations for this endeavour were almost identical to those that informed the education of the Innu. As Dr. Tony Paddon argued in 1966, the problems of providing education for mixed settler-Inuit populations on the coast "arise from the fact that there is a strong Eskimo racial and cultural element in an isolated population." It was "the Eskimo influence and attitude towards education, and the language problem in these bilingual groups . . . [that] we wish to mitigate."[9]

The provincial authorities, with only minimal contact with the Innu at the Hudson's Bay Company posts, and acting upon the folk wisdom of priests, physicians, and traders, were seldom deterred in their efforts to "integrate" the Innu. By the early 1960s this still appeared to be at best a rather partial success, mainly because of the continuous pull of hunting in the interior, and the sometimes lacklustre performances of the Innu with the fur traders. In a report from 1959, Rockwood boldly stated that while education was necessary, other impediments to integration also needed to be attended to. "Neither is it to be assumed that the mere teaching of English or even trades, will solve all the problems," he reflected, before the diagnosis that "there are deeply rooted psychological attitudes to be overcome" (Roche, 1992). Similar sentiments were expressed a few years later, in the 1963-64 Annual Report of the Department of Public Welfare (quoted by Budgell, 1984: 47), where it was maintained that:

> Indians must be taught the three R's, and will also need vocational training, but it would be naive to think that this will automatically solve all the problems overnight. As with the Indians elsewhere there are deeply rooted psychological problems to be overcome before the process of integration is complete.

The Indians' minds needed to be attended to as a matter of some gravity. "Deeply rooted psychological attitudes" were barriers to integration. These pathologies were equated most emphatically with patterns of thought that lured families out into the country in search of animals, made them relax at the posts and avoid paid employment, spend days in chaos drinking alcohol provided by the traders, and – in comparison to the British settlers of Newfoundland and Labrador – allow their children greater liberties. These were the qualities, observed by the austere traders and Roman Catholic priests at the posts, that "required correction." The teachings of Christ imparted by the priest at Mass and the secular example of the ledgers and balanced books of the traders were not sufficient. Institutions were needed as a more permanent corrective. These were modelled not so much on the more rigorous conception of the European school, as indeed they were in other areas of the world with larger literate populations,[10] but under the harsh conditions of the landscape, the makeshift frontier schoolhouse.

Learning suddenly became an autonomous sphere, organized by others, and wrenched away from the activities of travelling, hunting, and the dynamic pedagogy of the country. The school started to split apart two ways of learning and living, separating them by the vast chasm of "civilization." The establishment of formal instruction was directly linked to the systematic invalidation, through verbal and physical reprimand, of nomadic hunting as a way of life. From the outset, schools were conceived as a means to both salvage and transform the Innu. *Principles for a Theory of Instructing Adult Nascappie Indians*, a document produced by the Protestant school authorities in Schefferville in the mid-1960s, concerns itself with Mushuau Innu adults who, because they were children before settlement, are often "socially retarded" and in need of "social recuperation." It positions the education of "the Indians" within the overall process of regional "progress":

If Quebec is to develop well, we must stress the fullest education possible for all our Indians, no matter what the cost or sacrifice. No Province can be socially, politically or economically secure and progressive in the long run until all the Indian segment of the population is constantly improving, developing, and strengthening their ideas, ideals and minds. Minds are golden. No gold "mine" can be compared in value to the golden mind of an individual. For those who think only in dollars and not in "sense" I make the plea for the complete development of the golden minds of the Nascappie Adult Indian Student which can be developed at eventual great profit and benefit to Quebec. (Slesar, n.d.:1)

Because they are founded on the conviction of Native primitivism, one of the original intentions of schools for Native peoples was to illustrate to the children the vast gulf between "civilized" and "savage" ways. The Newfoundland administrators, somewhat like their Jesuit predecessors, but without the nuance or literary flare of the *Relations*, imagined the binary world. In Labrador, as elsewhere in the history of colonization, the creation of a divide between the dynamic and civilizing forces that Europeans offered to the location and the static and backward qualities of the Innu who were merely existing there, was summoned up on numerous occasions. Here, if Frantz Fanon is any guide, the differences between the French colonization of North Africa and the Canadian colonization of Labrador, both in the 1950s, were not so great. The "Manichean world" that Fanon (1963: 41) describes is similar to the one invoked by the authorities in Labrador at the time. Speaking of Christian evangelizing and education, Fanon (1963: 42) remarks that:

The customs of the colonized people, their traditions, the myths – above all their myths – are the very sign of that poverty of spirit and of their constitutional depravity. That is why we must put the DDT which destroys parasites, the bearers of disease, on the same level as the Christian religion which wages war on embryonic heresies and instincts, and on evil as yet unborn.

Like the French efforts that Fanon refers to, the Canadian policies of the same period assumed that Innu beliefs and practices were at best insignificant and at worst dangers to their acceptance of the kind of economic, social, and political forces that were about to be thrust upon them. In the administrative literature of the period, the path to progress required toil, industry, commerce, wealth, homeownership, and rationality. To remain as Natives would be to remain socially retarded and psychologically impeded, and such attributes in a future population were unthinkable to the authorities of both Quebec and Newfoundland, so eager to exploit all the natural resources, including "golden minds."

Serving to avert the conflict that could follow from any sense of loss or morbid reflections on the ways of the hunter, rapid moves were made to educate the younger generation of Innu at the settlements. It was the young people whom the authorities banked on as being in the vanguard of "integration." While adult education would eventually be put forward for the hunters, it was important that the first generation to live in the villages on a permanent basis be educated to accept the various assumptions upon which Euro-Canadian society was beginning to develop on the Labrador-Quebec peninsula, particularly the need to economically exploit the resources of the area. If they were to function in the society of those who were about to bring about such drastic changes to them, the socialization of children could not be left up to Innu parents, the hunters, who were deemed to have only a fragile grip on the skills, attitudes, and knowledge which the Euro-Canadian world demanded. From the very beginning, schooling drove a wedge between the older and younger generations of Innu, first by severing the tie between parents and children in the reproduction of knowledge, and secondly by educating children in buildings out of reach from the hunting camps that formed the basis for Innu knowledge of the world and the cosmos.

Unlike their parents, Innu children in the settlements were constituted by their teachers as participants in some wider Canadian, or even global, social order. On the whole, however, the education that the young Innu have received has not permitted many to function in what would be regarded as a "successful" manner outside or inside the Innu communities. While a rift was created between the generations, this has not produced the outcome of "integration" desired by the planners. As I shall explain, this is both a result of the sheer insensitivity of the Roman Catholic priests and teachers and a function of the desire of the Innu to maintain their own unique way of life. Not surprisingly, other indigenous societies of the Far North subject to abrupt immersion in schooling on the European model in a context of little familiarity with Western institutional and intellectual patterns have been "only marginally productive at . . . best and devastating at . . . worst" (Darnell and Hoem, 1996: 142).[11] This dilemma was described early on by the first permanent priest in Davis Inlet, the Flemish Oblate, Father Frank Peters. Referring to the role of education, Peters (1972: 28) wrote that Innu children were being prepared "*for a way of life that does not exist.*" They were gradually weaned out of the hunting life of their parents and grandparents and, at least in the villages, into a void.

THE TERROR OF THE LOVING GOD

In 1999, I was asked by the band council in Sheshatshiu to help with a study of schooling in the community. The evaluation study, as it was called, was part of the process required for the band council to take control of the school under the provisions of the Indian Act, which leaders were keen to apply for. In the process of this research and with the help of Louis Rich as an interviewer and translator, I spoke with about 60 adults about their experiences of schooling. The people that we interviewed told us of many different experiences of schooling. For some, going to school was a positive experience and they had happy memories of the priests and teachers. They recalled the excitement of being with other children, sports activities, good relations with teachers, and other rewards. However, for a much larger proportion of those interviewed, schooling in the Roman Catholic educational system was not a happy experience. Many were traumatized, and for some school was filled with a kind of terror that had left emotional scars. This was a major theme of the conversations we had with members of the community. People aged about 30 and over mentioned school-related trauma more commonly, but it was not limited to that generation.

In the years when schooling was first imposed and the Catholic clergy presided over teaching, Innu students of the time vividly recalled the beatings that were meted out at the school. According to numerous Innu in Sheshatshiu, the most notorious perpetrator of this kind of terror was Father Pirson, who taught in the community for 22 years from the 1950s until he departed abruptly in the early 1970s. Innu pupils said that he treated them very harshly, commonly using a stick, ruler, or leather strap to beat them across the palms of their hands or knuckles. Some people said that Father Pirson also beat them on the buttocks with a large stick. Others said that the priest used any implement that came to hand – leather straps, rulers, belts, and even broomsticks. Some told us that they were kicked when they did not know the answers to questions. One man said that he was even smacked over the head with a Bible, and after that incident he questioned the "loving God" that the priest had lectured on. Elizabeth Penashue, a woman of the same generation, recalled one school day in the 1950s when she "sat down with the girls in the class and, because I asked another girl to help me," she said, motioning to the area above her right eye, "Father Pirson hit me over the face with a ruler and blood came down my face. I went home to tell my mother and she went to speak to the priest. But, this happened to a lot of kids."

Severe punishments were dealt out for minor infractions of school protocol such as not paying attention to the lesson and arriving late. Even when students tried to avoid school by staying at home, the priest would visit the house and persuade the parents to force the truant child to go to school. Some people who migrated to Sheshatshiu from Davis Inlet had similar experiences. One man remembered Father St. Cyr, an Oblate in Davis Inlet before the permanent posting of Father Peters, hitting the students with a metal curtain rod. Because of the enormous respect accorded to the missionaries during the immediate post-settlement period, many children did not tell their parents about the beatings. So feared and revered was the priest that several of those who did tell their parents said that their parents refused to believe them.

Perhaps the mildest form of punishment that Father Pirson used was verbal chastisement. He routinely raised his voice to the children, became impatient, and shouted at them. Many Innu students were too scared to absorb anything that Father Pirson taught them. One middle-aged woman said that if the priest had not hit her she would now know how to read and write. She could not write any English and could only speak a little. Feeling that all hope is lost now, she thought she would be illiterate for the rest of her days.

The priest's punishments were performed in front of other children, bringing a sense of shame to the student being reprimanded. In the 1960s, one woman was sitting in the front row of the classroom when she was asked a question that she could not answer. Father Pirson then kicked her so hard that she fell over with her desk. Because the other students laughed at her she felt humiliated. The incident was so dramatic, that several others of her generation heard stories about it. Some of the older women we interviewed experienced sexually embarrassing punishments such as being spanked on the buttocks, kicked on the buttocks, and having their skirts lifted up by the priest. The memories of the beatings partly explain why so many adults in Sheshatshiu are distrustful of the school. The memories were so terrifying to some Innu that they said they would like to see the school building burn down.

As a key figure in the decision to pressure the Innu to settle at Sheshatshiu, Father Pirson believed that they needed to be subjected to the regularity, discipline, and control of European-style schooling in order to make any social or economic advances. Punctuality, the inculcation of literal adherence to orderings of mechanical clock time, was strictly enforced by beatings dished out to those arriving late at the school. Pirson is on record as a stern judge of Innu manners, constantly noting their deviations from

Euro-Canadian norms. He was concerned on some occasions that the various intermediaries (traders, government officials, and the like) were too generous to them. In a letter to Walter Rockwood, written somewhat impatiently in ungrammatical English, the priest singles out the government depot manager, Max Budgell, for negligence. For Pirson, Budgell's minor generosities were a "great mistake" hindering orderly settlement and education:

> I was told by the Indians that Mr. Budgell is letting the Indians have yeast cake – by relief is given to them. Lately it has been disturbance which was caused by drunkenness.
>
> Another result of that great mistake – some families now staying away from here – and near to Happy Valley. Consequently the children are not attending school. You know as I do that they need badly.
>
> I did wait few weeks before to write to you. It is my feeling that Mr. Budgell gives too much to the Indians and that he does not refuse anything to them. This feeling is shared by other people here at North West River and as well at Goose Bay. For two months, I asked some Indians for fire wood which I was paying them 10 ¢ a piece and nobody did. Nobody wants to work or to hunt or to fish. (Roche, 1992)

Despite the obstacles erected by the generosities of the depot manager, the sale of yeast cake to make alcohol and the siting of Innu campsites out of the reach of Pirson's schoolhouse, the priest persisted in his efforts to school the younger generation. Discouraging the Innu from nomadic hunting and luring them to camp for longer periods of time at Sheshatshiu near the North West River post was central to Pirson's projects. Schooling, however poor its quality, required settlement, and this led Pirson to employ various techniques, including physical intimidation and bribery, to discourage *nutshimit* life. A common method that he used to pressure parents not to take their children to the country was to threaten them that their Family Allowance would be discontinued if they did not send their children to the school. In a letter to the Newfoundland Superintendent of Schools in 1959, Pirson asserted:

> I think the time has come to give a true picture of what is going on here. Looking at this monthly report, you will notice that there are 21 pupils attending school here at North West River (I mean Indians). But according to the census of the Indian population 53 children are supposed to attend school . . . I think that I have to do something. I told the parents many time I am afraid to do that but I will suggest in inform Family Allowances Department and ask them to discontinue allowances to parents who are careless. (Roche, 1992)

Hence, for the many parents who had become dependent on these funds, the continuation of Family Allowance came at the cost of subjecting their children to Father Pirson's reign of terror and forgoing the opportunity to hunt and live with other families in the country. Judging from Pirson's poorly written English, it seems likely that Innu students did not even receive competent instruction in exchange for the sacrifices their parents were making in staying in the village.

Over time, the persistent proselytizing of the priests, combined with the carrots and sticks of welfare to be collected at the settlement and the emergent problem of alcohol abuse, began to wear down any resistance the Innu might have offered. Shortly after settlement, confused and disoriented, many of the older generation became heavy drinkers. They had little or no facility in the English language and Pirson himself addressed the Innu in *Innu-aimun*. *Nutshimit* became an uphill struggle, an engagement that first had to overcome the intimidation of the Oblates, then later the provincial Social Services Department, which also made similar threats.[13] As Jean-Pierre Ashini described:

> Me and my sister didn't go to school. We went to the country in the spring of 1966, returning to Sheshatshiu in September. Then the priest came to the house telling us we had to go to school to become doctors or lawyers even though my father didn't like the priest or accept the non-Innu religion. He thought the priest was brainwashing the Innu kids. My grandfather knew that something would come wrong out of it. When we didn't go to school again, the priest hired a truant officer from Goose Bay to chase us all around the community and take us to school.

Even those of a younger generation who attended Peenamin McKenzie School in the 1970s and 1980s have similar memories. For this generation, the punishment may have been less painful, but it was nonetheless equally humiliating. Punishment such as ear twisting, kicking on the backside, and verbal chastisement was commonly experienced. Many also remember not being allowed to go to the washroom when they requested it, and many people said that they occasionally had to urinate or defecate in their clothes in the classroom. Some people indicated that this happened in fairly recent times either to themselves or their children. Others remember being hit by Sister Coffey, a principal in the 1970s and 1980s, with a belt or strap. Some people said that they were asked to stand in the corner or leave the classroom for not listening to the teacher. One young man said that he was whipped with a ruler for speaking *Innu-aimun* with a friend. At the time he was confiding about his parents drinking at home, which was bothering him. Other young students were told to stand in an empty room or in the corner of the classroom for what was deemed misbehaviour.

In some ways, it is not unusual that this terror was perpetrated in the Innu schools and became part of the pedagogical regime. Such pedagogy was standard practice in Native schools across North America. What is remarkable is that terror continued for so long. In a report entitled *Breaking the Silence*, the Assembly of First Nations (1994: 50) examined the impact of residential schools on Native people in Canada. "Every one of the people interviewed either saw other children beaten or were themselves beaten. The beatings were often public to teach the children a lesson." While corporal punishment might have been common in schools generally at the time, its use in schools for Native peoples had added ramifications. Most transparently, it was a graphic reminder to Natives of their own subordination to Euro-Canadians. Not only were Euro-Canadians taking it upon themselves to socialize and educate Aboriginal children in accordance with European values, but also they were brutalizing them in a way that almost all Native peoples would have found deeply offensive. Whereas Europeans have long tolerated, even encouraged, physical punishment as a spur to learning, such conduct towards children was seen by Innu, as Father Le Jeune and his successors discovered, harmful and counterproductive.

SEXUAL ABUSE

"In school, he [the priest] stood up behind me, and pressed himself into my back," said one older woman, "and, with one hand right down there inside my pants, he was trying to tell me how to write something down. I felt shame and then thought I would never have a boyfriend. I was 11 or maybe 12." A young Innu woman spoke of the gym teacher sexually abusing her when she was 15 years old. She was aware at the time that the same teacher had abused other students. She quit school as a result of these incidents and believed that the sudden outbursts of anger that she now experiences stem from these incidents. A teacher sexually abused three teenage boys within another family. The teacher in question was trusted by the family and was sometimes asked to look after the boys when the parents were away. After the incidents and a public court case, the boys were called "queer" and "gay," and adult men in particular teased them about the incidents as if they were the boys' fault. In 1999, one of these young men put a shotgun barrel in his mouth and blew away most of his head. Another man in his early twenties recalled being fondled by a teacher when he was in Grade 2. As a result, he grew up thinking that this kind of exploitation of children was normal. Often, as a consequence, those who were victims became victimizers in adulthood. Yet another man, now in his late twenties, told us that he was sexually abused in Grade 2 and stopped going to school as a result of it. He then returned and was abused again when he was in Grade 4.

While it is impossible to say exactly how widespread school-related sexual abuse was, we do know from our interviews that a considerable number of young Innu were sexually abused by priests and teachers. As a result of the abuse, Davis Inlet Chief Simeon Tshakapesh argued that "an entire generation of young people was abused at the hands of the church and state."[14] Innu sexual abuse victims have not spoken out sooner for a number of reasons: the fear of shame, the perception that others would not believe them, especially when it involved a respected figure such as the priest, and the feeling that others would think that the victim was a sexual pervert or deviant. What many Innu have revealed indicates that sexual abuse has been a fairly constant feature of their experience of schooling and that it has involved a number of teachers and clergy stretching back to the early period of settlement until the mid-1990s, when two teachers were exposed as child sex abusers.

While many priests and teachers have acted honourably, several have been charged and convicted of sexual abuse offences in the courts. By 2001, Innu in Sheshatshiu and Davis Inlet had filed almost 50 cases of sexual abuse against the Roman Catholic Church, individual Oblate missionaries, the local diocese, and the Vatican. These complaints date back to the early 1960s and are widely regarded to be only a fraction of the total number of sexual abuse violations on Innu by clergy that took place in the villages. There is evidence that as late as the early 1990s the Roman Catholic Bishop responsible for the parish was fully aware of the abuse and made every effort to cover it up. Fuelling further speculation by the Innu of a cover-up, the Canadian Department of Justice upheld a decision not to extradite an Oblate Brother from the United States who was charged with three counts of sexual assault against Innu boys in Davis Inlet in the 1960s.[15]

The dark shadows of sexual abuse hang over the school and colour the perceptions of many of those who have attended it. As recently as 1995, a male schoolteacher faced multiple accusations of molesting and sexually abusing young boys. He even adopted a young Innu boy who was used for this purpose. As the accusations mounted for court proceedings to take place and his eleventh-hour attempt to bribe his adopted son to lie on his behalf failed, the teacher soaked his arms in hot water, slashed his wrists, and walked through his small white house on the beach road in Sheshat-shiu until he collapsed in a bloody heap. One of his victims, curious at not seeing him for a while, peered through his window and raised the alarm.

But, again, the sexual terror inflicted upon the Innu was not unique. It occurred across Canada. As the Assembly of First Nations (1994: 51) study remarks:

> The most profound form of physical wounding occurred through sexual violations. Reputed violations vary, with incidents of fon dling, intercourse, ritualistic washing of genitals and rape, and in some cases instances of pregnancy and forced abortion.

Partly in response to hearing tales like this the federal government of Canada issued a "solemn offer of reconciliation" to Aboriginal peoples. Speaking at the unveiling of *Gathering Strength: Canada's Aboriginal Action Plan* in 1998, Jane Stewart, Minister of Indian Affairs, singled out the residential school system as a cause of embarrassment and contrition. Noting the sexual and physical abuse suffered by Aboriginal children, she said, "to those of you who suffered this tragedy at residential schools, we are deeply sorry." The Innu of Labrador, of course, were not in residential schools. The acts perpetrated against them are disturbing for different reasons in that they occurred within the community itself and continued after the residential school system in Canada had been dismantled. Thus far, the non-Native officials at Peenamin McKenzie School and the Labrador School Board have remained silent about the abuse.[16]

In the face of all this maltreatment and abuse, one obvious question is why Innu parents did nothing about it. In the 1950s and 1960s, the older generation had great respect for priests and teachers. The missionaries were the main mediators between them and a government that had been instrumental in abruptly curtailing their nomadic way of life. This was done under the banners of Christianity, progress, and civilization, which the Innu were told were the ways of the future. Some were so affected by this that they became ashamed of the Innu way of life. These missionaries instilled what one Davis Inlet resident referred to as "a psychology of fear." In many ways, Catholicism imparted not devotion but fear, and its dull traces infuse the melancholy Sunday morning services.

ARE YOU REAL?

While many *Tshenut* still attend Mass with this memory of fear, Catholicism is now made to appear as if it belongs to some mutual spiritual consensus. The clapboard church in Sheshatshiu is decorated with Christian symbols that have been fashioned out of Innu materials and icons, such as the drum, once banned by the church. The priest's vestments are made of caribou hide. A large beaver pelt is mounted on one wall, caribou antlers on another. The shelves and stands supporting small statues of Jesus and Mary are decorated with pelt and hide trimmings and fringes. On another wall are two paintings. One features Jesus in a northern landscape being greeted by what appear to be northern Aboriginal people at the shore. The Natives are bending on one knee and looking up at him. In the background another Native paddles a canoe towards Jesus and the kneeling flock. Most of the Mass, including the singing of hymns, is conducted through translators in *Innu-aimun*. Priests in the 1990s preferred "the Great Spirit" as an alternative to God, but this pan-Native deity was presented in the context of the Christian God. "He will give us strength to fight alcohol abuse and to make political decisions," Father Fred told the congregation one summer morning. "The Great Spirit will help us contemplate our sins and help us move towards solving our many problems."

Out at the Easter gathering place of the Mushuau Innu at Kamesteuishikashish, opposite Sango Bay, the Mass inside the church tent starts late, but there is excitement as six children are prepared for baptism. The ritual begins with Father Jack, a priest nearing retirement and posted in Goose Bay, asking the parents, "Why have you come here?" Not knowing what to say, there is only silence. At this point Father Jack instructs the nun and school principal, Sister Joan, to "Tell them to say 'baptism.'" The communications become garbled and several people speak over one another and out of turn, so the priest then tries another tack, "Tell them what to say." Eventually, through the the nun slowly rephrasing the priest's questions in English, the ritual is completed and all six infants baptized. The sermon then continues in a cheerily upbeat manner. Saccharine humour is delivered throughout, but it barely keeps the attention of the Innu youngsters. I glance up to notice one lad darting around the tent wearing a baseball cap emblazoned with the word, "Devils." My own attention span is likewise sporadic. I tune in to Father Jack telling the congregation that many people see the church as a serious place, but it can also be a happy place. He says that he would like to tell a lot of jokes, but he checks himself, telling only one. Every single tent at the gathering site, he observed, has a cross stitched above the door flap, except one. He pauses for effect, then revealed that the one in question is that which belongs to the two priests and the nun. There is mild amusement, then he returned to his happy, upbeat sermon. The young gradually filtered out, and the Mass ends with most of the original congregation already having departed.

Roman Catholic Mass at the Mushuau Innu gathering site at Kamesteuishikashish. Photograph by author.

That evening, I enter the tent without a cross. Inside, the clergy are playing Scrabble. The mood is cozy and things are ordered as if the tent were actually a house, with neat compartments, boxes, and books neatly stacked. It has all the appearance of being a refuge from the surroundings. Not long after I enter, I see dismay course across the faces of the clergy as a trail of Innu children from the tent I was staying in follow behind me. The kids are instructed exactly where to sit, and as ginger snaps are passed around, Joseph, one young boy, takes a wedge of three cookies. He is reprimanded by one of the priests, "Whoa, if you take that many, there won't be any left for Joan and us." The child is chastened and I think slightly confused by these *Akaneshau* who ration, plan, and partition everything. The Scrabble game was continuing under strain and disruption. As a disingenuous ploy to have the children evacuated, Sister Joan asks the oldest child a meaningless question, "What time does your mother expect you home?" The children all fall silent and I can do nothing to help or hinder either party, for I know that their mother presumes the children are safe in the camp and would never specify a particular hour when they have to be in their tent.

If the clergy believed that their view of the world and that of the Innu were gradually converging, and that the Great Spirit and God were becoming one, here was surely a glimpse of their own disbelief. Apart from the ritual of the Mass and some anodyne banter displayed around the camp, their impulse was to separate. The clergy acted as if there were really an Innu world that was best left to the Innu, and another world that needed to be cloistered away from the Innu. These two worlds coincided with their vaguely middle-class North American suburbanism and the "Other," neither assimilated nor untouched, but not close enough to keep company with. It led them to have two faces, jolly and amiable inside the church tent and elsewhere in the camp, and judgemental and set apart inside their own tent without a cross. I imagined that Kamesteuishikashish, on the borderlands of stretches of featureless sea ice on one side and the brooks, rivers, forests, and tundra of the interior on the other, and a considerable distance even from Davis Inlet, was a place that unsettled these Christians' certainties and led to their emotional unease.

Here, I think, one of the boys grasped something of the contradictions. Charlie appeared behind Father John, asking him, "Are you real?" Receiving only a bemused look, he repeated the question to the other clergy. Trying to change the subject, Father John, possibly thinking that Charlie was much younger than he actually was – he was a teenager – repeatedly patted him on the back as one would a pet, unconvincingly repeating the phrase, "You're a nice boy, you're really a good boy." This did not appease Charlie, and the existential bite to the questioning soon became too much for Father John, who took Charlie outside the tent where I heard the priest saying, "What do you want from me?" When pressed, Charlie told him that he wanted to know what was really underneath him. If he were to peel the skin off the priests would he find human beings underneath? Receiving only patronizing diversions from his questions, eventually Charlie left. The Scrabble game was then quickly resumed. Father John, losing his cool, told me, "That guy is a real shithead, he has nothing inside his head, no brains." Continuing the board game without the Innu children, the conversation became mannered and polite. Any turn to topics related to the Innu on my part was instantly diverted or parried. Charlie had clearly revealed that all was not as ordered as the Scrabble game, that the clergy were showing outward joviality in the church and camp and displaying control, separation, and distance within the confines of their own tent when the Innu boys disrupted the Scrabble game. Legitimately, the boys could wonder whether *Akaneshaut* are real.

It does not take much observation to see that the spiritual concern for the Innu on the part of the clergy is strained. Their edgy benevolence and lack of attention to the realities of the Innu predicament is an admission of their belief in an almost intractable cultural gulf. In addition to Masses and interactions at gatherings, I have witnessed confusion among the clergy in several funerals in both communities. Typically, priests who cannot honestly share in the grief of the villagers or understand why early death is so ubiquitous are thronged by masses of emotional and tearful people. In the midst of this, the priests seem unable to do more than proceed with a scripted Roman Catholic ceremony.

In 1997, Father John, a recruit from India, presided over the funeral of the 34-year-old Yvonne Asta. No one knew exactly how Yvonne died. Most said that she had hung herself, although others said it was a heart attack. The nurses told me that there were burn marks on her neck. To the throngs of grieving Innu mourners, however, cause was not at issue. Over the three hours of the funeral, children, adults, and the elderly were crying and wailing over the casket. One by one grieving friends and relatives stood up and spoke of Yvonne and her life. This emotion contrasted with the priest's formalism, which began with his recitation of the Easter benediction, not the funeral oration. Some few minutes into his delivery, he realized his error only after being jogged by the nun in attendance, and shuffling papers and Bibles, Father John eventually came up with the correct script. His motions then became noticeably strained as if realizing the absurdity of his rituals amid the sorrow engendered by the death of a young mother. His forced and nervy oration as much as admitted that he was not really being real. Nevertheless, he plowed on, ending with: "Whatever her failings and negligences were, we ask God to accept her into His heaven."

Teaching Lies   6

. . . if the guiding hand is ill qualified, an instrument is murderous in proportion to its sharpness.

– James Agee, *Let Us Now Praise Famous Men* (1941: 267)

My kids don't go to school. I don't force them because it was like a nightmare to me. We were supposed to be doctors and lawyers, but we ended up in jail, committing suicide and being drunks and bums. Nowadays, that's called progress.

– Jean-Pierre Ashini, Sheshatshiu, 1999

"MORE INNU"

There had been a break-in the previous night. Kids had raided junk food stored for an end-of-year party, smashed windows, and stolen a compact disc player. Despite this disturbance to the institutional sense of order, the school had a languorous atmosphere on this June afternoon just before the summer holidays in 1995. Children wandered the wide corridors, curious, yet aimless. The harshness of the long unbroken walls was softened by Native decor: skins here; a drum there; a wall panel of photographs of the "old days" and of Peenamin McKenzie after whom the school in Sheshatshiu is named; a naive northern landscape painting; the blue, green, and white of the Innu Nation flag; a glass cabinet of old hunting implements. Teachers sat in offices, chatting. Some classes were half-heartedly in session. It was hot outside. Across from the principal's window, a neat row of clean and shiny cars and pickup trucks were parked. At the close of school the teachers would be driving them to their homes in North West River and Happy Valley-Goose Bay.

Like most of the *Akaneshau* involved in a professional capacity with the Innu, the principal, Cynthia Fleet, manages a positive impression. While there were problems of attendance and motivation, she told me that she was presiding over a move to make the Roman Catholic-run school "more Innu" by incorporating the Innu language in teaching and bringing in the elders to talk to the children about "culture." Her story line was one of gradual improvement, as small changes and innovations to the curriculum were made to mark out the milestones of progress. The principal recognized that the school was alien to the parents – "the white man's culture," she called it in her high-pitched Newfoundland intonation. But the task at hand was to improve the school so that more Innu parents would be enticed into sending their kids there. Nonetheless, there was a certain sense I detected, which grew with every subsequent visit I made, that the optimistic exterior disguised insecurities – and these were not just about the integrity of the school in its own terms, but the very concept of education for the Innu youngsters. If the school is improving, what is it an improvement upon? If the school is on an upward ascent, what is it ascending to and for whom? What is signified by progress?

On the school premises I detect a lurking sense of inertia, a semi-paralysis, brought about by the ambivalence embodied in the very notion of a Euro-Canadian school in a Native community with strong ties to a hunting way of life. If this hunting life, *nutshimit*, continues to draw the Innu away from the settlements, the task of education is Sisyphean. Within the standard Newfoundland school model, teachers can only teach if the young are contained in buildings and minds are applied to the lesson at hand. But here such continuous application is rare. Hence, a hesitation is apparent when the principal considers the values of the people in the community – the great love for children, the free play and independence of the young, all the childhood liberties denied by white society with its demands for disciplined dedication to work and study from the earliest possible moments. If the Innu keep these values, attendance will remain low and sporadic, and making education "more Innu" will be a moot point.

However, if the school, like the church, projects syncretism – caribou bone scrapers in glass cases and the Innu Nation flag alongside books on Newfoundland history and the Internet – then perhaps standard Newfoundland education can be delivered with less friction. By emphasizing the merging of the cultures, the school presents young Innu with a world that appears mutually constructed and consensual. Any thoughts that the villages, or indeed the school itself, might have been imposed can, at least momentarily, be suspended. Making the school "more Innu" can assist in the gentle dislodging of the binary division between the Innu, in need of instruction, and the Euro-Canadian architects of the civilizing project. This is important because the older Innu are well aware that those individuals – priests, traders, and government agents – who set out to change them did so in the conviction that Innu were somehow inferior. Any awareness of this on the part of the young Innu could be a deeply destabilizing factor in the school. To guard against the possibility of the Innu or anyone else thinking that schooling is part of a colonial mission to destroy their difference, the school presents itself as both the product of syncretism and "more Innu." According to educational sociologist Basil Bernstein (1996: 26), "the long socialization into the pedagogic code can remove the danger of the unthinkable, and of alternative realities," making such notions inconceivable.[1]

The present-day village schools have been able to bypass the words and actions of the authorities during the sedentarization phase, with its pejorative judgements and stark choices of assimilation or death that were grounds for establishing these institutions. Forty years into sedentarization, the teachers start not with *tabula rasa*, but with the raw materials to create affinity and to dissolve the binary divisions of civilization and savagery that were invoked so persistently when ending nomadic hunting was the order of the day. The school is rife with conjured symbols of incorporation that have been made to appear as affinity. The caribou bone scrapers, the drum, the skins, the moccasins are in their glass case to mark the association, to designate that they are part of a heritage that is now entrusted to the school to pass on. The objects in the glass case are now unused, dead, static. The school display helps the Innu children connect with an imagined people of the past. This is like preserving "the family Bibles without any longer believing in their content, but because of a certain poetic quality they possessed."[2] The power and sense of connection of the objects themselves are now safely encased.

The afternoon I visited the principal was designated a "sports day." The games played in the gym supplied a relief from the chasms of understanding that frequently surface in spite of the "more Innu" strategy, syncreticism, and the artfulness of the decor. Sport operated on the lowest common denominator of physical energy and amusement, a sort of bridge between the young Innu and some of their more athletic Euro-Canadian instructors. A diverse group of Innu children and adolescents were divided into teams named after North American sports outfits such as "Eagles" and "Falcons." The children lined up and raced perhaps 10 yards to a mat where they popped a balloon by jumping or sitting on it, the goal being to do this task before the other teams. The proceedings were not orderly. Children would wander off, play private games on the side, chat and laugh among themselves while the teachers tried to impose structure. Some of the children did not know which team they were on, and indeed, given their lack of proficiency in English, could not have known. Even after they burst the balloon, they sometimes did not realize they had to run back to their team. Many children did not grasp the competitive nature of the game with its divisions into opposing sides. The competitive team concept was common to many of the sports day's events. Another game consisted of children, as "Jets" and "Eagles," propelling themselves around the gym on skateboards. They also played a game called the "Owl Game," a Native, but not Innu, game. The teacher who instigated the Owl Game told me that she had tried to find an Innu game to play, but even though she consulted people in the community, she had not discovered one such pastime, although she presumed the Innu *did* have games.

However clumsily, games combine disparate sensibilities. They blend the Innu child's love of physicality with the insistence on competition as the meaningful way to channel bodily energy. They evoke nature, mixing the names of feathered creatures with the quest to win. Physical competitiveness gradually imposes itself on a people who have long rejected the kind of organized one-upmanship present in the Western approach to sports. Even when the Innu adopted North American sports like baseball, they adapted them so as to eliminate the harshness of competition that produces winners and losers. George Rich (2000: 6) explained Innu baseball in Davis Inlet:

> We only used two bases. The idea was that you had to hit the ball three times, and if you did, you had to run to the other base before somebody hit you with a ball. If the ball hit you, you were out. If a teammate got stuck at first base, it was your job to get them back, to get them back to the home base without getting hit with the ball. If the other team managed to catch your ball while in the air, your team was out. There were usually two teams but no score was kept; it was just for fun.

In the context of the school, games are light and create high spirits, breaking the laboured classroom situations where teachers must contend with endemic boredom, sporadic attendance, and cultural and linguistic misunderstandings. Such games are not so much conscious efforts to assimilate or acculturate as they have been for other Native North Americans in organized residential schools.[3] Even though competitive games bulldoze over Innu sensibilities, they function more subtly, filling in the voids and moments of doubt that arise in an enterprise that involves the conscious social

and psychological transforming of real differences into homogene-
ity. They mix fun with infantilization and bring all ages together in
the spectacle of the competition. The hard ontological questions of
colonial education – What is it to know? How can we know *this* and
not *that*? Why do "They" not answer? Why do "They" think the unthinkable? – can momentarily be forgotten.

THE REDEMPTION OF CULTURE DAYS

Since the schools in Utshimassits and Sheshatshiu have until recently been controlled and run by the Roman Catholic Church, the
same institution that played a central role in ending Innu nomadic
life, profound spiritual and cosmological conflicts necessarily come
to the fore. These have been addressed by the school redefining itself
as "more Innu." The "more Innu" program as pursued by Fleet's suc-
cessor, Steve MacDonald, meant soft-pedalling on Catholicism, in
the wake of the expulsion of the local priest after allegations of sexual abuse of a child in 1996, and promoting more Native spirituality
in the school. Tapping into New Age representations of Native American and Asian spirituality, MacDonald envisioned dream-work,
creation stories, and energy chakras in his arsenal of spiritual tools
for the young Innu. Perhaps the new "Native Christian School" could
start each day with meditation, he mused, when I spoke to him in
1996.

Enthusiastically embraced as part of what was to be yet another
short-lived leadership of the school, MacDonald pointed to "culture
days" and "life skills" programs as fortifying the Innu content of the
curriculum. One of the reasons why there is a need for "culture
days" is that the academic calendar used in the two communities
rigidly follows Newfoundland regulations and results in the school
being in session when many families would like to go to the country
(the spring and fall) and being out of session when Innu largely stay
in the settlement in the summer when blackflies, mosquitoes, and
heat make hunting prohibitive. The numerous attempts made by
the villagers to modify the school calendar for hunting activities
have fallen on deaf ears among the non-Native school administrators of the province. Even if their children do not attend school,
many Innu parents feel a certain compulsion to be present during
the school terms and to forgo opportunities to go to the country.

When they do go to the country during the school year, many
parents feel that they are perceived by *Akaneshau* teachers as preventing their children from being "educated." Thirty-year-old Greg
Pastitchi told me, "I remember the teacher saying that 'in 10 years I
can see this or that student as a manager or a leader.' He said, 'Greg

can probably do some kind of manual work.' He acted as if he knew my future. He thought I was a slow learner because my parents went to the country and I went with them, so I would be assigned to a special class. That's maybe why he thought I wouldn't do well, because I was in the country with my parents." Absences caused by going to the country often result in children missing long sequences of instruction and facing the humiliation of either being considered backward or in some instances being held back a grade. Under these pressures to stay away from the country, the Innu way of life is increasingly conveyed to young people as culture days.[4]

The "culture days" at Peenamin McKenzie that I observed were co-ordinated by Frank Phillips, a representative from the local Forestry Department, with the help of Dominic Pokue, a *Tshenu* who speaks very little English. One "life skills" classroom session for teenage pupils was on trapping and furs. It was conducted entirely in English. A video aided the presentation. As well as factual information on the seasonal variations in types of pelts and a geography lesson showing where animals are located on the map of North America, the video emphasized how pelts are measured and graded. Several computer-generated graphs presented the Innu students with "primeness curves," indicating the times of the year when pelt values peak and trough. A shot of men in suits bidding at an urban auction room was accompanied by the commentary – "grading guarantees that pelts will be sold at their true value." The "true value" was measured in units of money, not use, spirituality, hunting life, or anything else that Innu hunters would also recognize. To help the Innu students grasp the concept of "true value," an analogy was given by the white teacher. "When you go to a supermarket there is a difference between buying hamburger meat and a T-bone steak," he asserted. "The T-bone steak costs more, but it tastes better." Like the consumer goods and meat of domesticated animals in supermarkets, there are natural hierarchies within nature and these are reflected in the monetary value for which the products of nature sell. The strong implication of the presentation was that the relationship that people have to the animals is mediated through cash. Like all commodity relationships, it was essentially a materialistic connection.

The culture day functions not to reinforce pride in Innu practices, world views, or history, but to upstage them – to impose a materialistic conception of nature and to allow the Animal Gods, dreams, shamans, and other forms of spirituality to recede into the background like Dominic, an expert hunter himself, watching the video without being able to understand the commentary. Echoing this incomprehension, some of the pupils amused themselves with graffiti on the chalkboard at the back of the room. Ironic comments such as "Boring," "You won't understand nothing in here," and "You crazy Indian girl" juxtaposed themselves against the stolid Canadian earnestness of the "primeness curves," the four grades of fur from XXL to 5, and the method of measuring the pelt from the tip of the snout to the base of the tail.

Following the video presentation on pelts, instruction was carried out in the tent that Dominic and his wife Philomena had erected outside the school. While Philomena prepared caribou stew and Innu doughnuts on the sheet-metal stove, instruction on skinning actual pelts was provided in a mixture of *Innu-aimun* by Dominic and English by Frank Phillips and another *Akaneshau* instructor. Although Dominic's skinning was skilful and laced with jovial bantering with the students, most students were going about their tasks in a half-hearted way. As they took turns to remove the fur from the animals, it seemed they were not trying to do anything well or to copy Dominic's assiduous precision. Some attempts were made to impose structure, but these were largely unfocused, as knives flew about and boys and girls chased each other in and out of the tent. The scant attention paid to the lesson was broken when one of the teachers lifted up the door flap and announced "recess," taking orders for pop, candy, and potato chips. These were duly delivered and soon the tent was littered with aluminum cans and junk-food wrappers. Hardly anyone touched the caribou stew.

Culture days simulate and parody. The gulf between abstract classroom knowledge and lived and living experience, not lost on the students, makes the exercise more one of institutional self-presentation than one of Native knowledge. Culture days do not honour the Innu, so much as mark the sedentarization of the people and the domestication of nomadic hunting. To learn about *nutshimit* one must physically be in the country in much the same way as one has to see, rather than simply read, a play in order to understand theatre. To know the power of the elements, the tracks of the animals, the techniques of killing, and other skills requires an accumulated experience, not a representation of that experience in a classroom or in a tent specially constructed outside the school. Knowledge of the legends, stories, and Animal Gods, sometimes imparted to children by older people who have been asked to participate, is out of context and abstract in a school building in the community, far removed from the areas of importance to the Innu. The almost exclusive choice of the *Tshenut* on the part of the school authorities, as personal embodiments of this way of life, fixes Innu hunting in the past tense.

Although the triumph over nomadic hunting is incomplete, by simulation and parody, culture days anticipate a closure. The process, like many other simulations of Native Americans, is an attempt at the redemption of Euro-American acts of destruction. "The tragic wisdom that was once denied is now a new invention," as Vizenor (1994: 7) remarks of the film, *Dances with Wolves*, is equally applicable to the culture days. The difference is that the school system in Canada is taking no chances, anticipating the need for redemption well before there has been time to reflect on the gradual decimation of a way of life. The funerary plaudits are being mouthed while the body is still warm. What is commemorated in the culture day through its banal simulation in classrooms is the end of hunting. The students' lack of interest and derision mark the parody of Euro-Canadians instructing them on themselves. The miscreants in the classroom and tent gesture towards a refusal to be mocked and, at least momentarily, to mock the mockery.

'Culture Days' at the Peenamin Mackenzie School, Sheshatshiu. Photograph by author.

ANIMAL PEDAGOGY

Akaneshau teachers in regular classroom sessions frequently draw upon animal examples to teach children basic English language structure and composition. Besides being interesting to children in general, teachers are aware that animals are the central focus of hunting and play a large role in Innu views of the world. As with culture days, the animals are brought close, then abstracted and eventually reconfigured so that they end up being represented in ways that are often contradictory in themselves and at variance with Innu perceptions of them.

Students may eventually learn English sentence structures only through bizarre renderings of the animals that inhabit *Nitassinan*. One elementary school classroom exercise focused on "the bear." "What does the bear look like?" the teacher enthusiastically queried. This was met by blank expressions from the assembled class. "The bear looks like a ____" was then inscribed on the blackboard, further abstracting the bear from any lived context. Finally, the 13-year-old class jester, perhaps bored with the extensive prompting, broke the stalemate by announcing that "the bear looks like a moose." Amid some guffaws, this was duly written on the board and copied out by the students into their exercise books. The ice having been broken, other students joined in the construction of what were taken as hilarious absurdities. Many of their responses, by turns incoherent and playful, were reconfigured into standard English and rendered into grammatically correct but nonsensical constructions, especially in terms of how Innu would know and encounter bears in the country. Thus, another jester suggested that "Bears are mean and cruel to other animals because they are hungry." This attribution, which the teacher also asked the students to copy into their notebooks, involves the attribution of "mean and cruel" qualities to the bear that have no meaning in the hunting world where Innu encounter bears. An attribution of "mean and cruel" can only be made outside of any lived relationship with the bear because hunters would see the actions of bears as either intelligence or survival instincts.

The animals the Innu know are routinely given surreal and fantastic classroom representations – caribou eating flowers, rabbits crazy for carrots, and ducks that pray for water. The jesting shows that the children do not always passively absorb what they are being taught. They play with the images of the animals, supplanting the surrealism of the teachers with their own impromptu trickster versions. In relation to repeated questioning of junior high school students as to the sounds made by certain animals, the students played to what was expected with the dog, "ruff," the cat, "meow," until one young man authoritatively told the teacher that the owl sounds like a cow.

Animals that have no relation to the Innu or their land also feature in elementary classroom sessions, and they do so even more frequently than those that they are familiar with purely because the domesticated animals of southern agriculturists turn up as examples more often in textbooks. These animals and others will have been experienced by the children only vicariously – in their picture books, or perhaps on a nature program on television. From a very early age, Innu children are fed with a myriad of bizarre animal imagery – goats are on railroad tracks, elephants at animal fairs, monkeys jump on a bed, the adventures of the tiger-catcher's kid, and incy wincy spiders.

Another source of animal imagery is the generic Native American animals. Under the presumption that the Innu are connected to a vast pan-Indian reality, a "Native" story will sometimes be used as a lever to engage the students. In one junior high class in Utshimassits, the teacher, a fresh college graduate from Newfoundland on her first assignment, introduced a Mohawk creation story from a textbook by trying to get the students to identify the local Native groups. "What are people in Hopedale and Nain called?" she asked. "Eskimos," volunteered one student. As this was not the politically correct response, a further prompting was necessary, "What else do we call them?" "Killers," announced one boy to uproarious laughter. "Inuit" was only enunciated by the teacher, who then went on to what was closer to home. "People in Davis Inlet and Sheshatshiu are called what?" The students did not respond. "M-o-o-o-o-o-sh . . ." she prompted, but still received no answer. "Mushuau Innu, right?" Again, there was no answer. This line of inquiry must have been perplexing since at least some of the children would have known that not all people in the two communities are *Mushuau* Innu and, in fact, most in Sheshatshiu are not.

This was not the perfect entrée into the Mohawk creation story, but the story was duly read aloud and at its conclusion the teacher asked whether the students had any questions about the story. Several mumbled "No." "Was it good?" Again, the "No's" were clearly audible. The rest of the period was then devoted to a quiz about the story. Again, the students had a lot of fun with the questions. To the question, "Who makes the animals?" they variously responded, "You," "My dad," and "Jesus," the latter being dubbed "a pretty good guess" by the teacher. The dialogue proceeded in this vein as a series of questions about how the Great Creator, a deity only recently introduced to the Innu by the Roman Catholic priests, "made" certain animals the way they now appear.

In these examples, the Innu children were not passive victims of a colonial pedagogy. They resisted through their playful and witty responses to nonsensical animal juxtapositions. They mocked the mockery, and through humour survived the onslaughts on their sensibilities. As well as bringing levity to what were often tense classroom encounters, humour became an important tool of cultural survival. And so, there were similarities with the strategies of the working-class lads in Paul Willis's *Learning to Labour* (1977), a landmark ethnographic study of a school in the English Midlands in the 1970s. The "lads," constantly alert to a school standard that functioned according to the hegemonic values of the British middle class, operated to subvert the educational system that destined them for failure. Like the Innu, one of the techniques that the lads used was humour. As Willis (1977: 29) relates, "the 'laff' is a multi-faceted implement of extraordinary importance in the counter-school culture." Humour is used "to defeat boredom and fear, to overcome hardship and problems – as a way out of almost anything." But the young Innu, unlike Willis's "lads," do not end up "learning to labour." Their acts of resistance are purely momentary, helping them survive ontological assaults of the moment.

ASHAMED TO BE INNU

Formal schooling is seen almost universally in the Western world as a necessity for the continuation of orderly society and the transmission of knowledge. Although inheritances of wealth and status count for a lot, education is still one of the most important determinants of the life chances of individuals. In Newfoundland and Labrador, very few non-Innu parents would disregard education, and although they may be critical of particular facets of their local school, there is no disagreement that schools are a fundamental requirement of economic and civic life.

This is not so for the Innu. Almost every adult in both Innu communities in Labrador is apprehensive about schooling. Many Innu think that little is learned in school about who the Innu are and believe that the school itself is a tool of both cultural assimilation and culture loss. According to this view, not only do the teachers provide misinformation about who the Innu are, but schooling encourages children to adopt values that run counter to those that are important to the Innu and that have collectively sustained them as a people. Although there are some exceptions, many Innu parents admit that, in one form or another, the school is attempting to

transform their children into *Akaneshaut,* white children. "The
school has done a lot of damage to our culture and our children,"
opens the discussion of the school in Davis Inlet in *Gathering Voices*
(Innu Nation, 1995: 65).

> It has really changed our lives. The school is not working as it is
> supposed to. The biggest problem is that our children are not learn-
> ing their culture in school. They are learning the white culture. This
> is a foreign culture. The school has prevented us from learning our
> own history. Too many of our children are dropping out.

This refers to the 1990s, but Apenam Pone, speaking of his school
days 30 years earlier, echoes this theme:

> Instead of being proud of my grandparents, I learned to be proud of
> the Queen. She doesn't even live in Canada . . . . I learned to disre-
> spect the elders. It was more important to listen to white teachers
> and priests than to the elders. They were to be respected as knowl-
> edgeable. The priest was "a man of God." I thought that what I had
> to know was what the school taught me. Kids today are the same;
> they think the elders are not educated.

Several people to whom we spoke as part of the Sheshatshiu
Innu band council study in 1999 made the point that the effect of the
school has been to erode the sense of being Innu among the young
people of the community. Because formal schooling instructs children in the subjects that are seen as important in Newfoundland
and the wider Canadian society, it socializes them primarily as Canadians and reinforces an image of them as "minorities" in Canada,
under the all-embracing authority of the Queen.

Many Innu remembered the first days of school as a kind of "culture shock." Suddenly, they were placed in a strange environment,
their freedoms were curtailed, they were removed from their parents, and they were addressed in a foreign language. Soon they
discovered that they would be physically punished for behaviour
that was accepted and tolerated in their homes. In the first two decades of the settlement, teachers punished them simply for not being
able to adequately learn the subjects being taught. For example, Father Pirson required children to memorize passages from the Bible.
If they did not do this or were not able to do it faithfully, many Innu of
this generation, as we saw in the previous chapter, were beaten with
sticks and other objects. The objective of Pirson and the school
authorities was to inculcate Euro-Canadian beliefs and values as
rapidly as possible. This meant that it was not simply academic
knowledge that had to be conveyed, but manners and attitudes towards the care of the self. Thus, in the 1960s and 1970s Euro-
Canadian ideals of hygiene, cleanliness, and appearance were en-

forced upon the Innu children as if they were prison inmates. Several people remembered being told to drink a foul-tasting brown liquid in bottles issued to them every morning. It was not explained to them at the time, but this was probably cod liver oil. Others remembered being given pills, probably vitamins, and powder for lice each morning. Some former students said that teachers would remark on how bad they smelled, and this was at the time when very few households had any running water.

At a very basic level, the school contains a linear rhythm and an enforcement of discipline that the Innu not only experience as difficult to adjust to, but find alien and even absurd. Parents must make sure that their children, those who attend the school, arrive "on time." That is, they must adhere to a notion of time that is divorced from the landscape and from lived experience. School time, as time in the European world more generally, is abstracted as hours in the day, marked off according to the hands on the clock. The school system demands that children and teachers be at the school at a certain hour rather than according to other factors such as their own feelings, the weather, and the disposition of others. Related to this, punishment is used to enforce not only punctuality, but also other desired behaviours in a way that is foreign to almost all Innu households. In general, Innu parents are very reluctant to discipline their children in the way that Euro-Canadians, especially Newfoundlanders, who have made up the bulk of the teaching corps, do. Most parents regard their children, even the very young, as autonomous agents. While they express love and affection in abundance, the Innu method of learning has been via direct experience and imitation rather than verbal injunctions or punishments. In the school, however, while discipline is now more subtle and verbal in character, it is still tied to a negative behaviourist understanding of how human beings work. If desired actions are not forthcoming, punishments, or the withholding of privileges, are used as inducements.

Of all the subjects taught, history was perhaps most vividly recalled by the first generation to experience schooling in Sheshatshiu. History consisted of heroic tales of European explorers such as Christopher Columbus and John Cabot, and then funnelled down to the more local history of Newfoundland where they were taught the finer points of fishing lore, the design of schooners, the sale of cod, the tune and lyrics to the "Ode to Newfoundland," and the political accomplishments of former Newfoundland Premier Joey Smallwood. In effect, they were, as one woman put it, "taught a lie." She continued, "my grandchildren are still taught about John Cabot, even though we teach them differently. The kids find it confusing." For several decades Innu children were taught that their descendants were merely "discovered" and that the most important events of the past were the dramas of explorers and settlers. The message students derived from the absence of any significant teaching of Innu history, the Innu way of life, Innu views of the world, and Innu achievements was that their parents and ancestors were barely worthy of consideration.

Greg Pastitchi said that he was "made to feel ashamed to be Innu." His schooling led him to believe that there was something shameful about being Innu because it attached so much importance to Newfoundland and world history and none to the history of the Innu. It was the history and development of fisheries, the single economic focus of the Newfoundland settlers, that Greg felt the teachers regarded as most important. He remembered being given an exercise in which he had to describe a schooner in 100 words or less, but, as he said, "I was not given an opportunity to learn my own history." Only some years later when an Innu history course was offered at a local college did he learn from a student who attended it the genealogies of the families in Sheshatshiu, including his own.

Many people in the first generation to grow up in the settlements looked back regretfully at how their education concentrated on the Newfoundland and Labrador settlers' experiences at the expense of Innu history. Likewise, the indoctrination both of Christianity and of science highlight Innu world views, not just as different, but as backward and prior. This was often conveyed, not by any overt criticism of Innu history and society, as it was by the early missionaries, but through omission. Members of the younger generation who have recently finished their schooling or who dropped out also expressed similar sentiments, feeling that they would have liked to have learned more subjects relevant to the Innu way of life. One young man said that he got the distinct impression at the school that the Innu way of life was hardly worth living and that it was much better to stay in the community than to be in the country. In effect, the first generation in the settlement missed out on knowing their history by omission. The second generation, currently in the schools, is learning Innu history as a confused pan-Indian spectacle, further distorted through the lens of some of the Newfoundland teachers who are only dimly aware of Innu history and supplemented by the theatrical quality of culture days.

The presentation of the jumbled pictures of who the Innu are occurs not only through the staging of culture days, but when the *Akaneshau* teachers fumble around to present a picture of the Innu to the Innu. Due to a lack of textual material on the Innu in English (there is a great deal more in French produced by the Innu schools on the North Shore), images, stories, and legends from other peoples, often Iroquois or Plains Indians, are produced. While there are some parallels between these peoples, the many differences are overlooked and certain perversities occur. Even when the Innu teaching aides teach *Innu-aimun*, they are often required to provide illustrations in which Innu are shown as generic "Indians" wearing feather headdresses.[5]

Child's classroom exercise drawing. Peenamin Mackenzie School, Sheshatshiu.

Only when the students became teenagers did some realize that they had lost something of value. If they did not go to the country, their continued exposure to the English-speaking world, in the school and elsewhere, created a bewildering array of images of Innu identity. As this exposure continued, some began to feel increasingly removed from any concept of Innu uniqueness and their ability to express themselves in *Innu-aimun* was compromised by not being able to go to the country where the language is most vital. Thus, one man in his twenties said, "I am ashamed to say that I went to the school at all . . . I wasted my years in school." Another man in his late thirties said that it changed the way he thinks. It made him "think English" and gave him "white thoughts," leading him to prefer the non-Innu way of life with its technologies and conveniences. He found this regrettable, saying that "I lost part of my life." The sense of losing something of one's history and identity that can never be reclaimed was an overwhelming sentiment. For many people, the end result of this process was not a smooth "integration" into Canadian society, but a kind of double bind. One young woman expressed this as a conflict between the *Akaneshau* and Innu ways of thinking, leading to a constant struggle within, as if she had two selves that she had to alternately turn on and off. She was judged by *Akaneshau* for her facilities in English and potential to obtain a job, while the *Tshenut* had very different expectations of her.

Along with the desire to make the school "more Innu," the school authorities claim to be teaching "both cultures," as one principal put it. While Innu parents are often not able to evaluate fully the Euro-Canadian content of the curriculum, many believe that it is inadequate and nearly everyone regards the presentation of Innu reality as bizarre and distorted. A deep cynicism pervades about the professed aim of teaching children in the ways of both cultures. Confused as to what kind of Innu cultural knowledge is being imparted in the school, many parents say that only *Akaneshau* knowledge is being taught. For example, the Innu teaching aides in Sheshatshiu observed that the school helps children only in the ways of one culture. For them, whatever Innu content the school had was not Innu. Although they were Innu themselves and actually taught much of it, they freely admitted that the school cannot represent what it is to be Innu.

This distortion arises not only from learning in the abstract, away from lived experience, but because the juxtaposition of Euro-Canadian manners and Innu realities tends to cast the latter in an unreal and often pejorative context. As Greg Andrew, a former Chief of Sheshatshiu told me, "the only thing that kids are able to learn in school is to be embarrassed by our culture." Similarly, Simeon Tshakapesh of Utshimassits recalled that "I was ashamed of who I was. I didn't want my parents to come to school wearing moccasins." The manners, dress, and sensibility of the teachers naturally impress themselves upon the children. Differences between teachers, who, for example, usually wear clean and different clothes every day, and the parents, who generally do not, is easily taken by Innu parents to be emblematic of their inadequacy within the world that their children are operating within.

EXTINGUISHING INNU-AIMUN

As Innu children are increasingly exposed to the school, each generation's oral facility in the Innu language has diminished. Many Innu believe that this is because the school has heavily biased instruction in *Akaneshau* subjects in the medium of the English language. "Because education was forced upon us," began one

Tshenu, "we have lost our heritage and culture. The school has had a damaging effect because of the lack of Innu teachers. There's a lot more *Akaneshau* teachers teaching the *Akaneshau* way. Because of this the language is being lost, and we're losing it fast." The imbalance between English and Innu language instruction in the school leads many parents to feel that they are unable to communicate with their children. With ever more exposure to the Euro-Canadian world through the school and the mass media, young people are increasingly unable to communicate with those who have a knowledge of the pre-settlement world. This leads them to attend and respond to the non-Innu cultural forms – sports, television, fast food – which in the community have become more immediate.[6] As with the middle-aged woman quoted in the following passage, many older Innu feel that in the context of the imposed settlement, gains their children make in English coincide with losses of *Innu-aimun* and Innu values:

> When kids go to school an emphasis should be on how they treat their parents. Kids now talk back to parents. That comes from the school. They don't pay attention at all. They don't listen to parents because in school they get a lot of English. They are gradually losing their language. Kids are starting to talk to each other in English.

At a more fundamental level, however, *Innu-aimun* is a language that developed from, and relates to, the activities of the Innu as nomadic hunters of the Labrador-Quebec peninsula. Its vocabularies are tied to place, landscape, animals, and techniques of survival. It contains words and phrases for which there are no direct translations in English. Many of these are associated with the landscape – the flow of rivers, the solidity of ice, the body parts of animals, and so forth. Other vocabularies are needed to understand how to make and use the tools that Innu require in the country, such as the chisel, the crooked knife, the salmon spear, and the many forms of snowshoes. While more effective European devices have replaced some of these tools, many Innu implements, as well as snowshoes and moccasins remain more practical. Yet other vocabularies articulate the vital spiritual relationship that maintains between hunters and the land and animals. In addition, grammatical structures, syntax, and other language categories, if not unique to *Innu-aimun*, substantially differ from English.

When *Innu-aimun* is transferred into the villages, many of the basic categories, rules of correspondence between words and things, colloquialisms, humour, metaphors, and meanings no longer hold. A whole host of cultural, conceptual, and cognitive dilemmas surface when *Innu-aimun* is taught in the school in the earliest grades by Innu teaching aides. There is a certain existential absurdity in the learning of *Innu-aimun*, the language of a dynamic and mobile hunting society, in the confines of a classroom in a village. Learning the Innu language in the school involves stripping words and expressions of their referents, since what is being referred to in the language often does not exist in the community. And, conversely, many of the words and concepts that are central to village life have no equivalent in *Innu-aimun*.

Efforts to teach *Innu-aimun* in the classroom salvage something of Innu identity in the younger generations, but this entails the huge compromise of learning *Innu-aimun* away from experience in the country, where the language originated and where meaning relates to concrete situations. The Innu teaching aides at the Peenamin McKenzie School believed that if English was also being learned, *Innu-aimun*, even the watered-down version necessary for classroom teaching, would not be inculcated as strongly. They recognized that the colonial relations between Canada and the Innu extended to the relations between English and *Innu-aimun*. Although *Innu-aimun* is still the first language in Innu households, English is the more practical language for communicating many of the most important aspects of a villager's life.

Innu-aimun is at the vortex of a host of political processes. While there have been few outright attempts to eradicate it, as there were with other Native North American languages through boarding schools, the imposition of the settlement itself, as well as the church and English as the medium for school instruction, made it less important to the younger generations of Innu. The assimilation drive in Labrador at mid-twentieth century was predicated on the notion that in order to function in employment, at the very least, English would be needed. *Innu-aimun*, if it ever was considered, would have been an irrelevance to those who worked to transform the Innu. In this context, the Innu language is an inheritance from a way of life that has been depicted as archaic and largely irrelevant to the future of Innu schoolchildren in Canadian society.

The indigenous tongue is more than a medium of communication, it is a central element of cultural survival, and since colonialism is concerned with the overturning of cultural difference the language is an object of broader political processes that both explicitly and tacitly, have undermined Innu self-confidence. I am suggesting that there is an intimate connection between this sabotage and the gradual relegation of particular ways of thinking, orientations to space and time, and a number of assumptions about the world.[7] With Keith Basso (1996: 69), I would argue that "there is a need for an expanded view of linguistic competence in which beliefs about the world occupy a central place." This does not mean that a creative bilingualism or hybridization will not occur, only that severing *Innu-aimun* from *nutshimit* against a backdrop of aggressive assimilation pressures is likely to have profound effects on both the richness of the language itself and on how young Innu think about themselves and the world.

More generally, schooling creates cultural duality or double consciousness in young Innu. While cultural diversity in other settings can be a positive experience, broadening the horizons of the young, fostering toleration and open-mindedness, young people in Sheshatshiu and Utshimassits must bear some profound cognitive and ideological contradictions. As novice English-speakers, they learn about a Euro-Canadian society of which much is gleaned vicariously through television or else experienced through the settler cultures of Goose Bay and Newfoundland. But as Innu, they are connected to, but cut off from, the way of life of their parents and grandparents. The pervasive feeling, nonetheless, is that the cultural importation of Euro-Canada via the school and the media actually banishes what is important about being Innu. As Elizabeth Penashue of Sheshatshiu remarked about the impact of the school:

> The school here is very important. It has too much stuff inside it and Innu culture gets driven outside. Kids go to school everyday. But when they have reached 16 years, the kids will have lost everything. They will be just like white people. Me, I never have accidents in the country. I'm afraid that they [young people] will get lost and die or have accidents in the bush. Now, the little ones speak too much English. English is in the head. I'm not saying that English is unimportant. But, some kids don't want to go to the country. They feel shame to say they are Innu. White teachers push too much for them to be like white people. Everything is white; school books are all white, animals in books are monkeys, whales, horses, and cows.

Everything may be "white," but this offers no avenues of contentment or advancement to the young Innu. Their double consciousness, a parallel to W.E.B. DuBois's (1969: 45) memorable description in his essay on post-slavery black identity, leads the young Innu to "see himself through the revelation of another world." Eventually, DuBois (ibid., 47) believed "the would-be black *savant*" would not be able "to articulate the message of another people," and "this seeking to satisfy unreconciled ideals has wrought sad havoc with the courage and faith and ideals of ten thousand people," making them "ashamed of themselves." The Innu teaching aides are at the centre of this double consciousness. They risk failing at conveying both Innu and Euro-Canadian knowledge, since the official terms of what constitutes knowledge for both are set by the structures of the school itself and the *Akaneshau* educational authorities. They risk ending up like DuBois's (ibid., 46) black *savants* as "poor crafts-men," having "but half a heart in either cause."

Mindful of the need to pay attention to the Innu language, but adding to the general cultural confusion, it is the task of the Innu teaching aides to compose English – *Innu-aimun* "dictionaries" and translate English textbooks. In Sheshatshiu this job is delegated to Francesca Snow and Judy Hill. They feel that they are treated like "robots" by the school authorities, who assume that the task of translation is largely literal and unproblematic. Working with noth-ing except inherited Canadian textbooks and their Native tongue, the only possible result of their efforts is a certain bastardization of the Innu view of the world as conveyed in language. Innu words for colour, for example, change according to context – is it moving? still? animate? inanimate? alive? dead? Colours, of course, are fairly ba-sic concepts in the English language and are vivid and evocative means of teaching children how to use the language. But in *Innu-aimun* there are no separate categories for colours. It is easy to see that this could lead to the diminution of *Innu-aimun*, as it is simpler for children to remember one word for a colour than the complexities of colour specification by context. If this persists, then *Innu-aimun* will be reduced and Anglicized because the way of learning inherent to the school system presupposes the grammatical and syntactic structures as well as the perceptual divisions encouraged by Eng-lish. Furthermore, the switch from learning a language through constant engagement with a world that it expresses to learning it by books is likely to further reduce the emphasis on oral transmission. Rasmussen (2000a: 23), in his study of the effects of education on the Inuit of Nunavut, claims that the emphasis on book learning en-courages the decline of orature. Because personal memory of language, place, and events is so vital for peoples who pass down knowledge orally, the introduction of alphabetization and literacy-based schooling also necessarily contributes to the "atrophying of memory, and a loss of personal connection to relevant history."

The profound forms of knowledge of *Nitassinan* contained in Innu thought and *Innu-aimun* vocabularies are becoming lost, as the generation of men and women who were born and raised in the country slip into old age. Young people are constantly found wanting in their own language because they have learned *Innu-aimun* pri-marily in the context of the villages. Older people and those who spend more time in the country are keen to notice these gaps. "A lot of kids have lost or forgot or don't know the name of things in Innu," said Simeon Tshakapesh, a relatively young man himself. "They don't know how to say 'chisel' or 'crooked knife,' and they don't learn anything about Innu culture in school. There are four names for boughs, for example."

At the same time as Innu vocabularies are being lost, terminology from completely alien traditions and geographical spaces is introduced and restated in *Innu-aimun*. Holidays such as Halloween and Christmas provide focal points for learning at the Peenamin McKenzie Shool. Francesca Snow and Judy Hill participate in these even though they say they do not believe in them. At these times, they are busy translating words such as "pumpkin," "witch," and "virgin birth." They must also work on translations for the picture-book presentations of animate and inanimate objects, the vast majority of which have no presence or relevance to the experience of the students or their families. In one book that I perused the first five examples of words beginning with the letter "C" were "castle," "cabbage," "cauliflower," "caravan," and "chapati."

The promotion of these unfamiliar vocabularies in the village schools inevitably leads to curious, and often unkind, juxtapositions with the experience of the children. Forcing relationships between words and concepts that have little connection with Innu life at best creates a kind of incomprehension, but at worst results in the shaming of the students because, in not being able to relate to particular words or ideas, they are exposed as ignorant and somehow wanting in what is taken for granted in the settler society. To parry these attacks on their selfhood, the children were often silent or made nonsensical responses to classroom questioning. I witnessed many occasions when children were exposed and embarrassed in this way. For example, in an attempt to elicit the word "cream" in a sentence completion exercise, the following dialogue took place:

Teacher: What do you put in your coffee?
Student: I don't know, miss.
Teacher: Sugar and what?
Student: I don't know.
Teacher: Haven't you ever had coffee in a restaurant?
Student: (No response)
Teacher: Or, your mom, what does she use?
Student: Milk?
Teacher: What's another word for milk?
Student: I don't know.
Teacher: Cre-e-e...
Student: Cream.

The word "cream" was finally uttered, but only after the student had been exposed by the teacher's questioning. As a young person, he probably did not drink much coffee, yet it was assumed that he did. Because he probably did not drink it often, if at all, he had little experience of putting anything in coffee. Hence, his truthful answers. Yet, "I don't know" is rarely a satisfactory answer in the school and this may be a reason why many students opt for the surreal. The embarrassment was then transformed into humiliation by asking whether the young boy had coffee in a restaurant. There are no restaurants in Sheshatshiu, and eating in restaurants is well beyond the welfare budgets of most Innu families. Even when they may treat themselves to food out in Goose Bay, this would generally be at a fast-food outlet rather than a sit-down restaurant. Contrary to what the teacher takes as a commonplace activity, this child is exposed as someone who does not eat in restaurants. Finally, the correct answer is only elicited with the aid of a false analogy – cream is milk – and parroting the sound of the word.

As Western cultural and political dominance and, along with it, the English language spread over virtually the entire globe, rationalistic knowledge of the cosmos has been accorded most relevance in thinking about global problems. Colonization of peoples like the Innu, the introduction of schooling, and the displacement of peoples from the land precipitate an untold diminution of the diverse ways humans understand the world. Observing recent trends among the Inuit in the High Arctic, Barry Lopez (1986: 277) noted that "whole areas of the language are starting to disappear because they refer to activities no longer much practiced, like traveling with dogs; or to the many different parts of the animal like the walrus which are no longer either eaten or used; or to activities that are discouraged, such as the intercession of shamans." If local languages are increasingly split apart from the landscapes in which they were long associated, our collective human knowledge rooted in place also diminishes. When indigenous knowledge is simply transliterated into Western languages and materialist modes of thought, it will become more difficult, as Nancy Lord (1996) points out, "to ask and answer the tough questions about how the human and non-human can live together in a tolerant and dignified way." If linguistic anthropologists such as Daniel Nettle (1999: 113) are correct in their projections that at least 100,000 speakers are needed for a language to survive "the cultural-economic juggernauts," almost 84 per cent of the world's languages, including *Innu-aimun*, are at risk.

SOCIALIZATION INTO A VOID

Few children attend the school with the regularity required for it to function as it is supposed to – as a socializing agent of local populations within a larger social order. On weekdays when the school is in session, most children in Sheshatshiu are out playing in the streets or watching television in their homes. On days when there is plenty of snow for sliding, there are often more students at the Nukum Mani Shan School in Utshimassits playing on the roof of the school than inside the classrooms. In the spring, especially, a large proportion of the pupils are in the country. Innu parents are generally non-directive towards their children attending school, neither encouraging nor discouraging. Given the choice, many children opt to stay away from school, attending erratically. Although few graduate from high school and attendance at all levels is sporadic, virtually all children are exposed to the school for much of their childhood and adolescence. Despite low attendance, the school has a palpable presence in the community.

The dropout rate from the school is astronomic for a variety of reasons. In the course of carrying out the research for the Sheshatshiu Innu band council study in 1999, we were told by several Innu that they had quit school as a result of the physical and sexual abuse they experienced or witnessed at school. Others quit because they saw no point in what they were learning. The school curriculum neither prepared them for jobs in the local economy nor facilitated their ability to perform in *nutshimit* and to think as an Innu person. Few students could see how they could become doctors or lawyers, or how, even with a high school diploma, they would obtain a job in Goose Bay. The vast bulk of the jobs open to people from Sheshatshiu remain office jobs in the band council or Innu Nation, and these jobs are both limited in number and often conferred through family ties. Throughout the 1990s, many teenage girls quit school when they became pregnant.

As an illustration of a typical pattern of school enrolment, Figure 1 shows the progress of the 38 students who began kindergarten in 1986. Enrolment remained fairly stable until the sixth grade, when there were seven students less than the previous year. There is an apparent rise in Grade 8, but this is accounted for by the ungraded system in operation at Peenamin McKenzie. The 61 students listed for that year are junior high students spread over several years, and do not necessarily relate to the original cohort. Assuming that students progressed from one year to the next, only one of the original 38 graduated in 1998 from Grade 12. However, we know that only rarely does a student move through the school system in this fash-ion. Rather, progress is more haphazard, so that even the few who do graduate usually do so at a more advanced age than might other-wise be expected as a result of dropping out for periods of time.

Figure 1: Enrolment of Cohort that started Kindergarten in 1986 to Grade 12 in 1998, Peenamin McKenzie School

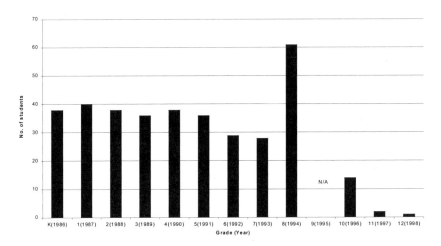

There is very little to say about graduation other than the fact that a tiny fraction of the overall student-age population of Sheshat-shiu graduate from Peenamin McKenzie School. Figure 2 compares the high school retention rates with those of other schools in the province.

Figure 2: High School Retention Rates at Peenamin McKenzie as Compared with Provincial Schools, 1990-1997

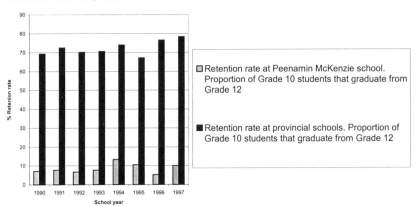

One of the most obvious features of Peenamin McKenzie School is the low level of attendance. The typical school year starts with a large enrolment, which at the end of the 1990s was close to 360. After the first few weeks attendance steadily drops off, with sharper declines in the spring when many children join their families in the hunting camps. By the end of the school year only a fraction of those enrolled are attending. Some teachers literally have no students to teach in May and June. Attendance is not only low but erratic, with students attending almost randomly.

Figure 3: Monthly Attendance Report for Peenamin McKenzie, 1997-98

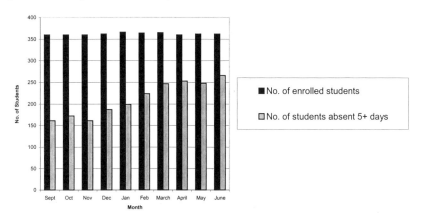

Figure 4: Attendance Rate for 1984-85 and 1997-98, Peenamin McKenzie School

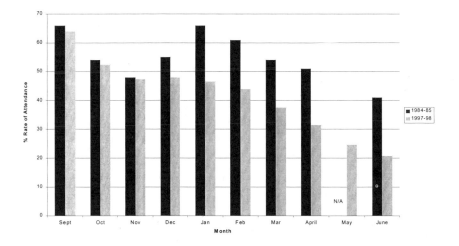

Figure 3 shows the monthly attendance at the school for the 1997-98 academic year. Over that year enrolment remained stable, while absenteeism, as measured by the number of students absent for five days or more during each month, increased steadily throughout the school year. Over the year, as Figure 4 indicates, attendance started off at about 64 per cent, then declined month after month, plummeting in the spring and ending up in June with a rate of just 20 per cent. I have incorporated into Figure 4 the attendance rates at Peenamin McKenzie for the 1984-85 academic year that Ryan (1988a: 15) calculated. These show that there has been no improvement over time. In fact, when we compare attendance rates between the years 1984-85 and 1997-98, rates were consistently higher in 1984-85, especially for the period from January to June. Double the proportion of students were attending in June 1985 than in June 1998.

One of the consequences of the low level of attendance is that children are being socialized in ways that have no clear precedents and for a society that has yet to be clearly defined. *Tshenut* are adamant that in the past Innu effectively socialized young people in *nutshimit*. Children were with their mothers and fathers over a long period of time. Thus, girls would watch their mothers undertaking such tasks as collecting boughs, making tents, setting snares, fishing, making moccasins, webbing snowshoes, and cooking. Boys would watch their fathers practise firearm safety, hunting different kinds of animals, making snowshoe frames, and setting up camp. In contrast to the general social and familial stability of Innu life in the country, in the villages there are a large number of Innu households where one or both parents are, at least periodically, heavy drinkers. In these families, children often get little or no direction, must fend for themselves, do not eat regularly, and have erratic sleep patterns. Under the circumstances, the values expected by the school – punctuality, attention to lessons, and orderliness – are difficult if not impossible to conform to. Some of these families regularly go to the country, and this means that some socialization in the Innu hunting world can be achieved before the return – often descent – to the village. Other families, more common in Sheshatshiu than Davis Inlet, are stranded in the villages for long periods with no employment, little security, and few diversions except bingo and drinking.

Thus, many Innu children are not being socialized through any established cultural process. A vast number of children are denied the opportunity to be socialized as Innu because they do not go to the country, or only do so infrequently, and at the same time their sporadic attendance at the school ensures that they are not socialized to function in Canadian society. They are, in effect, in a kind of social and psychological void, simply surviving as best they can and drifting from one pastime to another. Because many children faced long stretches of time at home, one means by which young Innu are being socialized is through television. Many homes have satellite hook-ups that allow for a more or less continuous diet of North American talk shows, game shows, videos, computer games, and action films. Television, like schooling, is widely perceived by Innu adults as inculcating materialistic values and encouraging young people to aspire to a non-Native lifestyle that none will have the means to achieve without going to school, and as the experience of many Innu testify, even this is no guarantee. Many people believe that television influences young people to believe that the values of North American society, including violent retribution, greed for money and material possessions, and the ideals of romantic love are normal and preferable to the values that Innu people have for sharing, generosity, and an outdoor hunting lifestyle. As one woman interviewed for the schooling study said:

> our children now get the white man's negative influence, which is affecting their attitudes and mood. It was different when I went to school. There was less TV, and no computer games. These things make children aggressive. Kids are now talking back to their parents. They do things their own way now.

Several people observed that children are often up until the early hours of the morning watching television. As a result, it is difficult for them to adapt to the rhythms of any day with a purpose. Both television and schooling are seen by some *Tshenut* as part of the same process of assimilation, functioning to encourage young people to lose interest in Innu skills and the Innu way of life. Tshenish Pasteen, for example, pointed out that children take television to be more real than hunting. Many Innu adults believe that the values imparted by the North American mass media lead people to become selfish, and this creates the sustained interpersonal conflict that has become a prominent feature of village life. In one of my conversations with him, Tshenish drew a straight line between television and social implosion – suicides, divorce, infidelity.

THE TEACHERS' WORLD

As part of the Sheshatshiu Innu band council study in 1999, I interviewed the teachers at Peenamin McKenzie School in groups. The non-Innu teaching staff openly discussed a number of problems they believed the school faces. Despite a lot of frustrations, most of the teachers said they enjoyed their work, were proud to be working with young Innu, and found the Innu students especially bright. Some pointed out how talented Innu students were in oral and visual tasks.

On the whole, the staff did not believe that the school was providing a lower standard of education than other comparable schools. However, they did indicate that Peenamin McKenzie faced particular difficulties that were fairly unique, partly because they were teaching a student body whose second language was English. The lack of proficiency in English was highlighted as a major obstacle to the achievements of the students. Until recently, teaching from kindergarten to Grade 3 was entirely in *Innu-aimun*. Some students may not have been required to converse in and comprehend English until Grade 4 at the age of 9 or 10. As the children had not been expected before this age to have a command of English, either orally or verbally, the teachers pointed out that young Innu lack the basics of many other subjects on the curriculum.

Because most of the subjects taught presume sequential learning – mastery over a subject through a gradual accumulation of knowledge that must be completed in a logical order – the low rates of attendance were identified by the teachers as the greatest impediment to effective teaching. The patterns of low and sporadic attendance made teaching particularly taxing for them and futile for the students. In any given class teachers might be faced with students who attend every day, others who come in once a week or month, and yet others who turn up only when there are special activities such as sports, swimming, skating, Christmas concerts, and the like. Because the teachers must deal with students at widely differing stages in the sequence of learning, it was impossible for them to use a general lesson plan. On any given day, some students in a classroom would be at the level that others were at on the first day of school. This pattern generally became exacerbated as the school year proceeded and meant that teachers were often attending to individual students instead of teaching the class.

As noted earlier, attendance dips gradually as the school year proceeds, so it is commonplace, as one primary teacher explained, to start off with 30 students in a class and be left with two in the spring. By May and June, some teachers have almost no students to teach. Some teacher aides spent many hours in the staff room idling on the computer as a result of the scarcity of students. Many of the teachers felt that the low and sporadic attendance of the majority of students negatively affected the morale of other students who attended regularly. The tendency of parents to bring their children who very rarely attended to graduation ceremonies, Christmas concerts, and public sports events where achievement was honoured was said to have a similar effect on those students who were regular attenders.

Despite the low level of attendance, teachers admitted that students passed from one level to the next fairly fluidly. One teacher used the example of a student who had missed four years of schooling and was currently in Grade 10. Teachers confronted a particular dilemma at the end of each year when they must decide whether students who had hardly attended should pass from one level to another. In order to spare the feelings of many students, teachers end up passing those who had hardly appeared at school. As one teacher put it, "What do you do, keep them back even though they are 17 years old in Grade 8?"

The low rate of attendance also negatively affected the morale of teachers. One teacher described how he sometimes had to wait in the hallways for a single student to appear to populate his classroom. The teachers realized that spring hunting accounted for a large number of their absentees, but they primarily attributed the attendance patterns to a lack of value placed on education by the Innu parents. The teachers believed that the problem stemmed from parents' allowing children a choice as to whether or not to go to school. Thus, instead of attending school "eight-year-olds often choose to stay home and watch movies all day long," as one teacher put it. Fuelling this belief that the Innu parents were non-committal or even apathetic about education was the observation that only a small fraction of parents attended the parent-teacher meetings. Teachers said that they had made every effort to make parents feel welcome, but despite this only a handful of parents came to the meetings. The low level of homework completion was also a concern of the teachers. Some believed that there might be either cultural factors or problems in the home environments that prevented students from doing homework. The lack of homework completion was partly attributed to a different orientation to time and work among the Innu. The teachers also believed that, to a certain extent, the band council encouraged students not to attend school by sponsoring volleyball and hockey teams to tour Quebec during school time. They noted that after such tours, some students lose the momentum they had built up at school and simply stopped going.

Almost as grave a problem as low attendance, in the teachers' view, was "poor communication." Teachers indicated that they had sent out letters and made phone calls in an attempt to involve community groups such as the band council and the Innu Nation, but these bodies had ignored their requests. They felt that the various activities and deliberations of the Local Education Committee (LEC) of the band council were not relayed to them. Therefore, they could not benefit from any insights that the committee might have gained from its various activities. For example, members of the LEC had toured band council-controlled schools in Quebec, but none of the findings of this tour were relayed to the teachers at the Peenamin McKenzie School. Within the school, communication between *Akaneshau* teachers and Innu teacher aides, although not entirely strained, was not fluid and open. One teacher described the physical separation of Innu and *Akaneshau* teachers in the school as a kind of "apartheid."

All of the non-Native teachers expressed a strong desire to know more about the community, the Innu as a people, the Innu language, and Innu child-rearing beliefs and practices. Many times in the school day they were presented with behaviour that they did not understand. Teachers enthusiastically embraced the idea of a thorough cultural orientation, including exposure to *nutshimit*. One teacher noted that during her time in Davis Inlet, the leaders took her and other teachers into the country. This gave them a much-needed exposure to a highly valued feature of Innu life. Another somewhat frustrated teacher asked, "why can't we be taught *Innu-aimun* at lunch times?" The teachers' opinions were to a large extent understandable. As Euro-Canadians, they found themselves in an alien environment that they knew little about. Some of them were newly trained teachers. Many were genuinely curious about the Innu and sincerely believed that more knowledge of all things Innu would help them in their work.

In the context of low attendance and support from the Innu community that was lukewarm at best and hostile at worst, it was almost impossible for the school to act according to any strategy or plan. Its administration lurched from year to year with little planning. Teacher turnover was high at all levels. Records were not kept according to any standard method of bookkeeping, but rather were randomly deposited in boxes in the school basement. Between 1995 and 2000 there were five principals, some of whom were appointed through last-ditch phone calls just before the beginning of the school year. Consequently, there was little continuity of policies and virtually no meaningful leadership in the school, which of course depressed morale and made it more difficult to establish any genuine connections between the community and the school. It also meant that individual staff members were not accountable to the community for any extended length of time. Teaching assignments at Peenamin McKenzie were often brief.

Almost all *Akaneshau* teachers lived in Goose Bay. There was hardly any interest in extramural activities. One teacher indicated that virtually no staff – Innu or non-Innu – would volunteer to participate in such activities. The successful Sheshatshiu youth hockey team was organized and run with little or no support from the school or any of the staff.

While nearly all *Akaneshau* teachers expressed a general bewilderment towards the Innu, some, at least in private, confessed to a feeling that their work was basically irrelevant. After a biology class on sense receptors a high school teacher admitted that what he had just patiently outlined was of little meaning to his students. One young teacher in Davis Inlet told me that the students felt threatened by the English language because it was not their own. "They don't own it," she said. "If someone was trying to change me, I'd feel threatened too." Teachers realized that although their knowledge of the Innu was at best fragmentary, they were responsible for educating Innu children into accommodating to a world that was by turns distant and bizarre, through the medium of a language that is still not spoken to any appreciable extent in Innu households. However jarring this realization might be, it was usually tinged with a kind of grim fatalism – that is, that things could be no other way. One cannot go back to the "old world," as the biology teacher put it.

The teachers' frustrations were understandable, yet teachers with whom I spoke rarely showed any appreciation of the history of Innu schooling, although several M.A. and Ph.D. dissertations have been written on the subject (Ryan, 1988a; Heimbecker, 1994; Schuurman, 1994). Had they taken account of the fact that the schools were intended as instruments of assimilation and denied young Innu their own histories, and at the same time often subjected them to physical and sexual abuse, the Innu reactions to the school would have seemed more intelligible. Furthermore, the ignorance of Innu history, sensibility, and contemporary circumstances, which was admitted by teachers and exuded in the classroom, was fuelled by the physical separation between Euro-Canadian professionals and Innu in the two communities, and even within the schools themselves. This is particularly evident in Utshimassits, where the teachers actually live in the community. However, they live in their own quarters in a community within a community, socializing almost exclusively with themselves and other outside professionals such as the priest, social workers, and nurses. Their dormitories, unlike the shacks of the Innu, are well furnished and are provided with running water and sanitation. Teachers rarely stay more than one or two years. Many vacate the community at every opportunity. Rapport with the Innu children and parents is at best superficial. According to one Davis Inlet man, there was only one teacher he could remember who socialized with the Innu, and he was fired. Some of the teachers were known for taking snowmobile trips to Hopedale, where they could drink and socialize away from the objects of their work.

Like other "human services," teaching in Sheshatshiu and Utshimassits involves working on as well as with people. But it is a kind of work that is at arm's length from those who are its objects. Although many teachers were warm and empathetic in the classroom, rarely were they in any other ways engaged with the students or their families. The teachers had almost no stake in the community and their participation in community affairs has been negligible. More pertinent, teachers have virtually no role in assisting with the many traumas that the Innu children suffer. This is a vast turnaround, since the school and church were the institutions that were supposed to be the saviours of the Innu, rescuing them from living on "garbage dumps," as Walter Rockwood once put it (Roche, 1992).

POST-SECONDARY EDUCATION

After several generations of village life, many Innu are now wondering what happened to the doctors and lawyers that priests and educators told them they would become when they were first sedentarized. Among the many young people who now have only a tenuous connection with *nutshimit,* some would like to be able to achieve according to Euro-Canadian standards of success. This route has been attempted by several Innu who have gone on to higher education.

In the past many young Innu students were required to leave the community and travel to Newfoundland to stay in boarding houses and complete their high school education. For most although not all of those who were interviewed as part of the band council study, this seems to have been a traumatizing experience. The students were given little preparation for life outside the village, often being singled out for placements by teachers without any discussion with parents. Some said they experienced "culture shock." They found it difficult to adjust to life in towns and cities where they were visibly different and where they were required to function in the English language. Many found the school programs more demanding and the work more complicated than that which they had been used to at Peenamin McKenzie. As a result, large numbers of former Peenamin McKenzie students have done poorly on the intelligence tests that were required when they entered schools in Newfoundland. Nearly all Innu students in Newfoundland have been assessed to be functioning several grades below the grade that they were in when they left Peenamin McKenzie. Many Innu tell stories of defeat, and as they got further behind with their academic work they turned to alcohol and drugs while in college. This often ended in calls to return home with their studies incomplete.

While high school students receive instruction in science, mathematics, and English that is preparatory to university, hardly any Innu students attend university. Although a few Innu from Utshimassits and Sheshatshiu have been to university, mostly Memorial University in St. John's, only one had graduated by 1999, and most survive only for a short time. Not only were they not academically prepared for university, and thus end up suffering the humiliation of failure, but in the all-white environment they are subject to discrimination and racism and often became homesick for their communities and families. There are, of course, a few exceptions.[9] However, for the mass of students who never even consider university, the extremely low standards expected by the school are not good preparation to enter into employment or further education outside their communities.

Through bitter and often humiliating experiences, the Innu discover that they are the products of what Father Frank Peters (1972) called *a way of life that does not exist*. Jerry Gregoire, a high school graduate from Utshimassits, was sent by Innu Nation to a pilot training school. Soon after he arrived he was told that his basic science and mathematical knowledge fell far short of what was required. He was sent back for more training, but has been unable to receive what is necessary to return to the pilot training school. When George Rich decided in his mid-thirties to pursue a high school equivalency diploma in Goose Bay, he soon discovered that the textbooks used in Goose Bay were completely different from those used in the school in Davis Inlet. It led him to believe that they had special books for the Innu – books that presupposed stupidity.

Greg Pastitchi was among the first graduates of the Peenamin McKenzie School. When he went on to pre-university training in Halifax he couldn't keep up with the work assignments. His grades were low, despite having a counsellor and extra tutoring. Eventually the school began to give up on him. One instructor told him, "you didn't go to school, you were just babysat." Urged to work on his academic weaknesses, he left his studies for a year. Instead of returning to Halifax, he went to the Saskatchewan Indian Federal College in

Regina. Although Greg lasted four semesters there, the story was the same. His marks were low, despite extra tutoring, and eventually he was told that he didn't belong in a university and should pursue some line of work more suited to people with lower capabilities. He started drinking before returning to Sheshatshiu.

Over the last 20 years, a rudimentary high school curriculum has got off the ground. Despite the efforts of teachers and principals, in terms of the general standards applied across Canada, it is widely perceived in Sheshatshiu as a relatively inferior program of study that does not prepare Innu students for anything outside the village. "Our school is not like other schools," Lionel Rich, a middle-aged man, told me. "My kids don't like going to the school. They don't learn nothing . . . . If it was more academic, more of them would go. The teachers treat them different than they would white kids. The kids are totally lost, I would say, because there's nothing academic and the standards are not very high."

THE ALTERNATIVE SCHOOL – TSHISKUTAMASHUN

Over the years, members of the community have developed a number of positive responses to the perceived inadequacies of the formal school system, particularly in regard to the perceived loss of culture. From 1995 to 1997 the band council sponsored a project called Nutshimiu Attusuen, a program of instruction for students of all ages to learn skills needed for *nutshimit* life. In 1999 an alternative school or *tshiskutamashun* was established with band council funding. Planning for this began in 1998 with a proposal to the Local Education Committee. The original proposal to teach both Innu and non-Native subjects changed during the course of planning to focus solely on the teaching of Innu life skills and *Innu-aimun*. A group of parents, who comprised the advisory group on the alternative school, accepted this change of plan. Since it officially opened in January 1999 with 17 students, three Innu instructors, and one non-Innu co-ordinator, the aim of the alternative school was to teach young people how to make the tools, hunting equipment, and camp equipment necessary for *nutshimit* life. In addition to this the school sought to improve the language skills of the participants, teach Innu history and genealogy, and generally provide support for the continuation of country life among the younger generation. In recognition of the fact that many young Innu feel confused about and in some cases ashamed of their Innu heritage, the alternative school had as its mission the improvement of self-esteem among young Innu.

The alternative school operated to a different rhythm than formal education. It did not begin abruptly, but gradually. The students did not all have to begin work at the same time. The work was always co-operative, even though students made their own products. The senior Innu instructor, avoiding the need for punishment, had handled conflict between students with humour and gentleness rather than the public humiliation that has been common in formal schooling. According to the co-ordinator, disruption was dispelled easily and comfortably. While instructors made most of the decisions, leadership was always subtle rather than rigidly hierarchical. The "Western way of organizing the delivery of education services is the antithesis of the typical social structure of indigenous societies," as Darnell and Hoem (1996: 141) point out. Recognizing this, one of the aims of the alternative school was to make learning coincide with the sensibilities of the people of the village.

The school co-ordinator believed that the alternative school made a real difference in the confidence and self-esteem of the students. During one of my visits, one student proudly held up a pair of snowshoes he had been working on. After making crooked knives, snowshoes, komatiks, mittens, moccasins, stoves, and other items, the students were taken out to the country by the Innu instructors. The first trip was to Mista Miskamit, where the 16 students participated in hunting, cleaning animals, gathering and chopping wood, setting up camp, gathering boughs, baking bread, and cooking. While there were some difficulties in the camp – some students were disrespectful of the animals, some food items ran out because they were used more heavily in teaching, and there were differences of opinion between staff members – these would be expected in any experimental program. Upon returning from this trip the students continued to make items necessary for life in the country.

From this point on, however, the school experienced further problems. As a result of confusion over the times when students were supposed to assemble for departure, only one student went to Sapeskashit, the second camp location, and only small numbers went on subsequent trips to camps on the Churchill road in April and May of 1999. Nevertheless, the classroom element of the school continued with students engaged in the making of snowshoes, moccasins, and other necessities of country life. However, some of the students found that the curriculum, sometimes consisting of several days at a time on one task, lacked variety and they became bored. To remedy this, some English and mathematics were introduced and an additional Innu teacher was hired to teach crafts. These changes caused some friction and division among the staff.

Outside the alternative school, concerns were raised at Peenamin McKenzie School that because it was not consulted, a significant number of its students were simply transferred to the alternative school.

Despite these difficulties, virtually every person we spoke to in our interviews supported the idea of an alternative school and urged that such a school be supported and funded on a regular basis, operating every year just as Peenamin McKenzie. A few younger people, however, did point out that a specifically Innu school would not help them obtain jobs. These are a sampling of the opinions on the alternative school.

A middle-aged man:

> I don't object to this school, but I heard that there were not many students taking the course. . . . There should be more students taking the courses. It is very important to the community. It should continue to be supported and funded. It is good for kids because it gets them away from the community and all the social problems that exist here. . . . They should learn in the country where everything is there. How would an Innu instructor look if he only stayed in a building?

Another man said:

> The alternative school is a good school. It should be kept up. Kids must feel good about themselves. I would like to see that continued. Young people need to know who their grandparents are. A lot of young men don't know how to put up a tent. It is okay to learn English, but the important part of life is to know who you are. If you lose that, then who are you? There are other ways to survive than jobs. That is why it is so important to know how to hunt and fish. Instead, all that a lot of people do is go to Social Services and pick up $80 a month. In the country there is all kinds of food. I think what we need most in the community is the alternative school. That is how you know who you are.

A young man:

> That school looks excellent. I would like to go there. It should be funded and continued. I really liked the place when I visited it. There were lots of pictures posted up on the walls. It made me feel that I wanted to be involved in it. I would like to see us support people who teach Innu things and set up Innu history courses.

One man said that the need for such a school was urgent because "When the old people go we will lose everything. We will only be able to talk about being Innu and dress up in costumes, Hollywood style."

The following year funding for the alternative school was not made available by the Sheshatshiu Innu band council, despite widespread community support for it. Although most of the hunting families were solidly behind the idea of an alternative school, there was no strong advocate for it within the Sheshatshiu band council. At the same time, there were also opposing political pressures to continue with the conventional school, since it already had a well-established funding base and was deemed to be the precondition for any devolution of education to Innu control. The Newfoundland-model school was also thought to be essential to meeting the criteria for how success was being measured, and accordingly how funds could be released for Innu education. Nevertheless, in both Sheshatshiu and Davis Inlet, a group called the Tshikapisk Foundation, independent of the political bodies, initiated further proposals to teach young Innu in the country along the lines of the alternative school.

We Are Always Sick 7

Since we have clinics, we are always sick.
– Manikinet, Sheshatshiu woman (Innu Nation, 1993: 42)

I see fear in their eyes when they are in hospital . . . and I can't blame them.
– "Akaneshau" nurse in Davis Inlet, 1998

With medicine we come to one of the most tragic features of the colonial situation.
– Frantz Fanon, *A Dying Colonialism* (1965: 121)

Murder has also been committed if society places hundreds of workers in such a position that they inevitably come to premature and unnatural ends.
– Friedrich Engels, *The Condition of the Working Class in England* (in Samson, 1999: 280)

VALENTINE'S DAY

One of the most beautifully haunting vistas in Utshimassits is that from a levelled-off area near the crown of a hill, where Kanuekitat, known also as John Poker, placed a tall wooden cross. The view across the inlet, over the frozen water and to the mainland and the old Davis Inlet trading post, is especially exhilarating on cold, clear days. Standing there, I looked out over the community, but because of the steep incline of the hill, I could only be seen from a few of the houses. The contrast of the green-turquoise cross, the snow-covered ground, and the deep blue sky was irresistible. Yet, it gave me only a flicker of pleasure. I felt something wrong about being here, camera in hand, peering *through* a marker of calamity. I surveyed the charred metal appliances on the other side of the cross, but I could not photograph them. Then, fiddling with the polarizing lens to get a good contrast between cross and sky, I was struck by the bad taste of my undertakings, a sense that I was a violator, attempting to produce something aesthetic from the lingering sorrow of others. The power of this place created a disturbing effect in my mind. Breathtaking as the scenery was, I could only stay briefly with these mixed feelings and images of what had happened at this very spot a few years earlier on Valentine's Day.

Cross on the hill at the site of house fire in Davis Inlet. Photograph by author.

The cross symbolizes the collective mourning for the tragedy of 14 February 1992 when six young children, left alone for an evening, burned to death in a house fire. Katie Rich (1995: xiii), a former Chief of Utshimassits, described the scene:

> February 14 is usually a day when one gives a loved one a Valentine's present, message or card. But February 14, 1992 is a day the Innu . . . will never forget. It marks the death of six innocent children in a house fire. Helplessly the community stood and watched the house burn to the ground. There was no water to put the fire out. Confused about whether or not there was anyone in the house, men went from one house to another to look for the children. Daylight came, and we saw the bones. All day elders, women and children came and examined the ashes, stood around in the freezing cold and cried.

On the first anniversary of the event, six more children between the ages of 10 and 16, depressed at the deaths of their friends and intoxicated from sniffing gasoline, barricaded themselves into an unheated shack in temperatures of -40 degrees Celsius. As adults tried to help, they threatened collective suicide, spat at the helpers, and declared their wishes to die (though in this instance they did not die). So disturbed was Simeon Tshakapesh, an Innu police constable at the time, that he videotaped the incident and distributed the tape to the Canadian news media.

The Valentine's Day tragedy has done much to seal an image of Iliukoyak Island as an evil place, the "devil's island" as a resident Inuit man once said to me in the heights of a liquor binge. Some Innu believe that the erection of the houses over Inuit graves along the shoreline has brought bad luck. Another circulating story tells of the ill omens connected with settling on the island. A common view is that premature deaths are related to the loss of respect for the animals and the erosion of Innu spirituality. This is symbolized by the frequent sight of dogs dragging caribou bones – which should be stored safely and eventually used for *mukushan* – around the community. The spiritual performances such as the drum dance and the *kushapatshikan*, which protected them in the past, are now abandoned after being persistently condemned by the Oblate priests.

Another story tells of Shushebish, the Mushuau Innu chief appointed by the priest, who believed that the people would be safe on the island only until he died. Unfortunately, Shushebish met his death only a few years after the establishment of the settlement in 1968. In 1997, Stanley Rich, a sharp, intelligent, and handsome teenager, the great-grandson of Shushebish and the son of my friend, Angela Pijogge, shot himself through the head on Valentine's Day. Numerous other descendants and relatives of Shushebish have followed the same fate, both in Davis Inlet and Sheshatshiu, where Stanley's 16-year-old cousin, Sylvester, hung himself in the summer of 1999.

REPRESENTATION AND TRAGEDY

Violent deaths of the young and other unnatural deaths brought Davis Inlet, a community of only 600, to the attention of the international mass media in the early 1990s. "Among the children, petrol sniffing has reached epidemic proportions, as has alcoholism among their fathers and mothers," read a story in *The Independent* of London (Roberts, 1994: 10). "Attempted suicides are commonplace. John Poker's brother, sister-in-law and four of their children died in an alcohol related boating accident in 1977," said the same article. In "Island of the damned," an apocalyptically titled report in the London *Observer*, journalist Tim Cornwell (1993: 41) claimed that Davis Inlet "may fairly be described as a piece of frozen hell. . . . The despair is palpable," Cornwell continued, "especially in early summer, when the ice is breaking up but not yet drifting away, and access to the mainland is impossible by either snowmobile or boat." An article in the *New York Times* referred to "the drunkenness and desperation, the foul water, the raw sewerage, the poverty and debilitating dependence endured on this rocky island off the northern coast of Labrador" (DePalma, 1996: A1).

A photograph of a dilapidated pool hall in a *National Geographic* feature on Labrador was underlined by the terse caption, "Taking aim against boredom, an Innu teenager shoots a solitary game of pool at a youth center in Davis Inlet – an impoverished community of once nomadic caribou hunters and their kin, now wracked by gasoline sniffing and suicides" (Poole, 1993: 29). The rest of the article tells of the hardy endurance and recent economic trials of settler and Inuit families in "Canada's desolate corner," the land of "strange, wild beauty." But there is none of the strange, wild beauty in this photograph. To the non-Native viewer, the photograph is a glance at a bleak and melancholy world where one would not wish to linger. The photograph creates the impression that *they* would like to be like *us*, but *they* are doing it in the wrong way. *They* are not there yet. Like photographs of urban slums, it provides just enough of a glimpse into Davis Inlet life to suggest both familiarity and a gulf between the viewer and the subject. This one, however, is momentarily unsettling for its inclusion of familiar consumer objects in states of obvious disrepair and decay in a starkly empty, dirty, and uninviting room. Daylight shines in through a paint-peeled doorway. Kit Kat and Reese's peanut butter cup wrappers are strewn with other debris, including spent lottery tickets, on an unswept floor. A tattered broom head lies unused by the door. The hooded Innu youth in the centre has his back to the lens, setting up a shot behind the cue ball. The game is solitary, the room is dirty, the subject is merely passing time. In photographs like this in which no subject gaze is visible, viewers must infer some wider commonalities of the Other, and as Lutz and Collins (1993: 203) suggest in their study of *National Geographic*, "communicat[e] a sense of nameless others." The disarray of the room, with its lone pool player, clearly demarcates a boundary between viewers and the nameless others.

Yet, the photograph does not really shock. It merely opens a window onto the world of nameless others that the article quickly glosses over in its upbeat assessment of hardy settler folk in an ethe-

Taking Aim Against Boredom. Photograph by Richard Olsenius.

Source: Robert Poole, "Labrador, Canada's Place Apart," with photographs by Richard Olsenius, *National Geographic* 184, 4 (Oct. 1993): 2-35.

real but rugged northern landscape. As Susan Sontag (1977: 15) remarks, "a photograph that brings news of some unsuspected zone of misery cannot make a dent in public opinion unless there is an appropriate context of feeling and attitude." Even though the photograph and accompanying text communicate something of the suffering in Davis Inlet, no context is provided for understanding why the community is so "wracked by gasoline sniffing and suicides." However, it is not only that a context for recognition of suffering is missing, but a paradoxical context is suggested. Earlier in the *National Geographic* article, the journalist relates an account of an interview with Peter Penashue, the President of the Innu Nation in Sheshatshiu, which is presented in similarly gloomy prose – "the street gouged with potholes and littered with trash" (Poole, 1993: 18). While life in Sheshatshiu and Davis Inlet may be grim, readers of *National Geographic* are informed that "the Canadian government *grants control* of Labrador to its 1,500 Innu Indians" who are nevertheless "*demanding* hunting and fishing rights over huge areas of Labrador" (Poole, 1993: 15, 30; emphases added). Another photograph, at once more warm and candid, of an Innu family in a tent, accompanies this latter commentary.

But it is the image of the hooded pool player that expresses many of the paradoxes of Euro-American representations of Natives. *Their afflictions are communicated, but recognition is lacking.* Recognition is lacking not only because photographs and international newspaper stories are necessarily scans and snapshots, but because any sense of Innu life in such representations is static. There is no story of how the Innu youth ended up behind the cue ball, for this would mean telling something of how his parents became "*formerly* nomadic hunters." With the cast of government officials, priests, and intermediaries that so persistently demanded settlement all absent, we simply have the generation of *former* hunters "wracked by gasoline sniffing," detached from time, but fixed in a place that has no "strange, wild beauty." At the same time – and here is the paradox – they are said to have been granted control of most of Labrador, while simultaneously *demanding* ever more hunting and fishing rights. In the end, the portrait of the Innu fits a broader contemporary Euro-American conception of Natives who are seen to have immense privileges, sometimes in the context of white losses (in this case the decline of the Newfoundland and Labrador fisheries prominently mentioned in the article), yet they are shattered by the scourges of alcohol, gas-sniffing, and suicide.[1]

Acts of self-destruction – threatened, attempted, and fatal – occur with regularity in Utshimassits and Sheshatshiu. According to an estimate of the band council, one-third of all adults in Utshimassits attempted suicide in 1993 (Wilson, 1994). In the 1980s, northern Labrador as a whole, which is populated by both Inuit and Innu people, had twice the Canadian Aboriginal rate and almost five times the national rate of suicide (Wotton, 1986: 141). Between 1990 and 1998 there were eight successful suicides in Utshimassits – equivalent to a rate of 178 suicides per 100,000 population, compared to a Canadian rate of 14 per 100,000. This means that Innu are almost 13 times more likely to kill themselves than the general population of Canada, and if this figure could be generalized, it would make the Utshimassits Innu one of the most suicide-ridden people in the world.[2]

In Sheshatshiu there is at least one suicide attempt per month, and during certain periods, particularly the spring when there is a lot of drinking after people have returned from the country, there can be several in any given week. While we were in Ottawa together, Simeon Tshakapesh showed me his constable's logbook for one arbitrary week in December 1999. Ten suicide attempts, all of which he had to rescue, were recorded. Nearly all successful suicides and suicide attempts are those of teenagers and young adults, both male and female. Two young men killed themselves during one week in the summer of 1999, a time that coincided with a spate of gas-sniffing among teenagers. Shortly after these, a 16-year-old boy in Davis Inlet attempted to kill himself by fire. The RCMP officer on duty at the time noted that an eyewitness saw the boy stamping on a gasoline bag that was on fire. The witness approached the boy, who told him to stay away because he had another bag of gas in his jacket. The boy then started running around the house and within seconds was ablaze, screaming, taking his jacket off.[3]

Suicide is widely interpreted by the Innu themselves as connected to the periodic drinking sprees of the adults. So pervasive and seemingly uncontrollable were the drinking and gas-sniffing problems in 1999 that the Sheshatshiu band council temporarily set up a road block outside the community to stop alcohol from coming in, and called on Health Canada officials to discuss the situation. Tragically, the situation was exacerbated in November 1999 when "Mr. T," the 15-year-old son of Jean-Pierre Ashini, fatally shot himself in his house in Sheshatshiu. Jean-Pierre received the news when he arrived in London to appear at a press conference to launch the human rights report, *Canada's Tibet* (Samson et al., 1999). The dramatic and ironic character of the suicide and the brave determination of the bereaved father to face the press, combined with the strident condemnation of the Canadian government, partly over this issue, received wide media coverage in Canada. Reporters focused on the sorrow of Jean-Pierre and his family, the suicide statistics, and the defensive reactions of government ministers. Virtually all the major newspapers in Canada carried the story, but none provided much context for understanding how so many young Innu end up on the wrong end of the gun.

Suicide is a communal tragedy. Almost every Innu in Sheshatshiu and Utshimassits attends the long and emotional funerals. Because members of the community are closely related to each other by blood and marriage, funerals are reminders of the collective trauma of the Innu as a people. A flood of Canadian journalists were dispatched to Sheshatshiu for the funeral of Mr. T. As it happened, his death was a time of double grief as his infant cousin had inexplicably died in her cot a few days earlier. The two cousins shared the same funeral. The Innu interviewed at the time said that they are inextricably linked to each other as a people and that the conditions the government had created for them in the communities contributed to their early deaths. Thus, Peter Penashue, the newly elected President of Innu Nation, told a reporter, "it is true to say that Canada is killing the Innu in the context that this country does not make it easy for us to live as a people" (*St. John's Telegram*, 1999: 1). Mary May Osmond, an Innu counsellor whose 27-year-old son Clarence had shot himself a few months earlier, was quoted in a *Maclean's* magazine article as saying, "everything that is wrong here is passed on from generation to generation" (DeMont, 1999: 40).

Amid the tears and charged emotions, non-Native health professionals in the Innu communities are largely silent. This is evident in the euphemisms used in the death registers compiled by the nurses in Davis Inlet, who frequently do not enter "suicide" but "gunshot wound to head" in the logbooks. The few and somewhat fragmentary health and mortality statistics that I have been able to collect shine only a cold, befuddled glare. They generalize and agglomerate the family breakdown, abuse, drunkenness, and alcohol-related disease, violence, accidents, and self-harm. Even though no detailed figures are kept in Sheshatshiu or Utshimassits, at the hospital in Goose Bay, at the Health Department in St. John's, or with Health Canada in Ottawa, it is obvious to the local health workers that life and death for the Innu are not what they are for people in other parts of Canada.

The frequency of infant deaths, alcohol-related deaths, and suicide does not tally with the figures for most of Canada. Significant numbers of Innu die in what are called accidents when they have been drinking heavily – falling through ice, being run over on the road, or simply passing out and freezing to death. The local doctors and nurses say that diabetes, heart conditions, respiratory conditions, skin diseases, arthritis, ulcers, obesity, alcoholism, and accidents are also very common. Many diseases occur at younger ages than are usually found in other populations; diabetes, for example, affects some teenagers. The nurses speak of "epidemics" of impetigo, skin infections, and gastric problems among young children. In both Utshimassits and Sheshatshiu very high numbers of children and adolescents sniff gasoline. Sometimes these erupt into wild sprees of mass vandalism of buildings, snowmobiles, and whatever machines are to hand, as well as interpersonal violence and suicide attempts. Each year that I have returned, the friends I have made tell me that things are progressively becoming worse. Several Innu say they would like to leave the communities – a drastic measure since this would cut them off from family, friends, and the hunting way of life – but few have been able to make any specific plans.

This deterioration in the quality of life is apparent not only among the youth. After a gap of about a year since our last meeting, Cecilia Rich, a 40-year-old woman, said that she found it difficult to carry on living, not only as a result of the youth crisis but because so many "middle-aged" people in the community were dying. Just a few months before our conversation, her brother-in-law, who had frequently threatened suicide, had choked to death on caribou meat and her sister had died of cancer. She thought that people were coming down with fatal diseases at increasingly younger ages. Along with this, marriages were splitting up, teenage girls were becoming pregnant, people seemed to be drinking more than before, and more kids in Sheshatshiu were sniffing gas. Her matter-of-factness never suggested exaggeration.

Table 1 gives a rough idea of the vast gulf between the life and death experiences of the Innu and Canadians as a whole. During the last two decades more than half of all deaths in Innu communities were of people aged under 30; this was the case for only 5 per cent of Canadians and 4 per cent of Newfoundlanders. Conversely, while at least 80 per cent of Canadian and Newfoundland deaths involved people over 60 years old, only a quarter of Innu deaths were in this age range – ages to which people are expected to live in industrialized countries with liberal democratic traditions.

Table 1: Age at Death in Canada (1990), Newfoundland (1993), and Innu Communities (1975-1995)

Age	Canada	Newfoundland	Innu Communities
0-4	3,325 (2%)	60 (1.5%)	34 (30%)
5-14	814 (0.4%)	22 (0.5%)	8 (7%)
15-29	4,817 (3%)	89 (2%)	18 (16%)
Total Under 30 Years	8,956 (5%)	171 (4%)	60 (53%)
30-44	8,762 (5%)	146 (4%)	9 (8%)
46-59	19,546 (10%)	412 (11%)	15 (13%)
Over 60	153,577 (80%)	3,161 (81%)	29 (25%)
Total	190,841	3,890	113

Sources: Adapted from United Nations, *Demographic Yearbook 1993* (New York: UN, 1993), Table 19, 414-15; Statistics Canada, *Annual Demographic Statistics 1994* (Ottawa: Statistics Canada, 1995); Roman Catholic Church records; local informants. The chi square for this table is 769.5347 with a p-value .001, indicating that the differences between the age at death of the three populations are statistically significant.

Infant mortality rates provide another measure of the chasm between the Innu and the rest of Canada. Table 2 shows that an Innu child is between three and seven times more likely to die before the age of five than the average Canadian child. There are also dramatic differences between the two Innu communities. The rate in Utshi-massits, where there is no sewerage or household running water and the nearest hospital can only be reached by plane, is more than twice that in Sheshatshiu, which does have these basic amenities and is within an hour's car journey of the hospital in Goose Bay.[4]

Table 2: Mortality Rates for Infants 0-4 Years in Sheshatshiu (1983-94), Utshimassits (1984-94), and Canada (1990)

Location	Births	Deaths	Rate Per 1,000
Sheshatshiu	446	12	26.9
Utshimassits	208	12	57.7
Canada	404,669	3,325	8.2

Sources: Calculated from Roman Catholic Church records, local informants; United Nations, *Demographic Yearbook 1993* (New York: UN, 1993); Statistics Canada, *Annual Demographic Statistics* 1994 (Ottawa: Statistics Canada, 1995); *Canadian Almanac and Directory, 1996* (Toronto, 1996).

HEALERS AND RECOGNITION

Two nurses running the Utshimassits clinic spoke long and pas-sionately about their work with the Innu. Here is the unprompted and mostly verbatim account of one of them:

Mothers are not able to look after their babies. They don't know how to keep the bottles clean and they feed babies while their hands are dirty. They do not teach their children how to be clean. But this does not worry them because they expect to get medicine at the clinic and will return time and time again. Innu houses are not well ventilated. Inside you sometimes find all burners on the stove on full blast and the kids put their hands on it. Mothers do not have even a basic knowledge of safety. Kids play everywhere, even on top of roofs. They jump off and the parents do not say anything. In the cold, kids play outside without shirts and shoes. They have no idea of nutrition and give greasy pork, which has a high fat content, to babies. Kids eat irregularly and consume a lot of junk food. Sexu-ally transmitted diseases are common, especially clamydia, because they start sex very young – as young as eight. The kids go to the top of the hill and sniff gas until very late.

They do not have strong coping skills. They want to take pills over the smallest things. There are many overdoses over trivial is-sues such as "someone said something about me." They are all like kids, but they don't know how to cope. They have no control of the children. Kids can do anything they want. Liberation starts from the age of one. Even the police don't do anything about gas-sniffing. There is a 12-year-old girl who has attempted suicide three times.

Once with a gunshot wound through her arm near the carotid artery. She did it because her father was sleeping with someone else and she was addicted to gas-sniffing. But everyone gives support. We sent her to Goose Bay. Parents lie too much to get a free flight to Goose Bay. They say they are sick. The midwives say they have no pain when they have babies. They say they don't want to die, so I think they are asking for help. Often the parents are drinking all night and there is no food. They don't teach young people to cook. In the day they are sleeping. They don't have any values for the children. The government gives them too much.

In my country [in Latin America], people don't have money but they are clean. Bathtubs are available here and are in use all day, but it is only some people who use them sporadically. In my country, children have rules. Here, parents don't control the children. They don't believe in punishment. This happened with the fire [mentioned above, in which six children died, and for which the Innu oppose the prosecution of the parents for manslaughter]. Tents are better than houses. They are more comfortable and not as dirty. The boughs are changed every week. They are okay for the elderly, but not for those who have been here 20 years. They've had white people to teach them, but still they're dirty. It can't be "identity" for young people. They have to blame someone.

Winter is better. They melt the snow and wash with it. They seem very disorganized to us. I teach them. Then they come back dirty and I have to teach them slowly. Self-help is a good thing. We will have a pajama party and teach the children about sex. We will teach the young mothers simple things that mothers do all over the world. The kids eat everything, even money.

Grown men come to see us even for small cuts. They want antibiotics for everything. Skin diseases, scabies, lice, eczema, these are all hygiene-related. We are going to start going to houses with Social Services and the alcohol program – if they allow us – to teach them how to clean the house. There is garbage everywhere. Kids and dogs play in it. I recently saw a kid with a bleach bottle, drinking water from the ditch.

Children don't speak any English. We have very good personal care assistants who are Innu. There has been some success. Some are clean now. They're like mad cows. They destroy everything in sight. Work is very tiring. We are always on call – every second night. Often we work all night. On the phone, they blame you if you don't come. John Poker refused to take medication for his stroke and high blood pressure. He had a stroke in the country and they couldn't get the chopper in there very quickly. Simeon [the chief] swore at me for not getting it there sooner. They blame nurses for everything. It was John Poker's choice not to take medication. Maybe now he is happy [he died three days earlier]. They want medication for everything. Kids say the whites teach them to sniff gasoline, but sometimes parents also do it, as well as alcohol.

We don't have any time off at all. Even at home they knock on
the door or phone. They are very dependent. They cannot do anything for themselves. We had a call on Sunday night for condoms,
trying us out. They want everything free. The move to Sango Bay
[then the proposed relocation on the mainland] will be the same as
Davis Inlet if they don't change. That's bad because this is a beautiful place. We get frustrated. It's like talking to the air. They don't
appreciate anything.

The nurses' job is unenviable. It is tiring, thankless, exasperating,
and ultimately Sisyphean. The Innu spectacle, the undifferentiated
"they" of the narration that would never be delivered to "them," is at
once horrifying, chaotic, anomic. Ever vigilant for the weaknesses of
the Other, the nurse portrays Innu life as precarious, unhappy, and
yet carried out with a kind of wilful abandon. Death is never far
away. Dirt is everywhere. Their sickness is of their own making, yet
they blame "us," the nurses who have travelled far and forfeited
much to help them. They never strike the correct balance – John
Poker died because of his refusal to take medication as prescribed,
yet they all crave medication for the most trivial complaints; they are
recklessly dependent and childish, yet they are demanding of their
numerous entitlements at the clinic and elsewhere. The Innu in the
narration, like in *National Geographic*, actually have it rather good,
but they are throwing it all away in an orgy of foolish irresponsibility.

Lurking only slightly under the surface of these observations are
the insecurities, bewilderment, and social isolation that nearly all of
the nurses who come to Davis Inlet experience themselves. Although
their contracts are for relatively short periods of time – most only
spend a few months in the village – they are always thinking of leaving. Nurses see sickness, pain, and distress all around them, yet
they are unable to prevent any of it because the necessary measures
would require authorities to consider long-term public health
strategies rather than placebos and pain management. All of their
efforts are exerted towards immediate primary-care crises. Nurses
are trained as humanitarian workers, as healers of the sick, yet in
Davis Inlet it is difficult to summon the energy or empathy for their
patients that would be necessary to the task. Another nurse in Davis
Inlet expressed a profound sense of unhappiness and self-doubt
amid her general alienation in the community:

> They just about tolerate us. Sometimes I feel that they don't want
> us here. They call you a fuckin' nurse. We never get a response, only
> a giggle. I can't ever get away from work. I am isolated in this house.
> Most nurses don't really want to be in Davis Inlet. In a year they
> may see 15 nurses. A lot refuse to come here. Before I came, all I
> heard was that it was a very busy community. It is a very hard place

to be. In other places, I've made friends. Here, I am pleasant and I
reach out, but I don't get any response from them. No one prepares
you for the cultural response of no eye contact. They are people of
few words to outsiders. . . . We're not part of the community. Here,
people don't invite you to anything. It is more of a closed community. I feel that I am always outside the community. If someone said,
"Come down [the nurses live at the top of a hill overlooking the vil-
lage], I'm skinning a caribou," I would.

During the same conversation, safely inside the nurses' residence, her colleague interjected some similarly anomic remarks. For
her, Davis Inlet was an "interesting place" to live and "the children
were beautiful," but, "there's no escape. It's not a life. They don't
know anything about us. They think it's just the worst nurses that
come here." She went on to speculate that the Innu suppressed a lot
of generalized anger that was vented on her and other nurses. The
problem was that "they think we should be like mechanics fixing
them. If we don't do it just right, we're awful people. They pester you
for Tylenol." The irony here is that Tylenol and other biomedical
remedies actually promote the mechanical interpretations of health
and illness that the nurses are castigating the Innu for expecting.
But what we have in these nurses' stories is not simply a condemnation of disorder, but a fear of the Other arising out of the inherent
danger, even power, as Mary Douglas suggests (1966: 114), when
order is lost. And here, with access to health care guaranteed by
band membership, each Innu in Davis Inlet can in theory call upon
the nurses with little restriction. Beneath the bewilderment of the
nurses, there is a hint of a fear of power surfacing from the massed
clientele who appear in the clinic and at their log cabin-style home at
the top of the hill.

Although their impulse is always to summon faint praise by ex-
tricating a few redeeming characteristics of the Innu, nurses in
Davis Inlet frequently drew out a line of cause and effect that moved
from wilful ignorance and irresponsibility to sickness. Causality
helped since it rationalizes their misfortunes and excesses as ignorance. Impetigo, for example, was thought to be caused by nutritional
factors and exacerbated by poor hygiene. According to a couple of
nurses in Davis Inlet, when *they* – the constant and unavoidable
Other of the narratives – wash, *they* leave soap in their clothes. This
gets into the skin and causes disease. Similarly, other ailments were
seen to flow from a whole catalogue of errors. *They* don't understand
that junk food is not good food. *They* don't know about vitamins and
nutrition. Consequently, there are lots of teeth extractions and ab-
scesses, and dental caries, a function of poor dental hygiene and a

lack of fluoride in the water, is common. The dentist only visits two days per month, but the band council shells out a lot of its funds on dentistry. Throwing money at the problem in this way, however, was meaningless, because as one nurse said to me, "I could give them all the toothbrushes in the world and it wouldn't help." If *they* cannot even muster the ounce of prevention needed, cures are all the more onerous.

In Sheshatshiu, nurses tell similar stories, tales that begin cautiously, then gain extra momentum as each new deficiency of their patients is rooted out. Fay Midgley is the home care nurse working in Sheshatshiu. She speaks of her work, attending patients who are mostly housebound. Although she mentions a few positive examples at the end of our discussion, she thinks that there is little responsibility among the Innu for caring for the sick. The carers of some patients drink and nearly all smoke cigarettes, and do so around mentally or physically ill people. She cites the instance of an elderly woman who is handicapped and contracts chest colds because the adults in the family around her are drinking. When the husband is drunk he leaves her in a diaper and does not cut wood for the fire. Everyone in the house gets cold.

She relates other cases of neglectful carers. There was a man who was physically disabled in a road accident and could not look after himself. He was forced to go from house to house because his wife had left him. The man in question was not taken care of, even though, as she put it, the Innu say that "we take care of our own." There are no voluntary organizations in the community, nor is there much family volunteering. Most handicapped people are not helped by their families because, in her view, Social Services is expected to do the caring. This narrative merges into more stories of other abandoned and needy patients. A young epileptic woman was used as a "drudge" by her grandparents as a child. When they died, she went to live with her parents, but this did not work well, so she, too, went from house to house looking for shelter. According to the nurse, the only reason why Innu would volunteer to be home care assistants is if they were paid for it. They are not willing to help unless they are paid. But, even here, things often break down, and Social Services must come in and take charge when paid carers abandon their responsibilities.

Signifying that they cannot look after their own, let alone others' health, the Innu are almost universally portrayed as having unhygienic habits. According to Fay Midgley, it takes a lot of persuasion for them to realize that they can bathe more than once a week. Again, another case in point is brought forward. This time, it is of a housebound woman whose family would only wash her once a week. Thanks to an *Akaneshau* nurse attendant, she is now washed five times a week. An Innu woman would not do this even for one hour every day, the nurse told me.

To all of my questions about the health of the Innu, the nurse's replies almost always included an attribution of immediate blame to the Innu themselves. Even the infant deaths that are so common are the fault of mothers. There are diabetic mothers who do not comply with their drug or insulin regimes, and consequently babies die during delivery. She cited a 20-year-old on her fourth pregnancy who did not comply with medical orders. Throughout her pregnancy, the woman preferred to eat randomly rather than have regular meals. Her baby died. Like this 20-year-old, Innu mothers, the nurse tells me, are very upset when their babies die. "They have the same reaction as us," she tells me, as if I would have thought otherwise.

Dr. Karen McDonald, a doctor at the clinic in Sheshatshiu, is another veteran observer of Innu manners. Her stories of the health problems of the Innu are part biology, part sociology, and part ethnology. Although her words are often more measured than those of the nurses, her accounts of the health dilemmas of Innu patients follow a similar format. This can be characterized as a linguistic contrast structure. A priori facts are stated, logical behaviour is identified as a response to the facts, but Innu are observed to act contrary to the logical response to these facts. Thus, x is a fact, therefore we should expect y as a response, but instead we get z from the Innu. She begins one of our first conversations by talking about iron. Many Innu children have very low iron levels, which leads to impetigo and anemia, *yet* Labrador has rich deposits of iron. Tea makes iron unabsorptive, *but* the Innu drink lots of very strong tea. Iron deficiency also affects mental abilities and causes bad behaviour in children. Despite her urgings, people do not purchase iron-rich foods. This then leads into a discussion of nutrition generally, which she believes is not an important issue for the community although it should be. There is an inconsistency in her view because "self-esteem," evidently a less pressing problem, *is* a community concern as evidenced in the numerous healing programs in operation (discussed in Chapter 8). The logic is impeccable, the indictment sharp. Fact: the children have low iron levels. Because Labrador is rich in iron we should expect them to avail themselves of it. But no, we find the opposite. They drink strong tea, which makes iron unabsorptive and they do not follow her advice to buy foods that are rich in iron. Even worse, they concentrate on self-esteem, when they should be concerned about their diets.

The doctor's account of the poor nutritional intake of the Innu then turns more ethnographic, drawing on her own observations from years working in the community. She observes Innu people eat only when hungry. They do not structure their day around scheduled meals. Cold spaghetti is simply left on the table for family members to pick at when they choose. In the overcrowded households, food is always consumed quickly. There is little concept of a budget and food planning is rare. The Innu in Labrador have adopted the Newfoundland diet, which tends to be heavy and stodgy. They combine this with canned foods, bologna, eggs, processed foods, chips, candy, pop, and junk food. This is further stimulated by television advertising. The television is almost permanently switched on in most Innu households. It is no surprise to her that many Innu adults are obese. They do not toil in the community as they do in the country and as a result some people have up to 50 per cent body fat. Diabetes, especially the Type 2 or 'adult onset' type, is a major health problem among the Innu, and Dr. McDonald believes that it is probably under-diagnosed because many patients don't come to the clinic. "They are very naughty patients." She believes this non-attendance for appointments is a form of denial. In turn, diabetes is a risk factor for hypertension, kidney problems, cerebral malfunctions, poor eyesight, and poor blood circulation. Like many others, the doctor emphasizes how alcohol contributes to this sorry state of health and how it is passed on to the younger generations. When parents are drinking, children are often neglected, and upon sobering up they "overcompensate" by buying junk food that their children enjoy.

Both doctors and nurses working in the Innu villages commonly locate the underlying causes of physical illness and disease in the conduct of the Innu themselves, particularly in their inability or unwillingness to teach their children basic safety requirements, their lack of coping skills, aversion to washing, their drinking, poor nutrition, and sexual promiscuity. These factors were frequently cited by doctors and nurses for the proliferation of illness in Utshimassits and Sheshatshiu.[5] Few health workers stopped to question the many complexities that inevitably surround compliance to medications in a place like Davis Inlet. Most *Tshenut*, even with coaching and translation, are unable to follow complicated instructions dictated by the movements of the clock. Others, for example young mothers in overcrowded households, will find it difficult to comply while there are numerous other crises in the household. Many people are not convinced of the efficacy of biomedicine, preferring to bear either their pain alone or to seek an Innu remedy. Furthermore, there is no cultural basis among the Innu for them to adopt the customary deference towards physicians.

The front-line efforts to help and heal the Innu display little recognition of the experiences of Innu either as individuals or as a people. Although they may be dedicated professionals, medical personnel usually have scant knowledge or, in many cases, regard for the histories and experiences of their Native patients. This is not because they are racist or prejudiced individuals – although this should not be ruled out in some cases – but because their medical training steers them towards a mechanical view of illness and the body that is relatively insensitive to cultural nuance. Doctors and nurses working with the Innu view their patients as bringing about much of their own sickness through a slovenly and carefree lifestyle that makes them non-compliant and insensitive to medical advice. As such, the Innu are often spoken of as intractable miscreants, objects for stern lectures, and fit only for palliative care. Medical work with the Innu reveals a massive chasm between Us and Them. The biomedical healer recognizes only the deficiencies of the Other. There is little that connects the two, and perhaps because of this there are few of the social and psychological powers needed to heal. Like the *National Geographic* photograph, suffering is communicated but the context for recognition is lacking.

In *A Fortunate Man*, a narrative of an English country doctor, John Berger (1967) pointed out how important recognition was to the healing relationship between doctor and patient. Berger's doctor is a "clerk of the records" of the community. He understands his patients through a kind of fraternal association with their trials, which are trials that he can imagine himself. Because illness severs connections with the world, it is up to the doctor to "reaffirm the social content of the invalid's aggravated self-consciousness" (Berger, 1967: 69). The doctor must intimately recognize the physical and psychological trauma of the patient. Further, the doctor should be "a comparable man." While this does not necessarily mean that the doctor must be of the same ethnicity as the patient, it does imply that a doctor's respect for the beliefs and practices of the patient is conducive to healing. In turn, patients must be able to sense this respect. "To find . . . a healing peace [patients] need to feel that a connection exists between themselves and the healer and between themselves and something larger than self or science," Carl Hammerschlag (1988: 137) tells us in his account of working as a doctor with Native Americans in the U.S.

If the doctors and nurses do not, and perhaps cannot, recognize the personal trials of their patients and the social content of their

trauma, healing efforts will be palliative at best, socially and psychologically damaging at worst. Their doctoring will be an enlargement
upon some of the most notorious features of Western medicine – its
mechanical rigour, invasiveness, and insensitivity to human desires, emotions, and histories. Both the social and the psychological
dimensions of illness experiences will be shunted aside. This is normal in biomedicine, as philosopher Jacob Needleman (1985: 31)
points out in relation to his own hospital experience: "Every day I
found the world of real reality was announcing its existence on the
ward and people behaved as though this world did not exist, as
though this world were not constantly pressing in upon us, insisting, demanding that we acknowledge it." The medical denial of an
external social reality has a more insidious character when it is imposed within a colonial order in which patients are the dominated
ethnic group and health professionals are members of the dominant
group and representatives of the imposed state. In Labrador and
other areas of the world where it is clear that colonial domination
has a tangible form, biomedicine frequently functions as an aid to
the hegemony of the state. By refusing to acknowledge and recognize
colonized peoples in terms of their histories and experience, medicine has concentrated on identifying what the natives lack and what
is necessary to absorb them silently into the mainstream of the settler society.[6] An impediment to this absorption, and a cause of
immense frustration to the local medics are the perennial illnesses
of the Innu.

One way in which this colonial relationship can appear blurred
is through the invoking of genetics as the cause of Innu afflictions,
and here diabetes presents a case in point. Diabetes is a new and especially debilitating disease for the Innu. It was never reported when
they were permanent nomadic hunters. Some say that it has only
appeared in the last 20 years. Yet, according to Stacey McIver, the
dietician at the hospital in Goose Bay, the vast majority of Innu patients that she sees are diagnosed with diabetes and obesity. The
two conditions are interrelated in that obesity is linked to a high fat,
high sugar diet, which is a risk factor for diabetes. Many of the dietician's Innu patients tell her that junk food is what they eat in the
villages. This may mean processed foods, sugared foods, fried foods,
and in the case of residents of Sheshatshiu fast food purchased at
the rapidly expanding number of such franchises in Goose Bay.

The medical authorities attribute diabetes in the Innu to genes
combined with the relatively new diet of junk food and mass alcohol
consumption. "A lot of diabetes in Native populations generally are a
result of genetic predisposition," the dietician told me, "which is

spurred on or quickened by their eating habits and their obesity."
However, when pressed on the causes of diabetes, the picture becomes more confusing, with the dietician seeming to admit that
enlightenment is the clenching factor:

> We don't really know what causes diabetes. There's some genetic
> factor in there. Not everyone who eats a lot of sugar gets it. Sugar
> doesn't cause diabetes. It's not the food they're eating that causes
> their diabetes. There's some genetic predisposition that the Native
> population seem to have. . . . The rampant diabetes is largely envi-
> ronmental. It's what they're eating. They're not eating the fruits and
> vegetables and low fat products. They're eating all the fat and
> sugar. They're gaining weight and getting bigger and bigger. And
> this brings on diabetes.

Although "the rampant diabetes is largely environmental," the
medical theories that contemporary views of the disease depend on
privilege the genetic factor. At the same time, health-care workers
(and the medical literature in general) are silent about the colonial
processes that drastically changed a people's way of life and placed
them in conditions in which they are unable to attain what they consider well-being. As Mary-Ellen Kelm (1998: 37) remarks of a similar
situation with respect to the deterioration of the health of British Columbia Indians in the twentieth century as a result of non-Native
territorial encroachment, "[t]ake away a people's access to adequate
quantities of nutritious food and soon you have a population of
weakened bodies who must struggle just to survive." Similarly,
Naomi Adelson (2000), in her study of the health beliefs of the Cree
neighbours of the Innu, points out how well-being is closely associated with the value of foods obtained in the country. While wild foods
are still available to the Cree, they are increasingly concerned about
the effects that industrialization is having on the quality of meat
found on the animals. At the same time, the healthy Cree diet was
being replaced by mass-produced "whiteman's food." For the Cree,
"eating whiteman's food to excess was likened to consuming alcohol
to excess . . . both lead to disease when taken in large quantities"
(Adelson, 2000: 104). Instead of looking into the historical and political factors responsible for the changes that "weakened bodies,"
genetic theories advance the notion that because there are high
rates of diabetes among indigenous peoples worldwide, and such
groups supposedly have a common gene pool,[7] the disease in question *must* have a genetic component, if not origin. That is, there is
something in the DNA of indigenous peoples that "predisposes" them
to the disease.[8]

However, few "studies to assess the impact of changing lifestyle and diet of American Indians have been reported in the literature" (Jackson, 1994: 394). This is a significant omission because it is well documented that, in general, the further away a Native group is located from Euro-Canadian population centres, the lower the rate of diabetes (see Young, 1994: 24-28). Moreover, it is well known that the nomadic hunting life, by contrast with settlement life, provides a diet far superior in basic vitamins and nutrients than what can be procured from community food stores (Mackie, 1987) and the exercise necessary for survival keeps people in good physical condition. These factors, however, play a distant second fiddle to the well-funded genetic research projects aiming to discover a genetic marker that would predispose Natives to diabetes. Local doctors have been quick to anchor themselves in these ideas, thereby avoiding any significant engagement with the political issues surrounding enforced changes to the lifestyle of the Innu. Yet, while genetics is used to explain some cases of Innu illness, such as diabetes, local medical discourses also lean heavily on attributions of individual fault as explanations for this and many other Innu afflictions.

THE POLITICS OF BLAME

Mary Douglas (1992: 15-16) notes the increasing tendency in Western societies to assess misfortune in terms of risk calculation, which in turn is a necessary ingredient in the subsequent determination of fault. Fault follows from the perceived failure of subjects to live up to prescribed expectations. To enforce such expectations, acts of retribution often flow from the attribution of fault.[9] This pattern of blaming on the basis of risk calculations, fault-finding, and subsequent retribution, albeit subtle, can be observed in the attitudes of medical staff in the Innu communities.

Health workers attending the Innu find blame in a fairly straightforward manner. It is not that the Innu are dying "natural deaths," as Douglas terms it, but deaths that are preventable. They are preventable, according to medical staff, by regimes of positive action and abstinence – regular meals, exercise, no junk food, little sugar, dietary supplements, no smoking, and no binge drinking. The underlying inference is that the Innu do not seriously consider the chain of causation and the risk probability linking their actions and behaviour to specific health outcomes. By using what Douglas refers to as "methodological individualism," common in the sciences, the medics draw a causal line between individual actions of particular Innu and illness, then extrapolate from this to comment on the health of the communities as a whole. Larger-scale political or historical events – colonization, sedentarization, the injustices of Canadian land claims policies – are either ignored or seen as only distantly relevant. More subtle psychosocial dynamics – the undermining of confidence as a result of living in the villages and severing permanent connections with the land – are also downplayed. Similarly, although domestic material conditions such as the lack of sewerage and running water in Davis Inlet can hardly go unnoticed, few health workers I have encountered place any great stock in such factors, preferring to emphasize the improvements that the relocation to a new community at Natuashish on the mainland might bring. Even the local Mennonite in Davis Inlet observed the absurdity of this position. Nurses, he pointed out, were treating hygiene-related health problems when nothing was done to collect the garbage in the community, when Innu faced the daily indignity of dumping "honey-buckets" outside their shacks, and when dogs raced around the village vying for the prize of a soiled diaper.

Any consideration of the contexts needed for recognizing the suffering of the Innu and apportioning blame must account for both personal (micro) and political (macro) levels, ranging from brushing teeth to the imposition of Euro-Canadian social institutions. While health workers are likely to adhere to methodological individualism and emphasize the more personal, the Innu often contextualize their health problems by invoking political factors. One important illustration lies in the reactions of the people in the two communities to the development of their land. Activities such as logging, mining, hydroelectric projects, and low-level flying, they believe, damage health not only directly by their toxic by-products, but also by disrupting the existing ecological balance and causing changes to the animal population. Such changes degrade the country, thus undermining the only healthy route out of the increasingly unhealthy social and material conditions in the villages.

The sequestration of the land at Emish for the Voisey's Bay mining operation in the 1990s provides a good example. Many Innu believed that the mine would simply exacerbate problems of alcohol abuse and ill health. The early reports of the effects that mining had on Innu workers certainly supported this. Right at the beginning of the speculation about mining in 1995, Simeon Tshakapesh told me, "the Innu will die from booze and drugs that the Voisey's Bay money will bring." At the time of the initial push to develop Voisey's Bay in the mid-1990s there was much apprehension towards it. At around this time I had a conversation with David Nui, then a health counsellor in Utshimassits. He was fearful that a rumoured liquor store would be provided for the workers at Nain, and this would make alcohol much more accessible to the Innu. The mine would also draw young men to jobs, and the dislocations arising from these would, he felt, break up families and marriages. At the same time, the mine would erode "our culture."

In response to the threat of the mine, Innu Nation set up a task force to interview members of the communities on the issue. Many respondents quoted in *Ntesinan Nteshiniminan Nteniunan: Between a Rock and a Hard Place* (Innu Nation, 1996a) drew direct connections between the development of mining operations and the ill health that they believed would follow in its wake. Here are a sampling of the views expressed:

> I think the first problem will be more young people will use drugs and alcoholism and the second thing will be that teenagers will commit suicide. (Francine Nuna, Sheshatshiu, in Innu Nation, 1996a: 56)

> The big problem is that there will be drinking, a lot of suicide, marriage breakdowns etc. (Frances Piwas, Utshimassits elder, ibid.)

> People will drink heavy. They will bring booze back into the community especially. This will end in drowning accidents. They will spend their money in a town and nothing will be brought to their families. Diseases will destroy the community. (Patrick Andrew, Utshimassits, ibid., 57)

These apocalyptic scenarios suggest that members of the Innu communities saw the proposed mine as a vector of affliction, trauma, and disease. To the Innu commentators, there was nothing inevitable about mining. It is created by choices of people, specifically the provincial and federal governments in cahoots with the mining industry. However, this did not mean that the Innu could not act in certain ways to reduce their susceptibility to the pathological impacts of the mine. Hence, in the task force report Etienne Pastiwet of Utshimassits made important qualifications about personal responsibility:

> There will be a lot of problems. Like alcohol abuse and disease. But each individual has their own responsibility to take care of themselves. They have a choice not to drink and not to fuck around with other people who has (sic) disease. (Ibid., 57-58)

Both personal responsibility and wider political processes were seen as contexts for future illnesses and misfortunes in the wake of mining. In a long discussion about the Voisey's Bay mine one morning at the alcohol centre in Utshimassits, Simeon Tshakapesh paused and asked, "Are we humans? We are not being treated as humans. They [*Akaneshaut*] make human rights, but they are not treating us as humans." By taking away Innu land for mining and other purposes, the Innu were being prevented not only from practising their way of life, but from exercising personal and collective autonomy, and these developments have human rights implications.[10] "The government claims that the land belongs to them. But, look at all the evidence that our elders left on the land, marks on the trees, burial grounds. We know the names of places in the country, but we do not see these names on maps. They don't recognize our names on maps." For Simeon and many other Innu in both Utshimassits and Sheshatshiu, mining has the potential to wreck some of the remaining contacts the Innu have with nomadic hunting, the cosmology of *nutshimit*, and the places where many obtain pride and self-esteem. In removing Innu hunting territory for industrial development, the authorities fail to recognize the Innu as a people. In doing so, they blind themselves to the connections between acts of cultural domination and the downward spirals in Innu health that are occasioned by removing autonomy over land. Removing autonomy in this way is a vehicle not to "recognize our names on maps."

Most medical workers' stories do not concern themselves with the continuing actions of the state to occupy the land of the Innu. None that I have met see any serious health consequences emerging from the development process. In fact, most see these projects as positive, either because they will provide employment or because the Innu Nation will, it is assumed, negotiate an advantageous settlement that will make the Innu rich. The alienation expressed by the Innu towards their lives in the villages and the exploitation of their land appears to most *Akaneshau* as only a kind of dull and discomforting presence. The Innu articulations of defacement, displacement, and pain are reconfigured as evidence of their own weakness and ultimately their complicity in the sicknesses that plague them. When Innu people attempt to contextualize and politicize their troubles, as they do in conversation and in such publications as *Gathering Voices* and *Between a Rock and a Hard Place*, this is often dismissed as what Dr. McDonald referred to as "blameology" – a pathological form of scapegoating whites, and as she and several others, most notably the clergy of the villages, stress, a failure to "take responsibility."

As I indicated earlier, the structure of health workers' narratives follows a familiar pattern: x is a fact of life, therefore it would be prudent to do y, but we discover z, and often, a denial of x on the part of the Innu. Cause and effect are neatly cordoned off in this severe and judgemental form of truth-making. The fault is with Them, with their obduracy and ignorance. While most health workers admit that the living conditions in Sheshatshiu and Utshimassits are frequently grim, some see the Innu as actually being in an enviable situation. Their narratives of the "progress" on land claims, the introduction of various new programs and institutions, and the promises of a flood of cash provide an upbeat counterbalance to the inebriation, suicide, and misery they see all around them. Such a discourse shares something with the *National Geographic* vision of the Innu controlling most of Labrador, demanding more of it, yet on the rack of misery.

DOUBLE BAD FAITH

In *Death without Weeping*, Nancy Scheper-Hughes (1992: 195-210) described the Sartrean "bad faith" of physicians treating shantytown dwellers in the northeast of Brazil. She showed how Brazilian doctors transformed despair, misery, and suffering into the language of sickness. The decisions of local doctors to treat social ills as bodily ills and to see hunger, widely experienced by poverty-stricken shantytown dwellers, as a nervous complaint rather than a symptom of the politics of economic distribution represented an extreme case of "bad faith." By medicalizing the ailments of their patients in the shantytown, the doctors were consciously deflecting attention from the more fundamental incubators of affliction that lie in social, political, and economic oppression. Medicalization is "bad faith" in that doctors and other health workers "pretend to themselves and to others that they are not really involved in or responsible for what they are doing or the consequences of their actions" (ibid., 209). Although medicalization has long been a feature of health and psychiatric services in Western countries, it is relatively new elsewhere.

While Scheper-Hughes describes various ailments such as hunger, depression, and nervousness, many of the afflictions of the Innu can be more easily accommodated within biomedical taxonomies ranging from dental caries to diabetes. As a result, there is, in biomedical terms, a less problematic fit between the diagnosis and the medicines prescribed. Whereas doctors in Scheper-Hughes's shantytown, Bom Jesus, appeared relatively blasé about the family lives and conduct of their patients, the health workers in Sheshatshiu and Utshimassits are at pains to emphasize the behavioural deficiencies of Innu patients. In Bom Jesus, the pill prescriptions had the effect of halting any further questioning about the distribution and patterns of sickness in the shantytown. By contrast, in Labrador, the medical encounters open up whole arenas of scrutiny. But this funnel of inquiry narrows rather than broadens.

We could say that the health workers in the Innu communities were maintaining a kind of double bad faith. Not only were they treating the afflictions they encountered primarily in terms of the biomedical diagnostic system – and thus masking the political circumstances and contexts of illness – they were then attributing the blame for these illnesses not just to the impersonal, material body but to specific individual and collective failings of the Innu. The first step of bad faith is inevitably tied up with that product of Cartesian dualism, the clinical gaze, as Michel Foucault called it. Western medicine is constantly dogged by this form of bad faith. As Foucault (1975: 8) tells us at the outset of *The Birth of the Clinic,* "in relation to that from which he is suffering, the patient is only an external fact; the medical reading must take him into account only to place him in parentheses." Being trained in North American and European medical schools, not surprisingly, the Labrador doctors are wedded to a mind-body dualism. While they admit that social and psychological factors are relevant to illness, they do not see it as appropriate to connect, for example, self-esteem or the loss of land to the body in either their broader views of the etiology of illness or their treatment plans. Rather, they adopt, as one local doctor expressed it herself, a "fix-it" attitude. That is, the patient inhabits a body that is a machine to be repaired. The task is purely technical, having to do with both the fight against disease within the mechanical body and the *immediate* biophysical environment under which the body is made vulnerable.

The second step of bad faith follows from the further, and wholly unnecessary, blaming of sufferers themselves. The resultant attribution of fault functions not simply as bad faith, but could be seen as retribution for the failure of the Innu to be healthily "integrated." To blame them not only for their ills, but for being blamers, for even entertaining the idea that there are wider social and political associations with their bad fortune, is a retaliatory gesture.[11] Although there are differences between the bad faith that Scheper-Hughes discovered among the physicians of Bom Jesus and that which is expressed by the health workers in Labrador, they have similar effects. Scheper-Hughes (1992: 202-3) describes why bad faith is so important:

> To acknowledge hunger, which is not a disease but a social illness, would be tantamount to political suicide for leaders whose power has come from the same plantation economy that has produced the hunger in the first place. And because the poor have come to invest drugs with such magical efficacy, it is all too easy for their faith to be used against them. If hunger cannot be satisfied, it can at least be tranquilized, so that medicine, even more than religion, comes to actualize the Marxist platitude on the drugging of the masses.

Bad faith in both places helps to consolidate existing power relations. It is in the interest of any state dominated by particular ethnic groups and economic powers to pass off the misery, discontent, and powerlessness of marginalized peoples as medical or psychological issues. There is a pressing need on the part of the Canadian authorities to depoliticize the mass misery, suicide, and premature deaths of Aboriginal peoples. To acknowledge a political content to Native peoples' traumas is to question Canada's very legitimacy as a state, the civilizing project of sedentarization and similar forms of confinement to "reserves" elsewhere in North America, not to mention Canada's much-touted concern for human rights. Politicizing the ubiquity of Innu health problems would also raise questions about the negotiating processes, such as over comprehensive land claims, in which the Innu are represented by Canada and in the media as fully rational game-playing actors. The current depoliticization of Innu sicknesses assists in insulating the vital political negotiations with Canada from the collective suffering of the Innu in the villages. While there is no direct evidence of collaboration between the medical and political authorities in either Brazil or Labrador, the intimate connections forged by common ethnicity, social class, and state funding of medical care are likely to result in a common front in the face of the sufferings of marginalized or indigenous peoples. Both cases demonstrate the immensely important ideological role of medicine in consolidating the hegemony of the state and existing distributions of power, land, and economic benefits.

This is not to say that health officials have always depoliticized illness. Scott and Conn (1987: 1653), two medical workers in Davis Inlet in the 1980s, for example, advocated a public health understanding of the problems of the Innu along the lines of the nineteenth-century German pathologist Rudolf Virchow, who argued that the morbidity of the miners in Upper Silesia was a direct result of their unsanitary and oppressive living and working conditions. Scott and Conn argue that the physician must "educate himself about the historical, political and sociological pathogenesis of disease in the community he purports to serve." A similar perspective has been offered by Dr. Peter Sarsfield, author of a book on being a doctor in the Far North (Sarsfield, 1997) and a physician to the Innu in the 1970s and 1980s. In a CBC interview, Sarsfield situated the continuing high mortality in Native communities, including those in Labrador, as a matter of control over land and resources. "We are a country based on extraction, exploitation of resources," he said, "in order for us to stop killing, figuratively and literally, aboriginal people we're going to have to give up that power." Although Sarsfield was pessimistic about Canada relinquishing power over Aboriginal lands, he situated the issue as one of political action, not inevitability.[12]

Dr. Mcdonald's "blameology" critique ignores the more subtle ways in which the Innu themselves locate context for their sufferings. While the Innu are often fully conscious of the historical and political roots of their current situation and the role of the colonizing forces, such as the state and the church, they also blame themselves personally for their unhappiness. They situate fault in their lack of purpose, inability to maintain relationships, alcoholic indiscretions, lack of motivation, and the like. This is one of the reasons why the number of people who take their own lives or who want to take their own lives is so staggeringly high. Young people especially feel that they have failed according to the standards of Euro-Canadian society and, thus, that there is no future for them. At the press conference for *Canada's Tibet*, the day after his 15-year-old son's suicide, a grief-stricken Jean-Pierre Ashini sat beside me saying, "in the community, my son was weak, but in the country he was strong. He was a good hunter. I don't think he could cope with the way we live." The high rate of Innu suicide testifies to the propensity to turn frustrations inward. Not being able to "cope with the way we live" is a humble admission of psychic frailty brought about by "having to stay in one place all the time," as Jean-Pierre put it earlier.

While the historical and political roots are openly discussed whenever Innu confront scenes of death, alcoholism, and abuse, rarely is blame directly attributed to any particular agent or any one factor elevated over another as a trump card. Judgement is often reserved and slow in emerging. Contrary to the views of the health workers, I have never met an Innu who would place himself or herself in the exclusive role of victim of white oppression. Rather, the events that have occurred, from the initial sedentarization of the people through to the last young man to point a shotgun into his mouth, are recognized as actions of people, as things that individuals did in particular contexts of meaninglessness, despair, and drinking, but nonetheless these are actions of people. There is no attempt to formulate any kind of hierarchy of causality, since causes are themselves believed to be multifarious and often elusive. Nor is there any rigorous attempt to separate a cause and an effect. Although wide-ranging associations and inferences may be drawn, these are always fluid and changing and never neglect the role of individual agency.

To illustrate the chasm between Innu and Euro-Canadian ways of understanding Innu misfortune, the following transcript of a radio interview between Chief Paul Rich and the journalist Cindy Wall is illustrative. The interview took place on 3 April 2000 shortly after a house fire claimed the life of an 11-year-old boy who had been sniffing gas with three older boys. Anne Budgell first sets the scene:

> Anne Budgell: In our news this morning we told you about a serious house fire in the community of Sheshatshui over the weekend. An 11-year-old boy was severely injured Friday night, four young fellows between the ages of 11 and 17 were in the home when the fire started. There weren't adults around at the time. Three of the youngsters escaped unharmed but one boy suffered external and internal injuries. He had been sniffing gasoline at the time. Paul Riche [sic][13] is the Band Chief in Sheshatshiu and he spoke with producer Cindy Wall about the incident.

> Paul Riche (PR): This is something that's not new and everybody that is listening out in Labrador, in Newfoundland and in the rest of Canada has known that the Innu of Labrador are the only group in Canada that has not been recognized. And when something like this happens people wake up and ask, who are the Innu? And what I feel sometime is that the whole world out there is not listening. And when I say the whole world I am talking about Canada and Newfoundland, Minister Robert Nault.

In stressing recognition, Paul Rich provides political context. He is referring specifically to the recognition of the Innu as Aboriginal people in constitutional terms and this requires a parallel recognition of the right of the Innu to control the institutions in their own communities. The Chief is concerned that because the Innu are not "status Indians" with First Nations equivalency, they are not able to run any of their own programs or services, as was agreed at a 24 November 1999 meeting. But he also implies a more general recognition of Innu suffering in the context of the overall political situation. The interviewer does not register this appeal for recognition despite the Chief making it several times. Each question finds her reverting back to the individual level, focusing on errant parents initially:

> Cindy Wall (CW): But why, though? Because this happened because children were in a house and there was no parent around. Somebody listening is going to say this falls right on the parents, this is the responsibility of parents to take care of their children.

> PR: Okay, let me finish my story first and then you can say whatever you want to say towards me after. But what I have to say is that we ask for infrastructure dollars so we could build an arena for kids so they wouldn't have to be doing stuff like that. And we ask for education control so we could teach the parents about parenting, class courses that they need. We know that we lack a lot of those areas and just look at the budget that was announced by [then Premier Brian] Tobin. He said $23 million for the Inuit. But does it say anywhere in there for the Innu of Labrador? No it doesn't. And the Premier says he is fully supportive of the Innu position of being registered. But then you don't see any of that into the provincial

budget that was allocated. These are the things that the community really needs.

In the remainder of the interview the Chief broadens the perspective by linking aversion of tragedy to control of community resources and the validation of Innu cultural experience, while the interviewer constantly wants to circumscribe the discussion to issues of individual and collective pathology.

CW: So you are lacking these things for people to do the same as on the North Coast, those social issues are identical. But nothing has been happening to get things moving in your community.

PR: There was an agreement that was signed on November 24, 1999, between Newfoundland and the federal government of Indian Affairs. But then since that nothing has moved. We are caught in between a tug of war between the federal government and the provincial government. The only losers in this war is the children and that's what happened this weekend.

CW: So because the children have nothing to do they are doing these awful things, they are sniffing gasoline.

PR: Well there is, if we had the tools and our own resources we would take those resources and the tools that we get and help each other within the community, but that's not in our control.

CW: What tools, you mentioned some specifics there, you talked about a parenting course and other things but what specifically do you need? What is going to attract children away from this habit of gasoline-sniffing?

PR: Well, what's going to attract the kids from all these things that they are doing that's negative are things like, the kids go to school there is thing in the school under our control the Innu culture will be taught in there. The kids will be taken out in the country, there is so many things for kids to look forward to.

CW: If you had your own education system?

PR: Our own educational system, our Innu running our own Innu program under education. Our own infrastructures, our own heath-care system, these are the things that we are going to be moving quickly to. But I am saddened that nothing has happened since we signed the agreement in November 1999.

CW: What can you do in the meantime if you know that you have families who are struggling, if you know you have children who might be in homes there by themselves and there could be some danger. Is there anything that can be done as a community to make sure that this doesn't happen again? To make sure somebody is watching out for children.

The interchange continues in this vein, with the Chief reluctant to speak in terms of personal or social pathology. Unlike the shantytown dwellers described by Scheper-Hughes, who accepted the diagnosis of their hunger as nervousness, the Innu in general have not internalized the bad-faith categorizations of their sufferings offered by medical personnel or prompted by journalists. While they are conscious of some of the derogatory judgements, they have yet to accept these as authentic depictions of why they become ill.

Because biomedicine has never seriously entertained the notion that conceptions of health and illness, as well as causality, might be relative, an even more subtle omission of medical stories is the idea that the Innu may not view etiology, for example, in the same way as Euro-Canadian health-care practitioners. The materialist philosophical foundations of medicine tend to limit attention to the cause-and-effect relationships inscribed upon the Cartesian body and the germ theory of illness. Dirt, as Mary Douglas (1966: 48) pointed out long ago, is "matter out of place." Biomedicine has universalized its association with pathology and, hence, danger. By doing so, it obscures both the political character of dirt – for example, that associated with the government-sponsored dwellings of the Innu in Davis Inlet – and dirt as a culturally specific product. Put differently, it does not distinguish between political dirt and cultural dirt. While both can be implicated in illness, political dirt is rarely perceived as such, while cultural dirt is highlighted as grounds for medical offensives.

Dirt is often not recognized by the Innu as "dirt" in the same sense that it would be by Euro-Canadians. Lice, for example, that scourge of European hygienists, were never demonized by the Innu themselves. In a memoir, the Innu hunter Michel Gregoire (Dominique, 1989: 30-31) tells of the fable of the *Mistapeo* (guardian spirit) who actually creates lice for the Innu to kill. While lice were common, they were never regarded in the same draconian terms as they have been for Europeans. They were, and are, dealt with by mothers plucking them out of children's hair and often couples do the same for each other.[14] Similarly, many Innu wear the same clothes for many days consecutively, but this is never judged as being "dirty." However, this would likely be a feature of Innu life that medical workers and other non-Natives single out for comment. The attacks on cultural dirt and the silence on political dirt are just one more instance of the bad faith of the health professions.

HOSPITAL STORIES

Dr. McDonald helped treat an umbilical hernia that I developed one spring after some Wonder Bread had stuck in my throat and induced violent coughing. She ensured that I received medical attention and a speedy operation in the Melville Hospital in Goose Bay. While setting up the hospital appointment, our conversation, like many I have had with *Akaneshau*, was a dialogue that quickly became a monologue intent on sweeping away any sympathy for the Innu. At the time I was working for the Sheshatshiu band council, undertaking the research on schooling presented in Chapters 5 and 6. I related to her my observation that the school was perceived as destructive to Innu students, especially in the 1960s and 1970s. Without allowing me time to elaborate, she countered that there was too much "blameology" in the community and that the Innu had to "take responsibility" for themselves. While setting up the hospital appointment, she delivered a case in point. Many children came to her clinic with dental caries and other tooth problems. She knew that they ate a lot of sugary foods, for she had seen the candy purchased at the junk food stores in their mouths. They wandered past her clinic window armed with cheap candy from the store at the bottom of the hill. She asked the parents why they allowed their children to eat so much sugar, and they had told her that it was because the kids liked candy. To her this was like saying that a child could play with a gun because he liked it. Again, the contrast structure – "if x, therefore y, but we get z"– equalled pathology.

The next day is set for the operation. My alarm rings at six o'clock. Having had nothing to eat, I drive the spruce-lined bumpy road from Sheshatshiu to Goose Bay in my friend's noisy Bronco. I check in to the former U.S. Air Force hospital and the admitting nurse assigns me to share a room with Penote Rich, a young man from Davis Inlet. He is splayed out on the bed; his breakfast is cold on the tray. The television station from Toronto is blaring information on the morning commute into downtown Toronto hundreds of miles away. I wait in a hospital gown about an hour until I am wheeled down to the operating room, where the friendly nurses chat and warn me of indiscretions that patients blurt out while coming round from general anaesthetics. While I hear the blood-curdling wails of a small boy, my predecessor under the knife, the doctors explain the procedure thoroughly. I am reassured, fall asleep, and awake to the jovial ribbing of the nurses. My stomach is heavy with a compress, and I am groggy and hungry.

By evening I discover that Simeon Tshakapesh is in the next room. The last time I had seen him had been on a journey to Ashuapun a year before. He had a stomach ulcer and had not eaten properly since December. It was now April, and I noticed that he was much slimmer than the last time I had seen him. He tells me that he was stressed and anxious with palpitations that started after he moved to Goose Bay from Utshimassits. He is hooked up to a drip that gives him sustenance and drugs. While I visit, his doctor, a young man with a goatee and baseball cap, comes in and makes amiable chat. The doctor tells Simeon that he has switched his medication to Clonazepam on account of his anxiety. He need not worry about it because it is being fed straight into the drip. The doctor did not explain what Clonazepam is and why it was being used. Clonazepam is a benzodiazepine, a type of drug that slows down the nervous system. A drug with considerable side effects, Clonazepam is used to treat epileptic conditions as well as "panic disorders."

Observing the presence of several Innu patients, Simeon jokes that the hospital would lose a lot of its business were it not for the Innu. At night, I drift in and out of sleep. An old man shuffles up and down the corridor, his slippers sliding on the linoleum. Penote next to me sounds like he is shovelling gravel with every laboured breath. He occasionally wakes and turns on the oxygen machine. Sleepless, Simeon walks along the corridor with his drip. Before dawn, a child cries. I hear the nurses scurrying about, talking, the smell of toast in a toaster. Blood pressure, temperature, and pulse are taken every few hours, recorded and filed. The nurse, while checking my vital indicators, is curious about why I live in Sheshatshiu. I tell her of my work on schooling with the band council, and this becomes the cue to another monologue on Innu manners. The blame for the distress of so many children in the community, she believes, is with the parents. So many of them are drinking, and when they are drinking, they are "savages." "Not even Indians," she adds, as Penote slopes back into the room.

Although young Penote enjoyed the attentions of the nurses, *Tshenut* generally do not like the hospital. Most do not understand English so, apart from the presence of a part-time translator or occasionally an escort, they are at a total loss to know what is being done to them in these strange surroundings. The Innu, particularly those from Davis Inlet, are almost totally severed from their family and friends. Nearly all *Tshenut* shun the hospital and only go there in extreme emergencies, and while confined in hospital they are often despondent. Some who are critically ill discharge themselves against medical advice, preferring to die at home. Hospital is a place of death and resignation for many *Tshenut*.

Several years ago there was an old Innu man at the Goose Bay hospital. He did not understand what the doctors and nurses were doing or saying to him. When Daniel Ashini, who told me this story, arrived as a patient, the elder's face lit up. He asked Daniel to request that they share the same room. They were granted this, and the old man talked to Daniel a lot. But after Daniel told him that he was going to leave the hospital, he stopped talking. At the moment when Daniel was leaving, the old man told Daniel to tell the doctors that he wasn't sick anymore. When this was relayed to the doctor, the doctor said that there was still evidence of pneumonia. A few days later he died in his hospital bed. Daniel put this down to a resignation of his spirit.[15]

While the *Tshenut* often resign themselves to a morbid fate in the hospital, children actively resist. One nurse in Davis Inlet told me that she had to fight Innu children to get them into bed or to take them to the operating theatre. "They are always fighting and screaming." Within the hospital, the personal autonomy that Innu enjoy at home is stripped from them. They find themselves at the mercy of professionals who presume to know what is best for them and overtly and inadvertently do what very few Innu would ever do – that is, make a decision on behalf of another person. Because of this autocratic tendency, a trait often associated with the practice of Western medicine, some people say that the doctors act as if the Innu patients are stupid. And here, my own experience in hospital is indicative. While doctors and nurses explained the fine details of my operation on several occasions, I did not notice anything like the same attention being paid to Simeon Tshakapesh and Penote Rich. From the doctor's bedside chat, Simeon would have had no idea what Clonazepam was or what it was meant to do. Penote said that he could not really explain to me what his treatment was because he had not been told.

Mary Pia Benuen, the only Innu qualified nurse in Labrador, explained this situation to me:

Older people find hospital strange. They feel that they have to do what the doctors and nurses tell them. They feel that they have no rights. They feel like they are not in control of themselves and that the doctor is controlling them. The Innu see white people as authority figures with the right to tell you what to do. Doctors try their best, but it slips out of their mind that this person [an Innu] is from a different culture with different beliefs. Doctors from the dominant culture think they are dealing with the same cases, the same as them. *They forget that Innu patients are different.*

Of course, many things make the Innu patients different. Having experience and histories as relatively independent nomadic hunters with a continuing attachment to a way of life – *nutshimit* – is only the most obvious difference. Most Innu *Tshenut* face a language gulf with their carers. All Innu live in familial and community circumstances that bear little resemblance to those of the nurses and doctors who live in Goose Bay or North West River. Very little commonality of experience can be assumed. Furthermore, Innu generally enjoy a kind of personal autonomy that helps to dissolve conflict. They are more accustomed to making their own personal decisions, a right denied them in the hospital.

TREATMENT FOR YOUR SENSES

Few Innu people see matters of health and illness in the same way as the *Akaneshau* authorities. Confident certainties are avoided. Cause is not severed from effect. Blame is not so readily dispatched. The body is not disconnected from the mind. In fact, for many the body is part of a whole living system – *nutshimit*. The fate of the body follows observances of respect for the animals, landscape, and other people.[16] When this order is disturbed – as it obviously has been by sedentarization, village conditions, and the alienation and exploitation of their land – it is not surprising that the assault on an established social order results in the kinds of afflictions that people are experiencing in Sheshatshiu and Utshimassits. Illness to the Innu is not simply a biological malfunction. It follows from community life. For them, the severing of a permanent link with the land, which is the flip side to their confinement to villages, has had a huge bearing on their well-being. The collective loss of autonomy occasioned by these processes acts as a sort of benchmark against which they situate illness and healing.

The *nutshimit* life is seen, even by Innu who do not go to the country very often, as synonymous with health. Although the Innu now do not hunt with dog teams, haul their possessions on toboggans, or paddle canoes up the rivers and lakes, vigorous physical exertion is necessary to make and maintain the camp, hunt for animals, and set up traps, snares, and nets for fish. Physical exertion is involved in the use, maintenance, and repair of snowmobiles, outboard motors, and other machines. Women working with hand sewing machines usually make canvas tents beforehand. The tents are then fitted over poles fashioned from spruce trees that have to be cut down, denuded of branches, and hauled to the location of the camp where they are cut to size and fashioned as supports inside and outside the tent. Camps may be moved often and rapidly, each time requiring a variation of tasks in different locations with different topographical and climatic challenges. Firewood has to be cut for warmth. Spruce boughs must be continually picked for the floors of the tents. Children must be watched, nurtured, and protected, but they also help by fetching and carrying.

Hunting expeditions almost always take a whole day and sometimes hunters may stay out of the main camp for several days in search of animals with no guarantee of success. They may travel vast distances, walking into forests on snowshoes and enduring extreme cold for long periods of time, sometimes sleeping in the open. When animals are killed, the hunters have to gut, skin, and haul them up onto their komatiks or boats for transporting back to the camp. Hunting for some animals can be very taxing. Beaver, for example, are sometimes taken by dismantling the lodge and shooting the mammal after prodding it out into the open water. Here, the hunter can spend hours taking apart, layer by layer, all the logs, sticks, and branches that the beaver has used to build the lodge, and at the end there is no necessary guarantee that the animal will be inside it. If a beaver is killed, however, a tasty and nutritious meal will be ensured for several families. Similarly, porcupine and ptarmigan hunting in the winter and spring involves walking through forests in snowshoes, vigilant for the signs of the animals as well as directions and the natural hazards of soft and deep snow.

Dominic Pokue and Colin Samson dismantling a beaver lodge. Photograph by Daniel Ashini.

Christine Rich butchering a caribou at Kamesteuishikashish. Photograph by author.

Even if they are overweight and physically unfit to begin with, the requirements of camp life are such that almost everyone will build muscle and develop great stamina and endurance over the time they are in the country. If hunts are successful, the wild foods such as caribou, beaver, ducks, geese, partridges, ptarmigan, porcupine, and several varieties of fish are far superior sources of nutrition than the food items on sale in the community stores and will aid the general strengthening of the body and the sharpening of the senses. In fact, when Innu speak about their life in the country, they almost always highlight the goodness of the food they eat.

While general physical fitness is enhanced by camp life, hunting families rarely attempt to push their bodies to the limits of endurance. When camp is set up, families work quickly and efficiently, but breaks, if only for a short period, are taken during difficult jobs. How one feels will dictate whether particular tasks will be done on any given day. Although sickness is taken stoically and hunters will endure much pain without complaint, hunting families rarely take risks that could imperil their health. If a woman is not feeling well, she will not go out in search of fresh boughs for the floor of her tent. Likewise, if a man is tired, he may forgo hunting for a day or more. There is no

Maggie Pokue preparing to singe quills from a porcupine. Photograph by author.

conception among the Innu that is analogous to the biomedical
metaphor of the body as a machine. While a Western body can be
continually tweaked by vitamins, pills, medications, and organized
exercise to enhance "performance," in the country the Innu rely on
judicious rest periods, close observance of weather and other environmental conditions, the nutritiousness of wild food, and the good
humour of camp life away from the multiple stresses of the villages.

Well-being is always collective. The animals, fish, and waterfowl
that are killed are shared. Hunters do not hoard meat for their own
exclusive consumption. Teamwork is vital to survival. While there
are occasional tensions, amity within the camps is necessary for the
success of hunts, and this, too, requires tolerance, respect, and consideration for others. With a long historical tradition of nomadic

hunting to connect with and the shared goals necessary to its realization, camp members say that they draw closer to one another in
the country. There is a strong sense of inclusion and belonging. The
contrast between the relative calm and equilibrium of the country
and the seeming chaos and animosities of the communities is experienced most intensely by *Tshenut*. "In the past," Lizette Penashue
told me, "we never had booze and drugs. In the past, we never heard
of suicide. We never knew drinking in the country. Now there is no
sharing and people don't care for each other. In the country people
only talked about our way of life and the animals. Now there is too
many arguments, and too much hating each other." Thus, on occasion the tensions of village life are carried over into the country,
making it less insulated from outside influences than it had been in
the youth of the *Tshenut*.

Nevertheless, the experience of several months in the country is
still refreshing and many older people experience the abrupt transition back to community life as profoundly depressing. Whereas in
the country their days were full with hunting, chopping wood, maintaining the tents, snaring, fishing, cooking, stories, humour, and
taking care of children, the day in the community will often be blank.
Time is filled by sleeping longer and sitting around the house and
watching television. If they do not speak English, *Tshenut* may have
no role in community life other than occasionally being called on for
largely ceremonial duties with the political bodies or as communicators of traditional knowledge and stories at the school. But it is not
simply the *Tshenut* who have virtually no place in community life, it
is also those who are not connected to the political bodies of the Innu
Nation and the band councils that provide access to the vast bulk of
the employment opportunities in the community.

For the many Innu who exist largely outside these institutions,
nutshimit provides meaning, purpose, and spiritual connections. After festering in the village of Sheshatshiu for about 15 years, in the
1980s many people returned to the country for as much as seven
months of each year. This corresponded to some dramatic improvements in health and morale. As Ben Andrew, an Innu hunter, and
Peter Sarsfield, a physician working with the Innu, pointed out at
the time, "Alcohol abuse suddenly stops. A combination of improved
diet, a rigorous lifestyle and the stable emotional and social environment offered by a functioning Innu society, make for a startling
contrast to life in the villages" (Andrew and Sarsfield, 1984: 429).

The separation from *nutshimit*, however, is recognized variously
as a source of a split or loss of self. "The country is our survival,"
Francesca Snow, an Innu teacher, told me in the uneasy surround-

ings of the Peenamin McKenzie School, "it is how you become who you are." To be Innu is to be a hunter, as Paul Pone, a young hunter, once said after returning from the country, "my self, my identity, my own religion is in the country. I go to my own school there. There are medicines there that I know about. Out there I am a worker, a hunter, a fisherman, an environmentalist and a biologist." *Nutshimit* helps people who have lost their way, who are confused or depressed. Being in the active, meaningful, and comparatively congenial environment of a hunting camp encourages young people especially to put their problems into a different perspective. It helps them see who they are or who they might be without constantly gauging themselves against the various yardsticks of Euro-Canadian society. "As for me," Paul Pone said, "it helped me. There is work without money. That's what I call help and what I call treatment. Its exercise and freedom . . . it's treatment for your senses – eyes, ears, nose, brain." Whereas boredom is a daily feature of community life, the difference in the country is that "work takes over from apathy," as Apenam Pone, an alcohol counsellor, told me.

Nutshimit is as much spiritual as it is physical. The Innu hunters, both in their own accounts and in my observations, are deeply respectful of the animals. Some ask for the life of the animal before they kill it. Killing an animal is not the end of the life of the animal just as death is not the end of human life. The wisdom of the animal is transferred to the hunter and forms part of his spirit. Hunting is a holy occupation to the Innu. The single most important factor in the success of a hunt is determined by how respectful one has been to the animals, rather than solely by the skill of the hunter or how technically proficient his equipment is. Hunting is governed by the Animal Gods who determine which animals will let the hunter kill them. Respect for animals may be demonstrated in many ways – by killing only what is needed, eating and using as much of the animal as possible and properly discarding anything that is not used, and by sharing what is killed.

A successful hunt for caribou is often followed by a *mukushan* feast, in which all of the leg bones of the animals are carefully cleaned of meat and the marrow removed. The entire animal is eventually used and any waste product is either burned or put up on a scaffold to keep away from dogs. The crushed leg bones are then boiled, and as the fat rises to the top it is left to congeal or harden in a separate container and eaten with bread and meat by members of the camp. This occasion serves to show the Animal Gods the respect that they are accorded by the Innu through their careful usage of all of the animal. When food was scarce, the *kushapatshikan* (the shaking tent) was sometimes set up to consult with the Animal Gods and attempt to ensure a future supply of food. Partly because of the suppression of the shaking tent by the priests in the early sedentarization period and partly because the Innu themselves lack confidence to practise it, the last *kushapatshikan* was held in the 1960s.

There have obviously been major changes in the way the country is experienced since sedentarization. The *Tshenut* are very clear about the changes and often speak nostalgically about travelling vast distances across the peninsula in the dead of winter, portaging canoes and supplies over steep hills, and going days without food. The Mushuau Innu life described by Georg Henriksen (1973) just before sedentarization in the 1960s – travelling by dog team and surviving primarily through hunting caribou and trading at the posts for essentials – does not exist anymore. *Nutshimit* has changed. Hunting families use the latest technologies, come back and forth between the country and the community often, and eat a range of processed as well as wild foods. But the sensibilities, observances, and world views remain.

In the country, the Innu have specific remedies for the accidents and ailments that people are likely to encounter. Although it has obviously diminished over time, the Innu possess a vast natural pharmacy as well as a range of medical theories and treatment procedures. Most *Tshenut* prefer it to Western medicine, and shun, avoid, and refuse hospitalization except in dire emergencies. Even in the community, many Innu still find Innu medicines more useful than those available at the clinic or hospital. Matthew Penashue of Sheshatshiu outlined some of the Innu medicines in the film, *The Two Worlds of the Innu*:

> When a person gets sick, he remembers the medicinal uses of different types of tree and that's what he looks for. Then he cuts it down, brings it back to the camp, where an old woman prepares it, because she has the necessary knowledge. The little tamarack, and spruce and all sorts of willow, they all have medicine in them. The ptarmigan eats the seeds of one type of willow that has medicinal uses. And the same with the sap from fir trees, you use that when a person has a sore chest cold, or when he cuts himself with an axe or knife, he uses the sap to close the wound. . . .
>
> We didn't have any white man's medicines back then. We treated ourselves with all the medicines we found on the land. But now, that's disappearing. The Innu seem to be giving it up. (Wilson, 1994)

"In the country I had a cut from an axe on my leg some time ago before radio telephones," Matthew's grandson, Peter recalled. "Nobody panicked. My leg was treated with baby urine. It healed. Same thing happened to my thumb. It was nearly cut off. It was treated and healed." At a hunting camp at Utshisk-nipi, about 90 miles into the interior from Sheshatshiu, Dominic Pokue showed me how to heal an axe cut on my hand with spruce sap. The sap is boiled and the froth on the top skimmed off as a medicine. The first animal that was killed after I joined the camp was a beaver. On the way back to camp in the canoe, Dominic said that the film on the scrotum of the beaver can be used as a balm for earaches. For certain infections, a muskrat's fur can be used to clean the pus, after which sap or gum can be applied. Another *Tshenut*, Pien Penashue, told me that medicines can be obtained from all of the animals in the country. Sponges can be made from caribou skin, diaper rash and skin irritations can be treated with the soft shavings from dead spruce trees. For toothaches and teething babies, the gums should be scratched with a pine needle, and then applied with berries. If the arm is infirm, one can eat the arm of a bear to regain strength, and similarly with other limbs. Other more psychological problems can be dealt with by substances found in the country as well as physical exercise, dreaming, and communicating with others.

Although I have met doctors and nurses who are mildly curious, I have encountered almost no medical interest in Innu beliefs about the body, remedies, or explanations for their many illnesses. The nurses stationed at Davis Inlet have no cross-cultural training before they arrive and once they are in post they almost always stay cloistered within their quarters, positioned on the hill above the Innu shacks. Certainly none of the medical personnel I have met (with the possible exception of one nurse in Utshimassits who had an Innu boyfriend, and who was frowned upon by the other nurses) contemplated Innu health in terms of the overall history of sedentarization and healing as a return to the Innu life of the country.

ARE WE HUMAN?

As I have suggested, the bad faith of the medical professionals is maintained by depoliticizing the sufferings of the Innu. This is done by not seriously considering much that is known about the health-enhancing qualities of *nutshimit*, on the one hand, and the deleterious effects of European contact and sedentarization, on the other. Ignoring all considerations of the health of the Innu in relation to progressive European encroachments on their lands and way of life is therefore another crucial aspect of the medical construction of Innu health.

Epidemics of infectious diseases were brought to the Innu and adjacent territories as early as the 1630s when measles were spread by the missionaries, decimating whole populations, most notably the Hurons further west (Starkey, 1998: 87). More recently, disease was introduced by the Europeans docking their boats on the Labrador coast, the North Shore of the St. Lawrence, and the eastern trading posts of the Hudson Bay, where another source of infection – livestock – was introduced. In his memoir, *Labrador Doctor*, Wilfred Grenfell (1920: 108) writes of watching a "load of rude coffins from the wharf" and recalling the epidemic of influenza suffered by the Eskimos of the northern Labrador coast, the germ of which was "doubtless imported by some schooner from the South. Like all primitive peoples, they had no immunity to the disease, and the suffering and mortality were very high."[17] In fact, Grenfell's hospital ship was probably a carrier of infection as patients and crew brought disease from southern Labrador and Newfoundland. William Duncan Strong (Leacock and Rothschild, 1994: 58) reported that influenza and measles, common among the Eskimos at Hebron, Okak, Nain, and Hopedale on the coast, reached the Barren Ground and Davis Inlet Innu in 1918.[18]

The deterioration of the health of the Innu is closely associated with their contact with Europeans. Not only were Europeans transmitters of diseases that the Innu had little immunity to, but the practices that made them a healthy and vibrant people began to erode under the influence of the Europeans. Often such changes were made merely because they may have offended delicate European sensibilities. In the 1860s, Henry Youle Hind (1863, I: 177) observed that the Innu had previously anointed their bodies with seal oil, which made them less sensitive to heat, cold, and moisture, as well as the attacks of blackflies in the summer. However, "since most of them have adopted European habits, and ceased to anoint their bodies with seal oil, they are very liable to colds and influenza, and numbers die every year on the coast." Hind also noted that at Sept-Îles and other locations on the North Shore the Innu were prone to illnesses related to the damp, such as rheumatism. At the trading posts, they also suffered from the lack of caribou and other animals that provided the mainstay of their diet. By contrast, further north at Fort Chimo where there was less European contact, Lucien Turner (1979: 106) remarked on the longevity of the Innu in the 1890s. "Both sexes attain great age," he asserted, "in some instances certainly living over seventy years. Some assert that they were well advanced in years before the white man came in 1827."

Although remarking on high infant mortality rates along with stomach and lung disorders, many of the life-threatening diseases – smallpox, tuberculosis, and influenza – mentioned by Vaino Tanner in his discussion of Innu health in the 1930s are European in origin. Otherwise, much of the picture he presents is positive. The Innu in the interior "suffer less from disease than the Eskimo on the coast" (Tanner, 1944:594-5):

> the Indian is unbelievably hardened against wind and weather, and his imperviousness to cold is phenomenal. He lies down to sleep out-of-doors in winter in caribou skin only, and examines his fishing nets in a howling snowstorm, dipping his hands in the water now and then in order that they shall not freeze. His children run about in the snow barefoot. His whole body seems as hardened as his face. . . . The women, too, are strong; a few days after childbirth the mother is up and about, the baby is stuffed into a fur bag with moss as a napkin and on goes the caravan. (Ibid., 594)

The "Nascaupee" further north were "said to be hardier than the Montagnais. They bear cold as well as the Eskimo. The little children show astonishing indifference to temperature; they sometimes run barefoot in the worst cold. The birth rate is said to be good and the natural increase in their numbers is satisfactory" (ibid., 663). Upon closer observation, Tanner described the Innu as "being healthy, families are large, the children fit and jolly . . . never did I see the brand of 'fire water' on the face of a Montagnais" (ibid., 599). The geographer was eventually won over by the peacefulness, calmness, and radiating friendliness of the Innu he met.

Although demanded by the Newfoundland authorities, the change from living in movable tents to stationary wooden shacks would have been a drastic change to hunting families. Even the self-proclaimed civilizer of the Subarctic, Sir Wilfred Grenfell, recognized the dire public health consequences of such a transition to the neighbours of the Innu, the Inuit of the Labrador coast.[19] "Among the Eskimos I found a great deal of tuberculosis and much eye trouble," he recalls (Grenfell, 1920: 90). "Around the Moravian mission-stations wooden houses had replaced the former 'tubiks,' or skin tents, which were moved as occasion required and so provided for sanitation." By contrast, Sir Wilfred notes, "these wooden huts were undrained, dark and dirty to a remarkable degree. No water supply was provided, and the spaces between the houses were simply indescribable garbage heaps, presided over by innumerable dogs. The average life was very short and infant mortality high." Then comes the moment of doubt, which is quickly swept aside: "the best for which we could hope in the way of morals among these people was that a natural unmorality was some offset to the existing conditions." What did the doctor mean here, that *a natural unmorality was some offset to the existing conditions*? The Eskimos did not feel pain, disease, and death in the same way as the British? The "unmorality" of the Eskimos in this case was perhaps their virtue, allowing them to tolerate and survive the devastation of *existing conditions.*[20]

If the Innu were considered to be the same unmoral brutes as the Inuit (and every indication is that Europeans perceived them as even more brutish[21]), then it is perhaps not as ironic as it might seem at first glance that the same type of housing was provided for the Innu who were sedentarized slightly later than the Inuit. Whatever problems hunters might encounter in imposed villages, their tough resignation to disaster – and the records of explorers and anthropologists of the region are full of accounts of the stoicism of "the Indians" – may have made such changes palatable. Apart from some enmity with the Inuit, almost all pre-sedentarization first-hand observations portrayed the Innu as a largely friendly and amiable people who were skilful in hunting and the arts of living in a difficult terrain. But as hunters, they were judged to have a rather poverty-stricken cultural and spiritual life. They were ruled by "the chase" and the quest for meat, and as such were destitute of any deep emotions. The following description by Henry Youle Hind (1863, I: 239) is fairly typical:

> Savage life, in such a wilderness as the one I am describing is sometimes joyous to the Indians if they can kill enough to eat. The excitement of the chase, the pride, delight and temporary comfort of success, more than compensate for privations to which they are accustomed, or for the anxieties which they do not trouble themselves about. They kill a caribou, store away a little, make a gluttonous and wasteful feast of the greater part, sing, boast and sleep, until hunger wakens them, and the cold reality of their desolation is before them again, to be relieved and forgotten in never changing routine.

This depiction of the Innu as psychologically impoverished, maintaining sustenance and psychic well-being almost exclusively through providing for the basic need of food, represents the backdrop to many European attempts to transform them. If they were as base as these accounts portrayed them to be then surely they would be hardened or oblivious to other types of suffering that might be incurred in such transformations, which were always presented as for their own long-term benefit.[22]

The British and then Euro-Canadian authorities – most notably Dr. W.A. "Tony" Paddon of the International Grenfell Association – believed that without the benefits of Western medicine and health-care facilities, the Innu would suffer from fatal diseases and premature death. These efforts led Euro-Canadians to take credit for saving the Innu and Inuit of Labrador from extinction. In his book on tuberculosis in Newfoundland and Labrador, Edgar House (1981: 185) heralds Grenfell as a saviour. "In 1892, there came to Labrador one of the greatest crusaders in the history of the New World," House reveals, "a man . . . whose efforts, combined with those of the earlier Moravian missionaries, ensured that the natives of Labrador did not meet with extinction as did the Beothuks in Newfoundland."[23] In the early part of the twentieth century, Labrador had the highest rates of TB in North America, although a high proportion of those stricken with the disease were the "liveyeres" whom Grenfell regarded as his principal patients. Although House and others rightly refer to TB as the "white man's disease," its place is not in the history of colonialism but in a history of taming the wilderness, clearing it for settlement and miraculously saving the aborigines at the eleventh hour so that they, too, could be part of the narrative of progress.

However, Wilfred Grenfell's work, concentrated primarily on the "liveyeres" and virtually insignificant in relation to the Innu, was not enough to abate some advances of European disease. In the 1940s, epidemics of tuberculosis and influenza had combined with a cyclical dip in the caribou population to make the situation of some Mushuau Innu desperate. In response, the Commissioner of the Newfoundland Rangers in 1943 argued that "the only alternative . . . is to try to settle them on the coast where they might be given facilities for fishing" (Roche, 1992). Visiting the Davis Inlet post in 1952, it was obvious to Frederick Rowe (1985: 151) that "to even the untrained eye . . . most of the adult Indians were seriously ill."

By the 1960s, the provincial government began to see an increase in the population of "Indians" at the newly created settlements and attributed this to the improved medical and welfare services provided by Grenfell and the state. At this time the authorities even began to see sedentarization as the final step in saving the Innu from extinction. Former Newfoundland member of Parliament Frederick Rowe (ibid., 151-52), for example, depicts settlement as motivated entirely by the benevolence of priests, Grenfell doctors, and a compassionate government. He places particular stock in the health benefits of removing the Innu from tents, where, he alleges, tuberculosis could spread more easily, to houses. As he argues:

> The combined results of segregating infected persons, improved medical treatment, the success of the Oblate priests in getting patients to go to hospital or sanitorium, the building of houses to eliminate the tent syndrome, and the institution of basic hygiene all combined to save the Nascopi Indians of Labrador from extinction. (Ibid., 152)

Yet, it is now clear that the authorities never ensured that conditions in the settlements were conducive to either physical or psychological health. Why else would the government locate the Innu on an island, which, for several months of the year, is cut off from important sources of nutritious fresh meat and fish and physical exercise? Why would large families be housed in shacks with no running water or sanitation? Why, at the end of the twentieth century, would the Davis Inlet store stock only junk foods, causing the dietician to tell me that it was a waste of time for her to inform Davis Inlet residents about healthy domestic foods since these were not available to them?[24]

In the early 1980s, the rate of tuberculosis in Davis Inlet was more than a thousand times greater than in Newfoundland or across Canada (Scott and Conn, 1987: 1651). Settlement in Davis Inlet had been undertaken with neither household sanitation nor running water, precisely those conditions that gave rise to epidemics of infectious diseases in the newly urbanizing regions of Europe in the nineteenth century. Although the rates of tuberculosis have now abated, for all other details, the Inuit community Grenfell described in 1930 could have been Davis Inlet in the 1990s or even elements of Friedrich Engels's working-class Manchester in the 1840s.[25]

On the same day that Simeon Tshakapesh asked the question, "Are we human?" a sad time in Utshimassits following the gruesome shotgun suicide of a promising 19-year-old high school student in the summer of 1995, the Latin American nurse who was called to the scene was passing time with me outside the clinic. I inquired about the suicide. Although expressing sadness and horror at the diabolical scene of death, the fact that this occurred on her first night on duty after a spell away from the community confirmed her earlier prejudices. "They are hardly human," she said, "they think they are the best, but they have not seen how other people live in cities such as Ottawa [where she had a residence]." Amid the grim aftermath of drinking, wailing, and a young man's life violently cut short by his own hand, the question was in the balance – are they human? The attending nurse was barely willing to answer in the affirmative. While few other nurses I have met would speak in such terms, I believe that a common view is that the Innu are somehow constitutionally more adapted to living under the constant shadow of death.

Contemporary doctors and nurses are in a paradoxical position. The conclusion of the narratives of health workers is that the mass ill health of the Innu is plainly an Innu issue to be resolved or endured depending on what the Innu themselves do. More recently, the lexicon of causality invokes negligence, ignorance and feckless-ness rather than Grenfell's "unmorality." The Innu themselves, according to the health professionals, bear responsibility for the suf-fering. And here the medical authorities – perhaps more than the Innu themselves – often look to the Innu political institutions for leadership. To them, it is up to the band councils to negotiate better funding arrangements from the government to introduce more heal-ing programs and projects of the kind that are continually being set up with the aid of *Akaneshau* intermediaries. While the authorities in the past saw to it that the Innu changed as a result of aggressive intervention, the attitude more recently adopted is one of laissez faire.

In contrast to the early aggressive efforts of the Roman Catholic missionaries and the provincial government to sedentarize the Innu for their own good, senior authorities in the health services who I in-terviewed adopted a distinctly "hands off" attitude. Their goals were barely articulated, their sensibilities apathetic, and their visions rooted in an ahistorical present. Labrador health administrators ar-gued that their institutions existed merely to facilitate specifically articulated Innu goals and ambitions. A senior health service ad-ministrator in Goose Bay used the metaphor of a vehicle for the role of his services. The Innu could either occupy the front or back seat, but progress on dealing with health problems depended on the Innu. A public health nurse portrayed the Innu culture as one that was "evolving" and changing as a consequence of the active choices of the Innu themselves. Others insisted that any public health measures, for example, altering the junk food diet in the community, would have to come from the Innu themselves.

Healing, Drinking, and Lost   8
Autonomy

When you are put in a house, and even if you have a job, you can't be what you were. My father had no skills, so he was less than a person. So, he became an alcoholic. He turned into something he didn't want to. So, then we inherited those learned behaviours of violence and drinking. I ended up not having the family I needed to support me.

– Jack Penashue, Sheshatshiu, 1995

We are cleaning up what the government has done to the Innu people. We are cleaning up the government's mess.

– Mary May Osmond, Healing Services, Sheshatshiu, 1996

People are sharpening their knives. The anger will come out in violence or protest.

– Mark Nui, Innu health worker, Utshimassits, 1997

The federal government collects revenue from the sale of beverage alcohol; the funds that are returned to tribal communities are used to establish new treatment bureaucracies that focus on individuals rather than on larger social problems.

– Gerald Vizenor, *The People Named the Chippewa* (1984: 122)

THE REMOVAL OF AUTONOMY

The Innu villages are "Innu" only insofar as Innu people largely populate them. All authority, apart from the band councils and the Innu Nation, is vested in non-Innu. In Sheshatshiu, *Akaneshau* are the main teachers and administrators of the school, although there are also aides who teach in *Innu-aimun*. Both Innu and non-Innu staff the Social Services Department, but *Akaneshau* hold the chief administrative posts. There are health clinics in Sheshatshiu and

North West River, but only the aides and translators are Innu. Doctors, nurses, and administrators are *Akaneshau*. The Goose Bay
hospital caters to a large catchment area that includes both Innu
communities as well as coastal settler and Inuit communities and
Happy Valley-Goose Bay itself, which has a population of almost
9,000. During the 1990s, the hospital employed one Innu nurse and
two Innu translators. There are also resident non-Innu carpenters,
accountants, and environmental advisers, as well as contract researchers and lawyers who fly in to participate in criminal justice
cases as well as to advise on land claims and other matters. Crucially for their conflicts over land and authority with the state, much
of the legal and political advice has been imparted, often through
telephones, faxes, and e-mails, to Innu Nation officials from lawyers
and anthropologists living in Ottawa, Toronto, and St. John's, and a
large proportion of the official correspondence and speeches have
been both drafted and sent out from these cities.

A similar pattern of *Akaneshau* dominion holds for Utshimassits. Those with positions of administrative and legal power are not
Innu. Because Utshimassits is relatively inaccessible for most of the
year, non-Innu must also reside in the community alongside the
Innu. Even with the close proximity of living quarters, however, the
Akaneshau world in Utshimassits is physically and socially set
apart from the larger community. For most of these professionals,
like the transient crews on offshore oil rigs, their work is the only
reason for their presence. Teachers and nurses receive enhanced
"isolation pay" for working in Utshimassits and these *Akaneshau*
live in segregated and cosseted style. Their dwellings are not only
fairly unique in having water and sanitation, but they approximate
North American suburban households, replete with items that are
rare or unknown to the Innu – carpets, new furniture, the latest
home entertainment equipment, kitchen gadgets, specially shipped
in dietary and culinary provisions.

There are, of course, some Innu-run services such as the Alcohol
Program and Healing Services operated by Innu Nation. These programs, which are almost entirely devoted to stemming the rampant
unhappiness in the communities, lack the statutory authority that
the school, Social Services, the health services, and the police operate under. This means that it is always possible for communal
conflicts, marital disputes, health and mental health problems to be
processed outside of Innu control by a "higher" authority. Most of
the daily affairs of Innu people, then, are controlled and administered, either directly or indirectly, by non-Innu. Innu must appeal to
outsiders for welfare payments, legal counsel, child custody, medi-

cal assistance, marriage licences, spiritual advice, and education. Most important decisions are either made by *Akaneshau* or with their promptings and encouragement.

A long clapboard edifice, the provincial Social Services Department office is one of several purpose-built institutions in Sheshatshiu. The only reception room is cramped and fitted with uncomfortable bench-style seats. Many Innu clients stand outside smoking, waiting and chatting. A Plexiglass barrier separates clients from office workers. Only one trained social worker, Lanny Marcelo, the director, an *Akaneshau*, is on the staff. "I only act in accordance with the wishes of the Innu," she tells me as I am ushered into her office. "Decisions are made by the Innu themselves." All the solutions to the problems brought to her attention are "through the Innu people." After reluctantly granting a short interview, she makes a point of emphasizing that she is the wrong person to discuss Social Services. I should be speaking to the Innu workers, she pointedly informs me. She ensures that this is the case by beckoning one of her Innu assistants to accompany us in the office. Many of my questions are deferred to the Innu assistant. Despite the explicit claim that the Innu were autonomous, during the course of our conversation several Innu workers entered the room to seek the director's permission or signature for various courses of action. Granting an advance on welfare payments was the most common request.

The director was explicitly depicting the Innu as having authority, while simultaneously that imputed authority was being exercised, in their presence, not by them, but by her. All important decisions required the director's authorization. I had no way of knowing whether the Innu employees and clients experienced these incidents as confusing or simply routine *Akaneshau* behaviour. But surely, being spoken of as powerful while others wield meaningful authority is part of their everyday experience in many other spheres, such as land claims, development of their lands, and control over community affairs. "The attribution of autonomy to someone who clearly is completely alienated from her autonomous self, by the persons who are perpetuating this alienation, albeit unwittingly, is surely most mystifying" (Laing and Esterson, 1964: 186). In this case, autonomy was being attributed to people who could act independently only in the most superficial sense – as messengers between the *Akaneshau* officials and the Innu clients.

The Social Services Department has complete jurisdiction over a wide range of Innu social life, including child protection and child sexual abuse. Significantly, this sensitive area, one of the most troubling aspects of Innu family life, is the sole domain of the province of

Newfoundland. A relatively large number of local men and women have either confessed to or been charged with abusive acts. A counsellor at the Innu Nation-funded Healing Services told me that almost every Innu girl has had some sort of "abnormal sexual experience." Almost always this is emotionally traumatic, but the level of trauma is exacerbated by the involvement of non-Innu institutions where Innu girls are confronted by strangers who have instant authority over them. If an abusive incident is disclosed to the Social Services Department, this must be legally reported to the police, who after an investigation to determine whether a crime has been committed will instigate court procccdings against the alleged abuser. During this time, children may be removed from their families. If the case is intra-familial, the victim will be removed from the home. In non-familial situations, the alleged perpetrator of the abuse will be charged, required to appear in court with the victim,[1] and, if the Crown prosecutor is successful, incarcerated or otherwise criminalized. Many cases of this type of abuse involve girls of 12-14 and 16- to 18-year-old-boys.

As a statutory service, the Social Services Department is bound by particular provisions of Canadian law, most pertinently the Child Welfare Act, which conveys powers to social workers to remove children from their families.[2] Social Services personnel I spoke with believed that these removals, controversial because they are opposed by many Innu, ensure that the children are protected and the abuser is held accountable. While acknowledging that the system is not perfect, Kay Graves, a professional social worker in Davis Inlet, told me that the "legal process is the only thing we have to deal with sexual abuse and to put some measures into place to stop it."

In the past legal removals of children occurred frequently for many different reasons, not limited to abuse. Over the years, several young and even middle-aged Innu have gradually made their way back from foster homes in other parts of Canada after such removals. Stripped of their families, language, and connections to *Nitassinan*, they are often at a loss in Sheshatshiu and Utshimassits and rarely stay long. "Now Social Services take the babies. They say you drink too much," Elizabeth Penashue told me. "'I'm sorry, I got to take this baby,' they say. They take the baby outside, St. John's or somewhere else, and never bring it back. Now we are finding that there are lots of babies that have been taken away. Social Services did many things wrong to the people." While the removal of Innu children still occurs, placements are now largely within the villages, as children deemed in need of protection go to relatives or to the group home in Sheshatshiu.

In an attempt to mitigate what they see as the heavy-handed and inappropriate interventions of Social Services, the Innu of both Labrador communities have established alternative methods of healing, although the models for these are largely imported. Relatives and *Tshenut*, sometimes within a "healing circle," have attempted to help both the victims and perpetrators of sexual abuse through open confessions and honest dialogue. However, these techniques, hardly radical or challenging to the authorities, are deemed "informal," and generally are not considered a serious way to resolve the problem of sexual abuse. Kay Graves, for example, was skeptical about these approaches:

> I don't know yet whether the community has come to terms with what exactly physical and sexual abuse does to a child and to the family, and so with the healing that needs to go on. They will just get everyone together and the offender can say, "I'm sorry" to the child and that's enough. It's not enough. There are still power imbalances going on there. What is the sincerity of the offender in that and what are the measures put in place to keep a check on this person, male or female, who has committed this?

She believed that such healing might be a "good first step," but, yearning for that certainty that all authorities dealing with delicate human situations like to impose, "there's no follow-up around it." The courts, too, have put pressure on the Innu to formalize these procedures. Thus, for members of the community to adopt a sentencing circle they must first make an application to the court and receive band council approval, and then they are only able to proceed when the plea is guilty. According to the lawyer who told me this, "the court wants formal outcomes," so that the offender will have to complete specified tasks for each time period of the modified "sentence." Importantly, while Social Services has been largely engaged with formalizing procedures for sexual abuse cases within the villages, no parallel concern has been expressed towards the frequent sexual abuse of Innu by priests and teachers since the 1960s.

Another domain that has come under the auspices of Social Services is adoption of children between families. Interventions in this area affect the long-standing permeable family structures common among the Innu, whereby children moved fluidly between families. It was never considered unusual that a child not live with his or her biological parents. Adoption of children with and between regional groups of Innu and between the Innu and the Inuit prior to sedentarization was common.[3] These practices carried over into the community so that children still move easily between different families. Sometimes an informal adoption is arranged, but at other times no specific agreement is reached between adults as children freely shift from family to family. In some circumstances, young mothers unable to take care of their babies hand them over to their mothers, grandmothers, or others to raise. Over time, the child may return to the biological mother permanently or just periodically. The Innu refer to nearly all others who are close to them as "brother," "sister," "mother," "grandfather," etc., even though, biologically, they may not have the relation specified by the English translation of the word. The Social Services Department, however, has attempted to bind children to one nuclear family by enforcing bureaucratic procedures and legal rules of adoption. According to Lanny Marcelo, the formal legal route was a protection against a biological mother taking her child back.

Social Services does have a therapeutic arm, which involves counselling under the supervision and direction of the trained social workers. While some Innu have undoubtedly benefited from these counsellors, in the early 1990s the scale of their sufferings from drinking, gas-sniffing, suicide, and sexual abuse led to calls for help from other quarters. By agreements between state authorities and the Innu political bodies, pan-Native healers were brought in.

A SPIRITUAL HEALING JOURNEY

Bertha and Ken, two Plains Indians I met in Davis Inlet during my first stay in the village, were also making their first visit. Rapidly, they had set up an Alcoholics Anonymous group and women's healing circle, and they were planning a bake sale and a Halloween dance to raise money. Bertha and Ken were looking forward to their first visit to "Border Beacon" (*Ashuapun*), a favoured Innu camping site some 135 miles into the interior, where they would be taking along a generator and VCR to play promotional material from their organization, the Nechi Institute. Videos of healing, psychology, alcoholism, and the medicinal qualities of sweetgrass and sage would be played in the midst of an area with myriad historical associations for the Innu. They spoke of their founder, Eric Shirt, who had had a dream instructing him to go to California. There, I was told, he met a psychologist named Dale Flowers, who helped Shirt initiate Aboriginal healing programs. "Nechi" was a name that featured in Eric Shirt's dream. A pan-Native therapeutic organization based in Alberta, the Nechi Institute has also established both training and treatment for Innu and has been funded to run mobile treatment programs in the country. Most, if not all, of those who work for the Alcohol Program were Nechi-trained by the end of the 1990s.

Over the last few years, Nechi (as well as other treatment and training programs) has exerted an increasing influence in the communities. Innu themselves have gone to Alberta for treatment and training. In turn, the Plains Indian healers have brought feathers, sweetgrass, and sage and introduced sweat lodges to the Innu. Their manufactured dream-catchers, icons of pan-Indian identity, now festoon the walls of the houses of many Nechi graduates, and their ponytail hairstyle was imitated by some Innu men. At Poundmaker's Lodge in Edmonton, a treatment centre connected with Nechi, Innu children, adolescents, and adults have been exposed to the healing properties of pipe ceremonies, sweat lodges, meditation, prayer, and the counsel of Plains Indian elders.

Nechi was established by Native professionals, often recovering alcoholics, in 1974 and developed primarily in the province of Alberta. It has since grown and provides a range of services to Native communities across Canada and in the U.S., Australia and New Zealand. While the Nechi publicity material recognizes what it calls "cultural oppression" and urges its clients to understand their own problems in terms of the history of colonial domination, its main focus is clearly the psychological and medical conditions of individuals. A Nechi pamphlet on Adult Children of Alcoholics gives a flavour of this:

> Today in our healing from the effects of alcoholism and other painful ways of living, we are re-discovering that what we are doing is a spiritual healing journey to be shared for the recovery of all our relations. In this century we have gradually come to know much about alcoholism and its effects. Medical research has shown that alcoholism is a disease with recognized symptoms and named progression. Consequently, we now know a great deal about how this disease can physically destroy people. Psychology has brought insights to the emotional pain resulting from alcohol. . . . This movement [Adult Children of Alcoholics[is guided by two spiritual principles; self-empowerment and mutual aid. Self-empowerment means that each person has the ability, as well as the basic human right, to direct their own life. Mutual aid states that people have the ability to help each other to grow and to heal. (White, nd: 1)

What we see in this passage (and other elements of Nechi literature could be produced to similar effect) is an appeal to the authority of scientific research wedded to "spiritual principles." Embracing the materialism of medicine and psychiatry and combining this with the AA philosophy, the program depicts "alcoholism and other painful ways of living" as "diseases," for which the prescription is a "spiritual healing journey." Embarking upon this "treatment" is the first step towards "recovery." This involves practical exercises, mastery of handout information, and self-disclosure to unblock the pain that lies underneath the alcohol and substance abuse. "Denial," the inability to admit to and accept past and present anguish, pain, and abuse, is considered one of the cardinal traits of members of alcoholic and other dysfunctional families. Nechi advocates often repeat these basic principles, emphasizing the role of denial in protecting the self against unpleasant truths. As one alcohol counsellor told me, "you have to deal with sickness first. To do this you have to go deep inside you. First you have to talk about why *you* drink, then talk about the immediate situation." He continued, "we must tell our own stories now. I must blame myself now, not my parents or the alcohol. That's the past." In the context of Nechi-style healing, these stories are often melancholy reflections of maltreatment, abandonment, and inebriation in a guided Nechi confessional.

Many of the Nechi handouts require memorization of key terms and definitions. Using the positivistic assessment criteria that infuse so much contemporary mass education, they stipulate particular learning and behavioural outcomes, the most important of which is permanent sobriety. Likewise, Poundmaker's Lodge employs a highly structured residential program, through which "Alcoholics Anonymous and Narcotics Anonymous philosophies are interwoven" (Saggers and Gray, 1998: 152). This may be why some of the people who have been through Nechi or have attended rehabilitation programs, such as the one at Brentwood in Ontario, often speak about their problems in formulaic ways, repeating the psychological and medical phrases that define the pan-Native healing process.

Tom Ritchie had experienced pan-Native healing. I was fortunate to have spent some time with Tom and his family at a camp near Sango Bay. While there he was constantly engaged in work and always acted with purpose, whether travelling long distances in search of animals or felling huge dead spruce trees for the stove in the tent. He showed me many places that he had known all his life and instructed me on the landscape, noting places to get fresh brook water and guiding me over fragile ice. At nights we would talk and get to know each other long after his family had gone to sleep. However, when we returned to Davis Inlet, he lost much of the energy he had in the country. When I was walking past his house, Tom would tap on his window and beckon me in. He poured out stewed tea and we shared cigarettes. Sometimes we played cards. His thoughts and words turned inward as he revisited his childhood with tales of his father's violence and drunkenness, his own crimes, and his history of incarceration. For Tom, "alcoholism is a disease, not a crime." He was a "patient." As a patient at the Brentwood treatment centre, he was able to let go of his anger and resentments and forgive himself for the things he had done to others while under the influence of alcohol. "I can't go on like this" was the conclusion he had come to many times. But, unfortunately, while increasing his powers of self-reflection, his treatment had led him only in circles. Believing he was sick, diseased, and possessed of an illness, his lapses into drinking and violence could always be consigned to a "condition." He struggled to control himself, calling this "body over mind" because when he drank his body could not control his mind's craving for alcohol and then he became a slave to the intoxication. When drunk, he admitted not caring about anyone.

Mixing the phraseology of "treatment" with the narrative of wounds, in Tom's stories the orientations to *nutshimit* were sporadic, perhaps evaporating as we spoke, and the village with all its misery, drink, anger, and resentments was the "reality" he had come to locate himself in, although he was in my observation and his own admission much happier in the country. Likewise, the inward focus encouraged by "treatment," combined with the magnitude of the suffering he experienced, made the momentous political realities facing the Innu seem superfluous. While the mining company was bracing to take the land not far from where we had camped and Innu autonomy was being threatened on all sides, many Innu like Tom found it hard to focus on what should be done to protect themselves from these onslaughts. To Tom, the whole community was "sick." The drinking, gas-sniffing, and suicides that occurred all around had affected everyone. There was no way to detach such problems from the community itself. Daily life was suffused with noise, interruptions, and crises. There was never enough money. Tom himself was broke, without even a snowmobile, and his recent job application to work at the mine at Voisey's Bay had been rejected. He had lost a job as an alcohol counsellor because he went on periodic bouts of drinking and was now awaiting a court appearance on a serious charge. The previous year his teenage daughter had committed suicide. In the midst of a recent bout of drinking, one of the teenage children had taken one of the younger children, his grandchild who lived with the family, to the Social Services. I ask where the child is now. " I don't know, somewhere in the community, I guess," he replies.

Although it has greater legitimacy as an invited rather than an imposed institution, Nechi and other pan-Native healing bodies propose certain solutions to the personal problems of Innu like Tom that derive from popularized medical and psychological formulas as well as certain beliefs and practices of largely urbanized and more assimilated Native people from western and central Canada, which are elaborated as pan-Native beliefs. Simply postulating that alcoholism is a discrete entity, and a medical condition, imposes a particularly *external* frame of reference on the personal trauma of the Innu. This is further compounded with layers of obfuscation by the claim that Nechi treatment for alcoholism somehow relates to the Native experience in Canada, and perhaps around the world. Although there are some similarities in world view that could be traced between the Innu and the Plains Indians, the pan-Nativism, like the imposed European world view, obliterates difference and uniqueness.

One example of this is the use of sweat lodges in the Innu villages by Nechi. The healing is a mix of Roman Catholicism and New Age psychology, fusing confession and disclosure with heat, darkness, sweat, and sometimes sage. Prior to the arrival of Nechi, the Innu used sweat lodges only in the country. These were set up after a strenuous hunt to help relax the hunter or for therapeutic reasons if a member of the camp fell sick. The use of the sweat lodge as a therapeutic device in the settlement differs significantly from the Innu use of sweat lodges because psychological healing through prescribed rules largely replaces Innu medicine and spirituality. To many *Tshenut* the Nechi sweat lodge is a travesty of their own histories. It is an agent of cultural assimilation in the same way that the school is. The only difference is that the personnel entrusted with transforming the Innu are now Natives themselves.

Nevertheless, many Innu enjoy the saunas and find them therapeutic. Since the time of my first sweat in Davis Inlet, when on a late summer night four others and I went through three rounds of searing hot steam interspersed with blunt and honest confessionals, I have always accepted opportunities to join sweats. Before one sweat in Sheshatshiu, I had a rasping sore throat that cleared up almost immediately afterwards. The heat seeps through every pore in the body. Everyone groans with pleasure. As the hot steam concentrates inside the airtight tent, it is hard to breathe, and after 15 or 20 minutes, the person nearest the entrance opens the flap and all go outside for cool air and cold water. Inside the pitch darkness of the tent where no one is visible, save in the haziest of profiles, people reflect on their past, their mistakes, and their regrets. Although borrowing Alcoholics Anonymous language, the Innu confessional is rarely smug or conclusive. I have never heard anyone presuming to have overcome their alcohol problems or ruling out any recurrences, even after many years of sobriety. For me, the sweats were an opportunity to say whatever I wanted without judgement. I often noted my own failings, my sense of being out of my depth, and occasionally my own homesickness.

Apenam Pone outside sweat lodge in Sheshatshiu. Photograph by author.

Although sweats may prove recuperative for some, other aspects of Nechi healing are more puzzling in the Innu context. For example, both Nechi and Poundmaker's Lodge advertise high "success rates." Success is defined in terms of specified percentages of its graduates who fall into such categories as returning to school, increasing their income, holding program management positions, or, in a more personal sense, improving their family life and strengthening their identity as Native people. These claims assume both a degree of cultural assimilation and a structure of employment opportunities that largely do not apply to the Innu. Furthermore, Nechi sees no conflict between, for example, holding a "program management position" and at the same time "strengthening one's identity as a Native person." Since Innu identity is much more bound up with hunting than with program management positions, it is difficult to see how becoming an office functionary would enhance one's appreciation of being Innu without either elaborate rationalization or, more likely, psychic confusion. Furthermore, the treatment administered by these organizations does nothing to address the difficulties the Innu encounter in the village. Neither does it address the degrading conditions in which almost all Innu have lived since sedentarization.

One of the first experiences the Innu had with Poundmaker's was a six-month treatment program for a group of gas-sniffing children in the aftermath of the release to the press of a video of children gas sniffing in an unheated shack on the anniversary of the house fire in 1992. Within months of their return, the children returned to their gas-sniffing. As Waldram et al. (1995: 93) put it, "Entire families were airlifted across the country to receive treatment and rehabilitation. . . . The children returned with their counsellors, accompanied again by much media fanfare. Unfortunately, the causes of the substance abuse, which are rooted in the poverty and despair of the community, remained unchanged."

Whether or not it is successful for particular Innu (and personal testimony suggests that it is for some), Innu remain as clients. The very presence of Nechi serves to marginalize remedies for social and psychological problems that already exist among the Innu. For Nechi, "healing means that you have gone through the program at Poundmaker's," George Rich told me, but "for me healing is laughing, crying, living, loving and hunting." While many people in both communities testify to having quit alcohol through using Nechi techniques and see no necessary conflict with Innu practices, others believe that Nechi trainees who "relapse" are more severely affected than they were before training. Yet others say that they had quit alcohol by themselves. Jean-Pierre Ashini, for example, told me that "the cure is in the mind." Some of the older Innu believe that Nechi is an unhelpful presence and, like other non-Innu institutions, also imposes alien interpretations and frames of reference upon the Innu.

The Nechi literature, although providing a pan-historical sweep of cultural and political oppression, necessarily ignores the particularities of Innu-European encounters and the role of liquor in Innu history. Alcohol has long been known to the Innu. It was probably first introduced by fur traders on the North Shore and at the Hudson's Bay posts, but seldom were Innu described as heavy drinkers.[4] One evening, Prote Poker recalled his father drinking in the country. "In the country, my dad when he was drunk would just sing and dance around the stove. He would talk about the trees and say that the trees can sing when they are swinging back and forth." Some years before this, William Duncan Strong (Leacock and Rothschild, 1994) in the diaries of his 1927-28 ethnographic visit observed that the Mushuau Innu drank spruce beer and home brew to celebrate a big kill. He records no particularly adverse effects. Speck (1977: 92) observed that after particular dreams, hunters would drink whisky to give their soul-spirits a libation to pay for the revelation of a caribou by a river and to induce its fulfillment. Similarly, Henriksen (1993a) argued that Innu used alcohol not only to celebrate but, along with drumming, singing, and dancing, to communicate with the Animal Gods. In the early sedentarization phase, alcohol, along with shamanism and the shaking tent or *kushapat-shikan*, was suppressed by the church, and as Henriksen (ibid., 8-9) put it, "The people were thereby deprived of some of their crucial means to obtain spiritual power."

While the Nechi disease theory does not use the word "sin," alcohol use is clearly conceived as an individual failing and much of the literature has a missionary tone. On a hot summer day in Utshimassits, Father Fred reinforced this association, telling me that Nechi was "the best thing that ever happened here." Like the earlier missionaries who did their utmost to reward the sober, punish the drunk, and instill guilt (see Henriksen, 1973: 77), Nechi establishes a binary morality, inflecting alcohol with the language of contagion and encouraging a divisiveness in the villages between those who drink and those who do not. Father Fred was in unanimity with every *Akaneshau* professional I have encountered in the communities, all of whom support the Nechi approach. Ernie, the last Mennonite in Davis Inlet, enthusiastically reported that "they [the Innu] find out what is wrong with them and question why they drink so much."

Although alcohol is sometimes consumed in the country, binge drinking and daily drunkenness are almost exclusively associated with village life. Importantly, drinking occurs when the means by which Innu can practise their way of life and spirituality has been severely compromised. Innu drinking in the villages marks a separation from any objects of celebration. It takes place against a background of chronic boredom, loss of purpose, forced acculturation, extreme material poverty, and, significantly, the tragedies, unnatural deaths, and illnesses that these have compounded. While these points may be acknowledged by Nechi and other treatment programs, the programs themselves assume the primacy of a psychological cause to the "disease." They tend to emphasize the individual roots of drinking, of taking to the bottle when the person is not strong and cannot deal with his or her problems in a healthier or more acceptable manner.

AKANESHAU AND INNU PERSPECTIVES ON HEALING

Coincidentally, several conceptual and practical similarities are apparent between the pan-Native and official Canadian understandings of the troubles of the Innu. Both, in order to grasp the problems, can only imagine the Innu through inventing them as "Indians," as disadvantaged relatives under the multicultural fraternity constructed by the state.[5] In this context, the various healing initiatives are trumpeted as an important dimension of the progress that *Akaneshau* professionals attribute to the Innu. Improvement is measured out in speculative sobriety counts or communal confessionals, while regression is noted in lapses into drunkenness, most notable at critical moments, such as elections and inter-community rivalry. "I see a lot of hope for the community," said Kay Graves, the professional social worker, in Davis Inlet. With characteristic optimism, she continued:

> There's been a lot of change over the last 15 to 20 years. In another 20 to 25 years, you'll see a lot of good changes as well. It's moving step by step. Sometimes it might fall back a few steps, but they keep moving forward. A lot of really committed people in the community are struggling with their own healing and waiting to give something back to the community as well and we [at Social Services] are trying to figure out what it is we can do that is meaningful for them in a Native way and not just wanting to take on the non-Native stuff and put that in.

The forward and backward movements, steps to and fro, are dizzying, but the direction in which healing leads is unmistakable and the "Native" help that her agency will render will be rallied to these ends. Like many other *Akaneshau*, the social worker held out high hopes for the move to Natuashish.[6] The training of Innu carpenters to build some of the houses in the new community was a "good healing process" because "they would learn how to build their own houses." In the process, and this was stated with no acknowledgement of what this might symbolize for former nomads for whom meaning and identity were developed in a wider landscape, "the community can build their own community."

However, the Innu loss of autonomy is only incurred transparently and in some ways superficially by the optimistic visions of *Akaneshau* professionals. In this case, the former nomads who have had a most troubled, even catastrophic experience as settled village dwellers are now being configured as a "community" that must build another "community." To provide some semblance of cohesion in the village, the social welfare and the pan-Native programs have become central to village life, marking Utshimassits and Sheshatshiu out as communities of pathology. In both villages new institutions to deal with sickness such as treatment centres, group homes, women's shelters, and clinics have been funded and established rapidly over the last decade and now provide a large segment of the little employment available for Innu.

Not all healing in the villages, of course, is filtered through the visions of Plains Indians or the *Akaneshau* social workers. The Innu themselves have set up a number of health programs and counselling services. Most recently, an institution in Sheshatshiu for children and adolescents with gas-sniffing problems was established by the federal government. The related problem of alcohol abuse is one that Innu have directly confronted, beginning with the move to intermittent and sometimes long-term sobriety by some of the young leaders in the mid-1980s. Because tragic acts of violence, sexual abuse, and self-harm regularly occur in both communities when people are drinking heavily, alcohol programs in Sheshatshiu and Utshimassits have been established. On-site counselling is provided and individual clients can be funded to go out of the community for up to six months to treatment programs throughout Canada. In Sheshatshiu, the band council established a Healing Services Department in 1993. The idea behind this was to establish non-conflictual and non-confrontational methods of healing. The Healing Services personnel strongly differentiate themselves from government Social Services, which insists on retribution and punishment for any admission of a crime and is co-ordinated with the courts and the criminal justice system. Healing Services provides support to anyone in the community who expresses a desire to be helped. Most of the people seeking help have problems related to alcohol and sexual abuse, and many are drawn to this venue in order to receive help and support in the court system, through which their problems and conflicts are channelled.

One of the main principles of Healing Services is that Innu problems are best resolved by Innu, not the RCMP, Social Services, or the courts. The emphasis here is on understanding, not blame. Professionals are not hired. Only Innu women and others such as Lyla Andrew, an *Akaneshau* woman who is married to an Innu man and has lived and raised children in Sheshatshiu for two decades, are on the staff. Lyla Andrew explained the philosophy with an example of a young man who, many years previously, had abused two siblings. Feeling alone, he drank and was full of shame and fear. He wanted to approach his sisters, but was fearful of the consequences. In order to defuse the tension, Healing Services encouraged him to confess and to speak out without the fear of retribution. This could be guaranteed because Healing Services is not obliged to report to Social Services or the RCMP. Freedom from retribution ensured against the humiliation and public exposure that results from court trials. In this case, the young man could speak to other Innu who may well know exactly what it was like to be in his position. Furthermore, all discussion could take place in *Innu-aimun* rather than English.

One of the major differences between the various programs is that Nechi and Social Services have much more secure sources of funding. Nechi has received more lavish funding than the more culturally sensitive Healing Services through Health and Welfare Canada and Social Services operates on secure provincial funds, while the Healing Services funds are funnelled through the band councils. Utshimassits and Sheshatshiu Healing Services compete for a fraction of the budget of the Nechi and statutory services. As it stands, the more external the sources of assistance, the more secure their entrenchment as means of healing the Innu.

EXPERIENCES OF DRINKING

The fact remains that despite the efforts of these programs and the ongoing destruction caused by alcohol, many Innu continue to drink excessively. But in contrast to urbanized people and Euro-Canadians, nearly all Innu drinkers are binge drinkers. Drinking coincides with certain junctures, situations, and events. When it starts, it often does not stop until the drinker either runs out of alcohol, falls asleep, passes out, or precipitates some action that brings all partying to a stop – one drinking session that I observed, for example, was terminated by the sudden wailing of a mother for her dead teenaged son. Others may come to a halt by violence or the intervention of the police. While context-specific binge drinking largely obtains among the Innu, Nechi and most other AA-influenced treatment models stress the addictive quality of drinking as a "disease."

Regardless of one's theoretical perspective, the negative effects of parental drinking on Innu children are clearly evident. There is growing evidence that this may start with fetal alcohol syndrome (FAS), which can cause physical abnormalities as well as serious learning and behavioural problems. FAS was detected in several Innu children and adolescents who were sent to St. John's for treatment in the winter of 2001.[7]

It is well known that when their parents are drinking, Innu infants are sometimes left in the charge of older children, often with inadequate food or warmth. Many children attribute their gas-sniffing to feelings of being neglected by drunken parents and many older people tell tales of abandonment, abuse, and fleeing alcohol-fuelled parents and elders. Alcohol particularly affected the first generation of children to grow up in Davis Inlet and Sheshatshiu in the 1970s. In 1990 a local health report covering this period found that between 80 and 85 per cent of residents over 15 years old were alcoholic and that half of these were intoxicated on a daily basis. As the report observed, "the behaviour and appearance of the majority of Davis Inlet people are characteristically consistent with chronic alcoholic populations. The people appear to be physically older (by ten+ years) than they are" (McTimoney, 1990: 7). When in 1992 the Innu instigated an inquiry into what was going wrong in Utshimas-sits, they found that between 1965 and 1992, 47 out of the 66 deaths in the community were alcohol-related (Innu Nation, 1995: 187). "When I was a child," Prote Poker told me, "I didn't trust my parents or anything they said. I used to be happy when my father got sick and went to hospital because when he came back he wouldn't drink for a while. When there was drink in the house, I used to run around making like I was playing and knocking over the home brew." Prote's parents were among the many Innu who died alcohol-related deaths after the move to Davis Inlet.

Although gas-sniffing, suicide, sexual abuse, marital dishar-mony, and neglect are all widely believed to be connected with drinking, Innu remain largely non-judgemental about alcohol. In-stead of seeing drinking as a disease called "alcoholism," many Innu view it as an expression of a host of other tragedies, such as the lin-gering effects of sexual abuse, linked to their living in the settlement. The gas-sniffing of the children is perhaps the most visible symbol of communal breakdown, as hunched and hooded children can often be seen on the ice inhaling fumes from plastic garbage bags or hauntingly shrill screams are heard from the woods where the chil-dren are hiding themselves away. Most Innu health workers and others relate gas-sniffing to chronically low levels of self-esteem. They depict many of the youth as feeling useless and lacking in con-fidence. As Simeon Tshakapesh said one day when we were talking about a recent spate of gas-sniffing in Utshimassits, "that's how I felt as a kid. I thought I didn't have anything. I'm not worth it. There was nothing to look forward to. I didn't realize that I had a future."

Gas-sniffing is commonly related to the drinking of the adults. In fact, there is a lot of graffiti in Davis Inlet to this effect and adolescent sniffers often corroborate it. When I asked him what it was like to live in Davis Inlet, a nine-year-old boy who visited the house I was stay-ing in replied, "bad, especially because of all the gas sniffers, because its something in their heads. When grown-ups drinks, they fights when they drunk. My daddy might fight my mummy and then my brother fights my daddy. And there is a lot of stealing. I never sniff gas, yet. I never smoke, yet." Here even the child of nine could not rule out following a prevalent pattern. When I asked him what were the good things about Davis Inlet he said, "I don't know, maybe when I go riding on bike or on the skidoo."

Despite the obvious importance of psychological factors such as lack of self-esteem and social factors such as parental drinking, it is important not to lose sight of the wider political context within which both operate. Every contemporary Innu family is affected by having had to shift from nomadic hunting to settled life in the village. While they have been domiciled in the villages, the land that they and their ancestors used has become progressively appropriated by developers. The connections between drinking (as well as other self-destructive activities and disease) and self-esteem, on the one hand, and removal from the land, on the other, are apparent to all Innu. Jack Penashue, a Nechi-trained alcohol counsellor, put this in perspective when he stated that, for many Innu, "their culture is not what their grandparents taught them and that's why they drink. Then when they drink, they lose a lot of things. I began to see my parents *just* as drinkers. I asked myself, why can't they be white? Why is there no food in our house? No heat? When we see white people with lots in their lives. Then, I said to myself, these are not my real family. We didn't have any family unity or gatherings. I didn't have any of that." In this brief account, drinking is related to both the loss of the nomadic hunting life and the desire on the part of the child for a whiteness that could not be attained. Even if his parents had been like "white people with lots in their lives," this would not have delivered contentment unless Innu values were radically redefined.

The same connections apply not only to the removal of the Innu from permanent nomadic hunting but also to the consolidation of non-Innu occupation of their homelands. During the initial period when nickel was discovered at Voisey's Bay, there was a widespread view in Davis Inlet that disease and alcohol problems would escalate as a result of the development of the mine. Since most Innu had no real information as to what the mining company was up to at the time, there was a feeling that the land was simply going to be taken away from them. The prospect of having something of value, even sacred, stolen influenced many people to drink. As one resident put it, "if everything's going to be taken, why not drink."

Unlike the society that Jack Penashue's parents were wrenched away from, in Euro-Canadian society status is displayed by "position" and the accumulation of material wealth. While some Innu, principally the leaders who have access to secure salaries and "joint ventures" with industrialists, have been able to acquire gleaming new trucks and snowmobiles, large television sets, and other accoutrements of middle-class life, such possessions have not generated status. If anything, the displays of these possessions are not seen by the bulk of Innu living in shacks as badges of accomplishment. The widespread cynicism towards the leaders and their possessions, particularly in Sheshatshiu, means that goods only tangentially deliver status.[8] The new-found material wealth of such individuals, often at the cost of massive credit card debt, may provide them with a kind of whiteness that some of the young crave as an escape route from drinking. But possessions are no victory for the leaders and fledgling capitalists, for even if they refrain from drinking their close relatives and sometimes immediate family members are often prone to binge drinking, wild partying, and tragic endings.

DRINKING AND POWER

While possessions only marginally provide status, drinking, on the other hand, does deliver, making the drinker a person to be reckoned with, if only to be remembered for some extremely good and bad times. As a drinker, you will be remembered for your drunkenness, your adventures, your fights. Alcohol gives people feeling and passion that, amid chronic torpor, the community itself expunges. Sheer boredom should not be ruled out as a powerful stimulus to take to the bottle. With the Innu, as in other colonial contexts, it is easy to see how drinking can help fill the cultural vacuum. Sociologist Edwin Lemert (1954: 335) explained Native American drinking in part as "a direct reaction to boredom induced by the disintegration and disappearance of . . . ritual." The material possessions, even if they are "legitimately" acquired, seldom compensate for the loss of meaning occasioned by settlement.

When *Akaneshau* are witnesses to drinking and drunkenness, either by accident or design, there is sometimes a clever reversal that takes place in which the *Akaneshau*, nearly always judge and jury to the Innu in other contexts, are judged, questioned, and interrogated. The Innu drinker turns the tables and marks himself or herself as a memorable person, a persistent teaser of white certainties. In one of my first encounters with drinking in Sheshatshiu, I met an inebriated couple walking along the beach road. Repeatedly, they asked me, "Who are you?" The reply of my name and where I was from was quickly brushed aside as they continued to probe, "Are you Jesus?" "Okay," the woman continued, "you're from England. Tell the Queen to fuck off when you see her." My amusement at this, however, was not appreciated, as they quickly sensed that as an *Akaneshau* in the community I might be in the pay of Innu Nation. My protestations to the contrary were met with disbelief, as they told me that the current President of Innu Nation was going to be kicked out because he only listened to white people like me. These commentaries continued as they motioned literally to kick me out of the community, before reverting to the earlier questions, "Who are you? What do you want?" Several years later the couple died in one of the spate of house fires that occurred regularly in the mid-1990s.

Over time, I have discovered that the accusations of the drinkers mirror the concerns of the day, particularly the pervasive perception of being duped, or violated by *Akaneshau*. Thus, at the height of all the environmental impact assessment studies over the Voisey's Bay mine. I would sometimes be accused by drinkers of taking money from the mining company. If I denied this, the counter-accusation was that I was taking money from Innu Nation, as the two were linked in the minds of the drinkers. There was nothing remiss about such a linkage, because several complements of aid had been dispatched from the Voisey's Bay Nickel Company to Innu Nation at that time. The complete refurbishment of the Sheshatshiu offices in 1996 was paid for by mining company funds and could be seen by all in the community.

One evening at dusk I was walking along the beach road in Sheshatshiu with Tom Green, an *Akaneshau* adviser at Innu Nation. At almost the same location as the previous encounter with the inebriated couple, we discerned several men weaving as they walked along the road towards us. One was pretending to "drive" using the handlebars of a child's plastic scooter. When we met, some jovial teasing of our gait and our ubiquitous backpacks rapidly gave way to questions about our dealings in the community. Each man interrupted the questions of the next in a sort of one-upmanship of interrogation. One man shouted, while another man was smoothly and persistently questioning. Soon, Tom and I were separated with two to three Innu men questioning each of us. In response to my protestation that I was helping to write a human rights report, one man with a loud rasping voice put his nose within an inch of mine and shouted, "Do you think we are *animals*?" His brother, an older, gentler man, quietly told me that what I was doing was the wrong thing for the Innu, that it led the Innu in the wrong direction. With no hint of either irony or the tease, there were no clues in his speech or bearing to suggest whether he was making a scathing indictment of my work, merely mocking it, or actually approving it – since going in the "wrong direction" could be perceived as positive if the "right direction" (e.g., the one approved by the Canadian government) was "wrong."

Meanwhile, Tom Green extricated himself and made off as quickly as possible, leaving me with the men. Before I could get distracted at his departure, the older brother pointed out into Lake Melville, asking, "Colin, what do you see there?" The answers I volunteered, "waves" and "water," were batted down like the summer blackflies. They were either "not right" or simply "wrong." Simultaneously, the brother with the rasping voice interjected a repetition of the question, "What are you doing here?" Between questions another man, a third brother, in fact, subtly asked more philosophical questions, which, at my own muddled non-response, were then mixed with his own maudlin reflections on the community. From this point, we entered the house of a man who a few years later was to commit suicide. The older brother introduced this man, clearly younger than him, as his grandfather. Cans of Labatt's Blue were opened and one thrust into my hand. As I took a swig of mine, a truck arrived outside and virtually the whole household, minus the children, evacuated to jump in the flatbed. Alone, I walked back to my lodging, which happened to be the next house.

In these incidents, I did not see drinking as simply an expression of powerlessness and disenfranchisement through displaced or misplaced anger. Nor did I see it as disease. Drinking was not, in Gerald Vizenor's (1998) terms, "victimry," nor was it, as some have suggested of Aboriginal drinking, "symptoms of underlying inequalities" (Saggers and Gray, 1998: 88). Rather, through their quick-witted verbal tactics, the drinkers were talking back to the power of interrogation and surveillance that they are normally subject to. And here, it is not simply an "act of aggression against white authority," as Lemert (1954: 336) described the drinking of British Columbia Natives in the 1950s. It is an ironic reversal of roles that makes *Akaneshau* aware of the colonial nature of the situation. Through these chance meetings, the drinkers not only expressed their own understandings of the Innu-*Akaneshau* encounter in *their* way, they gave me a glimpse of how it must feel to be Innu in many situations – in the courtroom, the Social Services office, speaking to the police, being subjects of "research," and even walking into the Innu Nation office to find salaried *Akaneshau* making major decisions on their behalf while they languish on welfare. In other similar situations, I have sensed what it must be like for the Innu to be repeatedly confronted with rules and expectations that they are uncomfortable with or dimly aware of or both, and to be found wanting.

Turning the tables again, some Innu say that drinking can be productive, in that it breaks down the nuclear insulation of village life. People get to know how others feel. When drinking, they do not have to pretend that the pain of all that has happened in the villages does not exist or that the *Akaneshau* colonization of their land does not matter or affect them. According to one intermittent Innu drinker that I know, drinking can be a useful, even therapeutic, activity because it puts people in touch with common experiences very directly. As Lemert (1954: 338) pointed out in relation to such drinking, "one cannot escape the impression that the reputation these Indians have as drunkards, makers of home-brew and 'Bad Indians,' is a powerful *sustaining factor* for them" (emphasis added). That is, drinking builds solidarity among Native peoples by constructing a contrast between them and the colonizing authorities. Echoing Nancy Lurie's (1971: 317) classic paper on Indian drinking as protest, with her, we could say that "Indian people are more likely to drink when they feel thwarted in achieving Indian rather than white goals or when their success as Indians or simply individuals apart from Indian-white comparisons is interpreted as success in achieving status as whites." Thus, several of the Innu who regularly drink do so when they cannot practise the Innu way of life and through circumstance are forced to return to the villages.

By the same token, many of the drinkers are sharp, witty, and articulate people whose politeness, deportment, spoken English, or some other factor when they are sober could be counted on as characteristic of a "good" Innu in the eyes of *Akaneshau*. However, few Innu, even the political leaders who are competent in their dealings with *Akaneshau* authority, would relish being seen as what Erving Goffman (1963: 25) once called "heroes of assimilation," for that would be an admission that the game is up and that the Innu are really only somewhat different types of Canadians.[9]

As well as providing a means for identifying with other members of the community and their experiences, drinking can also be seen as a way of refusing to collaborate in the imposed way of life, fashioning out a resistance to the order of assimilation. On lonely days, drunks can create havoc in the Innu Nation and band council offices. By doing so, they bring levity to the office workers' day, and sometimes through their tricky semantics cleverly challenge the assumptions of these torpid institutions. Along with the presence of the *Tshenut* and the closeness of *nutshimit*, they remind others that the village represents a fragile order of assimilation, as their own inebriation in the centres of contact with the *Akaneshau* world abundantly illustrates.[10]

People drink both to live and to die. They drink to feel that they are alive in a community that, after almost a half-century, is moribund. The villages have no echo in the history of the Innu as a people nor do they possess very much meaning or purpose. Drinking can cut through the phoniness, the pretense that Sheshatshiu and Utshimassits are somehow Innu. It can give courage to see a vision of oneself and one's webs of relationships in a more truthful light, not refracted through the prisms of Euro-Canada. Drinking is to live in another sense, for it helps to remove oneself from the constant haunting of death, fighting, sickness, material poverty, land theft, and failing to live up to the expectations of the *Akaneshau* authorities.

Certainly, drinking can be a pleasure, but it is also a poison that leads to destruction and death, as evidenced by the drinkers whose relationships have been permanently tainted by acts of cruelty and carelessness and whose own lives have been cut short by road accidents, house fires, freezing in the woods, choking on their own vomit, or by the gun in moments of despair and hopelessness. Drinking is perhaps the major precipitating cause of what has become normal – premature death.

House fires are fast becoming a major consequence of the toxic mix of despair and drinking. Around the villages, several charred and empty vacant lots between houses, often with a cross or small shrine commemorating the dead family, mark tragedies known to everyone. These fires almost always occur when people have been heavily drinking or adolescents have been gas-sniffing. Sometimes houses go up in flames during suicide attempts, but any boundary between heavy drinking, gas-sniffing, and suicide is difficult to draw. The substandard construction of a high proportion of Innu houses in Sheshatshiu and virtually all of the wooden shacks in Davis Inlet make the probability of high loss of life even greater. The following table documents the house fires in Utshimassits and Sheshatshiu.

In the face of tragedies like house fires, which as Table 1 shows are increasing dramatically, it is absurd to conceive of the problems confronting the Innu – heavy alcohol consumption, gas-sniffing, sexual abuse, suicide, and accidents – as anything other than *social* problems.[11] It is also problematic to compartmentalize the problems as, for example, stemming from a "disease" called "alcoholism," or "solvent abuse" or even "dysfunctional families." These problems may be an intelligible reaction to an extraordinary situation of total loss of control over one's life and future. In one of the earliest sociological studies of Native American drinking, Lemert (1954: 382) concluded by remarking that the disastrous effects of drinking on American Indians "in actuality may have been the *secondary effects* of a shattering of the fabric of cues and symbols which ordered their overt actions into appropriate spheres" (emphasis added). Georg Henriksen (1973: 77) explained the "incessant" drinking he observed in old Davis Inlet in a similar vein, stating that "alcohol

Table 1: House Fires in Sheshatshiu and Utshimassits, 1960-2000

1962? Sheshatshiu (Only a few houses existed at this time.)
Istuanishish and Maninush Michel. House destroyed. Maninush died.
1960s Sheshatshiu
Shimoish "Pasteen." House destroyed. No injuries
1971? Sheshatshiu
Tuma Rich and Tumaiskueu. House destroyed. No injuries.
1978? Sheshatshiu
Mishenis Jack. House destroyed. No injuries.
1979? Sheshatshiu
Penash and Tanien Pone. House destroyed. No injuries
1980s Sheshatshiu
Tsheniu Ispastien Nuna. House destroyed. No injuries.
1980s Sheshatshiu
Priest's house destroyed. No injuries.
1985 Sheshatshiu
Tent at Sebastien Penunsi's camp (established off Churchill Road) burned to the ground.
Baby died of burns.
1990 Sheshatshiu
Father Jim Roche's house burned to the ground. No human injuries. Dog died.
Kaskantshiskueu and Shamani Andrew's house. House destroyed. Unoccupied. They were
in the country. Set on fire by children.
1990s Sheshatshiu
Sebastien Nuna, Jr., house set on fire by children. Partly destroyed. Unoccupied. No injuries. They were in the country.
1990s near Sheshatshiu
Benoit Pokue's tent burns to the ground. Occupants sustain burns but no deaths.
1992 Utshimassits
Kanikue and Akat Rich. House destroyed. Six children die.
1996 Utshimassits
Mennonite house burns to the ground. Believed to be set by children. No one was occupying the house at the time. Mennonites do not return to community.
1998 Sheshatshiu
Puatshuna Pokue. House destroyed. Baby dies.
1999 Sheshatshiu
Tanina and Matthew Andrew. House destroyed. Young boy dies.
2000 Utshimassits
Eric Mistanapeu sets himself on fire and dies. House destroyed.
2000 Sheshatshiu
Johnny and Shushepin Rich. House set on fire by gas-sniffers. House destroyed. One adolescent dies of injuries.
2000 Sheshatshiu
Pinameish McKay (née Jack). House destroyed. No injuries.
2000 Sheshatshiu
Manimanikanet Nuna. House set on fire but extinguished before flames spread. No injuries.
2000 Sheshatshiu
Benoit and Nuish Pokue. House destroyed. Benoit and Nuish and three grandchildren die.
Source: Local informants.

probably plays a significant role in people's efforts to cope with the numerous interpersonal conflicts resulting from the inconsistencies between the Barren Ground world and the coastal world."

In *The Divided Self*, psychiatrist R.D. Laing identified a similar situation when he reinterpreted Emil Kraepelin's famous case study of a patient showing signs of catatonic excitement. After describing the humiliation of the patient in the case presentation in a medical lecture hall, Laing offered an understanding of why the patient may have behaved in what appeared to the psychiatrists as a "schizophrenic" manner, in view of his public humiliation at the hands of Kraepelin. Laing's (1959: 31) conclusion was that "[o]ne may see his behaviour as 'signs' of a 'disease'; one may see his behaviour as expressive of his existence." Like Kraepelin's patient, the Innu drinker also "wants to be heard." The point is that when medical or other authorities place individuals in particularly constraining situations, they may generate the behaviour on the part of the subject that forms the presumed pathology. The words or actions of the subject may be interpreted as a way of being heard, but instead the medical frame of reference leads only to their categorization as symptoms of illness. This has been shown in studies of "total institutions," the prototype of which was Erving Goffman's *Asylums* (1961). While there are obvious differences of scale and context, it is not too far-fetched to see elements of the "total institution" in the villages. Like "total institutions," the villages remove Innu identity and bring the Innu under a foreign authority structure, and attempts are made to mould the Innu self to conform with Euro-Canadian norms.

To suggest that the linked problems of alcohol, sexual abuse, gas-sniffing, suicide, and accidents are expressive of Innu existence is more than the morose refrain of the casualty or the dysfunctional consequences of domination. While all are extremely damaging, and recognized as such, those who act recklessly express not just the predicament of being between two worlds, but their individual and collective relationships to Canada. Sometimes, albeit often with high personal costs, the Innu in their drinking are able to overturn the power and resist the desired assimilation. At the same time, drinking may lead to the neglect of children who, feeling unloved and unguided, may start sniffing gas. In the ensuing chaos with the pain of past abuses of settlement and the callous actions of the priests, unwanted sexual activity often occurs. Or, in another scenario, the sufferings experienced may produce a spirit of abandon in which one's own individual life becomes disposable. Massive reservoirs of resentment have been created from cruelties that people have inflicted upon one other in the communities. Thus, Mark Nui, then a health worker in Utshimassits, told me that "our culture has been ripped apart and ourselves too. A lot of anger is locked inside us and it's hard to snap out of it."

DECIDING WHAT TO DO

In the midst of locked-up anger, confusion, cruelty, and sudden deaths, making decisions as to what to do about these linked problems is excruciatingly difficult. In both Sheshatshiu and Utshimassits there have been periodic enforced bans on alcohol, usually following a major tragedy such as an alcohol-related death or suicide. In Utshimassits, alcohol cannot be purchased in the community, but it is frequently smuggled in by plane after sojourns in Goose Bay or it is brewed locally.

The spring of 1996 was a turbulent time in Utshimassits. The spate of break-ins and vandalism by roving groups of children and adolescents had gradually become more menacing. At the post office, hunting and fishing gear and spare parts for snowmobiles, which had been sent cash-on-delivery from mail-order houses, were smashed and destroyed. There was a lot of damage. The post office was ransacked so many times that the Canadian postal service refused to make deliveries to Davis Inlet until eventually one of the members of the band council volunteered to have it delivered to his house. Gasoline was poured in the water supply used by the *Tshenut*. Perched on a hill above the Innu houses with a beautiful view out over the water and mainland, the house belonging to the Mennonites was torched. It was the most ostentatious dwelling in the community – a multi-storey wood frame house with running water, a flush toilet, a basement, and even a small greenhouse for growing vegetables.

On their rampages, the children were often high from sniffing gasoline. Sam and Marie Angela, with whom I was staying, often went out at night looking for their children. Teenagers would spend some nights out sniffing on the ice in sub-zero temperatures. I sometimes saw 20 or more children huddled around plastic bags, their forms looming up against the white snow and the moonlight. Their howls punctuated the crisp night air. While their children sniffed, some of the adults were on drinking sprees.

These incidents coincided with the annual gathering of the community at a place they called Mistashantshish, near Daniel's Rattle. Many people were glad to get out and away, although some were afraid that if they left their houses unattended they would be vandalized. A meeting was called in the large tent at the gathering. Only about thirty people turned up, including the Chief and some members of the band council. Of this number, about seven or eight people contributed to the discussion. Each person spoke only for himself or herself, often prefacing statements with such disclaimers as "this is just my opinion." Christine Rich started by saying that adult drinking was at the root of the problem and that something needed to be done to control it. Because parents were drinking, kids felt unloved and uncared for. Now the kids had started to control the community, she said. After a pause, a red-nosed man responded that he would not stop drinking. Even if he were being chased by the RCMP while drunk on his skidoo, he would not stop. He would just drive on. Edward Piwas, an older man, pointed out that the Nechi training program for alcoholism had not helped. Many Nechi graduates had gone back on the bottle. Another person thought that gasoline could not be banned because it was needed for snowmobiles and ATVs. Tshenish Pasteen said that when he was young he had learned from the *Tshenut*. He thought that the young people and the leaders should learn from them now.

The points of view were diverse. Each was expressed as a personal view. No one attempted to debate with another or overcome opposing arguments. No persons or factions were accorded any privileged voice. A further meeting was called, but the Chief was ill and could not attend. A final attempt to have a meeting failed. Most people in the camp were hunting and enjoying themselves in a series of Easter games. After a little over a week everyone returned to the village. Views were aired, but no decisions were taken. The Chief did not take it on herself to act on any particular sentiment or to put any proposition to a vote. Her opinions carried no more weight than those of anyone else. No orthodoxy was enforced. No one was excluded. Inebriates had the same standing and the same entitlements to speak and be heard as non-drinkers. Because there was no consensus, nothing was decided and no attempt was made to force any decision. However, even had a consensus emerged, the Innu, as non-status Indians, would not have had the autonomy necessary to put any plan into effect, since authority is vested in the state, its social institutions, and the local *Akaneshau* agents.

Justice and Judgement   9

They just arrest on words only. This is not right.

– Tshenish Pasteen, Utshimassits, 1996.

The Innu are the most honest people I've met. I've seen no cases of total fabrication. You get everything, warts and all.

– Wayne Kelsey, lawyer, North West River, 1997

White society often forgets that the Innu are different.

– George Rich, *Struggling with My Soul* (2000: 59)

THE RETURN OF THE COURT TO DAVIS INLET

The police arrive in two detachments. I can hear the rattle of a speed-boat in the waters between the mainland and Iliukoyak Island. It is carrying the RCMP men from Hopedale. They dock and immediately go about their business. With clipboards and a brisk step they soon locate the houses of those who are due to appear in court today. The village is still half asleep in the mid-morning sun as a gleaming Twin Otter from Goose Bay touches down on the gravel airstrip. A second detachment of policemen unload their cargo of Innu youth from the Goose Bay Detention Centre. The teenage prisoners are returning in leg shackles to have their day in court and awkwardly make their way past the houses of friends and relatives to the court building, where they are unshackled. On the plane, the man who holds the power to release or incarcerate and who, through considered rational argument, can tease out truth from lies, the appropriately named presiding Judge Powers, unceremoniously enters the village.

After a gap of some 18 months when no circuit court was held in Utshimassits, there are no visible signs of reaction to the return of these authorities. The last time a Circuit Court was held, the Innu, a generally tolerant people, were so insulted by their treatment at the hand of Judge Hyslop that they evicted him and his court by calling a halt to the proceedings and escorting Hyslop and his entourage to the airstrip. Hyslop had apparently sped through cases, allowing little time for explanation, abruptly curtailing Innu defendants' answers. Several Innu were asked to get down from the witness stand before they had completed their statements. With what one lawyer observing the scene called "indecent haste," he wrote out sentences before the defence lawyers had spoken on behalf of their Innu clients. Eventually, three women – Chief Katie Rich, Justine Noah, an Innu constable, and Nympha Byrne – were prosecuted for contempt of court for the eviction of Hyslop.

No court had returned since, but not for want of trying. In what the Canadian media referred to as a "stand-off," RCMP planes with cargoes of judges, lawyers, and detainees had circled the airstrip only to be rebuffed by oil drums rolled onto the runway.[1] This was, by all accounts, a period when the Innu felt a sense of solidarity in confronting Canada. "The eviction drew out the anger. We felt the power of that time," said Mark Nui about three years after the events. Only after the threat of military options, not inconceivable so soon after the Canadian army operations in response to Mohawk protests at Oka and after the suspension of land claim negotiations and funding, was the Canadian criminal justice system finally able to reassert itself. The eviction of the judge and the fire on Valentine's Day 1992 were perhaps the two defining moments of the last decade of the twentieth century in Utshimassits.

Now at eleven o'clock, the appointed starting time, only a handful of people mill about outside the room designated as the courthouse, a Sunday school room attached to the Roman Catholic mission where the judge will stay in the priest's quarters. All the wooden chairs have red felt crosses draped on their backs. Adorning the walls are children's drawings in felt-tipped pens of Plains Indians with feathers and war bonnets. Wall hangings drape from the ceiling. One depicts caribou, canoes, and tents in cut-out caribou hide, another shows a stark red candle; in yet another, Christ holding up his hands seems to be gesturing the flock to follow. The walls are profusely decorated with crucifixes.

More people are gathering outside. I get a closer look at the uniformed RCMP men. They are wearing what must be their summer uniform: crisp white short-sleeved shirts; pressed twill trousers with yellow striping along the side. Pistols are in leather holsters. Their hard black boots are shining in the dust outside the courtroom. With closely cropped hair and neatly trimmed moustaches, they all look like they are playing a part. So unruffled are they that they could almost be on a film set. They banter with children and as the day wears on begin to bat at the thick black flies in the air.

At a quarter to twelve, a handful of Innu are gathered inside the courtroom. A corpulent *Akaneshau* woman, the court reporter, looks out at those assembled in the room, all Innu except for me, and announces the arrival of Judge Powers by exclaiming, "All rise." Only a very few do as instructed. Rooted to their Sunday school seats, others are impassive, looking straight ahead as the judge in his black robe enters from a back door. Underneath all the symbolism of *Akaneshau* power – the crucifixes, the armed and uniformed officers, even a portrait of Queen Elizabeth II depicting the elderly Old World monarch as a woman in her prime – there are no concessions to the people who are being judged. With no introductions made, no names announced, no explanations of either the people or the processes involved, it is as if this were always a part of their lives, as though there had never been a time when the Innu were not judged by foreigners.

Under the terms of the negotiations to reimpose the court, the Innu Nation believed that they were allowing the court back into Utshimassits on an approval basis with discretion to remove it if they wished. But the local lawyer representing the Innu defendants told me that the court regards itself as re-entering without condition, being the impenetrable embodiment of "the law." Hence, there is no need for any special announcements, formalities, or explanations since it is merely executing the legitimate powers of the land. As the lawyers representing the Innu defendants and the Crown rise respectively to address "Your honour" in a wooden dramatization of Old World formality, the proceedings begin. Most Innu, not understanding what is being said, are visibly bored by the opening long-winded exchanges, which continue for nearly an hour. Children file out after only a few minutes of incomprehensible and self-referential legal debates between the two lawyers and the judge. John Joy, the Newfoundland lawyer representing some of the Innu clients, had requested a translator for the audience in the courtroom. After numerous objections to this suggestion on the part of the Crown attorney, Judge Powers comes down in support of the Crown, stating, appropriately without translation, that there is no right that everyone in the court understands the proceedings. To this, John Joy makes a formal request for full and complete translations, but again he is rebuffed, as the judge tells him that there is no basis in law for translations to the community and the public in general. This was an issue for public policy, not the courts. Besides, it would be virtually impossible to translate everything so everyone understands. With this, Powers's judgement rested and the court adjourned until after lunch. The many Innu who spoke little or no English were none the wiser. Many fewer appear in the afternoon. None of the *Tshenut* who were there to oversee the proceedings on behalf of younger family members returned.

THE RAPE CASE

After the recess, the court reporter again announced the arrival of the judge by commanding that "All rise." Even fewer do so this time than earlier. Elizabeth Michel, an interpreter from Sheshatshiu, is sworn in on the Bible. Her job will be to translate only those statements addressed to the defendant, not the entire proceedings. The first defendant in the first case to be heard in Davis Inlet since the eviction of Judge Hyslop is smoking cigarettes with his friends outside in the dust. The first witness is a teenage girl named Lori Rafael, a victim in a rape case. The interrogation begins:

> Crown attorney (CA): Do you live in Sheshatshiu?
>
> Lori's head is down. Not using the translator, she barely murmurs yes.
>
> CA: Do you know Tony Norris (TN)?
>
> Lori's answer is inaudible.
>
> CA: Is he related?
>
> Lori Rafael (LR): (softly) Second or third cousin.
>
> Judge Powers asks her to speak up.
>
> CA: Do you remember meeting TN?
>
> LR: Yes.
>
> CA: Where were you?
>
> LR: His house.
>
> CA: Who was there?
>
> No answer.
>
> CA: What time of day?
>
> LR: I don't know . . . 5 or 6.
>
> CA: Morning or evening?
>
> LR: Evening.
>
> CA: Who was in the house?
>
> No answer.
>
> CA: What room were you in?
>
> LR: TV room.

CA: Who was in the room?

LR: TN.

CA: Where was everybody else?

LR: They . . . (inaudible to court audience)

Judge Powers asks her to repeat what she said because he couldn't hear her. The repetition is equally inaudible.

CA: What time of the day?

Inaudible answer.

CA: Was it after 6? Yes? What happened then?

LR: Went to his room to listen to tape recorder.

CA: What happened then?

Silence

CA: You said? Did you see him again?

LR: Yes.

CA: Which room did you see him in?

LR: His.

CA: Why?

LR: He called out and said he wanted to talk.

CA: What happened next?

LR: We were talking.

CA: Is there a bed in T's room?

LR: Yes.

CA: What other furniture?

Silence

CA: Where was TN? Sitting straight?

LR: Yes.

CA: What happened next?

LR: Talk.

CA: Where?

LR: Bed.

CA: How close on bed? Close or far?

LR: Far?

CA: What happened next?

LR: He started touching me. He listened first, but wouldn't stop. I said, leave me alone. Then he was too strong for me . . . (pause). I couldn't stop him. He was too strong for me. He grabbed my pants and ripped them.

CA: What happened next?

LR: I tried to fight back, but he pulled me back and he had intercourse with me.

CA: What do you remember happening next?

LR: I went home.

CA: Who lives at your house?

LR: Parents.

CA: Did you tell your parents?

LR: No, because my sister was in labour.

CA: What happened next?

LR: I threw out my pants. I don't want Mom to see.

CA: How old were you then?

LR: I don't know, 13 or 14.

CA: How old are you now?

LR: 13, 14.

CA: Where did he touch you when he started touching you?

LR cries.

Judge Powers looks on. It strikes me that, with the exception of the court reporter, Lori is surrounded by middle-aged white men.

LR: Private parts.

CA: When Tony tried to take your pants off, did he use two hands?

LR: Yes.

CA: Were you laying down or sitting up?

LR: Laying down.

CA: How?

LR (now tearful): He pulled me down.

CA: On your back or face first?

LR: Back.

CA: Where was Tony?

LR: On top of me.

Judge Powers: I can't hear you.

CA: What did you say next?

Silence.

CA: When he was trying to pull your pants off, were his pants off?

Silence.

CA: When did he take his pants off?

LR: On top of me.

CA: Where was he when he took his pants off?

LR: Still on me.

CA: Did Tony say anything when this was happening?

LR (who has been staring at the floor for some time): No.

CA: Did you ever have a relationship? Dating?

LR: No.

CA: Is he older or younger than you?

LR: Older.

CA: By how many years?

LR: I don't know.

CA: Did you tell anyone about what happened besides the RCMP?

LR: My cousin.

CA: Shortly after or a long time?

Silence.

CA: Any reason why you didn't tell anyone about it before?

LR: Because they wouldn't believe me. They call me a liar. They call me a slut around here.

CA: Why didn't you tell your parents?

LR (crying again): Wouldn't believe me.

After asking Lori whether Tony was in the courtroom, the Crown attorney completed his questioning. The Legal Aid lawyer representing the victim, seeing her distress, then asked whether she wished to continue. As Lori weakly responded in the positive, the lawyer began a series of questions. These, while more empathetically phrased, continued to dwell on precise times, dates, and ages, and the dates of the sister's labour. It was established that Lori was now 19 years of age, about to turn 20. Because the attorney quickly realized that Lori literally could not have been "13 or 14" when the event was alleged to have occurred four years earlier, he asked why she indicated that age. She said she just guessed when she was asked. To a question on the supposed anomaly of her disclosure of the incident only to a cousin and not to her parents, Lori replied that "No one believes a girl when she tells anyone or the police." As the questioning proceeded, the issue of Lori's undergarments again was raised, the lawyer even inquiring as to whether she had shown them to the police, how she disposed of them, and precisely where the tear on the fabric was located.

Tony Norris then took the stand, for a much shorter period of time. Again, the questioning hinged around recollections of times, dates, and linear sequences of events. He denied the rape, stating that he was not at the alleged scene of the crime at the time, and suggested that Lori's motive for a false accusation might have been because of a fight she had had with his girlfriend. Later Tony admits that he had been charged for an offence on Lori Rafael in the past, but this remained obscure. The times and dates he provides also don't seem to add up in what becomes a thinly described sequence of girl fights and plans to leave Davis Inlet that never materialize.

In summing up, Judge Powers noted the "burden on the Crown" to establish "credibility" since there were only two individuals present at the time of the alleged rape. The judge went on to highlight the fact that Lori Rafael was not certain of her age and could not narrow the time of the offence down at all. There was also an inconsistency of her age at the time of the event in 1991 and now. She could not be 13 or 14 in 1991 and nearly 20 in 1995 – although she first said that she was 13 or 14 now, which probably meant that she didn't understand the original question. I imagine that this was not pursued because of the victim's evident distress. Furthermore, the judge noted that Lori had not told her parents about the event and had not explained why she destroyed her underpants. The two lawyers weighed in with their summaries before the judge reiterated that the case revolved around credibility and reserved judgement until nine the following morning. After the summing up, it was also noted that Tony was to be tried on another offence – damaging the wires of the Newfoundland Telephone Company.

Pondering exactly what "credibility" might mean to Innu teenagers as I walked out of the courtroom in the late afternoon, I heard two elderly women remonstrating with the priest about the police using the church, supposedly a sacred place. They had no doubt witnessed the uniformed men escorting their leg-shackled grandchildren into the church annex that doubled as a courtroom. In hoarse voices, mixing *Innu-aimun* and English, the furious women, devout with large crosses hanging around their necks, were crying, shouting at him, "I am not happy . . . I am not happy." The shaken priest made half-hearted and unconvincing apologies, but took no action to address their protests.

For many Innu, the police are associated with foolish interference, violence, and removing people to prisons. Presumably, the women found the seeming collusion between the Church and the police too much to stomach. Although they are often called upon by the Innu, the RCMP remain a troubling presence. This predicament was articulated by Shustinis, a court worker, interviewed for *Gathering Voices*:

> The R.C.M.P. stands for the Royal Canadian Mounted Police, but in
> our language we don't have those words. Many of us say R.C.M.P., or
> police, or Mountie. We say these words in English but we don't
> know what we should call them in our own language. We just see
> R.C.M.P. in the uniform. The word we use in our language, *kama-
> kunest*, means, "the man who locks people up." (Innu Nation, 1995:
> 103)

Despite some jovial bantering with a few of the younger boys, the presence of several of these *kamakunest* in the community sometimes made for a tense atmosphere. The irate *Tshenut* could not understand why such disruptive forces were to be given charity from the Church, and how it was that the men who locked people up could be allowed the freedom of the Sunday school room to do more of it. Added to this was the insult of shackling the young detainees. So upset were many Innu by this blatant shaming of the young men that Katie Rich, the Chief, called the RCMP in to register the offence that many Innu felt for the humiliation of the youngsters. In order to placate the community, the RCMP later issued an apology.

Nevertheless, by nine the next morning when the court assistant announced "all rise," none of the accused from the previous day's proceedings was present. The RCMP men, perhaps having a lie in or enjoying the good weather of the morning, were also not in the courtroom, and it being their responsibility to ensure that the accused appeared, they were delinquent in their duties. An assistant was dispatched in search of them. The judge announced to the handful in the room that this was the "first time that the RCMP haven't done what they say they are going to do."

It took another hour and a half for the court to resume its proceedings. The resumption, however, was by no means slick. A huge group of young children found the presence of this official occasion an opportunity for play as they wildly swung in and out of the doors. The now frustrated Judge Powers told a small contingent of children that they "must either leave or stay for the duration." Visibly irritated by the wailing of a baby in the rear of the room, the judge embarked on a lengthy disquisition, untranslated and untranslatable, on the evidence, meandering into considerations of its "credence" and its "correspondence to the truth." Later he threatened to lock the door, then realizing his error of law, withdrew the threat: "I guess that would be against the fire regulations." The court was not to be anaerobic, but it might as well have been. The law, that self-affirming, impermeable yardstick of judgement and punishment, was as sealed as the proceedings themselves from the society of those who were being judged.

Gradually, as the judge's monologue on the rape case zeroed in on "the missing links in the chain of evidence," it was easy to see what was coming next. The times, dates, and ages iterated by the complainant did not correspond with the evidence. The date of the sister's labour was discovered to be an anomaly. In conclusion, the judge restated the crux of the issue, "credibility." Before announcing the verdict, "charges dismissed," Judge Powers indicated that the case was not "beyond reasonable doubt and does not necessarily indicate that Lori Rafael [who was not present] was lying."

So ended the first case of the court, which had returned only under duress by insisting that the Innu choose between the suspension of land claim negotiations and acceptance of Canadian criminal justice. Other cases involving vandalism, breaking into the school, breaking and entering the Innushare Centre, drunkenness as a breach of parole, and the case of the parents charged with manslaughter in the now famous house fire of Valentine's Day 1992 were all dispatched quickly or set over to another date.

DRIVING A WEDGE BETWEEN TRUTH AND FALSITY

One important task of the court is to separate the truth from fabrication. Through questioning, cross-examination, the probing of memory, and the filtering of these data through the prisms of logic and reason, the judge must arrive at a "verdict" on what happened and match this up to the taxonomy of crimes. This is no easy task, as we have seen in the rape case. Here, the judge admitted that the victim was not necessarily lying, but dropped the charges as a result of her not being able to align the events or her own narrative history in linear time. This raised the question as to whether the rape happened or not. Lori Rafael was not there to hear the verdict, but even had she been present, as was Tony Norris, it is unlikely that she would have been able to follow the disquisition on "credibility" or comprehend how the fact that she was not necessarily lying could have resulted in the dismissal of the charge. The disquisition itself revealed that the court was not so much interested in exact truth but in the presentation of a "credible" case.

"Credibility" was what was at stake, and to establish this, the Innu teenager Lori Rafael was required to answer to older male *Akaneshau* strangers the details of sexual violation. The state of the fabric and disposal of the underwear she wore at the time and the co-ordinating of the whole distressing experience in linear time were what the case turned upon. Little consideration was given to the fact that such a public exposure of a harrowing event, and one that was orchestrated by the protocols of strangers, would be experienced as shameful, and possibly be damaging to Lori Rafael, not even a resident of Davis Inlet at the time. Even though no one could say that the rape did not take place, the conclusion that is often drawn when a defendant is acquitted is that the accuser has lied. Likewise, no one considered that, like most Innu, it would have been considered absurd to locate her experience in terms of a specifically linear temporal sequence, carefully lining up "age" with a narration of key events.[2]

In most contexts in Western societies where the criminal justice system operates, the antagonists speak the same language and share roughly the same understanding of fundamental concepts. Likewise, there is a common recognition of the lexicon of crime and punishment as well as understandings of the role that actors such as the police, the judge, and the attorneys play in courts and other legal arenas. In the cases I have observed involving Innu in the courts at Utshimassits, North West River, and Happy Valley, no such alignment could be presupposed. The law used to judge and the rituals deployed to ascertain credibility are entirely imposed.[3] Most Innu, as one defendant told me outside the Happy Valley courthouse, have no idea what the justice system is all about. There is barely an Innu person to whom the jargon, long words, and rarefied phrases are intelligible, either literally or conceptually, and the whole process both expresses and is rooted in cosmological assumptions that have emerged out of European history.

Although sometimes it was taken for granted that "credibility," for example, was something readily amenable to the understanding of a teenage Innu rape victim, no means of ascertaining whether she understood this or any other part of the court procedure were put forward. It was tacitly assumed that the language and protocols were meaningful to her and others, though these assumptions were never checked. For example, the need for an understanding of the technical details of the case, Latin phrases, dense jargon, and linear chronology that would have a bearing on what happened to the Innu involved was not acknowledged or appreciated. Most words used by the court officials were never translated and probably not translatable into *Innu-aimun*.

In several cases I have observed, readings from the Criminal Code were enunciated. But not once have I heard these being translated, although on occasion, some Legal Aid lawyers attempted to render them into oversimplified English for the benefit of their clients. The problem of translating technical legal concepts, often derived from Latin, into the very different cultural terms of *Innu-aimun* defeats even the most gifted interpreter. As the contributors to a group discussion on the law in *Gathering Voices* reported:

> The police should explain to the Innu about the laws, because no-body really understands them. Even when there is an interpreter there, he or she has a difficult time with the two different languages. They try to translate, but they can't understand how some of the words translate. We don't have any words for a lot of legal things. We as Innu don't know how to say these difficult words in English. We try to say in an easy way that we can understand. When a Crown prosecutor or a judge asks a question to the accused, wanting him or her to explain it better, sometimes the accused doesn't know how to. These things are hard for us as Innu. These questions take a long time to find the answer. But it is easy for them, because they have it all in English. They can say whatever they want because they speak English. (Innu Nation, 1995: 107)

However, even when translation was provided by an interpreter, the restating of some of the legal language and the phrasings of questions in *Innu-aimun* can never deliver what is actually meant, and the assumptions behind what is said by the judges and lawyers are never made clear as they might be in other court proceedings involving Euro-Canadians. The court simply ignores the glaringly obvious fact that a common universe of meaning does not exist. The court's failure to ensure that its language, procedure, and assumptions about the world are meaningful to the Innu indicates three very fundamental processes at work.

First, although participants in cases are free to reject a translator, very few do so because they think the translator is part of the required court procedure. Interpreters from one extended family, for whatever reason, may not be acceptable to those from another who do not wish to have their dirty linen paraded in front of people from another family. Because there is no independent check on translations, the Innu, whether defendants or complainants in Crown prosecutions, are at the mercy of translators. The interpretations of the English they hear and renderings of what Innu participants say can have a profound influence on how the case goes, the verdict, and consequently what may happen in the future to the individual defendant (or complainant) and that person's family.

Second, there is a naive presumption that English words can be rephrased as meaningful words in *Innu-aimun* and that these words connect to a common imagery of the world. This is patently false given that all of the concepts used in the courts are European, from the notion of "crime" itself to the arcane subsections of the Criminal Code. The level of detail enveloped in the court proceedings and the

distinct possibility that a case can turn on subtle shades of semantics render translation into *Innu-aimun* absurd. The difficulty of this
in Davis Inlet was compounded by the court's hiring of a translator
from Sheshatshiu with a different dialect and a whispering delivery.

Third, the courts are not particularly interested in ensuring that
the Innu understand all of the language, procedures, and protocols.
In the Western political tradition, the court is an institution for the
universal arbitration of all human conflict, guided by the law, which
regulates social relations. As such, its mandate is provided by the
established laws of the state, which are adapted from precedents
and established and modified by its legislative apparatuses. The
Innu, as "Canadians," albeit non-consenting on the whole, are simply assumed to be one among many other social groups to fall under
the umbrella of the state and hence the law. Only through this combination of myopia and indifference towards difference can facts,
verdicts, and eventual punishments in the truth-making machinery
of the court be established. This produces bizarre reversals of testimony and retractions as Innu defendants switch between pleas,
trying to fathom the meaning and implications of their utterances,
the minutiae of which could be significant to their fate.

For example, at a very fundamental level, the simple distinction between guilt and innocence does not exist in *Innu-aimun*. If something
happened, then it is true. If the incident was painful, hurtful, or damaging, this does not necessarily imply that the perpetrator will adopt
anything like the Anglo-American concept of guilt, although the person
may be haunted or shamed by the event. The absence of guilt and tolerance of a wide range of activity that did not threaten the group directly
were targets of largely unsuccessful correction of generations of missionaries from Le Jeune onward. As Eleanor Burke Leacock (1980: 39)
remarked of her travels with the Innu in the 1950s, "conditions in the
north woods were still such that the traditional Montagnais-Naskapi
ethic of cooperativeness, tolerance and nonpunitiveness remained
strong." From my own discussions with Innu, I learned that in most
cases people maintain that all events are connected to a web of circumstances that make them intelligible. As such, these events are rarely
considered to be attached to any definitive, and certainly not a public,
judgement. This is why in meetings that are called by the Innu, all may
speak and may do so for as long as they please. It is more important to
allow individuals to speak their mind than it is to watch the clock and
curtail the fullness of opinions or stories.

The adversarial nature of courtroom procedure, on the other
hand, produces decisions that are much more clearly the product of
artifice. Verdicts are arrived at not by the full enunciation of the

story of how something came to be, but through a rapid sequence of questions chosen by lawyers in order to "win" the case rather than to understand if or how something occurred. This creates a "staccato effect" that cripples the ability of Innu court participants to speak in their own way. As such, it is both psychologically destabilizing and often deleterious to the interests of the individuals involved in obtaining justice on the criminal justice system's own terms. In *Rape and the Culture of the Courtroom*, Andrew Taslitz (1999: 115-16) has made the point specifically with regard to rape victims in American courts. Rape victims are unable to narrate freely what happened to them and must constantly tell their stories through very specific questions, the answers to which are frequently interrupted, and which are designed primarily to create a particular *impression* of events that will provide support for one side to "win" the case. Because the personal narration of events is particularly important to rape victims, the "staccato effect" is a way of displacing the victim's own understanding of what happened. In a similar way, by ruling out Innu narrative, banishing their right to tell their own story in their own way, the courts are manufacturing false selves with false histories and thereby basing judgement on presentations that they have required the Innu to fashion.

In one case that I observed, after an Innu defendant was called for sentencing on an assault charge, he was asked his plea. Through a translator, he said "guilty." Then, as the judge was about to set a sentence, he entered into a long conversation in *Innu-aimun* with the translator. After the conversation, it emerged that the defendant had a mitigating explanation, which the translator started to articulate in some detail. Part way through the explanation, the judge stopped her, indicating that the plea would have to be changed to "not guilty." This was then translated back to the defendant, who, shrugging his shoulders, agreed to the revised plea. At this, the judge issued him with a revised trial date, and seeing that he had not even had the benefit of the lacklustre Legal Aid attorney who plied his trade in Goose Bay, informed him, "You may wish to get legal counsel before that date." It appeared that the defendant in this case was attempting to sketch out a long sequence of events, which helped to provide a context for the "crime" and render it intelligible in light of the alignment of circumstances. But because all trials must hinge on a defining culpability with some precision, the narration at this time was "inadmissable" and, consequently, was cut short. The defendant would be required to reappear, fashion his narrative in line with the new plea, and adopt the stance that he was not guilty.

Guilt as it is incorporated into the Anglo-American judicial system has its roots in a very different cosmology and view of the self in human society than that which obtains among the Innu. It can be traced to the Old Testament and is a basis for Judeo-Christian civilization, developed according to codes of personal conduct and social order laid down by God.[4] Contemporary justice is premised on the establishment of fault for the violation of rules and the specification of schedules of punishment. The initial determination of guilt is then a determination of fault and, hence, culpability, which implies the adoption of a guilty frame of mind by the person found to be the author of the wrongdoing. Violations of social rules and crimes are transgressions of the boundaries of acceptability established within a society and are deemed to require retribution. Punishment alone is not sufficient since this could lead to repeat offending. The violator must both fear punishment and internalize the negative feelings towards wrongdoings and, by extension, oneself as the author of a crime. This adoption of a hostile attitude towards oneself – thinking of oneself as one imagines others do on account of being responsible for actions that others regard as reprehensible – is the subjective, and most important, aspect of guilt.[5] In *On Guilt and Innocence*, the legal philosopher Herbert Morris (1976: 89) argues that "We associate being guilty and feeling guilty with pain, with pain inflicted upon us by others, and pain that we inflict upon ourselves. The verdict in a court of law is 'guilty,' and this by itself may make for suffering."

Morris (ibid., 59, 63) contrasts guilt with shame. Shame operates in "a world devoid of moral criticism and punishment," and is inferior to guilt, which finds "a natural role within law." He then sketches out a variety of reasons why "we" should prefer the conception of guilt in law and other affairs. Presupposing the social need to maintain a balanced distribution of freedom through ordered adherence to rules specifying rights and duties, Morris suggests that only guilt can best uphold social order. While he may or may not be right in relation to Western societies – hence, the ubiquitous "we" of his and other legal narratives – the imposition of guilt on peoples such as the Innu is a direct attack on their way of ordering society and dealing with conflict. If the Canadian authorities are concerned at all, it may be their intention that by exposing Natives to courts for long enough they will effect the internalization of guilt and hence the correct orientation towards punishment. However, if this is the goal, it is, as the following case shows, far from being realized.

WEARING THE CROWN A LITTLE THIN

In a case involving the defendant Matthew Pone at the improvised courthouse in North West River, an initial plea was stated and then reversed. After the charge of multiple assaults on Matthew's wife was read out, it was noted that the wife, the complainant, had refused to be interviewed by the RCMP. The Crown prosecutor then withdrew the charges. But, at this point the Legal Aid attorney bizarrely announced that Matthew Pone wished to change his plea from not guilty to guilty. Sensing something was amiss but not knowing quite what it was, Matthew asked for an interpreter. The judge then began a long and rambling legal disquisition on the technicalities of the reversal of plea, which were delivered too quickly for the interpreter to translate except in rough summary. Using words and phrases such as "recognizance," "breach," and "fail to keep the peace," the facts of the case were summarized, but much of this was mumbled between the lawyers and the judge, as if there were no audience. The charge was read out again, and Matthew pleaded not guilty. Surprised, the Crown prosecutor responded, "That's not my understanding." After whispered translations from the interpreter, Matthew switched his plea again to guilty. These switches were not surprising, because it emerged that there were multiple charges, each detailing a different incident. One of these was a charge for violating a previous court order to stay away from his family, although at the time of the alleged breach he was actually chopping wood outside the house for the family. Further charges of assault against his wife were also read out.

The contest began in earnest when the two constables who had been at the scene of one of the assaults were called to testify. They described arriving at the Pone household to find Mrs. Pone covered in blood. Matthew was said to be "severely intoxicated," swaying as he walked and slurring his speech. Mrs. Pone's demeanour was portrayed as also "under the influence of alcohol, crying, wishing that her husband be removed from the house." While a statement was taken from her, one constable said that he noticed her lips were swollen, but she did not require any medical treatment.

Mrs. Josie Pone, who up to this point had been sitting passively next to her husband, was called to be sworn to the Bible in *Innuaimun*. "Do you know a gentleman by the name of Matthew Pone" was the first question from the Crown prosecutor. Josie pointed to the compact man in a jacket and baseball cap whose side she had just left. Other questions, such as "Are you married," the answers to which were obvious, were fired at Mrs. Pone before the actual incident of 18 months earlier was brought up. The prosecutor, working on behalf of Mrs. Pone to convict her husband of the assaults, although she had since apparently reconciled with him, asked questions designed to elicit a picture of the scene and of the participants on the night of that first assault.

> Crown prosecutor (CP): Do you remember the RCMP coming to the house on 16 November 1996?
>
> Josie Pone through the translator (JP): (after a long pause) Yes.
>
> CP: Why did the RCMP come to the house on 16 November 1996?
>
> JP: She cannot remember. They told her that she called the police.

Questioning then led to a description of the dramatis personae in what was a house party. Mrs. Pone "thinks they were all drinking." The exact times of comings and goings, trips to Goose Bay for beer, and the disposition of the other partiers, Helen and Jean-Marie Asta, were queried, although Mrs. Pone did not commit to anything with any degree of specificity. Then came the questions intended to replay the actual assault:

> CP: Do you remember getting a punch on the nose that day?
>
> JP: I can't tell you, I'm not allowed.
>
> CP: What happened?
>
> JP: She cannot say.

Then, after further prompting:

> JP: She was drinking and went up to Goose Bay.
>
> CP: Why?
>
> JP: To get some beer.
>
> CP: Where then?
>
> JP: Went back home, but then Matthew was already taken by the police.

My interpretation here was that since there were many things that happened on that day involving drink and procuring drink, Mrs. Pone's recollection of events did not follow the same linear sequence the Crown prosecutor was seeking to extract:

> CP: So you weren't even there when Matthew Pone was arrested?
>
> JP: She don't know.
>
> CP: What time did you start drinking that day?
>
> JP: She didn't look at the time.
>
> CP: Was it in the morning or the evening?
>
> JP: In the morning.
>
> CP: When did you stop?

JP: Two in the evening.

Then, perhaps seeing that this testimony was not leading in the direction required if Matthew Pone was to be convicted, the Crown prosecutor quickly switched to another later assault incident:

CP: Do you remember anything happening with Matthew Pone on 9 November 1997?

JP: She doesn't remember.

CP: Do you remember Matthew Pone hitting you with a board?

JP: (after a long pause) No, she don't remember.

CP: Do you remember making a statement?

JP: She don't remember.

At this point, I noticed that the increasingly frustrated Crown prosecutor and the RCMP constables were all shaking their heads.

CP: Do you remember being with constables?

JP: Yes.

CP: Do you remember if you had any injuries?

JP: She didn't think she had any injuries.

CP: None?

JP: No.

CP: No further questions.

In an unusual step, the Legal Aid lawyer, acting on behalf of Matthew Pone, deferred asking any questions of the witness for the prosecution. This raised the question of whether this normally lethargic lawyer simply could not be bothered or whether he thought that Mrs. Pone's testimony had actually helped his client and further questions would only muddy the already murky waters. The next witness for the prosecution was Helen Asta, who did not need an interpreter and so was sworn in in English. Her testimony, delivered in response to rapid-fire questions from the Crown prosecutor, revealed a few more details of both 1996 and 1997 assaults, but when it came to the crunch, she could not recall any details that would pinpoint the crime to Matthew Pone. "I remember the statement [to the RCMP]," she said, "but I can't remember what happened." After Helen Asta had admitted to having drunk four dozen cans of beer, the judge, either because he didn't believe the amount or because he was not paying attention, asked, "Any reason why you didn't remember your statement." To this, Helen Asta replied that there was no reason, but when prompted again, said, "I was drinking when I made the statement."

The final witness for the prosecution was Jean-Marie Asta, who proved equally incapable of playing the assigned role of nailing Matthew Pone to the crime. However, his testimony, through an interpreter, exposed both the ethnocentric nature of the proceedings and the way in which Innu attitudes on the relationship between the self and alcohol differ from those of Euro-Canadians and the Western system of justice in general. The questioning went as follows:

CP: Do you remember going out with the group?

Jean-Marie Asta (JA): He was drinking and he was drunk. He was drinking all night.

CP: When?

JA: Around ten.

CP: Where?

JA: In his house.

CP: Who with?

JA: They're gone to the country. (Jean-Marie here answers by reference to where the people are now, not who they are.)

CP: (obviously not following Jean-Marie's logic) Not Matthew Pone and Josie?

JA: No.

CP: How much did you drink?

JA: Ten cans.

CP: Then what happened after ten cans?

JA: I drank more.

The Crown prosecutor then asked Jean-Marie to describe the scene at the Pone house when he arrived on the night of 16 November 1996. Through a series of short answers, he said that although he did not see Matthew Pone hit Josie, he did physically restrain Matthew to prevent him from hurting Josie. Questioning then quickly switched to the night of 9 November 1997.

CP: Had you been to the home [of Matthew Pone] on other occasions?

JA: No.

CP: No, not on the 9th of November 1997?

JA: He don't know. He can't remember.

CP: Do you remember the incident with Matthew Pone and Josie and the two-by-four?

JA: He was drunk at the time. He cannot recall anything.

CP: Do you remember your statement to the RCMP?

JA: He thinks he probably gave a statement, but he was drinking and he was sick and he can't remember anything.

At this point, the Crown prosecutor looked exasperated. None of his witnesses were performing the adversarial roles necessary for the prosecution. Assertions of clear recall of events were few and far between and the witnesses could not remember their statements to the RCMP. "Your Honour," exclaimed a rather bedraggled looking Crown prosecutor, "it is now twenty-five to five. This sort of evidence is wearing a little thin on the Crown." He suggested an adjournment, to be followed by cross-examinations on the actual statements made to the RCMP. Judge Powers moved quickly to set over the case until another date in Goose Bay, but Jean-Marie put a spanner in the works by saying that he could not get there because he is on Social Assistance. After a brief hesitation, the Crown prosecutor reluctantly told the judge, "He's our witness. We'll pick up the tab. We'll get him there."

After the reading of a list of conditions for Matthew Pone – so rapidly that it would have been impossible to translate everything – the rotund Jean-Marie let it be known that he wanted to make a statement to the court. The interpreter told the judge that Jean-Marie "wants to know why statements made by Innu people when they are drunk are taken." This crucial point, touching on a core difference between Innu and Euro-Canadian concepts of the self and the role of alcohol in the accountability of the person, was summarily brushed aside by the judge, who told Jean-Marie that he could not answer the question and that the court "may have to get into that issue" when it reconvened. That is, Jean-Marie's clear implication, that all of the recollection of events and the statements existed only in a haze of heavy drinking and therefore should not be taken as "statements" of anything binding since they were made while people were inebriated, was simply sidelined. More fundamentally, it is clear to Jean-Marie and most Innu that one is not the same person when one is drinking. There is no attempt to construct a continuous single narrative self. Such a self is, of course, functional to systems of retributive justice, since an individual can always be nailed for a crime, no matter what circumstances may have influenced the commission of it because the individual is deemed to be accountable across all contexts. Although there are some exceptions, such as the insanity plea, certainly the fact that someone was drunk at the time of a crime is no mitigation in criminal justice, as it would be for the Innu. Rather, in the eyes of the court, drunkenness actually compounds the crime since it demonstrates a double failure – to keep sober and to keep the peace.

Suffice it to say Jean-Marie's point went unheeded. Notably, while one would not expect the Legal Aid lawyer to be a champion of cultural relativism and to develop the implications of the role of alcohol in the accountability of the self across cultural contexts, it is notable that he did not pick up on the practical implications of Jean-Marie's statement. He seemed as indifferent to it as the judge. Opening up a debate on the legitimacy of statements from inebriates could certainly have aided his client, Matthew Pone. But now, at five o'clock as the lawyers were looking at their watches, the judge called the proceedings to a halt. The Innu filed out, lighting up cigarettes as they walked out the door. Matthew and Josie, the Astas, and the interpreter, adversaries in the replaying of conflicts that clearly no longer existed, all walked home together, across the bridge, in jovial good humour.

The court manufactures a direct confrontation between individuals who are constituted as antagonists, even though, as in the above situation, the couple had obviously made up or settled to live with what happened. In the courtroom, they were forced to relive a painful clash from the past, which, for this couple, was buried in a dense fog of drinking, trips to Goose Bay, and slurred statements to the police. The Crown and defence lawyers buttress this expectation of antagonism through often aggressive questioning of "their" witnesses, who are expected to rally to the defence of their side. The consequence of this, as many Innu have pointed out to me, is that true resolution is hindered by the prohibition against co-operation and the insistence on direct frontal attacks between two competing sides.[6] Many times, as when Jean-Marie Asta started to wear down the patience of the Crown, the Innu are able to subvert this by not playing the expected roles and by questioning legal certainties. Nonetheless, the confrontational approach does result in what many Innu regard as obstacles to both reconciliation and truth. Not long after these events, Matthew Pone hanged himself.

MORAL AUTHORITY

In the courtroom dialogues, judges and lawyers constantly exert a moral authority over their Innu charges. I have yet to attend a court hearing in which the judge did not, at the end of a case, issue gratuitous advice to defendants. While this can be trivial and easily forgotten, the judge's moralism can often insinuate itself into the conditions that are stipulated in sentencing. In a case I observed at the courtroom in North West River, David Rich, again after inquiring about the implications of a change of plea from "guilty" to "not guilty," admitted to the "facts" of an incident of domestic violence.

The Crown, as always pressed for a custodial sentence, while the Legal Aid lawyer made a mumbled appeal for a fine on account of various factors, including presence of children for whom David had joint custody, it being his first offence, and his seasonal work. In summing up and sentencing, the judge used the opportunity to impart a kind of homespun moralism into the conditions he imposed. First, David Rich's relatively short criminal record was noted, but the judge offset this against the seriousness of the charges. This was followed by the judge repeating the sordid details of the intoxicated assault. The defendant was continuously chastened for his actions, and at the same time given faint praise for the fact that he had not undertaken other "criminal" acts very often. "This was unacceptable behaviour, drunk or not," the judge prefaced his consideration of incarceration, before settling on "six months' incarceration at Her Majesty's Penitentiary at home" – that is, house arrest.

While at "Her Majesty's Penitentiary at home," the defendant was told that he "must" abide by a long list of stipulated conditions. The first was that he not go to his wife's house (meaning that there would be a serious obstacle to any potential reconciliation). Next, although he had already told the court that Innu Nation had covered the damage to the house, David was required to make an estimate of the costs and pay her within 60 days. Emphasizing the economic aspects of the incident, the judge added, "I'm sure she can't afford you breaking up her property." Next, he was to participate in counselling for alcohol abuse, even though he had admitted in his testimony that he had not drunk since the unfortunate event many months earlier. Commensurate with this stipulation, he was not to enter any bar or consume or possess alcohol. His domicile amounting to a virtual penitentiary, David Rich was to remain in the home from 4 p.m. to 12 noon. In addition, he was required to pay a court surcharge of $35, a $250 fine, and a $35 victim surcharge and was placed on two years' concurrent probation. All this required that he sign his agreement to the various specifications for his future actions and movements. Ending David's afternoon in the dock, the judge added, "these are the consequences, Mr. Rich, of your behaviour."

In other cases, particularly those involving the numerous teenagers who are filed into the courts, the moralism, mixed up again with the sentencing, is usually more powerfully delivered by the judge. In the case of James Michel, a teenager who had been involved in a violent attack on another youth, the judge judged him "to be aimless. You don't go to school. You don't have a job. This won't help you in the future." James was given "extended probation, which is extremely restrictive." He could only leave his family's

house under "prescribed circumstances." While out, he was required to seek counselling and provide community services, and not
associate with his friends who were co-accused of the offence. His father was told that James had "to be supervised at all times." His
sentence was described as a form of "house arrest" and his curfew
would last from 10 p.m. until 7 a.m.

While the majority of Innu may not see the criminal justice system as legitimate, judges are beginning to impose a formal moral
authority that has been the preserve of the *Tshenut*, whose opinions
were and are treated with regard and even deference in certain contexts. Increasingly, however, the most difficult situations that have
arisen in the community are being negotiated through the moral
authority of the courts. In contrast to the judges, *Tshenut* are likely
to see "crime" as the activity of a troubled person who has not been
able to endure community life and who has suffered from not being
exposed to the Innu life in the country. But "when the elder testifies
in court, the judge doesn't care what he says," Eric Rich told me. He
continued, "Elders are supposed to be listened to and respected.
What they say encourages the offender to be treated rather than
punished." Eric was unable to detect any understanding of the *Tshenut* or the role they play in the community on the part of the judges
he has seen in Davis Inlet. "I felt really angry," said Eric, speaking of
his own case. "A lot of people had encouraged me to go to treatment.
The judge didn't listen to what my supporters were saying. I felt in
my heart that he wasn't listening."[7]

RETRIBUTION AND PUNISHMENT

Various Western philosophical assumptions underpin the workings
of the Canadian criminal justice system. Images of human nature
found in a long line of political theorists from Thomas Hobbes and
the nineteenth-century utilitarians to behavioural psychologists –
that human beings are selfish and egoistic, responding best to
authoritative incentives and disincentives – have been incorporated
into the law. One essential element that these versions of human nature share is that social wrongdoing or "crime" should be met with
punishment so long as the accused is adjudged to be competent and
responsible.[8] While there have been recent moves to incorporate
therapy and community service into sentences, there is still hardly
any dissent in the Anglo-American world to the idea that punishment is the central component of a societal response to crime.

As well as incorporating punishment as a central tenet, virtually
every criminal justice system slavishly follows a deterrence model,
applying sanctions to people found guilty of activities deemed to be

criminal (see Zimring and Hawkins, 1973: 18). Through the sanc-
tion of imprisonment, fines, community service, or other means, it is
assumed that the behaviour of the offender will modify even though
there is virtually no evidence that punishment is a deterrent (Ten,
1987: 8). Deterrence relies on the tired assumption that punishment and actions will be irretrievably linked in the mind of the
offender. It assumes a nineteenth-century version of "rational man,"
an individual constantly calculating costs and benefits and weigh-
ing up losses and gains for all avenues of action. The pains,
discomforts, and losses of the punishment will be so irretrievably
associated with the crime that all future activity of the same nature
will be discouraged.

In turn, deterrence relies on some concept of guilt, which, while
firmly rooted in the Judeo-Christian cosmology, has never found a
place in the traditions or world view of the Innu. Guilt is predicated
on the internalization of individual error and culpability, for which
relief comes only through certain acts of redemption. This is largely
foreign to the Innu. To the extent that they are aware of such a doctrine, it is through the teachings of the Oblate priests, which have
been discredited and discounted as a result of the widespread sexual and physical abuse these men inflicted on Innu who trusted
them. Furthermore, as I have indicated earlier, even the binary divide between guilt and innocence is an absurdity. As Judy Hill, an
Innu teaching aide once told me, "there is no such thing as 'guilty.'
You either did it or you didn't." Many defendants that I observed in
the courtroom had a difficult time separating the two, often changing their pleas and relating stories that, while freely admitting the
crime, contextualized events within a complex mesh of circumstances and relationships. Indeed, the Innu language is equipped
with no word for "guilty." Hence, when the court interpreter trans-
lates an invitation to a plea, the defendant is asked, "Did you do it?"
Katie Rich, the Chief who instigated the eviction of Judge Hyslop
from Davis Inlet, once told me, "There is no word for guilty. There is
only, 'I am telling the truth.'" This is rather different from asking
whether one pleads guilty or not, but nevertheless the court imputes
a state of mind in the defendant that does not exist – the *mens rea* of
English common law. Furthermore, "telling the truth" in Innu society is never associated with an immediate moral judgement as it is in
the guilty plea of the criminal justice system. Being the author of an
act, no matter how harmful, is rarely if ever followed by an attachment of guilt to the person or the internalization of guilt. Also, acts
themselves are not evaluated according to a hierarchy of moral approval. There are no firm principles that underlie actions and

events, and the history of the Innu as hunters, living with unpredictability and wild nature, has mitigated against the static moral rationalism that is pervasive in Western thinking.

Incarceration – the deterrent of last resort in the Canadian criminal justice system – is seen by the vast bulk of Innu as counterproductive and even harmful, both to individuals and to their families. No matter what offence someone may have caused, jail offers no solution to the after-effects of the events. The problems an individual may have had before imprisonment will be, if anything, more severe upon release. The prison merely wastes the prisoner's time and makes it more difficult for the family to get along without his or her contributions. Echoing these problems with jailing, Apenam Pone, an alcohol counsellor, said, "when the court sends a father to jail, it splits families apart. Look at the victim. She is more hurt by the court than she was hurt before. Then there is the trauma of the wife. She needs the husband to bring in wood and other things and the judges don't understand that. When the child is sick, they need the father. He is needed to protect the home."

Penal institutions exist not simply to prevent an offender from offending further; through entrenching guilt, they symbolize the total rejection of the individual from others in the community and aim to foment remorse within his or her own mind. No matter how psychically sheltered the Innu may be from the Anglo-Saxon philosophy of criminal justice, the imposition of a jail term is surely a strong test for any Innu. While many recognize their prison sentences as acts of *Akaneshau* domination, the experience can lead young Innu in particular to feel they are worthless, and suicides of teenagers have been known to occur prior to court appearances. While in the jail, Innu prisoners miss the outdoors, find the confinement oppressively hot and boring, and often gain a lot of weight from the combination of stodgy food and lack of exercise. The experience of incarceration either leads to no improvement in the offender's life chances and self-esteem or, more commonly, a marked deterioration in the position of the offender, who is released not "deterred" but with considerably lower self-esteem.

Despite the jail being considered unhelpful, damaging, and degrading by many Innu, some people look back on it without a trace of self-pity. Describing a period of 11 months in 1976 in a girls' home in St. John's when she was 13, Matnen Benuen told me of the prohibition against Innu girls addressing each other in *Innu-aimun* and being scolded for laughing at the dinner table. Reminiscent of the "mortification" process in an American mental asylum in the 1950s described by Erving Goffman (1961), on their first day of incarceration Matnen and the other Innu girls were stripped naked by the wardens who, suspecting lice, applied vinegar to their hair. Her account, however, was a humorous, nostalgic tale. It was not tinged by any bitterness. She simply related what had happened. No judgement was attached.

However, the very presence of criminal justice now means that Innu can use courts as a new weapon in inter-communal conflicts. Although there are various initiatives for Innu – controlled healing and sentencing circles, for example – the formal system of the court is increasingly an instrument of individual or familial retribution that has no history in the experience of the Innu people. Already, it is clear that the courts function to exacerbate the divisiveness fostered by village life itself. This does not negate the fact that some people may portray their experience of punishment without rancour or victimhood (as with Matnen Benuen) or that they can subtly, and perhaps inadvertently, subvert the intentions and premises of the court (as with Jean-Marie Asta).

Nevertheless, the criminal justice system has a marked destructive effect communally. The retributive element of the system can and is used by members of the community in such a way that it exacerbates rather than eases the tensions that have already been occasioned by large numbers of Innu all living in one place. Imposed law in the guise of criminal justice is harnessed for the purposes of tackling interpersonal problems flowing from the earlier imposition of the village itself. Almost all court cases involve more than just two parties – immediate relatives, extended families, neighbours, and in some cases the whole community may be affected by a particular court case. The public rituals of degradation and exposure ensure that reverberations of conflict often run deep, as the justice system becomes a means of settling scores for those who have been hurt by others. The court can be an instrument for sharpening divisions that may have, without it, simply dissipated or at least been resolved without humiliation and punishment.

The results of court cases have a knock-on effect within the community. While many Innu are reluctant to treat a criminal record as having any necessary bearing on the worth of a person, the more formalized the community institutions become, the more such records are taken into account. Many very capable people who have been convicted of alcohol-related offences, for example, may be seen as less suitable for jobs, education, and training opportunities and for the benefits that the political bodies dispense. Exacerbating the rifts that the court already creates is the feeling of many Innu (and this was also noted by the local lawyer, Wayne Kelsey) that members of the community are not treated equally either by the courts or by the police. As Kelsey observed, the "out-groups" in the community are more likely to get harsher sentences, while those related to prominent, politically involved families are likely to get lighter treatment. "This is how the court displays its sensitivity to the Innu," as Wayne Kelsey put it. While I was never able to verify this with any precision in my many observations of court cases, it would fit that the courts, as arms of the Canadian state, would seek to appease those Innu who are most crucial to the harmonious conduct of inter-ethnic relations and whose signatures are required for land claims and development projects.

In Labrador, as in other colonized territories where alien legal systems have been imposed and enforced, conflict is exacerbated and indigenous methods of resolution become displaced, while "crime," once it has been codified, increases.[9] That is, the advent of courts and police actually contributes to the rise, if not the invention, of the very conflicts that they are intended to control. It is not clear exactly how this comes to be, but there are many possible reasons why it should be the case. The sedentarization of the Innu creates a novel situation of people living in much closer proximity than ever before. When the Innu were permanent nomadic hunters, conflict was attenuated by constant movement, but this exit has now been largely closed, thus exacerbating tensions between conflicting parties. With this form of resolution blocked and the authority of those in the camps who would have helped to build consensus usurped by foreign laws, judges, and the police, it is easy to see how confusion can spread, thereby leading Innu to feel that they have no control over their own lives. When a people have no access to their own methods of resolving disputes or when these methods have been delegitimized, an attitude of careless abandon easily takes root since it is now not they, the Innu, who control how conflict is managed and "crime" is defined.

THE JUSTICE OF JUSTICE

It is clear that the Innu experience the imposition of an alien legal system as profoundly oppressive. First, and most fundamentally, the law as formulated in Canadian society is in many ways a bizarre institution that presents them with radical methods of dealing with conflict, ascertaining wrongdoing, and providing retributive resolutions. In addition, it relies on a Judeo-Christian notion of "crime," an elaboration of what constitutes the deviant and the abnormal, which is foreign to the Innu and most other Aboriginal peoples of the Americas. Canadian law, as a final arbiter of all conflict, presents a "no-exit" situation for the Innu. This represents a direct assault on the self, as Svennson (1979) has pointed out in relation to Native Americans under imposed law generally. It removes the right to be a Native person.

The law incorporates various binary conceptual divisions – right and wrong, guilty and innocent, truth and falsity, accused and accuser, victim and victimizer. Subject to the formal confrontations I have been describing, it prescribes largely institutionalized solutions to the conflicts between people. Such conflicts can only be resolved, contrary to the more consensual manner in which Innu have made decisions, by one party winning and another losing. Someone has to lose face and another has to claim victory, albeit meaningless as it may be. Like the concept of sovereignty with which it is entwined, the law is a trump card over all appeals to cultural difference. The law banishes the Innu acceptance of wide spans of conduct and stems the flow of understandable contingency ("I was drunk") and fluidity ("I may not blame my assailant when I sober up") and the relief from punitive retribution favoured by the Innu.

In addition, in the enforcement and execution of the law itself the Innu feel that it operates incompetently and largely to their detriment. In the immediate courtroom situation, the visibly lackadaisical performance of the Legal Aid lawyers appointed to represent Innu defendants hardly instills any confidence in "justice." I have observed several cases in which the lawyer supposedly defending Innu from Sheshatshiu has consistently demonstrated little or no understanding of their lives and experience, mispronouncing common Innu names, seldom visiting the community, and generally only meeting his clients for the first time when they arrive in court. In most court cases, lawyers only acquainted themselves with their Innu clients shortly before they were actually to appear in the dock. In Davis Inlet, clients and Legal Aid lawyers would meet with each other at the back of the courtroom discussing what were sometimes distressing and harrowing incidents within earshot of everyone else attending the hearings.

It is easy for the Innu to believe, as a vast number do, that the criminal justice system and, more broadly, "the law" comprise one more method by which the *Akaneshau* are dispossessing and diminishing them. As is clear to see, "the law" is a chain of regulations, injunctions, and remedies for conflict that links the state to the people and absorbs everything from land claims to the taking of statements from drunken Innu. In Davis Inlet, especially, outward appearances can easily be seen as a conspiracy against them. The entire team representing the justice system – judge, lawyers, police –

consists of *Akaneshau*. They almost always arrive on the same plane, stay in the same lodging, and depart on the same plane. While in Davis Inlet, they will be accommodated at either the priest's quarters or those of the teachers in the few dwellings in which Innu are not likely to be present. Crown and Legal Aid lawyers, adversaries in the courtroom, are under the same roof, sharing the same bathroom and breakfast table, often with the judge and the RCMP officers. All of the movements of the team in the community are made possible by the chauffeuring of the RCMP. Furthermore, the Innu accused are often treated disrespectfully, as with the young boys who, as yet unconvicted of any crime, were escorted through the community in leg irons.

Nearly all Innu I have spoken to about the fairness of criminal justice believe that in disputes between Innu and non-Innu, the police and the courts systematically favour the latter. There is a widespread perception that the law protects them less effectively than non-Innu and is used against them in ways that would not be the case if they were white Canadians. In fact, perhaps the most tormenting sequel to the house fire that killed the six children on Valentine's Day 1992 was the decision of the authorities to prosecute the two parents for abandonment of the children. Believing the parents to have already suffered enormously, the prosecution of the parents was generally met with anger and incomprehension in the village. The lawyer representing the parents told me at the time the case came up (the day the court returned to Davis Inlet) that only Aboriginal people had been prosecuted for this form of neglect. In Newfoundland there had been other cases in which children had died while parents were out, but thus far none had been charged with any offence. Alive to the wide scope with which all potentially criminal incidents are interpreted, many Innu believe that when the perpetrator of an offence is non-Innu, charges are more likely not to be pressed.

In the summer of 1996, a young man named William Pokue was struck and instantly killed by a taxi on the road from Sheshatshiu to Goose Bay. He had been drinking with his friends in Goose Bay that night. On the way home, the car in which he was riding stopped to let him out to relieve himself. Either because of an argument or a jest, the driver had continued home without William, who shortly afterward stumbled onto the road and was struck by the taxi. Almost immediately after the event, the RCMP announced that no charges would be brought against the *Akaneshau* taxi driver, Eric Hill. No breathalyzer test was administered. Feeling that had the reverse been the case, charges would have been filed without delay, the community became outraged at the seeming complicity between the police and the taxi driver. Only when more evidence came to light and the feelings of the community threatened to jeopardize the already fragile local relations between the Innu and the local settlers did the police charge Eric Hill with careless driving, a relatively minor offence. Some community members said that the taxi driver had been drinking that evening and "had a woman" in Sheshatshiu. I observed the hearing for Eric Hill on these charges, which amounted to "a slap on the wrist," according to one lawyer.

I heard many stories of such injustices. Daniel Ashini told me about a man in Sheshatshiu who was charged with beating his wife. Before the hearing he was put on probation and subsequently broke the conditions of the probation. When the case came up the charges were dismissed, but the defendant was still charged with breaking probation. He was thus punished for violating a procedural regulation attached to a crime that the court dismissed. Older people tell stories of rough treatment from the RCMP who, often at the behest of the priest, would break into houses in search of home brew, often inflicting violence and damaging possessions. On the other hand, when Innu need the protection of the police, many say that the police are slow to respond. Discussing this subject, Prote Poker told me, "When there are fights in the community and we call the RCMP, they would sometimes say, 'we'll look into it the next time we're there,' but if a white person calls, like a school teacher or the priest, they will be right there."

Conclusion

Canada, Extinguishment, and the Future of the Innu

For a minute imagine this . . .

You live in a very fine home, with all the comforts to meet your needs. But I move into your home, and I start selling off your furniture and belongings. I receive, say, $1,000 for the sale and give you $1. I tell you how you should live in your house. I tell you what you should think about. I tell you how you should feel and respond to things and when you do act I use my values to judge your actions. I tell you that it is now my house. After a while I suggest that maybe we could "negotiate" some changes to this arrangement but it will remain my house and I am in control.

. . . We don't have to imagine this, we live this experience.

– Daniel Ashini speaking on behalf of Shinepestis at a provincial court hearing in 1994

CANADA AND THE NATIVE OTHER

After cataloguing deplorable living conditions, rampant disease, suicide, poverty, unemployment, and the actions of the state to dispossess Native peoples, Matthew Coon Come, the National Chief of the Assembly of First Nations, contemplated the cultural, economic and political extinction of Native peoples in Canada. Although speaking to the World Conference Against Racism in South Africa, the National Chief was not merely playing to a crowd – he lambasted the United Nations and international law as well for their failures to challenge nation-states. Coon Come was echoing a sentiment present among the Innu and articulated without exaggeration by Native commentators across Canada. In fact, at the same conference, the Grand Council of the Crees (2001) distributed a report entitled, *Pushed to the Edge of Extinction.* This, too, was no mere hyperbole; the title of the report was taken from a quotation in a Royal Commission on Aboriginal Peoples report. Paradoxically, despite a raft of UN and human rights criticism for the "extinguishment" clause in land claims, for confining Aboriginal peoples in intolerable settlements, and for operating laws in insensitive and racist ways, Canada has managed to preserve a reputation for its commitment to human rights. However, as Coon Come pointed out, this reputation, while it may be deserved in the international arena, is not deserved "at home in Canada [where] the oppression, marginalization and dispossession of indigenous peoples continue."

For their part, the self-image of many Euro-Canadians is continually forged out against the looming presence of the United States and the distant tie of colonialism, the British Crown. In particular, it is through flattering comparison with what they see as the crass imperialism and violence of the U.S. that many Canadians view themselves as humble, honest, and peaceable guardians of the liberal conscience of the hemisphere. On visits to Cuba and Mexico in 1998, Prime Minister Jean Chrétien forcefully criticized the human rights record of the former country and the treatment of indigenous people by the latter. Instead, both Canadian politicians and academic commentators appeal to a vision of Canada as a haven of multiculturalism, tolerance, and diversity.[1]

One realm in which these liberal self-perceptions vividly emerge is in relation to Canada's relationships to Aboriginal peoples. In Canada, Indians were not slaughtered. There were no Trails of Tears, no Sand Creeks, and there has been no equivalent of a Chiapas. Indians may have been inequitably dealt with, but this bears meek comparison to the carnage inflicted to the south. The disgrace of the frontier experiences has long been a factor singled out to emphasize Canada's allegedly more benevolent approach. As a result, "people north of the border often looked smugly at their better record of dealing with tribal people when contrasted with that of the United States" (Nichols, 1998: 322). Comparing American and Canadian values, U.S. sociologist Seymour Martin Lipset (1990: 174) demonstrates how general Canada's benign reputation has become, arguing that Canada has shown "greater consideration" for and placed "less pressure" on its Native population. Peter Newman's (1991: 421) history of the Hudson's Bay Company ends with a stirring affirmation of

Canadian fairness that is "permanently woven into the marrow and dreams of this country." He, too, cannot resist the favourable comparison with the U.S., distinguishing the earnestness of trade and "peace, order and good government" from the brutality of American frontiersmen and the U.S. Cavalry. "In contrast," Newman writes, "the HBC established a long-term commercial relationship with the natives across the territory that would later become Canada. Its traders never shot their customers." A few hundred pages earlier, Newman had described how HBC factors Smith and Henderson had condemned great numbers of Innu to a death by starvation by refusing them ammunition. This fine line distinguishing legitimate and illegitimate expropriation of Natives, kind and unkind exploitation of "customers," deaths of commission and deaths of omission marks Canadian self-flattery.

Canadians, however, still agonize over the dishonest acts that enabled the state to assume control over Native territories. Although the Canadian Minister of Indian Affairs, Robert Nault, demanded an apology from Coon Come for his remarks in South Africa, many official communications to Natives are characterized by expressions of regret for various "wrongs" or "misdeeds" of the past. These are followed by invitations to integrate into the larger social and economic order. Natives are rendered visible only long enough to redeem their colonizers and give conscience and meaning to what is in effect a bargain involving the disappearance of real difference and Native sovereignty in exchange for a place in the mosaic of Canadian multiculturalism (see Day, 1998). In the report of the Royal Commission on Aboriginal Peoples (1996: xxiv), historic injustices are admitted to only in order to clear the way for a new relationship with "First Nations." After decades of "misunderstandings concerning the treaties," and "federal policies that ignored solemn commitments," Canada is now "opening the door" to more "participation" by Native people:

> Aboriginal peoples anticipate and desire a process for continuing the historical work of Confederation. Their goal is not to undo the Canadian federation; their goal is to complete it. It is well known that the Aboriginal peoples in whose ancient homelands Canada was created have not had the opportunity to participate in creating Canada's federal union; they seek now a just accommodation within it.

For Canada to deliver itself, Natives are told that their legitimate aspirations must now entail incorporation into the "Confederation" established on their "ancient homelands." "They seek now a just accommodation" within the state. Their involvement in federation, at once a vanishing act, irons out difference and neutralizes the confessed sins of the past. The Statement of Reconciliation issued by the Minister of Indian Affairs, Jane Stewart, in January 1998 reinforced such sentiments. Aboriginals and non-Aboriginals were to "move forward together in a process of renewal." The government was to "learn from our past." Natives were honoured in effusive New Age references to "the Creator," "spiritual values," "the Elders," and their role as "custodians" of the lands and waters. Then came the confessions – "as a country we are burdened by past actions" – and the apologies – "[t]he Government of Canada today formally expresses to all Aboriginal people in Canada our profound regret for past actions." The residential schools – sites of forced assimilation and physical and sexual abuse of Native children – in particular were singled out for confession. Significantly, *past*, not present, actions are the subject of the contrition. Finally, the minister invited Canada's Aboriginal peoples to "participate fully" and "work together" to "achieve our shared goals."[2] The invitation, however, was more of an admonition. The Natives, who were so enthusiastically honoured, were not given any other choice than to share and help to articulate new, but unspecific, goals of the state. In the process of apology and the proposal for Native inclusion in a national fabric, the state was cleansed. This is reconciliation-to-forget.[3]

As Jean Baudrillard (1992: 34) has pointed out in relation to events in Eastern Europe with the breakup of Communism, acts of repentance and commemorations are tiresome. Such statements – for words now replace acts – are boorish and contrived. The apology is merely talk that is purported to demonstrate a *volte face*, a sudden realization of grievous error. And what goes with the repentance is the invitation or insistence that those who are now pronounced victims by their colonizers join them in a "democracy." Aboriginal people are now to be included *in* Canada, a state that has renounced the acknowledged wrongs of past generations. But it is impossible for the peoples who have been handed the apology to determine what substance it has. Will it improve their living conditions? Help them regain stolen lands? Maintain their distinct ways of life? Is the apology merely restitution by promise of atonement through democratic inclusion alone?[4] And even this inclusion is dubious since in earlier times, when Aboriginals comprised more significant proportions of the Canadian population, they were prohibited from voting.

Atonement also characterizes governmental dealings with the Innu, but here expressions of regret are issued almost immediately after duplicitous deeds have been undertaken and publicized as inevitable progress. Soon after signing their accord on the Lower Churchill hydroelectric development in 1998, the Newfoundland

and Quebec governments turned to the Innu for expiation from the uncharitable deal they had just cut on Innu land. While negotiations were taking place and the land and rivers, used by Innu families for centuries, were staked out, Premier Brian Tobin of Newfoundland and Premier Lucien Bouchard of Quebec rebuffed all contact with the Native communities. Then, suddenly after the Lower Churchill deal had been announced, Premier Tobin expressed sympathy for the Innu. Although he did not acknowledge any lack of consultation over the new project, he confessed to the sequestration of the land for the original Churchill Falls project, albeit in the veiled but re-demptive language of not being able to "rewrite the past." By contrast, Lower Churchill became an exercise in "participation," with Tobin calling for "a new relationship, a new partnership, one that's fair, one that's beneficial to both parties" (quoted by Thompson, 1998b: A1). The benevolence offered by Tobin was directed only towards Innu collaboration in the project either through some sort of industrial venture, within which they would "participate," or through compensation for the loss of the land. Not having the project on their land was not an option.

The metamorphosis was swift and dizzying. The Innu trans-formed from being invisible people, who were of no account what-soever in the development of the second largest dam in the world, to victims who had suffered from injustices of the past. It was then just a short magnanimous step to making them new partners, perhaps even fledgling capitalists, who would help push the project through. The final switch in the depiction of the Innu was to present them as participants in a pluralist game on the level playing field of a benevo-lent state. According to the press, the protests involving placard-wielding Innu at the signing ceremony between the two premiers demonstrated that the Innu were starting to become "players." One report for the Montreal Gazette (Thompson, 1998a) credited the Innu with "flexing their political muscle" and becoming "a force to be reck-oned with." They were, the journalist asserted, "deft in public relations and political fights."

These plaudits and even the participation and gamesmanship with which the Innu are invested are redemptive creations of Euro-Canadians and the state. The starting point is always Native appear-ance from obscurity out of an admission of guilt for past sins; the middle is a testament to Native victimhood and noble virtue; the conclusion is the disappearance of Native difference as they become powerful game players and business partners. The gestures of Na-tive sovereignty, and moments when more subtle reasoning illuminates the colonial world the Innu have been required to enter, are ignored. Peter Fenwick (1998), a former provincial leader of the New Democratic Party and a columnist for the St. John's *Evening Telegram*, showed the pattern almost exactly. He began his column by confessing guilt, declaiming the "terrible wrong" dealt the Innu by the first Churchill Falls hydro project. This was followed by heaping praise upon them, tellingly in the past tense, as "probably the best cold climate woodsmen the world has ever known." He finished up by arguing that "I would be the last person to argue that the power projects not go ahead."

Canadian media coverage of Lower Churchill, Voisey's Bay, and other megaprojects represented the Innu as serious players in the political games that will determine the future of Canada. Colonial destruction is not the headline; rather, "capacity-building" is central in the jargon of the media and the white professionals who are sweeping into the Innu communities to facilitate these ventures. "Capacity" towards "governance" is being forged through the astute usage of political and other institutions. The Innu are now presented as being a force to be reckoned with in the larger Canadian political arena. The image of an empowered Innu shields against accusations of white intrusion, always an Achilles heel of the liberal conscience. At the same time, it helps to cloud any lingering memories of the deliberate policies of cultural transformation, for now the Natives are seen to be taking charge of their own affairs. They are now the authors of their own positive transformations.

These media images are reflected in local *Akaneshau* opinion. Far from being victims, the Innu are, in the eyes of many *Akaneshau*, skilfully taking advantage of both the largesse of the Canadian government and the opportunities coming their way because they are defined as Aboriginals with special "claims." In this view, they have learned to work the system, extracting the maximum funds and benefits and exerting the minimum effort. Always cheerily optimistic on the surface, Ernie, the last Mennonite in Davis Inlet before his ostentatious house was torched by young Innu, told me that "these people will get what they want from the federal government because they are hunters. They will hunt the government until they get what they want." One of the virtues of this folk wisdom is that it can be interpreted as charitable to the Natives, even politically correct, because it implies that the Innu are empowering themselves. The hunters are merely metamorphosing into a modern form of predator suitable to contemporary circumstances. Jenny Redfearn, a British public health nurse and settler of some 30 years in Labrador, adopted this kind of perspective. For her, the Innu had the best of both worlds – the country and the village. The two worlds are not in collision, really only two sides of the same coin. The young people want TVs, VCRs, ATVs, and snowmobiles, but they can still have the country, too – "How wonderful! How lucky they are." Like Ernie, she was confident that they would "get" some land, although neither specified how.

This type of stance, however, is fragile. If the Innu are in the midst of a self-propelled evolutionary process, they remain in transit. When it is believed that there exists some preordained outcome, a happy syncretic oneness, watching the changes is never comfortable. The *Akaneshau* must always keep an eye out for the things that go horribly wrong, when cultural evolution halts or even reverses. Suicides, gas-sniffing, and other tragedies become hiccups, consigned to side effects, or transient phases that may blur, but these do not change the direction of history. Nevertheless, observing the process by which the Innu are supposedly moving from the margins into the mainstream is a tense business in which the power that has been so cheerily invested in them often evaporates. Commenting on the connections between marginality and power, Mary Douglas (1966: 116) wrote that "danger lies in transitional states; simply because transition is neither one state nor the next, it is undefinable."

Over the four decades since sedentarization, the authorities have moved from intensive proselytizing about the benefits of village life, employment, and education to a less aggressive, complacent, and largely silent witnessing of a human catastrophe that they maintain is both transitory and largely the doing of the Innu themselves. Silent witnessing is broken only by a judgemental and decontextualized focus on pathology. The Innu are framed almost entirely as individuals and their individual problems are contained primarily within a bounded notion of "community." Thus, amid the well-publicized gas-sniffing epidemic in December 2000, Jane McGilivray, a physician in Sheshatshiu, spoke out in the media about her exasperation with what she saw among her Innu patients. After noting countless tragedies she had witnessed, an extended report to the media on her decision to resign as community physician thus ended:

> I know that the strength for change comes from the heart, from each person's heart, and not from the outside, not from people like myself, not from business, not from government. The task of accepting responsibility for our own lives, regardless of who we are, is a great challenge. It is my challenge as well as yours. (Quoted in Lindgren, 2000)

Dwelling on individual responsibility and failure in combination with the recommendation of individual solutions is a crucial permutation in settler, media, and official conceptions of Innu self-destruction. As a measure of how far the pendulum has swung, almost 10 years ago Henriksen (1993b: 14-15) insisted that the same problems among the Mushuau Innu "must be seen in light of the stress caused by the impact of White institutions and village life." He continued,

> It is obvious that medical or psychological diagnosis and treatment of the *individuals* who show these drastic signs of stress, are inadequate if considered alone. The problems experienced by so many Innu are caused by a feeling of being powerless, and not having the proper means of coping with the constraints and challenges confronting them as individuals and as a people . . . so must we look for *social*, *political*, and *economic* sources for the healing of the Mushuau Innu. (Emphasis in original)

Under the shadow of these paradoxes, contemporary health workers, social workers, advisers, environmentalists, and others continue with palliative ministrations while the suffering of the Innu from land appropriation, suicide, alcohol-induced sickness, sexual abuse, and gas-sniffing continues unabated. If Douglas (1966) is correct, then the danger of the transitional state of the Innu, at least in the white mind, is always a potential. As she suggests, such a state of being is associated with having contact with a source of power, and thus the judgements of the *Akaneshau* could be understood as a means of dealing with the fear that tragedy will unleash a more devastating energy. The cross on the hill, the Valentine's Day tragedies, and each new story of the young suicide victim or the children wishing to forget their lives in gas inhalation hold out the prospect of the uncontainable and the redundancy of the presence of these *Akaneshau*. But such reminders are tokens only of despair and anger turned inwards, for which the medical and psychological remedies of individual pathology can easily be forwarded.[5] What is feared is the potential for this energy to be directed outward, as when a judge is evicted, when there is a standoff with the RCMP, or when industrial sites are picketed and occupied. It is in these halting moments, when the state has mobilized political and police powers to subdue the Innu and quickly return them to the assimilationist groove, that the naked colonial relationship is exposed.

YOU ARE NOT WOLVERINE

When Innu people were given the opportunity to present their own stories in their own images and words in the numerous Innu Nation publications of the 1990s (Innu Nation, 1995, 1996a, 2000) as well as in the short documentaries, *Ntapueu* and *The Child Suffers*, neither a sense of power nor an overwhelming optimism came through. Each publication begins with an epigram to the deceased who have come to untimely deaths; each film ends by scrolling down a list of the young Innu who have taken their own lives during the time the film was being made. Conspicuously, these documents and films foreground the tragedies that ensue with the gradual loss of a way of life, graphically symbolized by ever more industrial developments on Innu land. Virtually all of those who are cited in these publications speak of maintaining the Innu world view and fighting developers as a matter of survival. They do not stir up any images of themselves as the political game-players presented in the Canadian media. To take one of many possible examples in the community survey of reactions to the Lower Churchill hydro project, George Rich of Davis Inlet remarks:

> Major developments attract more outside people. It means that the Innu will be shoved aside into a more stressful environment that will spark chaos and lead to the elimination of the Innu. A new hydro project means there would be flooding of ancient burial grounds. The history of the Innu would be flooded along with their proof of ownership of the land. The identity of the Innu would be lost forever. (Innu Nation, 2000: 45)

When young Innu were funded to make a film as part of the "consultation process" for the Voisey's Bay mine – a film whose central messages were subsequently ignored by the provincial government – the result, *Ntapueu: I Am Telling the Truth*, was a non-linear montage of images. Narrated in *Innu-aimun* by a host of different Innu voices accompanying images of community life, with all the ravages of alcohol, disease, and *Akaneshau* dominance, the film's central message is that the Innu are dying, literally and figuratively. A coffin in a hand-built wooden trailer containing the body of a teenage suicide victim is hauled by an ATV towards the cemetery in Utshimassits. The boy's young friends follow in the snow flurries. The music of an Innu rock band becomes the sound track. In another scene the camera catches the vice-president of the mining company asleep, his mouth agape, while the President of Innu Nation delivers a speech to a consultation meeting on the importance of the land the company is digging up.

Their encounters with Euro-Canadian officials and developers hardly inspire much confidence among Innu that their attachments to the land will mean very much or that any connections between development and tragedy will be recognized. All of these often stressful meetings are conducted in English (or French in Quebec), still second languages to the Innu, and are guided by a protocol and legal framework formulated by the state. The concession of their language constrains the Innu to formulate their position in the tongue of their antagonists. This means that the more culturally specific ways of understanding "rights" or the land, for example, are either jettisoned or rendered as best as possible into the European vocabulary. Thus, the Innu language does not recognize terms for "ownership," "claims," or "process" or for any of the many other fundamental concepts and principles of negotiation. On the other hand, the many kinds of expressions in the language that are contrary to the political or scientific spirit of these exercises must either be watered down in translation or expressed in such a way that they are ignored or dismissed.

In the film *Ntapueu* (Innu Nation, 1997), made by young Innu of Sheshatshiu and Utshimassits, a *Tshenu* forcefully shouts, "You [the Canadian government] don't own the land. You are not Wolverine (*Kuekuatsheu*)." In Innu legends, the Wolverine is always subversive. A mere assertion of sovereignty can never stamp out the Wolverine, who is a survivor, surviving in the present-day stories of the Innu. *Kuekuatsheu* was there first, even when the world was known to be all water and ice. After all, according to one version of the story, it was the heroics of Wolverine, soliciting *utshisk* the muskrat to swim to the bottom of the lake and bring back earth, that created this world. When *utshisk* returned, *Kuekuatsheu* blew air up into the muskrat's anus. The sod in his mouth shot out and provided the earth that we all walk on. Hence, the earth was created, and the creatures that inhabit it must be respected by the Innu.

To many Innu, this is much less fantasy than a parallel story, to that of the idea of European law, which dates back to the tablets handed down by God on Mount Sinai as recorded in the Old Testament. In legal discourse, English common law is construed to be based on the laws of nature that God mandated. Legal commentators, perhaps most famously that inventor of *terra nullius*, Sir William Blackstone, equated the laws of England with universal and natural principles formulated by the Creator. Hence, "this law of nature, being coeval with mankind, and dictated by God himself, is of course superior in obligation to any other. *It is binding over all the globe, in all countries, and at all times*: no human laws are of any validity, if contrary to this; and such of them as are valid derive all their force, and all their authority, mediately or immediately from this original" (quoted by Boorstin, 1973: 49; emphasis added).

The law, and the assertion of sovereignty that follows from it, is a Euro-Canadian creation story. It is never as rich, nuanced, and alive as the tricksters in Native creation stories. It is based on the universalization of abstract legal "principles," which as Boorstin (1973: 47-53) suggests ignore time and place and use reason to equate English law with natural law. Unlike *Kuekuatsheu*, these principles are connected to people who originate from distant places and whose God and scientific culture, have been made to bind all peoples to their authority. There is, of course, no Innu equivalent. Instead of trying to reduce the origins and nature of their world to a single, consistent narrative, they accept and explain different aspects of experience through a wide range of stories that, at a purely literal level, can often seem contradictory. For example, the adventures of *Kuekuatsheu*, a sly and cunning trickster figure, tend to dwell on the grotesque – unconstrained sexuality, flatulence, cheating and deception – and on the essential unpredictability of life, whereas the monster-slaying culture hero *Tshakapesh* generally features in uplifting tales that stress the importance of bravery and altruism. A third cycle of legends – which includes one of the most important Innu stories, "The Man Who Married a Caribou" – focuses on the loving and interdependent relationship between the people and the Animal Gods.[6] Innu stories revolve around their intimate and interdependent relationships with the lakes, rivers, forests, tundra, and animals that live in the interior of the peninsula. Their legends feature tricksters, animal-human communication and interchangeability, as well as sexual, scatological, and humorous adventures. Many others are serious moral tales of human humility towards all of nature. The vast wealth of the oral tradition situates the Innu in an inseparable relationship with *Nitassinan*.

In order that government representatives could appreciate some of the subtleties of the Innu relationships to the land, in the spring of 1995 Daniel Ashini, the Innu Nation land rights negotiator, invited Canadian officials to the camp at Utshisk-nipi, some 90 miles into the interior, where several families were hunting. Although preparations were made for firewood to be chopped and fresh wild food to be cooked for the visitors, the invitation was refused. The officials told Daniel that they were afraid of the cold, of insomnia, and of the wild food that may not have been to their liking. As a consequence, Daniel disrupted his hunting to fly back to Goose Bay to meet with the government delegation. In addition to visions of unfamiliar conditions, I suspect that the officials were also reticent to enter into a world where other rules apply, where even if their dominion is declared to have spread, it can be scarcely perceptible. Merely locating themselves at Utshisk-nipi would have immersed the officials in another ontological world, one with such deep roots in the very land that the Innu are allegedly "claiming" that it could raise doubts about Canadian sovereignty itself.

In his ruminations on scientific method, Paul Feyerabend (1987: 81) considers this very predicament:

> Colonial officials took it for granted that the Natives would either learn the Master language or could be informed by interpreters, again using the Master language as a basis. The Master language, applied in situations defined by the masters, was the official medium of formulating, presenting and solving problems. Can we take it for granted that using indigenous language and indigenous ways of solving problems would have led to the same solutions? To the same problems?

Perhaps because indigenous peoples would not identify the same problems and solutions, there are no attempts on the part of the Canadian government or its functionaries to enter into Aboriginal domains such as *nutshimit*. As such, there is no "just dialogue" between the state and Aboriginal peoples, as James Tully (1995: 55) has argued about the modern constitutionalism of Canada and the U.S.[7] Euro-Canadian methods of negotiation are simply imposed by fiat.

RESISTANCE AND CULTURAL CONTINUITY

The Innu have never simply acquiesced to the attempts to wrench control away from them. They have maintained their language, *Innu-aimun*, their beliefs, and their relations with the land, and they have done so by tenaciously upholding the value of all things connected to their nomadic hunting and by creatively reshaping that way of life. I have never met an adult who did not recognize the affirmative qualities of their cultural and political connections with the land or view *nutshimit* as a source of physical and spiritual well-being. As Paul Pone, a young hunter, told me, "when I was in the country, I feel that I was angry in the community, but I am at peace with myself out there. It was almost as if there was another Paul that I wasn't even connected to. I was really lazy in the community – I couldn't even wash the dishes." In a stuffy semi-furnished office in Davis Inlet, Simeon Tshakapesh, then an Innu police officer, expressed similar sentiments about these two worlds:

> Nutshimit is where people feel good, where they don't have problems. When I come back I think that Davis Inlet is not where I live.

The country is where we are given our own dignity back. It's where you feel alive and proud of yourself. Here is the white man's way. I have to write reports, that is not the Innu way.

On other fronts, the Innu have politically engaged with Canada, its agents, and developers and have sought out international assistance to challenge the state. Hence, although there is some substance in the representation of the Innu political bodies as game-players who have been able to promote Innu interests, the Innu Nation president, chiefs, and councils are participating on a very lopsided playing surface. Consequently, as the Innu political organizations have become more firmly incorporated into the procedures of the state, their resistance to cultural and political extinguishment has become channelled into the narrow avenues permitted by Canada. While Canada holds out cash compensation and the regaining of limited autonomy as bargaining chips in comprehensive land claims negotiations, this procedure preordains outcomes that are overwhelmingly favourable to the state. Although there have been spontaneous and confidence-building community-generated civil disorders to combat other indignities, such as low-level flying from Goose Bay air base and joint protests with the Inuit at Voisey's Bay mine, as well as the eviction of a judge in Utshimassits, and international human rights reports, most opposition is contained within Canadian formulas for conflict resolution. This includes the separate dealings that Canada has with the Innu peoples who are now located in villages on either side of a contrived frontier. Thus, the force that some 20,000 interrelated Innu in 13 villages spread out over a vast territory would have is vastly diluted by the insistence that the Labrador-Quebec border be considered sacrosanct. Increasingly, the state has endorsed plans to deal with the Innu on an even more segmented basis. Even the unity of the Innu Nation representing the two Labrador villages has been threatened. As we have seen in Chapter 2, for example, land claims maps drawn by Innu Nation advisers partition claims into two distinct "landscapes." On top of this, the cost of devolving policing, education, and other institutions to Innu control in Sheshatshiu and Utshimassits will be their incorporation as "wards of the state" under the Indian Act with separate "reserves" based around small Native villages.

Paradoxically, Innu resistance and cultural continuity have still survived, not only as a reaction to these policies and procedures, but in response to the sheer insensitivity of the authorities who planned and directed settlement. As we have seen in Chapter 5, the early experiences of village life were tarnished by the brutalities of the authoritarian and frequently pedophile Roman Catholic priests who were ministers, teachers, doctors, and middlemen to the first generation of village-dwelling Innu. Others who would go on to commit the same crimes then followed these missionaries into the villages. More recently, professional schoolteachers from Newfoundland with little or no knowledge of the Innu have been sent to work in the village schools. Over time, the corps of Euro-Canadian professionals has been progressively enlarged. The cast of characters includes unsympathetic medical workers, interfering social workers, culturally insensitive judges, and a remote and largely oblivious provincial government situated in St. John's, on the island of Newfoundland. This is not to say that all non-Innu professionals have acted maliciously and that some have been positive influences. But the myriad instances of brutalization and the lucidly exposed injustices, perpetrated both knowingly and unwittingly, have also served as grounds for Innu resistance, protest, and belief in the importance of maintaining a distinct way of life separate from that lived in the villages.

Resistance and cultural continuity are nonetheless hampered by the mushrooming numbers of Innu who are suffering the traumas incurred after intensified contact with Canada. New afflictions such as diabetes and cancer, alcohol abuse, gas-sniffing, and suicide have become hallmarks of life in Sheshatshiu and Utshimassits, as well as across Aboriginal Canada, as Matthew Coon Come emphasized to the World Conference on Racism. Not only is the pool depleted of Innu who can actively spend time and energy resisting, but the sheer volume of tragedies has led to the framing of their problems in terms of medical and psychological pathology. During the same crisis that the *Globe and Mail* editors responded to in the winter of 2000 by urging the Innu to join the "modern world," the Innu Nation made an impassioned plea to the government to finance detoxification and other treatment facilities for the gas-sniffing children. Speaking for the community of Sheshatshiu, Innu Nation President Peter Penashue told a journalist from the *Los Angeles Times* to "consider the money as royalties for what the government has taken from our land" (Farley, 2000). This statement indicates that the leadership considers the sufferings of young Innu so severe that it is ready to contemplate a monetary compensation of their land to fund medical treatment of the self-destructive activities that have arisen in the context of their removal from the land in the first place. New buildings to facilitate medical or psychological pathology are built almost every year. Sheshatshiu, a relatively small village, has a group home, an alcohol centre, a youth treatment centre, a women's shelter, and a clinic, but virtually no employment or recreational facilities. The very limited local economy is increasingly based on sickness and dysfunction and the procuring of government funds to contain these problems. Meanwhile, the use and occupancy of the land that sustained the Innu have diminished as funds that enabled Innu on welfare to go to the country under the Outpost Program have been scaled down, and the Innu Nation continues to be pressured to reduce its land claim even further.[8]

Both cultural continuity and physical survival will necessarily entail Innu access to educational and employment opportunities and to levers of power. This will have to involve a radical questioning of the assumptions upon which Canadian policies towards Aboriginal peoples are based. It will also depend on the abilities of the Innu to prevent the developers and their state sponsors from appropriating more of their lands. In this context, the willingness of Canada to consider how Aboriginal peoples such as the Innu see the world, rather than simply imposing assimilationist and development-based policies upon them, will be crucial. Nonetheless, the global character of the problems encountered by many small peoples lends itself to assistance from movements on the global stage – such as the UN conference at which Matthew Coon Come spoke – that are beginning to take issue with the policies of extinguishment operated by nation-states such as Canada. The Innu are by no means alone and need not stand alone in their quests to negotiate a *modus vivendi* with the state and to be recognized as a distinct people. They need not lead "a way of life that does not exist."

Notes

Prologue

1. Altogether there are 13 villages. Along the North Shore of the St. Lawrence in Quebec lie Pakua-Shipit, Unamen-Shipit, Natashquan, Ekuantshit, Maliotenam, Uashat, Pessamit, and Esipit. Mashteuiatsh is in the interior of central Quebec. Kawawatshimach and Matimekush are near the town of Schefferville in north-central Quebec. Sheshatshiu and Davis Inlet (also known as Utshimassits), with populations of some 1,200 and 600 respectively, are in Labrador. Most of the Innu living in Davis Inlet are known as Mushuau Innu or people of the barren gound. The population of Sheshatshiu are descended from Innu who hunted across the entire Labrador-Quebec peninsula and have particularly close relations with Innu now settled in the Quebec North Shore villages.

2. Utshimassits is named after Utshimass, the Innu name for the former Hudson's Bay Company trader at "old" Davis Inlet on the Labrador mainland, across the waters from present-day Davis Inlet. It has a wider connotation as "place of the boss." Beginning in 1994, the Canadian government authorized funding for a further relocation of the people of Utshimassits to Natuashish or Sango Bay on the mainland. Sheshatshiu, roughly, "the place where the river enters the lake," is alternatively spelled Sheshatshit and, less commonly, Sheshatsheits.

3. From 1999 to 2001, the Ojibwa community of Pikangikum in far northwestern Ontario, near the Manitoba border, made newspaper headlines on several occasions for extraordinary rates of suicide among adolescents. Over a one-year period 11 young people out of a total population of 2,100 killed themselves. Three of these occurred within one week. Noting inadequate housing, education, health care, drinking water, and fresh food, a visiting Aboriginal doctor told the Canadian Broadcasting Company that Canada was perpetrating a "crime against humanity" (CBC, 2001).

4. Technically, the plural of Innu is *Innut*, but I do not use this word in order to avoid confusion with the "Inuit."

5. Attempts to assimilate the Innu of course predated the impositions of twentieth-century Canadian authorities. The efforts of missionaries and fur traders, in particular, are notable and will be covered in this book. These supply the backdrop to the more systematic policies to transform them that were spearheaded by Canada.

6. A poll of young Canadians found that only 52 per cent could name a single Aboriginal issue in the news (Mofina, 2001).

7. Significantly, Axtell (1981: 272-315) indicates that when Indian influences on settlers were noted by Puritans and others in the early English colonies of North America, the Indians were nearly always charged with corrupting the mores of the whites in some way. By contrast, Bailey (1969: 25) emphasizes how much the French imported from Eastern Algonkian peoples. Besides food, materials, shelters, and tools, explorers such as Champlain and writers such as Rabelais, Rousseau, Voltaire, and Diderot gained insights from "le bon sauvage" that surfaced in their published writings. This leads Bailey to proclaim that "contact with American Indians . . . was a remote precursor of the French Revolution."

8. The collection of documents gathered by the former priest at Sheshatshiu, James Roche, are not page numbered. Hence my references to this source here and elsewhere lack page references.

9. During his times with the Pit River People in northern California in 1921, Jaime de Angulo noted the flexibility and aversion to firm plans among his hosts made any systematic methodology absurd. Waiting for a movement in the camp that never arrived, de Angulo (1990: 50) remarks that "the days went by. Not so many days, but four, five days, maybe. I don't remember exactly. I was not taking notes, I was living."

10. In a few cases where personally sensitive issues are discussed, I have used pseudonyms for Innu people. As a condition of my interviews with a few non-Innu professionals, other pseudonyms have been used for individuals.

Chapter 1

1. Europeans designated the more southerly Innu "Montagnais" and the more northerly peoples of the Labrador-Quebec peninsula "Naskapi."

2. Throughout the book, when no source is cited for a quote, this indicates that it came from one of my own personal interviews or conversations between 1994 and 2001.

3. It has only been in retrospect, however, that these procedures have been condemned as gross violations of the rights of the Innu. For example, an Assembly of First Nations (1993: 57) report on the relocation of Utshimassits noted, "the federal and Newfoundland gov-

ernments have repeatedly failed to meet even the most minimum human rights standards in relation to the Mushuau Innu."

4. Records of the housing arrangements are presented in Roche (1992) and Ryan (1988b: 14-15).

5. My comments here are merely a very brief summary of Durkheim's general approach in *Suicide* and *The Division of Labor in Society*.

6. Penote Michel, paper presented to provincial court on the occasion of a trial of Innu for trespassing on the runways at the Goose Bay air base, 1988.

7. Although this has been common knowledge for some time, the "booze for votes" tactic has only recently been covered by the media on account of a recent tragedy in Sheshatshiu. In January 2000, CBC reported, "The mother of a sexual assault victim in Sheshatshiu is blaming the assault on the election campaign for band council in the town. She says the assault happened because of alcohol supplied by one of the candidates in the election. And she's calling on community leaders to stop using booze to buy votes" <www.stjohns.cbc.ca/cgi-bin/templates/view.cgi?/news/2000/01/26/nf_booze000126>.

8. Under the terms of the comprehensive land claims, discussed in more detail at the end of the chapter.

9. The interpretation of Aboriginal self-government I offer differs from that offered by several prominent anthropologists. Referring to the Dene and Inuit, Hedican (1995: 177) believes that they "now have more political awareness, and internal organisation, than they have had at any time in the past." Scott (1993: 328) seems to agree with several official statements that self-government is essential to Native cultural survival. Summing up, he suggests that "cultural distinctiveness has been integral to the history of *exchange* between aboriginal nations and the Euro-Canadian state" (my emphasis). Even Asch (1993: 51) ends his otherwise critical essay with a statement that might have been drafted by the Royal Commission on Aboriginal Peoples: "aboriginal peoples are looking for means to enter into, not destroy, confederation." Henriksen (1993: 13, 15) writes of the young Innu leaders "breaking new ground by using the means at their disposal in the White man's world. . . . The path which the young Innu leaders are breaking is the path of self-determination – the right of a people to create their own future – which probably is the only path out of the present misery experienced by so many." These assurances accentuate a pervasive academic image of *realpolitik* in which "Aboriginal nations" are constituted as players within a national arena, squaring off against the state and industrial interests, and through negotiating and bargaining achieving their aspirations within the frameworks established by the state. The conception of power here is decidedly pluralist, a position that can only be maintained by ignoring or downplaying certain features of Aboriginal self-government and Canada-Native relations. These include the per-

sonal difficulties of leaders, the divisiveness of self-government, the undemocratic practices of many such organizations, the links between drinking, corruption, and such institutions, and the massive imbalance between the sovereignty of Canada and all Aboriginal assertions of autonomy as recognized by Canada.

10. Commander Donald MacMillan accompanied William Cabot on his expedition to Labrador in 1910 and led several other expeditions, including the Second Rawson-MacMillan Sub-Arctic Expedition, which included the anthropologist William Duncan Strong, in 1927-1928 (see Leacock and Rothschild, 1994).

11. If the need arose, any number of European principles could have been used in support of this. These would have included the doctrine of discovery in which Europeans who "discovered" Natives awarded themselves sole negotiating rights for land cessions, the observation that Indians were not Christian and hence not entitled to the same rights as Christians, and the Lockean theory that private property rights derive only from "improvement of the soil," which invalidated all hunting peoples' ownership rights (see Williams, 1990; Arneil, 1996).

12. For example, because of the destruction of buffalo herds in the 1870s, many groups of Plains Indians entered into treaties as an alternative to starvation (Wilson and Urion, 1995: 58).

13. According to various accounts I heard from the Innu in Sheshatshiu, many of whom originated from families now on the North Shore, much of this took place simply by government agents taking down the names of the Innu who emerged at the coastal settlements in the summers.

14. It was even noted during the 1927 Labrador boundary dispute, which created the border with Quebec, that the provisions of the 1763 Royal Proclamation applied to "the Indians" of Labrador. "The lands of the Domain therefore, are to all intents and purposes reserved, as hunting grounds to the savages, of which they are ever jealous, of the least appearance of an encroachment" (in Macmillan's testimony, Proceedings of the Legal Committee of the Privy Council on the Labrador Dispute, 435).

15. Obviously there has been little change in the position of Native peoples' relationship to the Crown since the earliest English colonies. Lepore (1998: 164) remarks of the "critical contradiction" in English arguments about the status of Indians at the time of King Philip's (Metacom) war in 1675: "On the one hand, Philip and his allies were said to be sovereign peoples, competent, though unwilling, to engage in negotiation and diplomacy with other nations. On the other hand, Philip and his allies were declared subjects of the King of England, with all the rights and responsibilities such subjection affords."

16. Several of my comments on the legal intricacies of comprehensive land claims, including terminology in quotation marks, are drawn from Asch and Zlotkin (1997).

17. See Agreement and Article 2 General Provisions, Part 7, 2.7.1, (a), as reproduced at www.tunngavik.com.

18. This is according to information provided by the Federal Treaty Negotiation Office in Vancouver and distributed by the Canadian High Commission in London.

19. Academic liberals often describe these agreements in positive tones. For example, in the latest edition of his well-known textbook on Canadian-Native relations J.R. Miller (2000: 371-72) describes Nunavut variously as "breathtaking" and "a great achievement." Liberal philosopher Elazar Barkan (2000: 167-68) describes such bargains with First Nations as a sort of win-win situation for all sides. Hence, "[t]he political transaction between the state and indigenous peoples involves restituting *limited* resources and rights to the indigenous population and legitimizing the indigenous legacy as part of the *national fabric.* By legitimizing indigenous culture, and to the degree that historical injustices imposed on that culture are amended, what was previously a colonial imposition of national identity is 'cleansed'" (emphasis added). Nonetheless, the process itself relies on the discredited doctrine of extinguishment. In 1999 the United Nations Human Rights Committee (1999) singled out this practice for criticism, recommending that "the practice of extinguishing inherent aboriginal rights be abandoned as incompatible with article 1 of the Covenant [International Covenant on Civil and Political Rights]."

20. This and subsequent quotations are taken from an interview with Ann Budgell on CBC-TV, 17 Sept. 1994.

21. From transcript of court proceedings of *Her Majesty's Attorney General for Newfoundland v. Katie Rich, Nympha Byrne and Justine Noah,* Supreme Court of Newfoundland, trial division, Happy Valley-Goose Bay, 20 Apr. 1995, 13.

Chapter 2

1. Tester and Kulchyski (1994: 339) go on to say that "expanded intervention" combined with the "tenacity" of the Inuit gave the Inuit a "new voice" that the state did not always want to hear. While they seem to indicate a shift from a colonial to a different role of the advisers, one that produces a greater political payoff, I do not share this view vis-à-vis the Innu, but rather see the advisers as mediating colonial power.

2. Henriksen (1985: 122) argues in relation to his own participation in land claims procedures in the 1980s that "we . . . worked with a sense of urgency: it was now or never that the Indians stand a chance to win what is rightfully theirs."

3. By the 1930s, the advent of aerial surveys had begun to make Native co-operation superfluous, as did scientific surveys of the coast, which could be done by steamers. Wilfred T. Grenfell (1933: 243-44),

founder of the public health mission, the International Grenfell Association, received a "psychic uplift" at the news of a British Admiralty survey of the coast in 1932. The survey would, in Grenfell's enthusiastic visions, "open up Labrador" for "a short, inexpensive, and exhilarating holiday trip."

4. The anthropologist's position is very similar to the broadly liberal stance taken by some North American commentators who wish to portray the kinds of encounters described here as evidence, not only of a new tolerance on the part of the dominant society, but of a renewal of Native American power. Using several examples, Warhus (1997: 211) portrays contemporary maps made by Native peoples as indicative of their greater power within the U.S. and Canada. GIS and other maps are "a symbolic expression of the move to reassert the Native Americans' place on the map of North America" and a "cartographic dialogue with the larger society." With a somewhat patronizing optimism, Warhus continues, "As these individuals and societies assert their place in the larger culture it is appropriate that the medium of the western map, with its power to shape our conception of the land, be used to preserve and pass on their cultural heritage." We get little sense from Warhus's book on Native American maps of the role of Euro-American advisers in the making of such maps or the political and epistemological compromises that Native peoples must make in order to produce them. However, in his discussion of "Nunavik," Warhus (ibid., 228) does admit that the gains made in terms of political and economic autonomy were made against the extinguishment of the Inuit's rights to much of their territory. Such compromises, Warhus believes, are part of "their recognition as part of modern Canada" (ibid., 229).

5. The advisers seemed to be following the land use and occupancy mapping procedures commonly used in land claims cases throughout Canada. Elias (1993: 243) provides an informative overview of the technical details of such research. Like the Innu advisers, he also views such research as lending support to Aboriginal land claims. This is in part because "courts and bureaucracies approve *orthodox* ways of doing things and map biographies are the result of what are now standard anthropological techniques and practices" (emphasis added).

6. William Duncan Strong documented the lack of boundaries in the past. As he put it in his 1927-28 journals, "the vast northeastern part of the Labrador peninsula is very generally divided up between four tiny Indian bands, but it is really only certain locales rather than definite circumscribed areas that the Indians regard with any jealousy. This is well demonstrated by the fact that no Indian could give any real list of boundary markers" (Leacock and Rothschild, 1994: 88-89).

7. Mailhot (1997: 130-164) also identifies various "bands" of Innu that are identified with particular territories. But these units are so flexible and cross-cut with changing marital and other affiliations that it is

impossible to equate any given territory with any specific bounded group of families.

8. This issue of "territoriality" of the Innu has preoccupied anthropologists and other observers throughout the twentieth century. Leacock (1954) first threw down the gauntlet by averring from Speck's (1935) assumptions that individual Montagnais hunters possessed discrete hunting grounds. Tanner (1944) emphasized another element – discrete "bands." Not only were the Montagnais and Nascaupee given separate designations but within each, distinct "bands" were identified. Hence, the White Whale River group, the Ungava group, and the Barren Ground group comprised the Nascaupee. Since then several others have pursued the debate. On the basis of interviews with various informants they have sought to modify the depiction of Innu hunting practices and links to the land. However, while there is a broad consensus on the absence of individual territories among the hunters who are now settled in what is Labrador (see Mailhot, 1986b), none challenge the validity of the border itself.

9. There is reason to believe that this tactic is commonly used by political liberals and others who seek to limit the demands of certain disenfranchised groups for social change. Steinberg (1995) points out that American white liberals in the 1960s commonly objected to black radical tactics over civil rights by arguing that the U.S. was fundamentally racist, and because of this brute fact, demands for civil rights must be tempered. As Steinberg (1995: 112) puts it, "the liberal retreat from race was rationalized in terms of *realpolitik.*"

10. Keith Basso (1996: 33) makes similar remarks about the Anglo-American depiction of Western Apache history, which to Apaches seems "distant and unfamiliar," "unspoken and unanimated," "silent and inert on the printed English page," and "[r]emoved from the contexts of daily social life."

11. Indeed, as Michel Foucault (1973: 66) notes, "Signs . . . have no other laws than those that may govern their contents: any analysis of signs is at the same time, and without need for further inquiry, the decipherment of what they are trying to say. Inversely, [and this is pertinent to our maps] the discovery of what is signified is nothing more than a reflection upon the signs that indicate it."

12. This form of map-making is well documented by Frank Speck (1935: 128-73) and William Duncan Strong (Leacock and Rothschild, 1994: 145). It was filmed by Arthur Lamothe in his 1977 documentary, *Memoires Batantes.*

13. Octavio Paz (1975: 108) depicts Euro-American cosmology as "abstract materialism." That which is valued, and accorded material value, he maintains, is abstracted from real lived experience and sensuality and rendered into abstractions such as money, "resources," and outward appearances.

14. Here Vizenor is referring to the allotment of lands under the 1883 Dawes Act in the United States.

15. In his work with the Apache, Keith Basso (1996: 32) makes a similar point in stressing the importance of place in social and personal life. As he puts it, "Answering the question, 'What happened here?' [people] deal . . . in the main with single events, and because these are tied to places within Apache territory, it [the narrative] is pointedly local and unfailingly episodic. It is also extremely personal, consistently subjective, and therefore highly variable."

16. *Katshemeitsheshu* are trickster spirits who inhibit the land. They often play tricks on people to ensure that they remain humble to the land, waters, animals, and spirits. The *Mistapeo* is one's guardian spirit.

17. Rundstrom (1995: 54) notes that the Bureau of Indian Affairs in the U.S. has encouraged the use of GIS systems, and over 150 geographic information systems had been set up for various American Indian tribes.

18. This is well documented in Evelyn Plaice's (1990) ethnography of North West River, the settler community across the river from Sheshatshiu.

19. Under the "salt water" or "blue water" doctrine, physical distance must separate one state from another in order that rights claims to self-determination and decolonization may be entertained by the United Nations. This means that settler states like Canada, which simply annexed the territories of indigenous populations, can go relatively unchallenged in international law. Relations between the state and such groups are strongly represented by Canada and other states with indigenous populations as internal affairs. See Morris (1992); Churchill (1999).

20. Rundstrom (1993) presents parallel examples of such colonizing by cartography in relation to projects on Zuñi land, Hopi toponyms, and the Cheyenne (Bighorn) Medicine Wheel.

Chapter 3

1. According to W. G. Gosling (1910: 420) "liveyere" is a corruption of the West of England pronunciation of "live here." Many of the "liveyeres" married Native, principally Inuit, partners. It was this population that Wilfred Grenfell ministered to and the descendants of whom currently claim Labrador Métis status.

2. The different spellings, "M'Lean" and "McLean" derive from two different editions of the fur trader's diaries.

3. The eighteenth-century British explorer Captain George Cartwright had some successes with vegetables, such as mustard and cress that helped prevent scurvy and beri-beri, by mixing fish offal and bone meal with the sandy soil (see Townsend, 1918: 280-81). Since the advent of the Moravian missionary stations on the northern Labrador coast in the late eighteenth century, a small range of vegetables have

been grown and berries cultivated (see Packard, 1891: 202). The Hudson's Bay Company traders, even those at Fort Chimo, attempted to establish small-scale vegetable plots. Donald Smith was noted for his successes with a wide range of fruits and vegetables, as well as cattle and sheep at the North West River depot (Zimmerly, 1975: 80).

4. The Lake Melville area is now the principal region of European settlement within the Innu territories. From these origins, the towns of North West River, Happy Valley, and later Goose Bay arose.

5. Grenfell, a British doctor, whose Christian-inspired philanthropic work on hospital ships along the Labrador coast earned him accolades and a knighthood, rendered assistance to the scattered families of settlers and fishermen. He was instrumental in the early development of hospitals, workhouses, and orphanages in Newfoundland and Labrador.

6. This was all listed on the Inco Web site <http://www.inco.ca.com>.

7. Not only were there massive environmental damage, losses of animal habitats, and the drowning of 10,000 caribou, but a major scientific report on the nearby James Bay dam project in Quebec characterized the damage done by the loss of Cree hunting grounds and fishing spots as "culturally genocidal" (see Churchill, 1993: 336). Margaret Sam-Cromarty (1996: 104) remarks of this project: "Try to imagine what it means for the Cree to have their traditional homes flooded and destroyed by the dams of James Bay. What if the oceans swallowed up the entire United States? No longer could anyone live as he or she had. If you imagine that, perhaps you might feel the pain of the Cree."

8. Although interestingly, John M'Lean, lauded by W.S. Wallace as the first European to cross the Labrador peninsula and the "discoverer of Grand Falls" (McLean, 1968: xxiii), did not speculate on any industrial use (M'Lean, 1849, vol. 2: 75-77).

9. Separate hydroelectric projects have been established on the ancestral Innu lands in Quebec. In 2001, the Innu villages of Maliotenam mak Uashat protested over the planned construction of a hydroelectric station on the Toulnustouc River. In a proposed $3.6 billion deal to compensate the Cree, a massive network of hydroelectric projects is currently in the process of expansion in the contiguous territories draining into the eastern side of Hudson Bay (Roslin, 2001).

10. For a concise account of the complex business transactions and intergovernmental dealings over the Churchill Falls and Lower Churchill projects, see Froschauer (1999: 108-37). Froschauer is pessimistic about the Lower Churchill project ever getting off the ground on account of the present power surplus in Quebec and what he imagines to be the high costs of compensating the Innu.

11. The Labrador Métis claim to be primarily Inuit-Métis, the descendants of unions between Inuit women and English men with some intermarriage with Innu, Mi'kmaq, Newfoundlanders, and Canadians.

Despite representing themselves as emerging from a history as a "nation" for hundreds of years, the Labrador Métis Association (now the Labrador Métis Nation) only formed in the mid-1990s when it filed a land claim. Innu Nation has disputed that the members of the Labrador Métis Association are Aboriginal peoples and has asserted that the claim to aboriginality was motivated by the prospect of a land claim (Innu Nation press release, 16 Sept. 1996).

12.   Letter from A.J. Bluck, Secretariat (Air Staff), Ministry of Defence, to Daniel Ashini, 9 June 1995.

13.   In his account of his times with an informant of northern California in the 1920s, Jaime de Angulo (1990: 71) recalled an incident that also vividly underlines the fundamental differences between Western and Native cosmology. An informant tells de Angulo, "Everything is living, even the rocks, even that bench you are sitting on. Somebody made that bench for a purpose, didn't he? Well then it's alive, isn't it? Everything is alive. That's what we Indians believe. White people think everything is dead." More recently, Vine Deloria (1997: 40) expressed this basic difference bluntly: "the major difference between American Indian views of the physical world and Western science lies in the premise accepted by Indians and rejected by scientists: the world in which we live is alive."

14.   Charles Townsend (1918: 276-77) observed the wanton squandering of birds, fish, and animals by the settler population on the North Shore in the early twentieth century. Of the "appalling wastes" involved in sealing, he evocatively writes, "Every year tens of thousands of seal carcasses are stripped of their hides and fat and abandoned in the same way the carcasses of the buffalo, destroyed for their tongues and their hides, were abandoned in the West. As a result, the same fate that befell the buffalo awaits the seal."

15.   Some Innu suggested to me that this metaphor related to the practice of electronic collaring of animals by biologists in Labrador.

16.   As Weaver (2000: 232) remarks, "even as colonizers seek an illusory indigeneity and are drawn to the image of indigenes within their claimed territory, they simultaneously fear that same indigeneity." Similarly, Johnston and Lawson (2000: 363) refer to this tactic as a central feature of the settler sensibility: "Increasingly, the white settlers referred to themselves and their culture as indigenous; they cultivated Native attributes and skills (the Mounties, cowboys, range-riders, gauchos, backwoods-men), and in a way cemented their legitimacy, their own increasingly secure sense of moral, spiritual and cultural belonging."

17.   For example, the settlers never mentioned the aggressive displacement of the Innu from their trapping territories or the expansionist methods of trapping as they extended their trap paths further inland. Unstated, also, was the fact that their historical attachments to the vast interior of the continent are hardly comparable to those of the Innu since the vast

majority maintained a coastal-based sedentary existence.

18. "Traditional ecological knowledge" would be, in Gerald Vizenor's terms, a simulation, a celebration of the *indian*, which is a Native absence. The EIA procedures engage in exactly the opposite of that which he recommends. Hence, "the point here, in the absence of Natives, is to counter the enterprise of reason that sustains the *indian* as a social science simulation of modernity" (Vizenor, 1998: 56).

19. Paul Feyerabend (1987: 21-22) makes a similar observation in relation to the scientific perception of non-Western medical ideas and therapies, the usefulness of which "were discovered by scientific means and must be confirmed with their help."

20. The indifference shown by many white experts to the Innu points of view mirrors the hearings on the Alaska pipeline documented by Brody (1981) in the Indian communities of northeastern British Columbia.

Chapter 4

1. A letter submitted to the Select Committee described the scene: "the Nascopie Indians had been dying from starvation in great numbers; whole camps of them were found dead, without one survivor to tell the tale of their sufferings; others sustained life in a way the most revolting, by using as food the dead bodies of their companions; some even bled their children to death and sustained life with their bodies" (quoted by Gosling, 1910: 443).

2. As the distinctions between various groupings of Natives in this area made by Europeans were not those that Natives themselves recognized, the "Cree" may well have been the ancestors of contemporary Innu trading at one of the posts on Hudson Bay. To the Innu all these groups speaking dialects of the same language are Innut, Ilnut, or Iyut.

3. As an Innu "chief" told Henry Youle Hind (1863: I, 84), "before my people had guns they . . . only killed for food and for clothing. Since the white man gave us guns, they kill them to sell the skins and the deer soon pass away."

4. This was true also in other areas of North America, and just as pronounced in such areas as British Columbia where Natives had adapted agricultural techniques. Kelm (1998: 27-29) describes how starvation among Natives in British Columbia was caused by the continual encroachment of settlers and large-scale agriculture, which drove away the wild animals and depleted the fish stocks that many depended upon.

5. For example, Charles Townsend (1918: 101-02) reports that during the period of the Great War in Europe, the price of furs increased, inducing competition from settlers in trapping. This forced the Innu of La Romaine and Natashquan into an impoverished state and reduced

them to hunting smaller birds and collecting eggs along the coast.

6. The fur traders' use of alcohol as a lever to obtain dependence as well as to exploit Natives was common across North America. Speaking of the nineteenth-century "frontier," Bonnie Duran (1996: 116) states, "By the 1800s, liquor was the basic bartering item on the frontier, as the Whites used the most deceitful tactics to make large profits. There are numerous reports of traders plying people with rum or whisky as a show of friendship, then trading watered liquor of the most vile nature (often poisonous) for the valuable furs that were often given away while Natives were intoxicated."

7. On other trips, such as those between Eastmain and Fort Chimo when they ventured out alone short of food and supplies, the Indians who happened to find them saved the HBC employees from starvation (Davies, 1963: lix).

8. One can find this broad theme in the leading "founding fathers" of both anthropology and sociology. Nineteenth-century figures such as Edward Tylor, Lewis Henry Morgan, Karl Marx, Emile Durkheim, and Max Weber all distinguished between "simple" and "complex" societies. Invariably, the "simple" societies were non-European and "pre-modern," while the "complex" societies of which they themselves were members were equated with modernity.

9. Thus, for example, when Émile Durkheim (1965: 13) went about studying the origin of religion in *The Elementary Forms of the Religious Life*, he started by looking at the "most primitive and simple" living religion, the Australian Aboriginal totemic cults. These, he believed, were to be found "in a society whose organization is surpassed by no others in simplicity." From these primitive origins, he inferred, more modern forms of religious belief and organization could be seen as developments.

10. There is a vast scholarship on evolutionary theories as related to human societies. Those that I have found useful include Teggart (1977), Bock (1980), and Nisbet (1969, 1980).

11. For his troubles, this "would-be pioneer of a new civilization in the sub-Arctic" (Grenfell, 1920: 197) received an honorary degree from Oxford and a birthday honour from King Edward.

12. Not all European representations of the Innu at this time had this evolutionary tone. Cabot's contemporary and New England acquaintance, the ornithologist Wendell Townsend (1918), for example, in his passing references did not allow his largely charitable observations to be tinged by the cultural evolutionism of the day. Mina Hubbard's (1981) memoirs of her trip from North West River to Ungava, meeting with Innu along the way, is also refreshingly free of such judgements.

13. Leonidas Hubbard Jr. led an expedition into Labrador in 1903 from North West River to Lake Meshikimau, a well-known Innu route, but shrouded in mystery and adventure for Europeans because it had not been "mapped." Hubbard, who lost his life on this poorly planned trip,

might well have survived had he taken Innu guides who would have known the much-travelled route. Taking with him only fellow American Dillon Wallace and a Cree guide, George Elson, he paddled up the wrong river (the Susan instead of the Naskaupi), encountering treacherous climatic and physical conditions and eventually dying of hunger before assistance could be reached.

14. The use of evolutionary imagery to depict non-Europeans has perhaps persisted in the Far North longer than almost anywhere else. Brody (1975: 92) explains a similar pattern of white perceptions in relation to the Inuit of the Eastern Arctic. Characterizing the white view, Brody remarks, 'It took us 3,000 years to get this far.' And the corollary is implicit: 'How can you expect *them* to get there in only 10 or even 50 years?' It follows that every Inuk is believed to contain in himself, at the central core of his being, an essential Eskimo-ness, a quality that can be finally dissipated by evolution alone."

15. Furthermore, agriculturalism was advanced as more efficient in that it could sustain many more people than hunting (see Dippie, 1982: 108-09). Hence, the very earliest policies to transform Indians in the United States under President Thomas Jefferson through the Intercourse Acts and the Indian factory system entailed instruction in agriculture, spinning, weaving, and the household arts (Prucha, 1962: 216-19). Jefferson believed that such instruction would not only render civilizing effects for the Indians, but would make them less reluctant to surrender lands for agricultural settlement.

16. One significant exception to this is the activity of the Mennonite Central Committee (MCC), which over the last 20 years has exerted some pressure (thus far to no avail) to encourage the Innu to grow vegetables, believing that this would lead more fluidly to Christianization.

17. In monetary terms, that is, the irreducible terms of European trade, Natives had much to lose. This exploitation can be traced back to the earliest instances of trade in Labrador. Hence, Captain George Cartwright, the eighteenth-century English settler and trader on the southern Labrador coast, received the following as a result of a transaction with the Eskimo in the 1770s: "3 cwt, of whalebone, 100 seal skins, 19 fox, 12 deer, 4 otter, 21 marten, 1 wolf and 1 black bear, at the expense of a small quantity of beads and trifling articles of hardly any commercial value. A representative transaction was the exchange of a comb which cost twopence for a silver fox skin worth four guineas" (Gosling, 1910: 230). While the terms of trade may have become less unequal over time, traders were always in a position to trade something of less value for something of more value in the increasingly global economy that the Innu and other Natives were being inducted into.

18. Very similar beliefs were held by the Moravian missionaries towards their Inuit charges on the Labrador coast at the same time. In 1960, the Moravian minister Peacock (1964: 454) could boast that "the ly-

ing, treacherous, and murderous Eskimo of Labrador has gone and in his place we have the law abiding citizen . . . moving quickly towards maturity." This advancement of the character of the Inuit would "make them admirable, well adjusted citizens of the Dominion of Canada."

19. As indeed did previous generations of Innu, who only ventured to the coasts for much briefer visits. Observing an encampment on the North Shore in 1861, Henry Youle Hind (1863: II, 170) remarks, "No sooner do the Montagnais hear the clang of the wild goose in the early spring than the old yearning comes back again and among the young who have never camped in the woods the feeling grows until it becomes a passion, which must be gratified at any risk."

20. As a consequence of substantial overspending and unaccounted expenditures, the report of which was leaked to the community by political rivals of the band council administration, the finances of both Innu band councils in Labrador were taken over by the federal government (MacDonald, 2001).

21. This testimony was Web-posted by Innu Nation at a time of heightened anxiety over the mining development <www.innu.ca> and was verified by my own conversations with Kanikuen Nuna in 1999.

22. Henriksen (1973: 79) noted this in the late 1960s, remarking that the Innu "are proud when they contrast their tradition of sharing and helping other people with the white man's demand for money in all undertakings." More recently, the fees levied by fly-in advisers and consultants, for example, are often astronomical, amounting to almost $1,000 per day. Despite the exorbitant charges, I have only heard of one case in which the Innu Nation rejected the services of an adviser on account of a consulting fee.

Chapter 5

1. New France consisted of three main territories; Acadia, which is now Nova Scotia, Norumbega, which is now New Brunswick and New England, and Canada, which was the territory north of the St. Lawrence River, extending to the north and west, and is now part of Quebec.

2. In addition to *The Jesuit Relations*, much of my discussion in this section owes itself to Gibson (1939), Kennedy (1950), and Blackburn (2000).

3. For example, the Franciscan friars presided over Indian slavery and a massive depopulation of Indians under the Spanish mission system from 1769 to 1834 in California (see Heizer and Almquist, 1971: 1-22).

4. As J.R. Miller (2000: 83) remarks, "[t]o many Indian nations, the French were merchants and soldiers who did not want to take possession of their lands but merely to trade for the fruits of the forest; the British, though some of them were merchants, were also largely agricultural settlers who inexorably dispossessed the original inhabitants

by means of their expanding farming settlements."

5. By drawing on the journals of Father Paul Le Jeune, Leacock stressed the relative autonomy of the sexes among the Innu. Referring to their culture as "communitarian" and "communistic," Leacock contends that missionaries introduced patriarchal relations into Native communities, prohibiting women from participating in hunting and decision-making and discouraging more assertive and permissive marital arrangements among women. The missionaries tried to impose the model of the European woman (chaste, fragile, and dependent) upon Native communities more accustomed to tough and independent women (see Leacock, 1980, 1981, 1995).

6. The correspondences of the new authorities in Newfoundland often made reference to "dying off," a kind of bleak Darwinian prognosis of the inevitable that occurs when two unequal peoples meet (see Roche, 1992).

7. The Oblates started converting other people such as the Sto:lo Salish people of the Fraser Valley in British Columbia much earlier. Between 1841 and the mid-twentieth century, the Sto:lo were subject to conversion through schooling. At the school, children were prohibited from speaking their Native language, and "their strong cultural beliefs were dismissed as mere superstition" (Archibald, 1995: 293).

8. In an illuminating essay on settler colonies, Johnston and Lawson (2000: 363) argue that the disappearance and even genocide of Native peoples served as a foundational narrative legitimizing the displacement of Natives.

9. Letter from W.A. Paddon of the International Grenfell Association to Edward Roberts, Secretary to the Premier of Newfoundland, 17 June 1966, St. John's, Office of the Premier Records Office.

10. Mitchell (1988) describes in great detail the efforts of Europeans who, with Native compliance, developed systematic, rational instruction based on the British "Lancaster model" to capture minds and bodies. This ontological division of the administrators created a power to order, discipline, and ultimately create colonial power in Egypt.

11. The authors here, of course, beg the question as to what exactly it means for a Native school to be "productive."

12. Until 1998 when it was taken over by the secular Labrador School Board, the school was run by the Roman Catholic School Board.

13. This policy of threatening to cut off welfare to those parents who did not ensure that their children attended school lasted at least until the late 1980s. James Ryan (1988a: 213) interviewed a local Social Services Department official who admitted to threatening Innu parents in just such a manner.

14. CBC, "Labrador Innu accuse church and schools of abuse," Web posting 26 Feb. 2001.

15.   On the number of Innu complainants involved, see "Labrador Innu ac-
      cuse church and schools of abuse," CBC, Web-posted 26 Feb. 2001.
      On the cover-up by the Bishop, see "Yvonne May, a former nun who
      worked as a counsellor in Sheshatshiu during the early 1990s, says
      the region's Bishop at the time covered up reports of sexual abuse,"
      CBC morning news, Web-posted 28 Feb. 2001. On the refusal to extra-
      dite the Oblate Brother, see "The Department of Justice has upheld a
      decision not to extradite Oblate Brother Gordon Paul Banem from the
      United States," CBC morning news, Web-posted 28 Nov. 2001. Fur-
      thermore, the number of sexual abuse claims by Aboriginal victims
      against the Oblates of Mary Immaculate reached 2,500 in Canada in
      2002, requiring the order to file a bankruptcy petition (Associated
      Press), "Lawsuits over past abuse force Roman Catholic Order to seek
      bankruptcy protection," Web-posted 9 Apr. 2002.

16.   In fact, in 1999 I was asked specifically to omit references to sexual
      abuse in my report to the Local Education Committee by the *Akane-
      shau* principal of the school.

Chapter 6

1.   Bernstein (1996: 21) has argued that pedagogy entails the internaliza-
      tion of classifications and distinctions in the world, which become
      unchallenged. Thus, "the principle of classification comes to have the
      force of natural order and the identities it constructs are taken as real,
      as authentic, as the source of integrity."

2.   As Alejo Carpentier's narrator writes of his Huguenot forebears in *The
      Lost Steps* (1991: 108).

3.   As for this aspect of Native schooling, Adams (1995: 185) writes, "foot-
      ball was a powerful tool for acculturating Indians to the American
      value system. From football, Indians would learn the value of preci-
      sion, teamwork, order, discipline, obedience, efficiency and how all
      these interconnected in the business of 'winning.'"

4.   One upshot of this is that young people are perennially exposed to all
      of the ills of community life, such as heavy drinking bouts, almost
      daily suicide attempts, and marital discord. Because it discourages
      them from spending time in the country, which nearly everyone
      regards as therapeutic, the school is symbolic of the "no exit" situation
      they have been placed in. Like other cornered people around the
      world, the children often live quickly and recklessly, turning to gas-
      sniffing, vandalism, and violence.

5.   I suspect that this might be because many North American children's
      spelling books use "Indian" as the example for the letter "I" and the
      teaching aides simply improvised from such a book.

6.   This rift in language between the generations may be part of a wider
      experiential and cognitive split that separates the pre- and post-
      settlement generations. In other instances when people have made a

drastic switch in their way of life or geographical location, similar divisions have occurred. A classic example in sociology is the Polish peasants who migrated to the U.S., as presented in the Chicago School study of W.I. Thomas and Florian Znaniecki. As they remark, "the members of the new generation who are brought up in this environment [Chicago], are more likely to show solidarity with one another as against the parents. . . . The traditional measure of exertion is lost; the parents have no standard of education, since the old standard is no longer valid and no new one has been appropriated. The natural result is a free play given to individual caprice, excessive indulgence alternating with unreasonable severity. Thus the moral character of parental authority in the eyes of the children is lost" (quoted by Shaw, 1966: 36). Although there are obvious differences in meaning and context, many of the details of these observations could be applied to the relationships between parents and children in the Innu villages.

7. A growing body of research on linguistic diversity has taken steps to delineate how speakers of different languages encode different cognitive appreciations of the world. Lucy (1996), for example, has demonstrated highly distinctive patterns of perception, classification, and memory recall through experiments with English and Yucatec speakers. Bowerman (1996) shows how spatial relationships are encoded in different languages and how different language speakers perceive space differently.

8. Older people's points of reference for judging how well someone can function as an Innu are almost always how they contribute to the life in the country. Here Elizabeth Penashue's measure of competence is how one conducts oneself in the hunting camp. This is what she and nearly all other *Tshenut* hold to be the most valuable part of socialization.

9. One recent high school graduate told me that she was not having any great academic difficulties at a Pentecostal Bible college in Ontario and was achieving average grades. Another young man had just graduated from the University of Ottawa Law School. But, these stories of Innu educational achievement are extremely rare.

Chapter 7

1. This assumption percolates up to the highest political levels in Canada. Noting that various fiscal outlays for Natives had not been cut, Prime Minister Jean Chrétien's response to *Canada's Tibet* (Samson et al., 1999) was that Canada had been "generous" with Aboriginals (*St. John's Telegram*, 9 Nov. 1999, 2).

2. These figures are calculated from Royal Commission on Aboriginal Peoples (1995). The highest national rate in the world for 1990 was 39 per 100,000 for Hungary (Lister, 1997). After a spate of suicides in Nain, an Inuit community of 1,200 people north of Davis Inlet, the rate there was calculated to be 250 per 100,000 (Saunders, 2000). While it

is difficult to arrive at an exact figure, the Ojibwa community of Pi-kangikum in northwest Ontario probably has a higher suicide rate than Davis Inlet. This community of 2,100 people has suffered out-breaks of several suicides in short periods of time on many occasions since the early 1990s (see Harries, 2001). Using hospital records, Ald-ridge and St. John (1991: 434) calculated the rate of youth suicide (ages 10-19) among Innu and Inuit of northern Labrador for the 1977-88 period to be 180 per 100,000 compared with a non-Native rate of 11.85 per 100,000 in Labrador as a whole. It should be noted that the Davis Inlet figure is derived from an average baseline popula-tion of 500, and potentially large fluctuations in rates can occur in small samples. For an extended overview of Aboriginal suicide in Can-ada from a social psychiatric perspective, see Kirmayer (1994).

3.   As reported on CFGB-FM radio, 18 Aug. 1999.

4.   In 1997, I sent the two tables detailing mortality differences to the di-rector of Labrador Health Services in Goose Bay, in the hope of getting some response to this clear indication of the plight of the Innu. I never received any acknowledgement or reply. The authorities in Newfound-land and Labrador have consistently ignored the advice and comments of researchers working with the Innu. Georg Henriksen (1993b: 6) remarks that his suggestions to alleviate some of the trou-bles of the Mushuau Innu – simply changing the school calendar and organizing a mobile school in the country – were not acted upon. The report to the Economic Recovery Committee in which he mentions this was similarly disregarded. In December 2000, I wrote a letter to the director of the Labrador School Board in Goose Bay, making simi-lar suggestions to those of Henriksen. I never received an answer, nor did the members of the Sheshatshiu Local Education Committee on whose behalf I had written.

5.   Physicians and nurses routinely complained of non-compliance with medical regimens and prescriptions. While on a home visit, a nurse in Utshimassits showed me an elderly chronically ill patient's drug con-tainer that had all of the days of the week marked on it. But it was clear to see that only a few tablets were absent from apparently ran-dom days. The patient, who spoke no English, was deemed to be non-compliant. While on their rounds, the nurses mentioned numer-ous other cases of non-compliance with dietary and exercise regimes advised for diabetics and of repeated missed appointments at the clinic.

6.   Being an arm of colonial domination, biomedicine has also contrib-uted to the eradication of indigenous health beliefs and modes of treatment. As Arnold (1988: 18) has pointed out in relation to medi-cine in European colonies, "seeing itself as rational, scientific and universalistic, western medicine defined itself in opposition to the presumed irrationality and superstition of indigenous medicine. The customs and beliefs of the people were treated as obstacles to over-

come, obscurantism to be brushed aside by the new scientific age."

7. This itself is a highly questionable assumption. To equate socially constructed ethnic or racial groups with particular gene pools is always arbitrary. "[P]opulations that belong to what we call major 'races' in our everyday usage do not cluster [in terms of gene frequency] together" (Rose et al., 1984: 122). The contemporary Innu, for example, have European (English, Scottish, Irish, French, Dutch, etc.) and Inuit ancestors.

8. Indeed, Natives in Canada may be up to six times more likely to suffer from diabetes than their white counterparts (Young, 1994: 22). The hypothesis this relies on is the "thrifty gene theory," which holds that the storage of excess fat would have been an advantage in conditions of varying food supply (e.g., hunting), so when food was scarce the excess fat would be mobilized as energy – but in conditions of a constant food supply the storage of excess fat and all the increased blood glucose that goes with it can be toxic, making the individual more prone to diabetes since blood sugar is not absorbed by body cells and builds up in the blood (see Jackson, 1994: 394). More recently, a Toronto-based 1999 study of the Sandy Lake First Nation (an Ojibwa and Cree community in northern Ontario) discovered a new genetic mutation – a gene that promotes fat storage. The study found that if a person had one copy of the gene, she or he had double the normal risk of developing diabetes. An individual with two copies (one from each parent) had 15 times the risk. The community itself has one of the highest incidences of diabetes in the world. Diabetes has only been evident in the community in the last 30 years, since the people became more sedentary (Web-posted CBC report, 9 Mar. 1999).

9. This is put into effect in many Western countries through the rationing of access to health care according to lifestyle.

10. For example, the sequestration of Innu land in this manner is in direct violation of Article 27 of the UN Covenant of Human Rights, which states that all minorities shall not be prevented from enjoying their own culture.

11. The depiction of the Innu as blamers or as being entrenched in a "blaming culture" is a fairly constant feature of the narratives of settlers and professionals in the communities. Besides medical workers, I have heard it from clergy, judges, and police.

12. Interview with Michael Enright on *This Morning*, CBN-AM radio, 10 Nov. 1999.

13. It is revealing that the reporters cannot correctly spell the most common Innu surname, "Rich."

14. A stark contrast between Innu and European attitudes towards the lice is presented in anthropologist William Duncan Strong's field notes (Leacock and Rothschild, 1994: 109-10, 138). Lice ruined portions of Strong's time with the Mushuau Innu. He comments about ill

effects from them on numerous occasions, but notes no strong reactions against them by the Innu.

15. A common explanation in Australia for the drastic decline in the Aboriginal population is that they had lost the will to live (Saggers and Gray, 1991: 66). The same reason is also cited for some Native North American deaths.

16. Among northern peoples, health is almost always not just a question of the integrity of the body, but is linked to the continuity of cultural traditions, relationships between the people and the land and animals, and the continuity of traditional activities. An excellent example of this among the Cree of Great Whale River is provided by Adelson (1998, 2000).

17. Some years later, noting the reduction in the Inuit population on the north coast of Labrador to just 1,000 by the 1930s, Wilfred Grenfell (1933: 88) argues that "[e]pidemic diseases and contact with white men have been the cause."

18. As Strong (Leacock and Rothschild, 1994: 59) noted some 10 years after the events, "[t]he Davis Inlet people were in the interior hunting at this time, but failing to get sufficient game, they were forced to come to Davis Inlet for supplies where they contracted the diseases rampant on the coast and several died. The epidemic seems to have hit the older people the hardest, and as a result there were no people of really advanced years among either the Davis Inlet or the Barren Ground bands at the time of my stay with them."

19. Devastating rates of casualty, especially from tuberculosis, coincided with the sedentarization of the Inuit in the Canadian Far North. In some settlements, such as Eskimo Point and Baker Lake, the *majority* of Inuit households were affected by the disease in the 1960s (Tester and Kulchyski, 1994: 358; Brody, 1975: 35).

20. In Grenfell's subsequent memoir, published in 1933, the last sentence of this phrase has been amended. Although the author claims the book to be "rewritten" as his "last testament," many sections are exactly as in *Labrador Doctor*. Thus, the passage reads verbatim as quoted up to the remarks on unmorality In the later memoir, *Forty Years for Labrador* (1933: 80) Grenfell makes an abrupt change of tack, "the features of Native life which appealed most to us were the universal optimism, the laughing good nature and contentment, and the Sunday cleanliness of the entire congregation which swarmed into the chapel service, a welcome respite from the perennial dirt of the week-days." It is difficult to know why the change of heart occurred to Grenfell. The altered picture still has the Eskimos ravaged by disease, but bearing up under their good humour, even turning out on Sundays to Grenfell's approval, despite "perennial dirt" on other occasions. Therefore, it is no longer their unmorality that helps them bear the casualties of European diseases, but their *joie de vivre* and Christianity.

21. This was a common perception of nineteenth-century Hudson's Bay Company traders, who, while noting "Eskimo ferocity," reported "standing by helplessly as bands of Indians bent on the murderous pursuit of 'Eskimo hunting' passed the posts on their way north" (Davies, 1963: xxxv). Grenfell (1933: 87-88) advanced the idea that the Montagnais "are the hereditary foes of the eskimos, whole settlements of whom have more than once been exterminated."

22. However, some of those who were living closer to them than these administrators and explorers were much more skeptical of plans to sedentarize the Innu. After noting the deep spiritual connections to nomadic hunting, the land and animals, and their hardy constitution, Richard White (1931: 3), a settler and trader on the coast near Davis Inlet, predicted dire consequences: "To attempt to civilize them or in any way hinder their nomadic form of life would undoubtedly destroy the Labrador Indians, for they would degenerate into mere hangers-on at the settlements, losing their self-reliance and dignity. Any effort, however well-meaning, to civilize them must inevitably have disastrous effects."

23. In 1921 the American explorer Donald MacMillan claimed that "[w]ere it not for the noble band of Moravians, not one Eskimo would be alive in Labrador today" (House, 1981: 181).

24. It has been shown throughout the world that virtually all hunter-gatherers who have been sedentarized have experienced drastic health consequences. Over a decade ago, Thomas McKeown (1988: 37), the historian of social medicine, wrote:

> Diseases such as cancer, obesity, diabetes, hypertension and heart disease [are] very uncommon in present-day hunter-gatherers and peasant agriculturists and only begin to appear when traditional ways of life are abandoned. Indeed it is the observation that primitive societies are largely free from non-communicable diseases which has led to the conclusion that so long as they are undisturbed by external influences, hunter-gatherers remain essentially healthy.

McKeown, of course, referred only to disease in the physical sense and not to the more psychologically damaging effects of European colonization, which achieve the same result. Summarizing the evidence on other destructive effects of forced changes to pre-existing modes of social organization, Kunitz (1983: 10) points out that "band-level [hunting] tribes were found to have higher rates of homicide and suicide than pastoralists, and pastoralists in turn had higher rates than sedentary agriculturalists."

25. For example, although Engels (1999: 281-82) referred to an urban context, the following description is in broad outline applicable to Davis Inlet in the 1990s: "They [the workers] are housed in the worst ventilated districts in the towns; they are deprived of all means of keeping clean. They are deprived of water because this is only

brought to their houses if someone is prepared to defray the cost of laying the pipes. River water is so dirty as to be useless for cleansing purposes. The poor are forced to throw into the street all their sweepings, garbage, dirty water, and frequently even disgusting filth and excrement . . . people are packed together in an exceptionally small area."

Chapter 8

1. I will relate an extended example of this in the following chapter.

2. This law has affected Aboriginal communities disproportionately. Aboriginal children are almost five times more likely to be in care of the state than other children in Canada (Shewell and Spagnut, 1995: 25).

3. William Duncan Strong (Leacock and Rothschild, 1994) mentioned several instances of adoption in his 1927-28 journals of his stays with the Mushuau Innu.

4. For example, HBC factor John McLean, who was stationed at Fort Chimo and North West River in the early nineteenth century, rarely mentioned alcohol among the "Nascopie," although he did display his disdain for drinking among other Natives. McLean (1968: 23) recorded a meeting with Natives on the Ottawa River in which "scenes of a revolting nature were of frequent occurrence. Rum and brandy flowed in streams, and dollars were scattered about as if they had been of no greater value than pebbles on the beach." Similarly, Samuel King Hutton (n.d.: 30), a doctor working with the Inuit on the north Labrador coast from 1903 to 1908, remarked that "it may be observed that alcoholism as a habit is not known among Eskimos. Occasional cases of drunkenness have arisen, but chronic alcoholism from the habitual use of intoxicating liquors is unknown." These Inuit communities, principally Nain and Hopedale, are now rife with alcohol-related problems as much if not more than the Innu communities.

5. I have commented on this in connection with the policies of the Canadian state, which require the Innu to configure themselves into political organizations sharing basic Western assumptions about land and rights and in relation to the policies advocated by the Royal Commission on Aboriginal Peoples and the Canadian Multiculturalism Act of 1988 (see Samson, 2001).

6. Some five years after my interview with Kay Graves, the Auditor General of Canada, Denis Desautels, did not share the optimism of local *Akaneshau*. In a report to Parliament on 16 October 2000, Desautels observed that the federal government had failed to identify what remedies were needed to address the "social pathologies" of the Innu. "There is a significant risk that the causes of these conditions will not be adequately addressed through the relocation," said the report ("Davis Inlet Innu may not be served well by relocation: auditor general," Canadian Press Web posting, 17 Oct. 2000).

7. As reported in "Innu children face more health problems," CBC web posting, 9 Feb. 2001.

8. The following encounter with a man at midday on the road in Sheshat-shiu is typical. The man tells me of his resentment that those who work at Innu Nation do not pay attention to the community and they get "fat cheques" for their work. While in their jobs, these employees appoint members of their own families to vacant positions. When he goes in the Innu Nation office, he tells me, "I feel like I am in a prison cell."

9. In *Stigma*, Erving Goffman (1963: 25) notes how members of stigma-tized groups can manage their "spoiled identity" by becoming success stories within "normal society" and providing "exemplary moral tales." Becoming a hero of assimilation in this way is precisely what most Innu avoid, even if it means fairly regular inebriation. The tendency is more pronounced in Sheshatshiu, where the white presence looms larger and where "good Innu" are continually sought out as models of assimilation.

10. Bonnie Duran's (1996: 124) assurances that alcohol "is viewed as de-structive of Native life" and that "abstinence becomes a symbol of protest and an affirmation of Native identity" do not fit the Innu situa-tion. While it is true that many Innu view and experience alcohol as destructive, it is not directly destructive of *nutshimit* life, from where it is largely absent. It is, however, destructive of drinkers' family rela-tionships and participation in village life. But this is not to say that abstinence per se is a symbol of protest.

11. As C. Wright Mills (1959: 9) put it, "When, in a city of 100,000, only one man is unemployed, that is his personal trouble, and for its relief we properly look to the character of the man, his skills, and his imme-diate opportunities. But, when in a nation of 50 million employees, 15 million men are unemployed, that is an issue, and we may not hope to find its solution within the range of opportunities open to any one in-dividual."

Chapter 9

1. When consulting the Canadian High Commission in London before my first visit to Labrador in 1994, I had been persistently discouraged by the senior counsellor from travelling to Davis Inlet as a result of this stand-off.

2. It is well known that many Native Americans do not emphasize linear chronology as Europeans do. As the Tewa anthropologist Alfonso Ortiz (1988: 11) explained it, "the kind of time considered most important by Indian peoples who live in unbroken communities is cyclical and re-petitive, rather than irreversible and linear . . . relationship[s] and cyclical passage of time take precedence over a Western sense of linear chronology."

3. Norman Forer (1979: 90-92) argues that law in Western societies is an outgrowth of the desire on the part of a ruling economic elite to protect private property. By its nature, it is "imposed," but it is more openly imposed upon American Indians who had occupied land without any notion of private property. We could extend this to say that the imposition affects not simply the relationship between collective entities such as the state and Native groups, but permeates the very core of the Native self as demonstrated in their exposure to the criminal justice system.

4. As George Steiner (1992: xi) remarks in the Foreword to Friedrich Ohly's *The Damned and the Elect*, "Guilt and chastisement, the Wrath of God and that of the Furies, literally generate the matter of biblical and classical narrative."

5. In a lucid discussion, Merold Westphal (1984: 74-89) distinguishes between objective guilt (being found guilty of an offence) and subjective guilt (the approval of others' disapproval of the self, which can be occasioned by the fear of punishment).

6. A young man in Davis Inlet, Eric Rich, while telling me of his experiences in court, related the absurdity of "the defence only believing the defence and the prosecution only believing the prosecution." Of course, this absurdity, driving all lawyers to pursue single-mindedly the perceived interests of their individual clients in "winning," militates against any genuine understanding of the troubles of the people of Davis Inlet and Sheshatshiu.

7. The only exception to this general view of judges was Judge Igloliorte, an Inuit judge from Hopedale. He was viewed as fair and impartial.

8. For a discussion of the various philosophical models that inform this need for punishment, see Acton (1969) and Ten (1987).

9. A compelling example of this phenomenon can be extracted from Irish playwright J.M. Synge. In his reflections on the Aran Islands at the turn of the twentieth century, Synge (1992: 50-51) notes how English jurisdiction over the islands coincided with an upsurge in crime that islanders claim was brought about by the advent of the police. A parallel with the Innu situation is also provided by the islanders' rejection of the assumptions of the justice system – the necessity of punishment and the "claims of abstract truth" that turn "the whole system of sworn evidence into a demoralizing farce." Like the Innu, the people of Aran also saw retribution as callous, futile, and counterproductive. As Synge tells us, "these people . . . are never criminals yet always capable of crime, that a man will not do wrong unless he is under the influence of a passion which is as irresponsible as a storm on the sea. If a man has killed his father, and is already sick and broken with remorse, they can see no reason why he should be dragged away and killed by the law."

Conclusion

1. In his book on English-Canadian identity, Ian Angus (1997: 146) even goes so far as to suggest that "multiculturalism as a social ideal in English Canada may make a contribution to the extension of democratic theory to include the public recognition of particularities." Richard Day (1998), on the other hand, argues that multiculturalism in Canada is a form of silencing real difference as a means of covering up the fact that Canadians have no particularly distinct characteristics.

2. These quotations are taken from the "Notes for an Address by the Honourable Jane Stewart, Minister of Indian Affairs and Northern Development on the occasion of the unveiling of *Gathering Strength – Canada's Aboriginal Action Plan*," Ottawa, 7 Jan. 1998.

3. As Derek Rasmussen (2000b: 2) puts it, "reconciliation-to-forget is a process of denial, justification, excuse, minimal grudging acceptance, carefully worded and fiscally cautious apology, and minimal negotiated compensation, concluded by a final resolution to settle matters once and for all."

4. "The democratic illusion is universal, linked as it is to the zero degree of civic energy," Baudrillard (1992: 36) tells us, then continues, "[a]ll we have left is an ad-man's illusion, that is, the zero degree of the Idea, and it is this which sets the tone for our liberal regime of human rights."

5. A prime example of this was a gas-sniffing crisis in November 2000. Both band council chiefs and the President of the Innu Nation called in the mass media to witness numerous young Innu sniffing gas. They first called for compulsory removal of the children for treatment, then, when the media attention had reached a peak, requested and received an agreement for the state provision of a detoxification centre, a family treatment centre, and recognition under the Indian Act. Although the leaders also stressed the wider political contexts for gas-sniffing, the Canadian media presented the issue as one of personal and family pathology, largely a medical problem. Even when a wider arc of consideration was brought into view, this largely dealt with improving life in the community, thus ignoring both the political bases of Innu misery and the health-sustaining alternatives in the country (see, for example, Morris, 2000: 5).

6. William Duncan Strong recorded a Wolverine legend and "The Man Who Married a Caribou" as told to him during his stay with Mushuau Innu in 1927-28 (Leacock and Rothschild 1994: 159-60, 165-67). These stories are also covered in great detail in James Wilson's BBC Radio 3 broadcasts, "The Enduring World of the Innu," 9-11 Dec. 1996, and in the Innu stories collected by Millman (1993).

7. A similar verdict is presented by the political philosopher Charles Taylor (1992: 64), who argues that for a liberal democratic order to

survive, diverse cultures need to be allowed to survive and to be recognized as of equal worth. He concludes: "Multinational societies can break up, in large part because of a lack of (perceived) recognition of the equal worth of one group by another. This is at present, I believe, the case in Canada."

8.   It was reported on CBC morning news on 15 March 2002 that recent maps presented by the Innu Nation covered a claim of "much smaller area than the Innu set out in an earlier land claim proposal in 1998."

Bibliography

Acton, H.B., ed. 1969. *The Philosophy of Punishment: A Collection of Papers.* London: Macmillan.

Adams, David Wallace. 1995. *Education for Extinction: American Indians and the Boarding School Experience, 1875-1928.* Lawrence: University Press of Kansas.

Adelson, Naomi. 1998. "Health Beliefs and the Politics of Cree Well-Being," *Health* 2, 1: 5-22.

———. 2000. *'Being Alive Well': Health and the Politics of Cree Well-Being.* Toronto: University of Toronto Press.

Agamben, Georgio. 1995. *Homo Sacer: Sovereign Power and Bare Life,* trans. Daniel Heller-Roazen. Stanford, Calif.: Stanford University Press.

Agee, James, and Walker Evans. 1941. *Let Us Now Praise Famous Men.* New York: Ballantine.

Aldridge, David, and Kimberly St. John. 1991. "Adolescent and Preadolescent Suicide in Newfoundland and Labrador," *Canadian Journal of Psychiatry* 36, 6: 432-36.

Amor, Mónica. 1996. "Dis-mapping America: Miguel Angel Ríos' Maps," *Third Text* 34: 23-36.

Andrew, Ben, and Peter Sarsfield. 1984. "Innu Health: The Role of Self-Determination," in Robert Fortuine, ed., *Circumpolar Health '84: Proceedings of the Sixth International Symposium on Circumpolar Health.* Seattle: University of Washington Press, 428-30.

Angus, Ian. 1997. *A Border Within: National Identity, Cultural Plurality and Wilderness.* Montreal and Kingston: McGill-Queen's University Press.

Archibald, Jo-ann. 1995. "Locally Developed Native Studies Curriculum: An Historical and Philosophical Rationale," in Marie Battiste and Jean Barman, eds., *First Nations Education in Canada: The Circle Unfolds.* Vancouver: University of British Columbia Press, 288-312.

Arneil, Barbara. 1996. *John Locke and America: The Defence of English Colonialism.* Oxford: Clarendon Press.

Arnold, David. 1988. "Introduction: Disease, Medicine and Empire," in Arnold, ed., *Imperial Medicine and Indigenous Societies.* Manchester: Manchester University Press, 1-26.

Asch, Michael. 1984. *Home and Native Land: Aboriginal Rights and the Canadian Constitution.* Toronto: Methuen.

_____. 1992. "Errors in *Delgamuukw*: An Anthropological Perspective," in Frank Cassidy, ed., *Aboriginal Title in British Columbia: Delgamuukw v. The Queen.* Vancouver: Oolichan Books, 221-43.

_____. 1993. "Aboriginal Self-Government and Canadian Constitutional Identity: Building Reconciliation," in Michael D. Levin, ed., *Ethnicity and Aboriginality.* Toronto: University of Toronto Press, 29-52.

_____. 1996. "First Nations and the Derivation of Canada's Underlying Title: Comparing Perspectives on Legal Ideology," paper presented at Socio-Legal Studies Association conference, Glasgow, July.

_____ and Norman Zlotkin. 1997. "Affirming Aboriginal Title: A New Basis for Comprehensive Claims Negotiations," in Asch, ed., *Aboriginal and Treaty Rights in Canada: Essays on Law, Equity, and Respect for Difference.* Vancouver: University of British Columbia Press, 208-29.

Assembly of First Nations. 1993. *Violations of Law and Human Rights by the Governments of Canada and Newfoundland in Regard to the Mushuau Innu: A Documentation of Injustice in Utshimassits (Davis Inlet).* Submission to the Canadian Human Rights Commission. Ottawa: Assembly of First Nations.

_____. 1994. *Breaking the Silence: An Interpretive Study of Residential School Impact and Healing as Illustrated by the Stories of First Nation Individuals.* Ottawa: Assembly of First Nations.

Axtell, James. 1981. *The European and the Indian: Essays in the Ethnohistory of North America.* Oxford: Oxford University Press.

Bailey, Alfred Goldsworthy. 1969. *The Conflict of European and Eastern Algonkian Cultures 1504-1700: A Study in Canadian Civilization,* 2nd ed. Toronto: University of Toronto Press.

Barkan, Elazar. 2000. *The Guilt of Nations: Restitution and Negotiating Historical Injustices.* New York: W.W. Norton.

Barron, Tracy. 2001. "US Company Scoping Churchill Hydro Potential," *St. John's Telegram,* 7 July.

Barrow, John, ed. 1852. *The Geography of Hudson's Bay: Remarks of Captain W. Coats, in Many Voyages to that Locality, Between the Years 1727 and 1751.* London: Hakluyt Society.

Barthes, Roland. 1973. *Mythologies,* trans. Annette Lavers. London: Paladin.

Basso, Keith. 1996. *Wisdom Sits in High Places: Landscape and Language among the Western Apache.* Albuquerque: University of New Mexico Press.

Baudrillard, Jean. 1983. *Simulations*, trans. Paul Foss, Paul Patton and Philip Beitchman, New York: Semiotext(e).

————. 1989. "Anorexic Ruins," in Dietmar Kamper and Christoph Wulf, eds., *Looking Back on the End of the World*, trans. David Antal. New York: Semiotext(e), 29-48.

————. 1990. *Fatal Strategies*, trans. Philip Beitchman and W.G.J. Niesluchowski. New York: Semiotext(e).

————. 1992. *The Illusion of the End*, trans. Chris Turner. Stanford, Calif.: Stanford University Press.

Berger, John. 1967. *A Fortunate Man: The Story of a Country Doctor.* New York: Pantheon.

Berger, Thomas. 1991. *A Long and Terrible Shadow: White Values, Native Rights in the Americas 1492-1992.* Vancouver: Douglas & McIntyre.

Berkes, Fikret. 1993. "Traditional Ecological Knowledge in Perspective," in J.T. Inglis, ed., *Traditional Ecological Knowledge: Concepts and Cases.* Ottawa: International Program on Traditional Ecological Knowledge and International Development Research Centre.

Bernstein, Basil. 1996. *Pedagogy, Symbolic Control and Identity: Theory, Research, Critique.* London: Taylor & Francis.

Blackburn, Carole. 2000. *Harvest of Souls: The Jesuit Missions and Colonialism in North America, 1632-1650.* Montreal and Kingston: McGill-Queen's University Press.

Bock, Kenneth 1980. *Human Nature and History: A Response to Sociobiology.* New York: Columbia University Press.

Boorstin, Daniel. 1973. *The Mysterious Science of the Law.* Gloucester, Mass.: Peter Smith.

Borrows, John. 1997. "Wampum at Niagara: The Royal Proclamation, Canadian Legal History and Self-Government," in Michael Asch, ed., *Aboriginal and Treaty Rights in Canada: Essays on Law, Equity, and Respect for Difference.* Vancouver: University of British Columbia Press, 155-72.

Bowerman, Melissa. 1996. "The Origins of Children's Spatial Semantic Categories: Cognitive versus Linguistic Determinants," in John Gumperz and Stephen Levinson, eds., *Rethinking Linguistic Relativity.* Cambridge: Cambridge University Press, 145-76.

Brody, Hugh. 1975. *The People's Land: Inuit, Whites and the Eastern Arctic.* Vancouver: Douglas & McIntyre.

————. 1981. *Maps and Dreams.* New York: Pantheon.

_____. 2001. *The Other Side of Eden: Hunter-Gatherers, Farmers and the Modern World*. London: Faber & Faber.

Budgell, Richard. 1984. "Canada, Newfoundland, and the Labrador Indians 1949-69," *Native Issues* 4, 1: 38-49.

Buell, Lawrence. 1995. *The Environmental Imagination: Thoreau, Nature Writing, and the Formation of American Culture*. Cambridge, Mass.: Belknap Press of Harvard University Press.

Bussidor, Ila, and Ustun Bilgen-Reinart. 1997. *Night Spirits: The Story of the Relocation of the Sayisi Dene*. Winnipeg: University of Manitoba Press.

Cabot, William. 1912. *In Northern Labrador*. London: John Murray.

_____. 1922. "The Indians," in Wilfred Grenfell et al., eds., *Labrador: The Country and the People*, new ed. New York: Macmillan, 184-225.

Canadian Broadcasting Company (CBC). 2001. "Doctor says Ottawa to blame for reserve's woes," 21 June, posted on CBC Web site.

Carpentier, Alejo. 1991 [1953]. *The Lost Steps*, trans. Harriet de Onis. London: Minerva.

Cartier, Jacques. 1906. "The First Relation of Jaques Carthier of S. Malo, 1534," in Henry Burrage, ed., *Early English and French Voyages Chiefly from Hakluyt 1534-1608*. New York: Barnes & Noble, 4-31.

Churchill, Ward. 1993. *Struggle for the Land: Indigenous Resistance to Genocide, Ecocide, and Expropriation in Contemporary North America*. Monroe, Maine: Common Courage.

_____. 1999. "The Tragedy and the Travesty: The Subversion of Indigenous Sovereignty in North America," in Troy Johnson, ed., *Contemporary Native American Political Issues*. Walnut Creek, Calif.: Alta Mira Press, 17-71.

Clifford, James. 1988. *The Predicament of Culture: Twentieth Century Ethnography, Literature and Art*. Cambridge, Mass.: Harvard University Press.

_____ and George Marcus, eds., 1986. *Writing Culture: The Poetics and Politics of Ethnography*. Berkeley: University of California Press.

Cornwell, Tim. 1993. "Island of the Damned," *The Observer Magazine*, 13 June, 41-43.

Cronon, William. 1983. *Changes in the Land: Indians, Colonists and the Ecology of New England*. New York: Hill and Wang.

Cruikshank, Julie. 1998. *The Social Life of Stories: Narrative and Knowledge in the Yukon Territory*. Lincoln: University of Nebraska Press.

Culhane, Dara. 1998. *The Pleasure of the Crown: Anthropology, Law and First Nations*. Burnaby, B.C.: Talonbooks.

Cumming, Peter A., and Neil H. Mickenberg. 1972. *Native Rights in Canada*, 2nd ed. Toronto: Indian-Eskimo Association of Canada.

Darnell, Frank, and Anton Hoem. 1996. *Taken to Extremes: Education in the Far North.* Oslo: Scandinavian University Press.

Davies, K.G., ed. 1963. *Northern Quebec and Labrador Journals and Correspondence 1819-35.* London: Hudson's Bay Company Record Society.

Day, Richard. 1998. "Constructing the Official Canadian: A Genealogy of the Mosaic Metaphor in State Policy Discourse," *Topia* 2: 42-66.

de Angulo, Jaime. 1990 [1950]. *Indians in Overalls.* San Francisco: City Lights.

Debord, Guy. 1995. *The Society of the Spectacle,* trans. Donald Nicholson-Smith. New York: Zone.

Deloria, Vine. 1997. *Red Earth, White Lies: Native Americans and the Myth of Scientific Fact.* Golden, Colo.: Fulcrum.

DeMont, John. 1999. "The Tragedy of Andrew Rich," *Maclean's,* 22 Nov., 36-40.

DePalma, Anthony. 1996. "Shedding Ashes of a Canadian Tribe's 'Evil Place'," *New York Times,* 22 Nov. A1, A6.

_____. 1997. "Canadian Court Ruling Broadens Indian Land Claims," *New York Times,* 12 Dec.

_____. 1998. "Canada Pact Gives a Tribe Self-Rule for the First Time," *New York Times,* A1, A10.

Dippie, Brian. 1982. *The Vanishing American: White Attitudes and US Indian Policy.* Middletown, Conn.: Wesleyan University Press.

Dominique, Richard. 1989. *Le Langage de la Chasse: Recit Autobiographique de Michel Gregoire, Montagnais de Natashquan.* Québec: Presses de l'Université du Québec.

Douglas, Mary. 1966. *Purity and Danger: An Analysis of Concepts of Pollution and Taboo.* Harmondsworth: Pelican.

_____. 1992. *Risk and Blame: Essays in Cultural Theory.* London: Routledge.

DuBois, W.E.B. 1969 [1903]. *The Souls of Black Folks.* New York: Signet.

Duran, Bonnie. 1996. "Indigenous Versus Colonial Discourse: Alcohol and American Indian Identity," in S. Elizabeth Bird, ed., *Dressing in Feathers: The Construction of the Indian in American Popular Culture.* Boulder, Colo.: Westview Press, 111-28.

Durkheim, Émile. 1951. *Suicide: A Study in Sociology,* trans. John Spaulding and George Simpson. Glencoe, Ill.: Free Press.

_____. 1964. *The Division of Labor in Society,* trans. George Simpson. Glencoe, Ill.: Free Press.

_____. 1965 [1915]. *The Elementary Forms of the Religious Life,* trans. Joseph Ward Swain. New York: Free Press.

Elias, Peter Douglas. 1993. "Anthropology and Aboriginal Claims Research," in Noel Dyck and James Waldram, eds., *Anthropology, Public Policy and Native Peoples in Canada*. Montreal and Kingston: McGill-Queen's University Press, 233-70.

Engels, Friedrich. 1999. "Results of Industrialisation," in Colin Samson, ed., *Health Studies: A Critical and Cross Cultural Reader*. Oxford: Blackwell, 280-93.

Fanon, Frantz. 1963. *The Wretched of the Earth*. New York: Grove Press.

_____. 1965. *A Dying Colonialism*. New York: Grove Press.

Farley, Maggie. 2000. "Tribe Sends Kids Away to Dry Out," *Los Angeles Times*, 19 Dec.

Fenwick, Peter. 1998. "Innu Owed a Debt in New Power Deal," *St. John's Telegram*, 25 Jan.

Feyerabend, Paul. 1987. *Farewell to Reason*. London: Verso.

Forer, Norman. 1979. "The Imposed Wardship of American Indian Tribes: A Case Study of the Prairie Band Potawatomi," in Sandra Burman and Barbara Hurrell-Bond, eds., *The Imposition of Law*. New York: Academic Press, 89-114.

Foucault, Michel. 1973. *The Order of Things: An Archaeology of the Human Sciences*. New York: Vintage.

_____. 1975. *The Birth of the Clinic: An Archaeology of Medical Perception*, trans. A.M. Sheridan Smith. New York: Vintage.

Friel, Brian. 1981. *Translations*. London: Faber and Faber.

Froschauer, Karl. 1999. *White Gold: Hydroelectric Power in Canada*. Vancouver: University of British Columbia Press.

Fumoleau, René. 1974. *As Long as this Land Shall Last: A History of Treaty 8 and Treaty 11 1870-1939*. Toronto: McClelland & Stewart.

Gibson, George. 1939. "Jesuit Education of the Indians in New France, 1611-1658," Ph.D. thesis, University of California at Berkeley.

Gibson, Gordon. 1997. "The Land Claims Ruling is a Breathtaking Mistake," *Globe and Mail*, 16 Dec., A21.

Globe and Mail. 2000. Editorial. 27 Nov.

Goffman, Erving. 1961. *Asylums*. Harmondsworth: Penguin.

_____. 1963. *Stigma: Notes on the Management of Spoiled Identity*. Englewood Cliffs, N.J.: Prentice-Hall.

Gosling, W.G. 1910. *Labrador: Its Discovery, Exploration & Development*. London: Alston Rivers.

Gosnell, Joseph. 1998. "The Nisga'a Treaty," talk given at the Canadian High Commission, London, 17 Nov.

Government of Newfoundland and Labrador. n.d. *Policy on Aboriginal Land Claims*. St. John's: Government of Newfoundland and Labrador.

Grand Council of the Crees. 2001. *Pushed to the Edge of Extinction: Racism Against Indigenous Peoples in Canada.* Nemaska, Que.: Grand Council of the Crees.

Great Britain, Privy Council. 1927. *In the matter of the Boundary between the Dominion of Canada and the Colony of Newfoundland in the Labrador Peninsula, between the Dominion of Canada in the one part and the Colony of Newfoundland of the other part,* 12 vols. London: William Clowes and Sons.

Greer, Allan. 2000. "Colonial Saints: Gender, Race and Hagiography in New France," *William and Mary Quarterly* 57, 2: 323-48.

Grenfell, Wilfred. 1920. *A Labrador Doctor: The Autobiography of Wilfred Thomason Grenfell M.D. (Oxon.), C.M.G.* London: Hodder and Stoughton.

_____. 1929. "Labrador in the Making," *The Listener* 2, 27: 709-10.

_____. 1933. *Forty Years for Labrador.* London: Hodder and Stoughton.

Gwyn, Richard. 1972. *Smallwood: The Unlikely Revolutionary.* Toronto: McClelland & Stewart.

Hallowell, A.I. 1929. "The Physical Characteristics of the Indians of Labrador," *Journal de la Société des Américanistes de Paris* 21, 5: 337-71.

_____. 1955. *Culture and Experience.* Philadelphia: University of Pennsylvania Press.

Hammerschlag, Carl A. 1988. *The Dancing Healers: A Doctor's Journey of Healing with Native Americans.* San Francisco: Harper and Row.

Hammond, Marc. 1994. *On the Use of Labrador by Quebec Naskapi Ancestors.* Schefferville: Naskapi Band of Quebec.

Harries, Kate. 2001. "Suicides haunt remote reserve," *Toronto Star,* 18 Aug.

Hedican, Edward. 1995. *Applied Anthropology in Canada: Understanding Aboriginal Issues.* Toronto: University of Toronto Press.

Heimbecker, Connie. 1994. "To School or Not To School: The Innu Dilemma," Ph.D thesis, University of Toronto.

Heizer, Robert, and Alan Almquist. 1971. *The Other Californians: Prejudice and Descrimination under Spain, Mexico, and the United States to 1920.* Berkeley: University of California Press.

Henriksen, Georg. 1973. *Hunters in the Barrens: The Naskapi on the Edge of the White Man's World.* St. John's: Institute of Social and Economic Research.

_____. 1981. "Davis Inlet, Labrador," in June Helm, ed., *Handbook of North American Indians,* vol. 6, 666-72.

_____. 1985. "Anthropologists as Advocates: Promoters of Pluralism or Makers of Clients?" in Robert Paine, ed., *Advocacy and Anthropology: First Encounters.* St. John's: Institute of Social and Economic Research, 119-29.

_____. 1993a. "Life and Death Among the Mushuau Innu of Northern Labrador," ISER Research and Policy Papers No. 17. St. John's: Institute of Social and Economic Research.

_____. 1993b. *Report on the Social and Economic Development of the Innu Community of Davis Inlet to the Economic Recovery Commission.* St John's: Government of Newfoundland and Labrador.

Hind, Henry Youle. 1863. *Explorations in the Interior of the Labrador Peninsula, the Country of the Montagnais and Nasquapee Indians,* 2 vols. London: Longman, Green, Longman, Roberts and Green.

House, Edgar. 1981. *Light at Last: Triumph over Tuberculosis in Newfoundland and Labrador 1900-1975.* St. John's: Jesperson Press.

Hoxie, Frederick. 1984. *A Final Promise: The Campaign to Assimilate the Indians, 1820-1920.* Lincoln: University of Nebraska Press.

Hubbard, Mina. 1981 [1908]. *A Woman's Way through Unknown Labrador.* St. John's: Breakwater Books.

Hutton, Samuel K. n.d. *Health Conditions and Disease Incidence among the Eskimos of Labrador.* Poole, England: Wessex Press.

Indian and Northern Affairs Canada. 1987. *Comprehensive Land Claims Policy.* Ottawa: Minister of Supply and Services.

Innu Nation. 1983. *Denial of the Right to Subsistence – Interviews, Sheshatshit, 1983.* Sheshatshiu: Innu Nation.

_____. 1996a. *Between a Rock and a Hard Place.* Sheshatshiu: Innu Nation.

_____. 1996b. *A Matter of Respect: Mineral Exploration in Nitassinan.* Sheshatshiu: Innu Nation.

_____. 1997. *Ntapueu: I Am Telling the Truth,* documentary film, produced by Marjorie Beaucage. Sheshatshiu: Innu Nation.

_____. 1998. *Money Doesn't Last, The Land is Forever.* Sheshatshiu: Innu Nation.

_____. 1999a. "Innu Release Details of Land Selection Proposal," Press Release, 9 Mar.

_____. 1999b. "Innu Nation Response to Voisey's Bay Project Release – Governments Fail to Implement Key Panel Recommendations," Press Release, 4 Aug.

_____. 2000. *Power Struggle: An Innu Look at Hydro Developments in Nitassinan.* Sheshatshiu: Innu Nation.

_____. and Mushuau Innu Band Council. [1993], [1992]. *Gathering Voices: Finding Strength to Help Our Children.* Sheshatshiu: Innu Nation.

_____ and _____. 1995. *Gathering Voices: Finding Strength to Help Our Children.* Vancouver: Douglas & McIntyre.

Inuit Circumpolar Conference. 1996. "Recommendations on the Integration of Two Ways of Knowing: Traditional Indigenous Knowledge and Scientific Knowledge," 15-17 Nov., Inuvik.

Jackson, M. Yvonne. 1994. "Diet, Culture and Diabetes," in Jennie Joe and Robert Young, eds., *Diabetes as a Disease of Civilization: The Impact of Culture Change on Indigenous Peoples.* Berlin: Mouton de Gruyter, 381-406.

James, William C. 1985. *A Fur Trader's Photographs.* Montreal and Kingston: McGill-Queen's University Press,

Johnston, Anna, and Alan Lawson. 2000. "Settler Colonies," in Henry Schwarz and Sangeeta Ray, eds., *A Companion to Postcolonial Studies.* Oxford: Blackwell, 360-76.

Kamper, Dietmar, and Christoph Wulf, eds. 1989. *Looking Back on the End of the World,* trans. David Antal. New York: Semiotext(e).

Kelm, Mary-Ellen. 1998. *Colonizing Bodies: Aboriginal Health and Healing in British Columbia 1900-50.* Vancouver: University of British Columbia Press.

Kennedy, J.H. 1950. *Jesuit and Savage in New France.* New Haven: Yale University Press.

Kirmayer, Laurence. 1994. "Suicide Among Canadian Aboriginal Peoples," *Transcultural Psychiatric Research Review* 31: 3-58.

Korsmo, Fae. 1999. "Claiming Memory in British Columbia Aboriginal Rights and the State," in Troy Johnson, ed., *Contemporary Native American Political Issues.* Walnut Creek, Calif.: Alta Mira Press, 119-34.

Kunitz, Stephen. 1983. *Disease Change and the Role of Medicine: The Navajo Experience.* Berkeley: University of California Press.

Laing, R.D. 1959. *The Divided Self.* Harmondsworth: Penguin.

_____ and Aaron Esterson. 1964. *Sanity, Madness and the Family.* Harmondsworth: Penguin.

Lamothe, Arthur. 1977, 1984. *Memoires Batante.* Documentary film, Montréal: Les ateliers audio-visuels du Québec.

Leacock, Eleanor Burke. 1954. "The Montagnais Hunting Territory and the Fur Trade," *American Anthropological Association Memoir* No.78.

_____. 1980. "Montagnais Women and the Jesuit Program for Colonization," in Mona Etienne and Leacock, eds., *Women and Colonization: Anthropological Perspectives.* New York: Praeger, 25-42.

_____. 1981. *Myths of Male Dominance: Collected Articles on Women Cross-Culturally.* New York: Monthly Review Press.

_____. 1995. "The Montagnais-Naskapi of the Labrador Peninsula," in R. Bruce Morrison and C. Roderick Wilson, eds., *Native Peoples: The Canadian Experience,* 2nd ed. Toronto: McClelland & Stewart, 150-80.

_____ and Jacqueline Goodman. 1976. "Montagnais Marriage and the Jesuits in the Seventeenth Century: Incidents from the Relations of Paul Le Jeune," *Western Canadian Journal of Anthropology* 6, 3: 77-91.

_____ and Nan Rothschild. 1994. *Labrador Winter: The Ethnographic Journals of William Duncan Strong*. Washington: Smithsonian Institution Press.

Lemert, Edwin. 1954. "Alcohol and the Northwest Coast Indians," *University of California Publications in Culture and Society* 2, 6: 303-406.

Lepore, Jill. 1998. T*he Name of War: King Phillip's War and the Origins of American Identity*. New York: Vintage.

Lewis, G. Malcolm. 1998. "Frontier Encounters in the Field: 1511-1925," in Lewis, ed., *Cartographic Encounters: Perspectives on Native American Mapmaking and Map Use*. Chicago: University of Chicago Press, 9-32.

Lindgren, April. 2000. "Doctor says parents must change," *St. John's Telegram*, 4 Dec.

Lips, Julius. 1947. "Naskapi Law: (Lake St. John and Lake Mistassini Bands), Law and Order in a Hunting Society," *Transactions of the American Philosophical Society* 37, 4: 379-490.

Lipset, Seymour Martin. 1990. *Continental Divide: The Values and Institutions of the United States and Canada*. New York: Routledge.

Lister, David. 1997. "Suicide in an International Perspective," *Suicide and Life Threatening Behavior* 27, 1: 104-11.

Lopez, Barry. 1986. *Arctic Dreams: Imagination and Desire in a Northern Landscape*. London: Picador.

Lord, Nancy. 1996. "Native Tongues: The Languages That Once Mapped the American Landscape Have Almost Vanished," *Sierra Magazine* 81, 6: 46-52.

Loring, Stephen, and Daniel Ashini. 2000. "Past and Present Pathways: Innu Cultural Heritage in the Twenty-first Century," in Claire Smith and Graeme Ward, eds., *Indigenous Cultures in an Interconnected World*. St. Leonards, NSW, Australia: Allen and Unwin, 167-200.

Lucy, John. 1996. "The Scope of Linguistic Relativity: An Analysis and Review of Empirical Research," in John Gumperz and Stephen Levinson, eds., *Rethinking Linguistic Relativity*. Cambridge: Cambridge University Press, 37-69.

Lurie, Nancy Oestreich. 1971. "The World's Oldest Protest Demonstration: North American Indian Drinking Patterns," *Pacific Historical Review* 40, 3: 311-32.

Lutz, Catherine, and Jane Collins. 1993. *Reading National Geographic*. Chicago: University of Chicago Press.

Mackie, Mary G. Alton. 1987. "Nutrition: Does Access to Country Food Really Matter?" presentation to the Fearo Assessment Review Panel Military Flying Activities in Labrador and Quebec, Montreal, 7 Oct.

MacDonald, Michael. 2001. "Ottawa takes over finances of Innu bands," Canadian Press wire story, 24 Jan.

Mailhot, José. 1986a. "Beyond Everyone's Horizon Stand the Naskapi," *Ethnohistory* 33, 4: 384-418.

_____. 1986b. "Territorial Mobility among the Montagnais-Naskapi of Labrador," *Anthropologica* 28, 1-2, 93-107.

_____. 1997. *The People of Sheshatshit: In the Land of the Innu*, trans. Axel Harvey. St. John's: Institute of Social and Economic Research.

_____ and Andrée Michaud. 1965. *North West River, Étude Ethnographique*. Centre d'études nordiques, Laval University, Quebec, Travaux divers 7.

Mamu Pakatatau Mamit Assembly. 2000. Mamit Innuat Propose the Canadian and Quebec Governments a New Territorial and Political Agreement Leading to a New Kind of Treaty. Sept-Îles: Mamu Pakatatau Mamit Assembly.

Marcus, George, and Michael Fischer. 1999. *Anthropology as Cultural Critique: An Experimental Moment in the Human Sciences*, 2nd ed. Chicago: University of Chicago Press.

McKeown, Thomas. 1988. *The Origins of Human Disease*. Oxford: Blackwell.

McLean, John. 1968. *Notes of a Twenty-five Years' Service in the Hudson's Bay Territory*, 2 vols., ed. W.S. Wallace. Toronto: Champlain Society.

McLean, Walter. 1998. "The Labrador Boundary Decision in the Privy Council." Available at: <http://www.geocities.com/ Yosemite/Rapids /3330 /constitution/1927priv.htm>.

McTimoney, David C., and Associates. 1990. *Davis Inlet Assessment*, prepared for Medical Services Branch, Health and Welfare Canada. Halifax.

Merry, Sally Engle. 2001. "Changing Rights, Changing Culture," in Jane Cowan, Marie-Benédicte Dembour, and Richard Wilson, eds., *Culture and Rights: Anthropological Perspectives*. Cambridge: Cambridge University Press, 31-55.

Miller, J.R. 2000. *Skyscrapers Hide the Heavens: A History of Indian-White Relations in Canada*, 3rd ed. Toronto: University of Toronto Press.

Millman, Lawrence. 1993. *Wolverine Creates the World: Labrador Indian Tales*. Santa Barbara, Calif.: Capra Press.

Mills, C. Wright. 1959. *The Sociological Imagination*. New York: Oxford University Press.

Mitchell, Timothy. 1988. *Colonizing Egypt*. Berkeley: University of California Press.

M'Lean, John. 1849. *Notes of a Twenty-five Years' Service in the Hudson's Bay Territory*, 2 vols. London: Richard Bentley.

Mofina, Rick. 2001. "Half of young Canadians unaware of any aboriginal issues," *Ottawa Citizen*, 31 July.

Momaday, N. Scott. 1976. *The Names: A Memoir*. Tucson: University of Arizona Press.

Moore, Brian. 1985. *Black Robe*. London: Flamingo.

Morris, Chris. 2000. "No Simple Healing Fix to Gas Sniffing Problems," *St. John's Telegram*, 25 Nov., 5.

Morris, Glenn. 1992. "International Law and Politics: Toward a Right to Self-Determination for Indigenous Peoples," in M. Annette Jaimes, ed., *The State of Native America: Genocide, Colonization and Resistance*. Boston: South End, 55-86.

Morris, Herbert. 1976. *On Guilt and Innocence: Essays in Legal Philosophy and Moral Psychology*. Berkeley: University of California Press.

Needleman, Jacob. 1985. *The Way of the Physician*. London: Arkana.

Nettle, Daniel. 1999. *Linguistic Diversity*. Oxford: Oxford University Press.

Newman, Peter C. 1991. *Merchant Princes: Company of Adventurers*, vol. 3. Toronto: Viking Penguin.

Nichols, Roger. 1998. *Indians in the United States and Canada: A Comparative History*. Lincoln: University of Nebraska Press.

Nisbet, Robert. 1969. *Social Change and History: Aspects of the Western Theory of Development*. New York: Oxford University Press.

_____. 1980. *History of the Idea of Progress*. New York: Basic Books.

Notzke, Claudia. 1994. *Aboriginal Peoples and Natural Resources in Canada*. North York, Ont.: Captus Press.

Oelschlaeger, Max. 1991. *The Idea of Wilderness*. New Haven: Yale University Press.

Ortiz, Alfonso. 1988. "Indian/White Relations: A View from the Other Side of the 'Frontier'," in Frederick Hoxie, ed., *Indians in American History*. Arlington Heights, Ill.: Harlan Davidson, 1-18.

Owens, Louis. 1998. *Mixedblood Messages: Literature, Film, Family, Place*. Norman, Okla.: University of Oklahoma Press.

Packard, Alpheus Spring. 1891. *The Labrador Coast: A Journal of Two Summer Cruises to that Region with Notes on its Early Discovery, on the Eskimo, on its Physical Geography, Geology and Natural History*. New York: N.D.C. Hodges.

Paz, Octavio. 1975. *Conjunctions and Disjunctions*, trans. Helen Lane. London: Wildwood House.

Peacock, Reverend F.W. 1964. "The Cultural Changes Among Labrador Eskimos Incident to the Coming of the Moravian Mission," in Jean Malaurie and Jacques Rousseau, eds., *Le Nouveau-Quebec: Contribution à l'Etude de l'Occupation Humaine*. Paris: Mouton & Co., 439-56.

Peters, Frank. 1972. "Acculturation Process Among the Naskopi Indians of Davis Inlet under Influence of the North-American Society," unpublished manuscript. Utshimassits: Utshimassits Band Council.

Plaice, Evelyn. 1990. *The Native Game: Settler Perceptions of Indian/Settler Relations in Central Labrador*. St. John's: Institute of Social and Economic Research.

Poole, Robert. 1993. "Labrador, Canada's Place Apart," with photographs by Richard Olsenius, *National Geographic* 184, 4 (Oct.): 2-35.

Prucha, Francis Paul. 1962. *American Indian Policy in the Formative Years: The Indian Trade and Intercourse Acts, 1790-1834*. Cambridge, Mass.: Harvard University Press.

Rasmussen, Derek. 2000a. "Dissolving Inuit Society Through Education and Money: The Myth of Educating Inuit out of 'Primitive Childhood' and into Economic Adulthood," *Interculture*, 139 (Oct.): 1-64.

———. 2000b. "Reconciliation-to-forgive Versus Reconciliation-to-forget," paper presented at Cultural Survival forum on "Justice before Reconciliation in Canada," Harvard University, Oct.

Rich, George. 2000. *Struggling With My Soul*. St. John's: Harrish Press.

Roberts, James. 1994. "Innu People Hunt for Lost Self-Esteem," *The Independent*, 8 Aug., 10.

Roche, James. 1992. *Resettlement of the Mushuau Innu 1948 and 1967: A Collection of Documents from the Provincial Archives of Newfoundland and Labrador and the Centre for Newfoundland Studies*. Sheshatshiu: Innu Nation.

Rockwood, Walter. 1957. *General Policy in respect of the Indians and Eskimos of Northern Labrador*. St. John's: Provincial Archives of Newfoundland and Labrador.

Rose, Steven, R.C. Lewontin, and Leon Kamin, 1984. *Not in Our Genes: Biology, Ideology and Human Nature*. Harmondsworth: Penguin.

Roslin, Alex. 2001. "$3.6 billion Cree-Quebec deal unraveling," *Montreal Gazette,* 10 Dec.

Rowe, Frederick. 1985. *The Smallwood Era*. Toronto: McGraw-Hill Ryerson.

Royal Commission on Aboriginal Peoples. 1995. *Choosing Life: Special Report on Suicide among Aboriginal People*. Ottawa: Minister of Supply and Services Canada.

———. 1996. *Looking Forward, Looking Backward*, vol. 1. Ottawa: Minister of Supply and Services Canada.

Rumbolt, Curtis. 1996. "Hot Rocks, Atlantic Provinces Mineral Industry Heats Up," *Atlantic Lifestyle Business* 7: 1, 8-17.

Rundstrom, Robert. 1993. "The Role of Ethics, Mapping and the Meaning of Place in Relations Between Indians and Whites in the United States," *Cartographica* 30, 1: 21-28.

———. 1995. "GIS, Indigenous Peoples, and Epistemological Diversity," *Cartography and Geographic Information Systems* 22, 1: 45-57.

Ryan, James. 1988a. "Disciplining the Innut: Social Form and Control in Bush, Community and School," Ph.D. thesis, University of Toronto.

_____. 1988b. "Economic Development and the Innu Settlement: The Establishment of Sheshatshit," *Canadian Journal of Native Studies* 8, 1: 1-25.

Saggers, Sherry, and Dennis Gray. 1991. *Aboriginal Health and Society: The Traditional and Contemporary Aboriginal Struggle for Better Health.* North Sydney: Allen and Unwin.

_____ and _____. 1998. *Dealing With Alcohol: Indigenous Usage in Australia, New Zealand and Canada.* Cambridge: Cambridge University Press.

Sahlins, Marshall. 1994. "Goodbye to Tristes Tropes: Ethnography in the Context of Modern World History," in Robert Borofsky, ed., *Assessing Cultural Anthropology.* New York: McGraw-Hill, 377-95.

St. John's Evening Telegram. 1997. "The Supreme Court and Land Claims," Editorial, 17 Dec.

_____. 1999. "Canada Blamed for Innu Strife," 9 Nov., 1-2.

Sam-Cromarty, Margaret. 1996. "Family Closeness: Will James Bay Be Only a Memory for My Grandchildren?" in Jace Weaver, ed., *Defending Mother Earth: Native American Perspectives on Environmental Justice.* Maryknoll, N.Y.: Orbis, 99-106.

Samson, Colin. 2001. "Rights as the Reward for Simulated Cultural Sameness: The Innu in the Canadian Colonial Context," in Jane Cowan et al., eds., *Culture and Rights: Anthropological Perspectives.* Cambridge: Cambridge University Press, 226-48.

_____, James Wilson, and Jonathan Mazower. 1999. *Canada's Tibet: The Killing of the Innu.* London: Survival.

Sarsfield, Pete. 1997. *Running with the Caribou.* Winnipeg: Turnstone Press.

Saunders, John. 2000. "Labrador Village Reels from Spate of Suicides: Liquor, Despair Combine in Deadly Potion," *Globe and Mail,* 6 Mar.

Scheper-Hughes, Nancy. 1992. *Death without Weeping: The Violence of Everyday Life in Brazil.* Berkeley: University of California Press.

Schuurman, Hedda. 1994. "Culture, Politics and School Control in Sheshatshit," M.A. thesis, Memorial University of Newfoundland.

Scott, Colin. 1993. "Customs, Tradition, and the Politics of Culture: Aboriginal Self-Government in Canada," in Noel Dyck and James Waldram, eds., *Anthropology, Public Policy and Native Peoples in Canada.* Montreal and Kingston: McGill-Queen's University Press, 311-33.

Scott, Richard T., and Selina Conn. 1987. "The Failure of Scientific Medicine: Davis Inlet and the Failure of Sociopolitical Morbidity," *Canadian Family Physician* 33, 1649-53.

Seed, Patricia. 2001. *American Pentimento: The Invention of Indians and the Pursuit of Riches.* Minneapolis: University of Minnesota Press.

Shaw, Clifford. 1966 [1930]. *The Jack-Roller: A Delinquent Boy's Own Story.* Chicago: University of Chicago Press.

Shewell, Hugh, and Annabella Spagnut. 1995. "The First Nations of Canada: Social Welfare and the Quest for Self-Government," in John Dixon and Robert Scheurell, eds., *Social Welfare with Indigenous Peoples.* London: Routledge, 1-51.

Shkilnyk, Anastasia. 1985. *A Poison Stronger Than Love: The Destruction of an Ojibwa Community.* New Haven: Yale University Press.

Silko, Leslie Marmon. 1991. *Almanac of the Dead.* New York: Penguin.

Slesar, R.J. n.d. *Principles for a Theory of Instructing Adult Nascappie Indian Students.* Schefferville: Protestant School Board of Schefferville.

Smith, Philip. 1975. *Brinco: The Story of Churchill Falls.* Toronto: McClelland & Stewart.

Sontag, Susan. 1977. *On Photography.* New York: Farrar, Straus and Giroux.

Speck, Frank. 1977 [1935]. *Naskapi: The Savage Hunters of the Labrador Peninsula.* Norman, Okla.: University of Oklahoma Press.

Starkey, Armstrong. 1998. *European and Native American Warfare, 1675-1815.* London: UCL Press.

Steinberg, Stephen. 1995. *Turning Back: The Retreat from Racial Justice in American Thought and Policy.* Boston: Beacon Press.

Steiner, George. 1992. "Foreword," in Friedrich Ohly, *The Damned and the Elect: Guilt in Western Culture,* trans. Linda Archibald. Cambridge: Cambridge University Press.

Sullivan, Deana Stokes. 1999. "Project Clears Environmental Process," *St. John's Telegram,* 4 Aug.

Svennson, Frances. 1979. "Imposed Law and the Manipulation of Identity: The American Indian Case," in Sandra Burman and Barbara Hurrell-Bond, eds., *The Imposition of Law.* New York: Academic Press, 69-87.

Synge, J.M. 1992 [1907]. *The Aran Islands.* London: Penguin.

Tanner, Adrian. 1983. "Introduction: Canadian Indians and the Politics of Dependency," in Adrian Tanner, ed., *The Politics of Indianness: Case Studies of Native Ethnopolitics in Canada.* St. John's: Institute of Social and Economic Research, 1-36.

Tanner, Vaino. 1947. *Outlines of the Geography, Life & Customs of Newfoundland-Labrador (The Eastern Part of the Labrador Peninsula),* 2 vols. Cambridge: Cambridge University Press.

Taslitz, Andrew. 1999. *Rape and the Culture of the Courtroom.* New York: New York University Press.

Taussig, Michael. 1987. *Shamanism, Colonialism and the Wild Man: A Study in Terror and Healing.* Chicago: University of Chicago Press.

_____. 1993. *Mimesis and Alterity: A Particular History of the Senses.* New York: Routledge.

Taylor, Charles. 1992. *Multiculturalism and the Politics of Recognition.* Princeton, N.J.: Princeton University Press.

Teggart, Frederick. 1977. *Theories and Processes of History.* Berkeley: University of California Press.

Ten, C.L. 1987. *Crime, Guilt and Punishment: A Philosophical Introduction.* Oxford: Clarendon Press.

Tester, Frank James, and Peter Kulchyski. 1994. *Tammarniit (Mistakes): Inuit Relocation in the Eastern Arctic, 1939-63.* Vancouver: University of British Columbia Press.

The Northern Miner. 1998. "Editorial: Voisey's Bay Becoming a Political Football," 16 Feb., 4.

Thompson, Elizabeth. 1998a. "Innu Show They Can't be Ignored," *Montreal Gazette,* 9 Mar., A1.

———. 1998b. "Premiers Shake Hands on Churchill Falls Deal: Innu Protesters Block Bouchard and Tobin as they Unveil Hydro Project," *Montreal Gazette,* 10 Mar., A1.

Thrower, Norman. 1996. *Maps & Civilization: Cartography in Culture and Society.* Chicago: University of Chicago Press.

Thwaites, Reuben Gold. 1896-1901. *The Jesuit Relations and Allied Documents,* 73 vols. Cleveland: Burrows Brothers.

Tompkins, Edward. 1988. *Pencilled Out: Newfoundland and Labrador's Native People and Canadian Confederation, 1947-1954,* a report prepared for Jack Harris M.P. on the impact of the exclusion of Newfoundland and Labrador's Native people from the Terms of Union in 1949. Ottawa: House of Commons.

Townsend, Charles Wendell. 1918. *In Audubon's Labrador.* Boston and New York: Houghton Mifflin Company.

Treaty 7 Elders and Tribal Council, with Walter Hildebrandt, Sarah Carter, and Dorothy First Rider. 1996. *The True Spirit and Original Intent of Treaty 7.* Montreal and Kingston: McGill-Queen's University Press.

Trudel, Marcel. 1973. *The Beginnings of New France 1524-1663,* trans. Patricia Claxton. Toronto: McClelland & Stewart.

Tully, James. 1995. *Strange Multiplicity: Constitutionalism in the Age of Diversity.* Cambridge: Cambridge University Press.

Turner, Lucien. 1979 [1889]. *Ethnology of the Ungava District and Hudson Bay Territory: Indians and Eskimos in the Quebec-Labrador Peninsula.* Quebec City: Presses Comeditex.

United Nations Human Rights Committee. 1999. *Consideration of Reports Submitted by States Parties under Article 40 of the Covenant Concluding Observations of the Human Rights Committee: Canada.* Sixty-fifth session. New York: United Nations.

Vizenor, Gerald 1984. *The People Named the Chippewa: Narrative Histories.* Minneapolis: University of Minnesota Press.

———. 1994. *Manifest Manners: Postindian Warriors of Survivance.* Middleton, Conn.: Wesleyan University Press.

———. 1998. *Fugitive Poses: Native American Indian Scenes of Absence and Presence.* Lincoln: University of Nebraska Press.

Wadden, Marie. 1991. *Nitassinan: The Innu Struggle to Reclaim their Homeland.* Vancouver: Douglas & MacIntyre.

Waldram, James, D. Ann Herring, and T. Kue Young. 1995. *Aboriginal Health in Canada: Historical, Cultural and Epidemiological Perspectives.* Toronto: University of Toronto Press.

Wallace, Dillon. 1977 [1905]. *The Lure of the Labrador Wild.* Portugal Cove, Nfld.: Breakwater Books.

Warhus, Mark. 1997. *Another America: Native American Maps and the History of Our Land.* New York: St. Martin's Press.

Weaver, Jace. 2000. "Indigenousness and Indigineity," in Henry Schwarz and Sangeeta Ray, eds., *A Companion to Postcolonial Studies.* Oxford: Blackwell, 221-35.

Westphal, Merold. 1984. *God, Guilt and Death: An Existential Phenomenology of Religion.* Bloomington: Indiana University Press.

White, John Allan. n.d. *Adult Children of Alcoholics: From Survival to Healing, Walking the Recovery Road.* Edmonton: Nechi Institute on Alcohol and Drug Education.

White, Patrick. 2000. "French Air Force Set for Low-Level Flights in Canada," Reuters News Report, 1 Nov.

White, Richard. 1931. "The Naskapi Indians: Notes Compiled for Dr. Frank G. Speck," St. John's: Centre for Newfoundland Studies.

Wilkinson, Charles. F. 1988. "Indian Tribes and the American Constitution," in Frederick Hoxie, ed., *Indians in American History.* Arlington Heights, Ill.: Harlan Davidson, 117-36.

Williams, Robert A. 1990. *The American Indian in Western Legal Thought: The Discourses of Conquest.* New York: Oxford University Press.

Willis, Paul. 1977. *Learning to Labour: How Working Class Kids Get Working Class Jobs.* London: Gower.

Wilson, Beckles. 1902. *Lord Strathcona: The Story of His Life.* London: Methuen.

Wilson, C. Roderick, and Carl Urion. 1995. "First Nations Prehistory and anadian History," in R. Bruce Morrison and C. Roderick Wilson, eds., *Native Peoples: The Canadian Experience,* 2nd ed. Toronto: McClelland & Stewart, 22-66.

Wilson, James. 1994. *The Two Worlds of the Innu,* BBC2 documentary film, produced by Ken Kirby, 7 Aug.

_____. 1998. *The Earth Shall Weep: A History of Native America.* New York: Grove Press.

Winichakul, Thongchai. 1994. *Siam Mapped: A History of the Geo-Body of a Nation.* Chiang Mai, Thailand: Silkworm Books.

Wotton, Kathryn. 1986. "Mortality of Labrador Innu and Inuit, 1971-1982," in Robert Fortuine, ed., *Circumpolar Health '84: Proceedings of the Sixth International Symposium on Circumpolar Health.* Seattle: University of Washington Press, 139-42.

Yakabuski, Konrad. 1996. "Tobin reveals secret pact on Hydro-Quebec agreed in 1984 to discuss altering deal, Newfoundland premier says," *Globe and Mail,* 16 Oct., 1.

York, Geoffrey. 1990. *The Dispossessed: Life and Death in Native Canada.* London: Vintage UK.

Young, Arminius. 1931. *One Hundred Years of Mission Work in the Wilds of Labrador.* London: Arthur H. Stockwell.

Young, T. Kue. 1994. "Diet, Culture and Diabetes," in Jennie Joe and Robert Young, eds., *Diabetes as a Disease of Civilization: The Impact of Culture Change on Indigenous Peoples.* Berlin: Mouton de Gruyter, 21-39.

Zimmerly, David William. 1975. *Cain's Land Revisited: Culture Change in Central Labrador, 1775-1972.* St. John's: Institute of Social and Economic Research.

Zimring, Franklin, and Gordon Hawkins. 1973. *Deterrence: The Legal Threat in Crime Control.* Chicago: University of Chicago Press.

Index

AGMV Marquis

MEMBER OF SCABRINI MEDIA

Quebec, Canada
2003